BATMAN – DETECTIVE COMICS

VOLUME 8
BLOOD OF HEROES

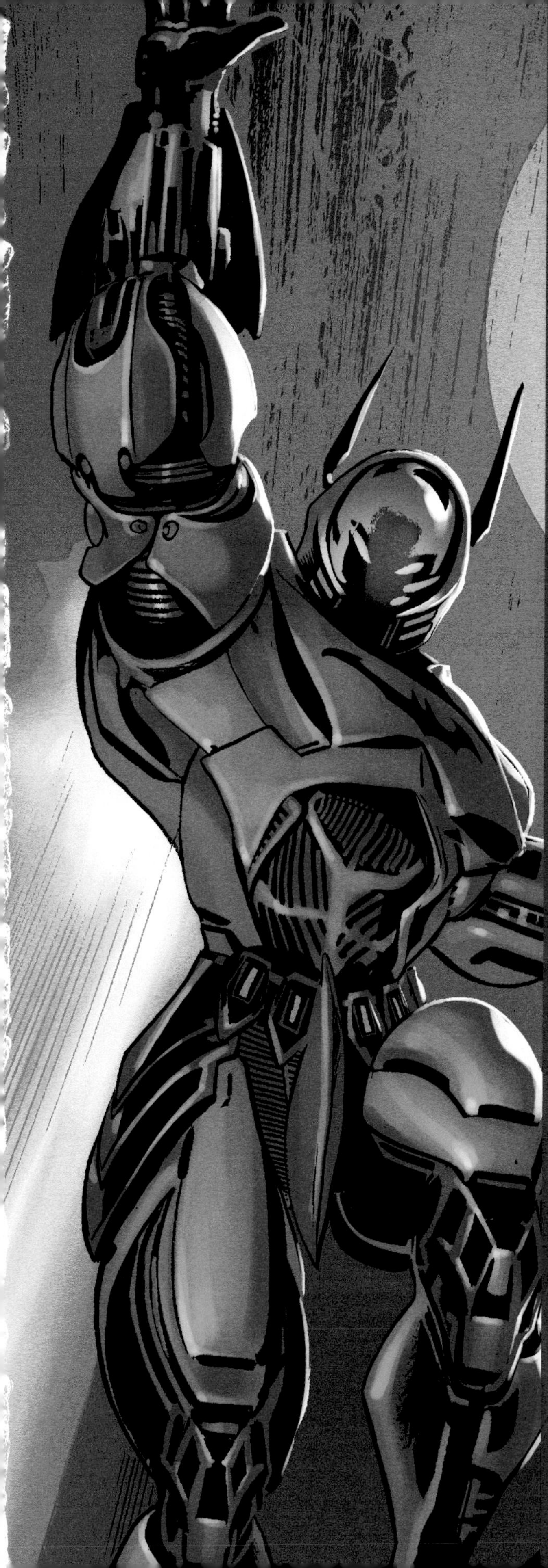

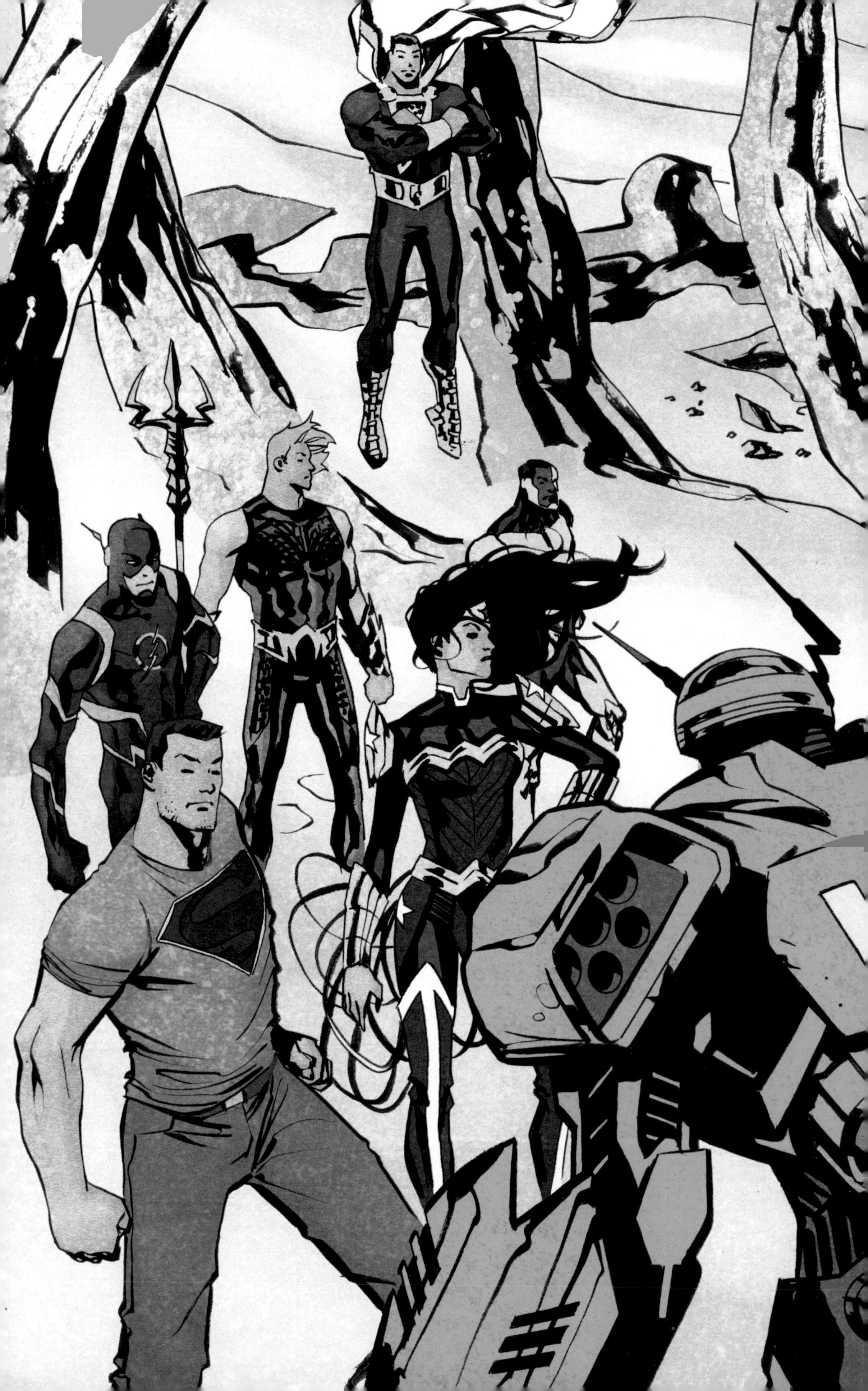

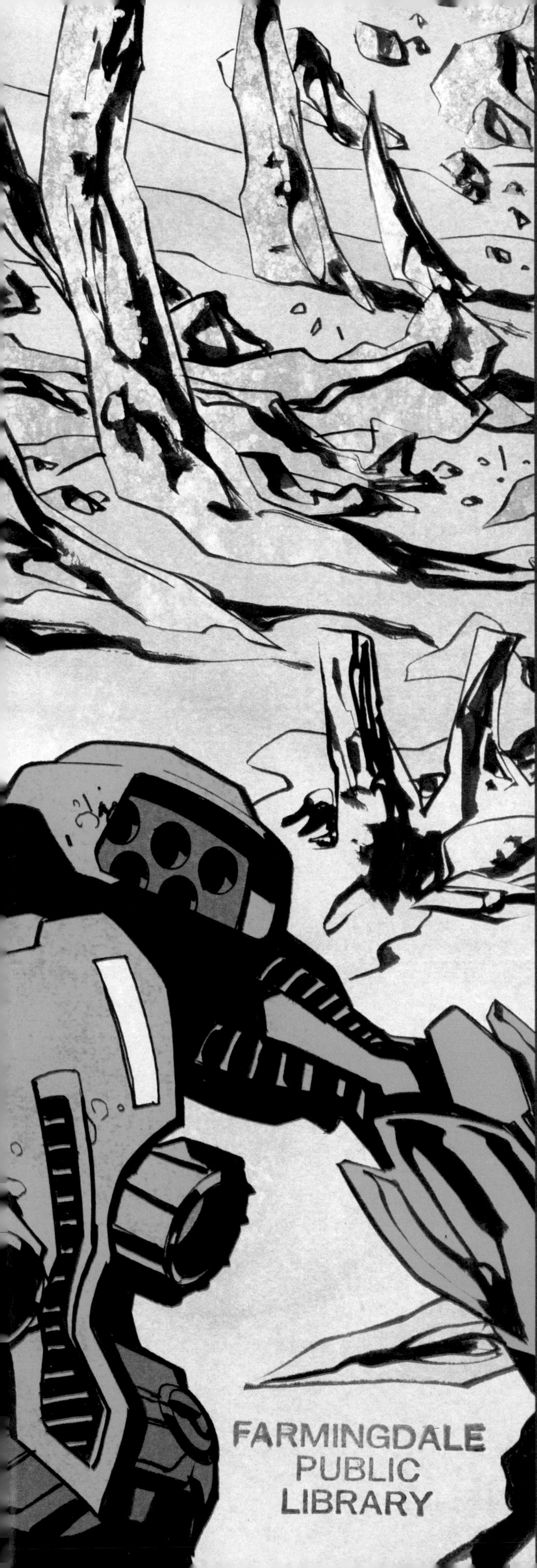

BATMAN – DETECTIVE COMICS

VOLUME 8
BLOOD OF HEROES

WRITTEN BY
BRIAN BUCCELLATO
RAY FAWKES
FRANCIS MANAPUL
PETER J. TOMASI

ART BY
FERNANDO BLANCO
FRANCIS MANAPUL
STEVE PUGH
MARCIO TAKARA

COLOR BY
BRIAN BUCCELLATO
CHRIS SOTOMAYOR

LETTERS BY
WES ABBOTT
JARED K. FLETCHER

COLLECTION COVER ART BY
FRANCIS MANAPUL

BATMAN CREATED BY
BOB KANE WITH **BILL FINGER**

SUPERMAN CREATED BY
JERRY SIEGEL AND
JOE SHUSTER
BY SPECIAL ARRANGEMENT
WITH THE JERRY SIEGEL FAMILY

MARK DOYLE, RACHEL GLUCKSTERN Editors – Original Series
REBECCA TAYLOR Associate Editor – Original Series
DAVE WIELGOSZ, MATT HUMPHRIES Assistant Editors – Original Series
JEB WOODARD Group Editor – Collected Editions
SUZANNAH ROWNTREE Editor – Collected Editions
STEVE COOK Design Director – Books
DAMIAN RYLAND Publication Design

BOB HARRAS Senior VP – Editor-in-Chief, DC Comics

DIANE NELSON President
DAN DIDIO and JIM LEE Co-Publishers
GEOFF JOHNS Chief Creative Officer
AMIT DESAI Senior VP – Marketing & Global Franchise Management
NAIRI GARDINER Senior VP – Finance
SAM ADES VP – Digital Marketing
BOBBIE CHASE VP – Talent Development
MARK CHIARELLO Senior VP – Art, Design & Collected Editions
JOHN CUNNINGHAM VP – Content Strategy
ANNE DEPIES VP – Strategy Planning & Reporting
DON FALLETTI VP – Manufacturing Operations
LAWRENCE GANEM VP – Editorial Administration & Talent Relations
ALISON GILL Senior VP – Manufacturing & Operations
HANK KANALZ Senior VP – Editorial Strategy & Administration
JAY KOGAN VP – Legal Affairs
DEREK MADDALENA Senior VP – Sales & Business Development
JACK MAHAN VP – Business Affairs
DAN MIRON VP – Sales Planning & Trade Development
NICK NAPOLITANO VP – Manufacturing Administration
CAROL ROEDER VP – Marketing
EDDIE SCANNELL VP – Mass Account & Digital Sales
COURTNEY SIMMONS Senior VP – Publicity & Communications
JIM (SKI) SOKOLOWSKI VP – Comic Book Specialty & Newsstand Sales
SANDY YI Senior VP – Global Franchise Management

BATMAN – DETECTIVE COMICS VOLUME 8: BLOOD OF HEROES

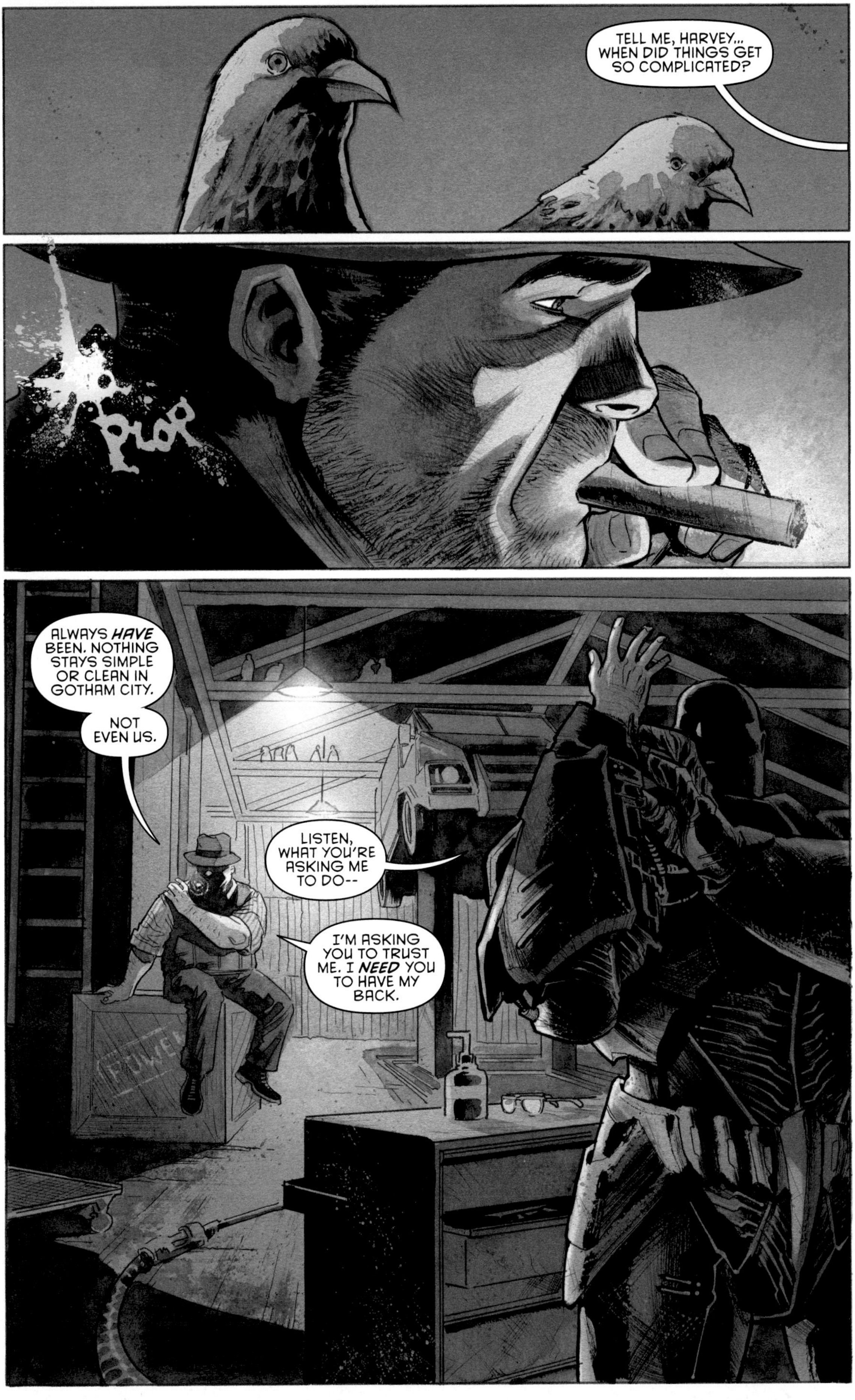
TELL ME, HARVEY... WHEN DID THINGS GET SO COMPLICATED?
PLOP
ALWAYS *HAVE* BEEN. NOTHING STAYS SIMPLE OR CLEAN IN GOTHAM CITY.
NOT EVEN US.
LISTEN, WHAT YOU'RE ASKING ME TO DO--
I'M ASKING YOU TO TRUST ME. I *NEED* YOU TO HAVE MY BACK.
POWER

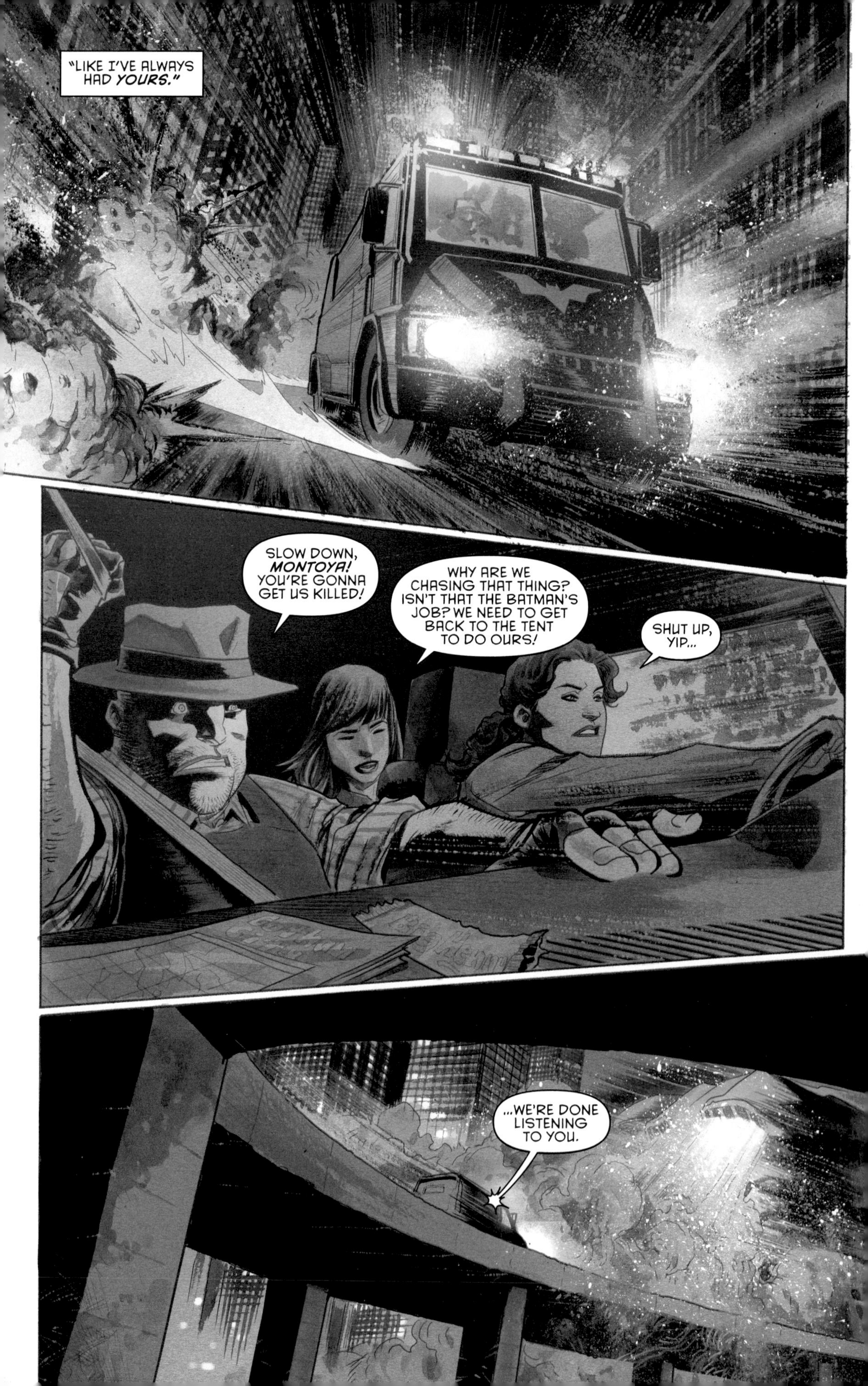
"LIKE I'VE ALWAYS HAD *YOURS.*"
SLOW DOWN, ***MONTOYA!*** YOU'RE GONNA GET US KILLED!
WHY ARE WE CHASING THAT THING? ISN'T THAT THE BATMAN'S JOB? WE NEED TO GET BACK TO THE TENT TO DO OURS!
SHUT UP, YIP...
...WE'RE DONE LISTENING TO YOU.

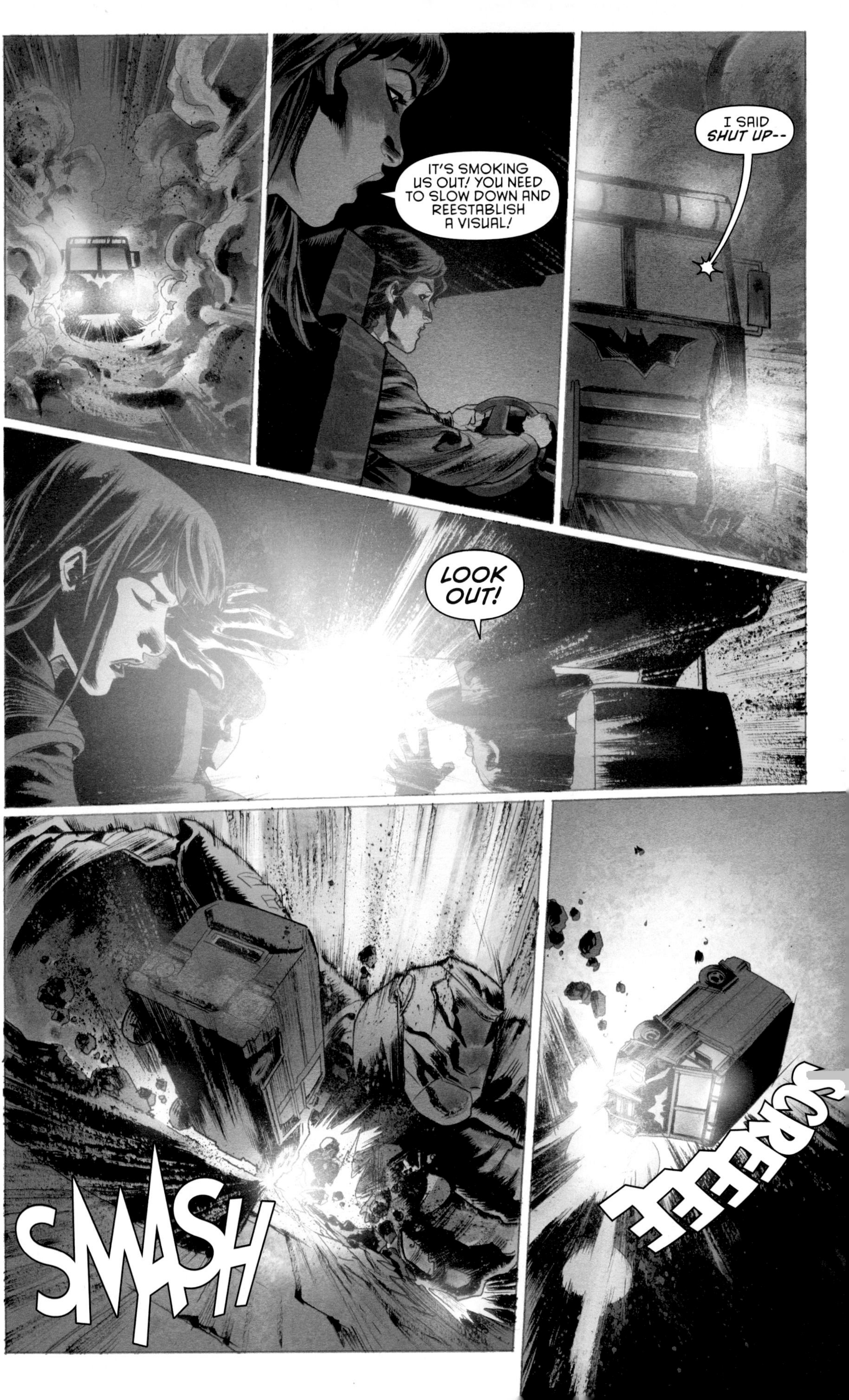
IT'S SMOKING US OUT! YOU NEED TO SLOW DOWN AND REESTABLISH A VISUAL!
I SAID SHUT UP--
LOOK OUT!
SMASH
SCREEEEE

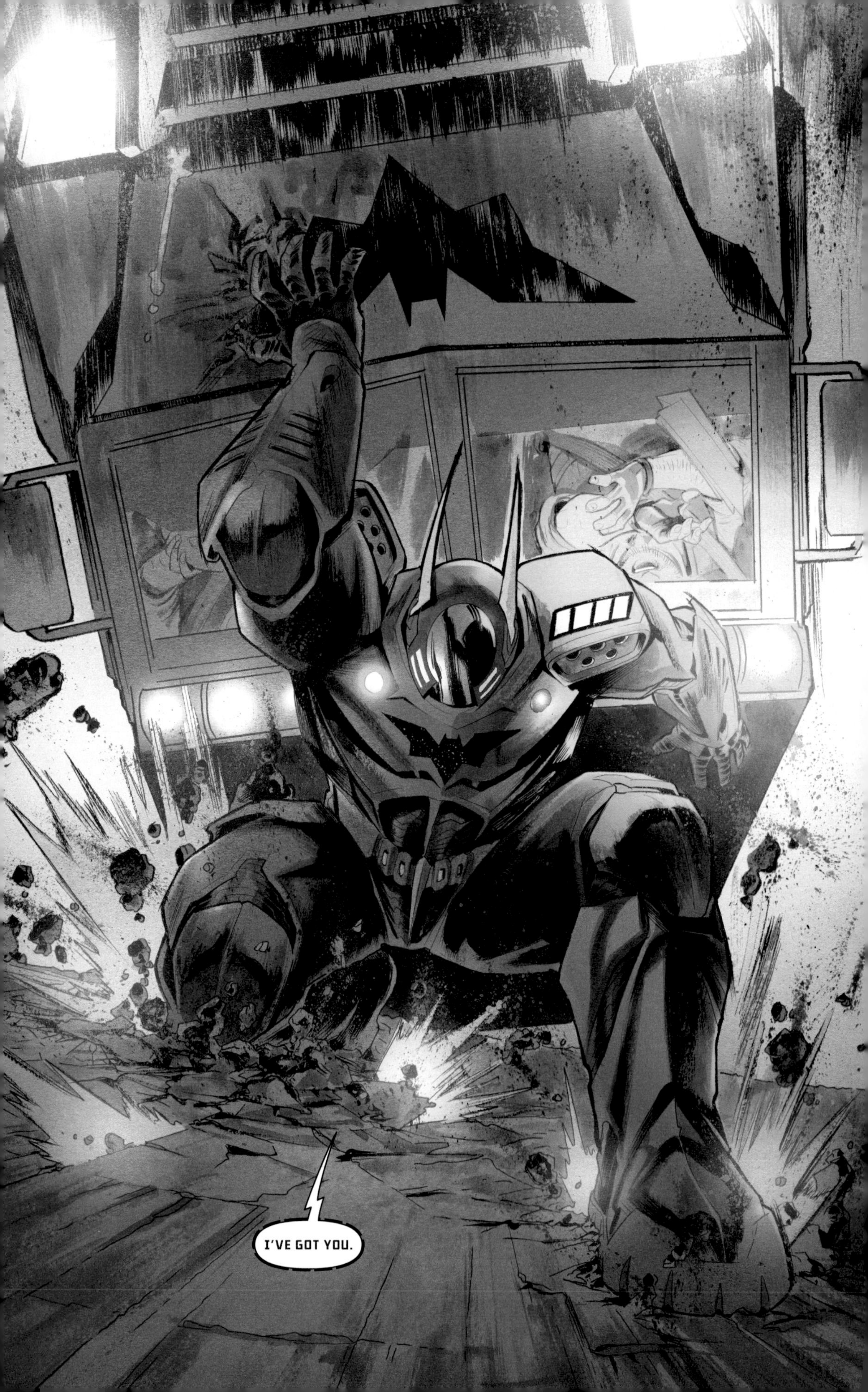
I'VE GOT YOU.

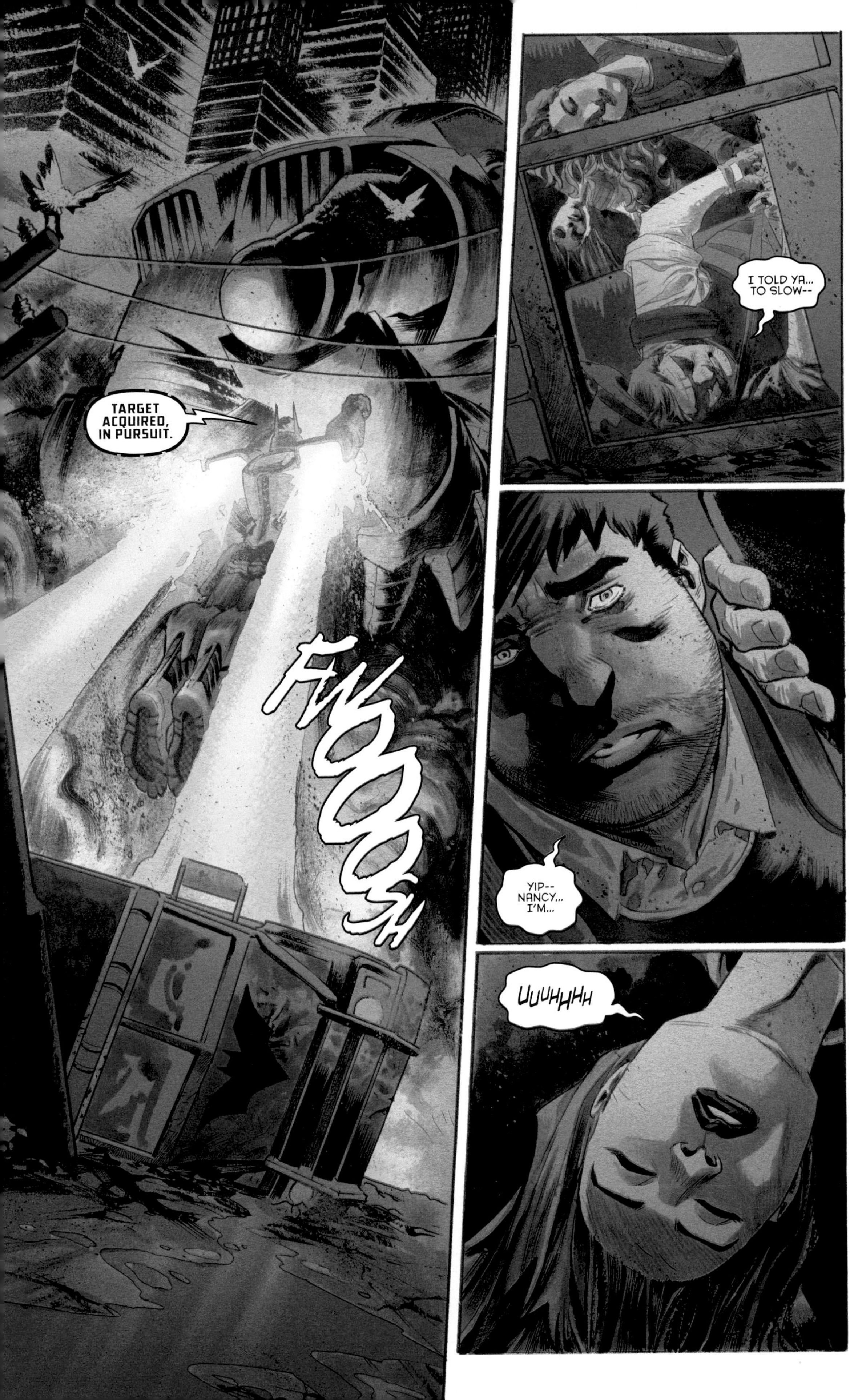
TARGET ACQUIRED, IN PURSUIT.
FWOOOOSH
I TOLD YA... TO SLOW--
YIP-- NANCY... I'M...
UUUHHHH

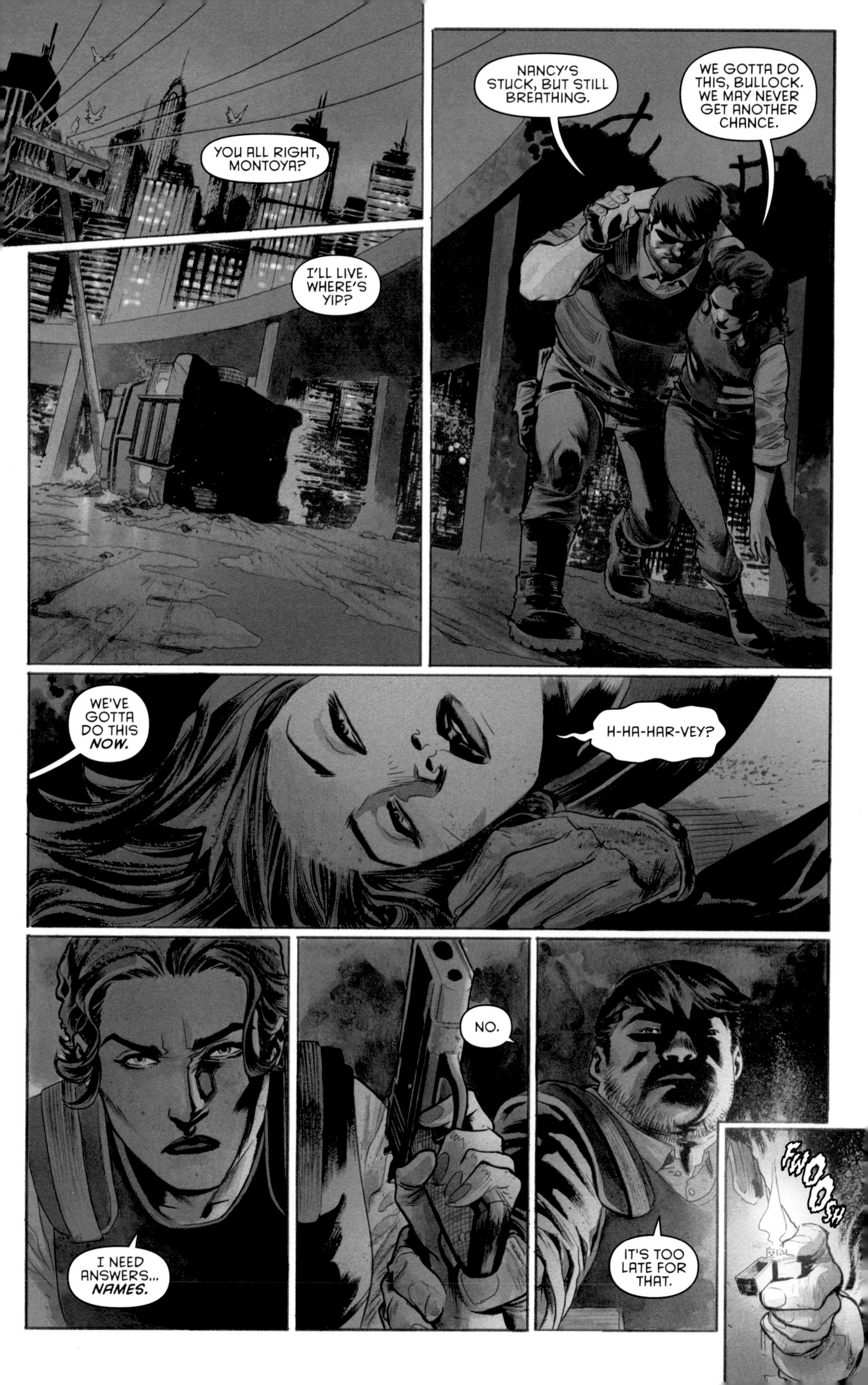
YOU ALL RIGHT, MONTOYA?
I'LL LIVE. WHERE'S YIP?
NANCY'S STUCK, BUT STILL BREATHING.
WE GOTTA DO THIS, BULLOCK. WE MAY NEVER GET ANOTHER CHANCE.
WE'VE GOTTA DO THIS *NOW.*
H-HA-HAR-VEY?
I NEED ANSWERS... *NAMES.*
NO.
IT'S TOO LATE FOR THAT.
FWOOSH

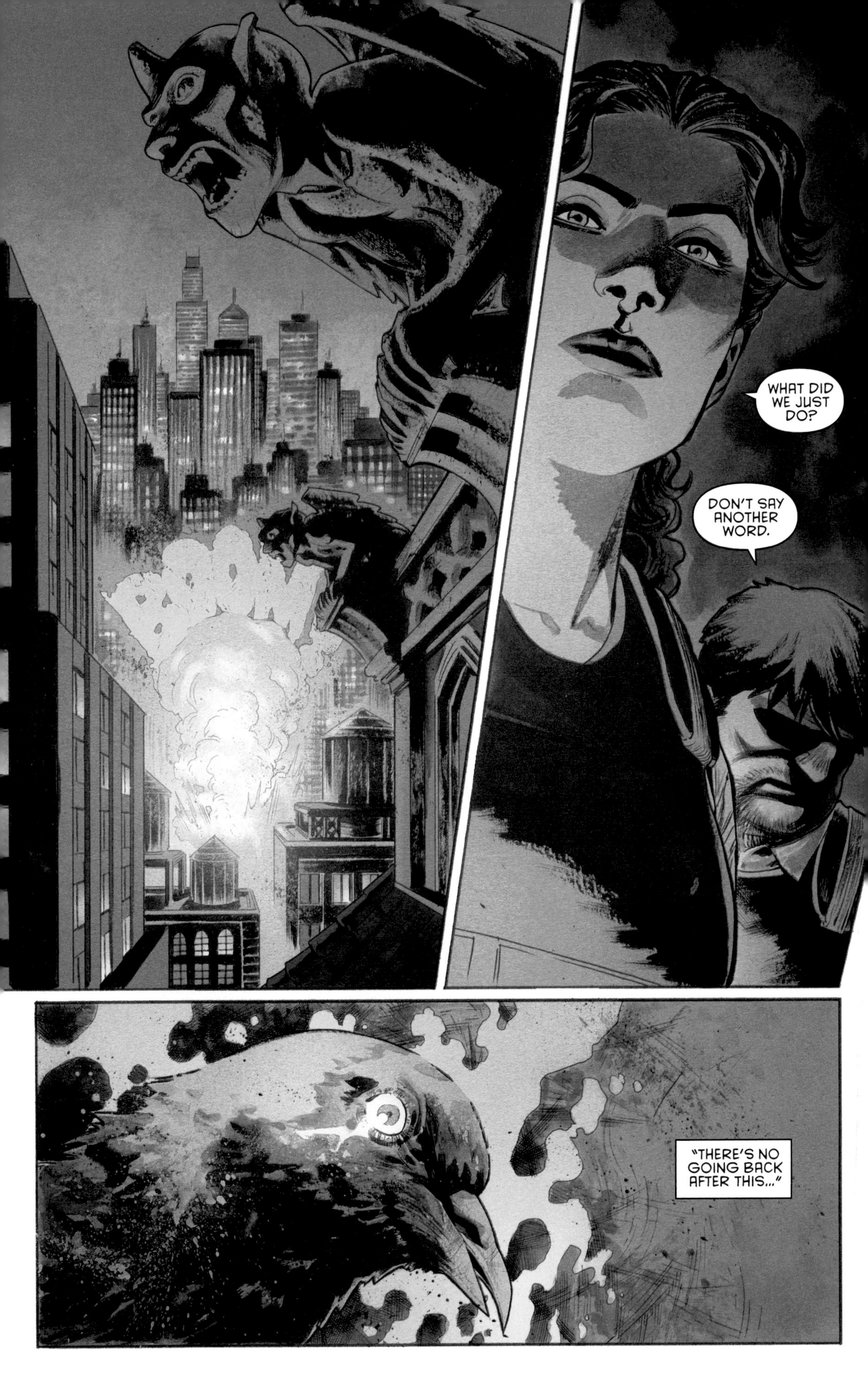
WHAT DID WE JUST DO?
DON'T SAY ANOTHER WORD.
"THERE'S NO GOING BACK AFTER THIS..."

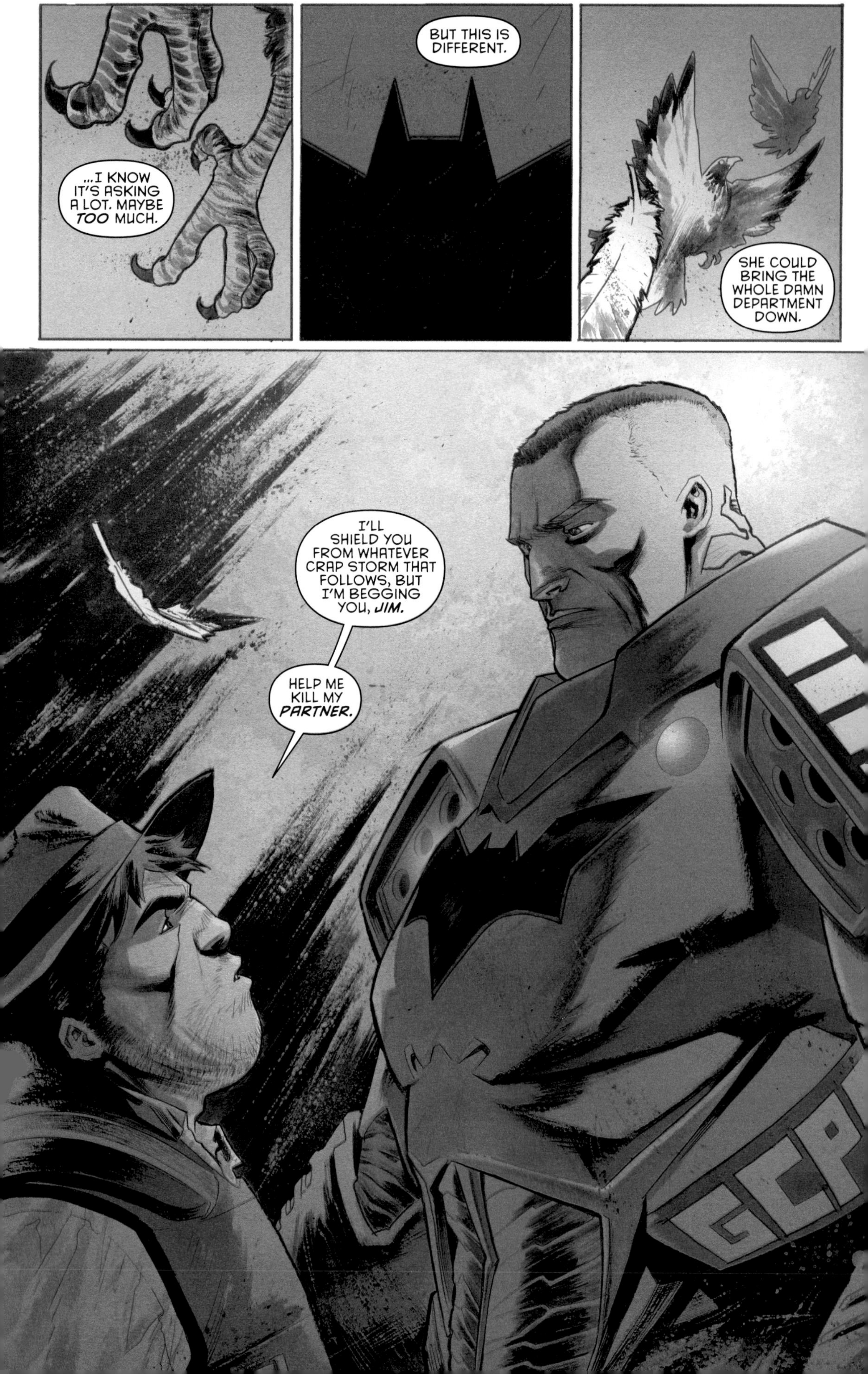
...I KNOW IT'S ASKING A LOT. MAYBE *TOO* MUCH.
BUT THIS IS DIFFERENT.
SHE COULD BRING THE WHOLE DAMN DEPARTMENT DOWN.
I'LL SHIELD YOU FROM WHATEVER CRAP STORM THAT FOLLOWS, BUT I'M BEGGING YOU, ***JIM.***
HELP ME KILL MY ***PARTNER.***

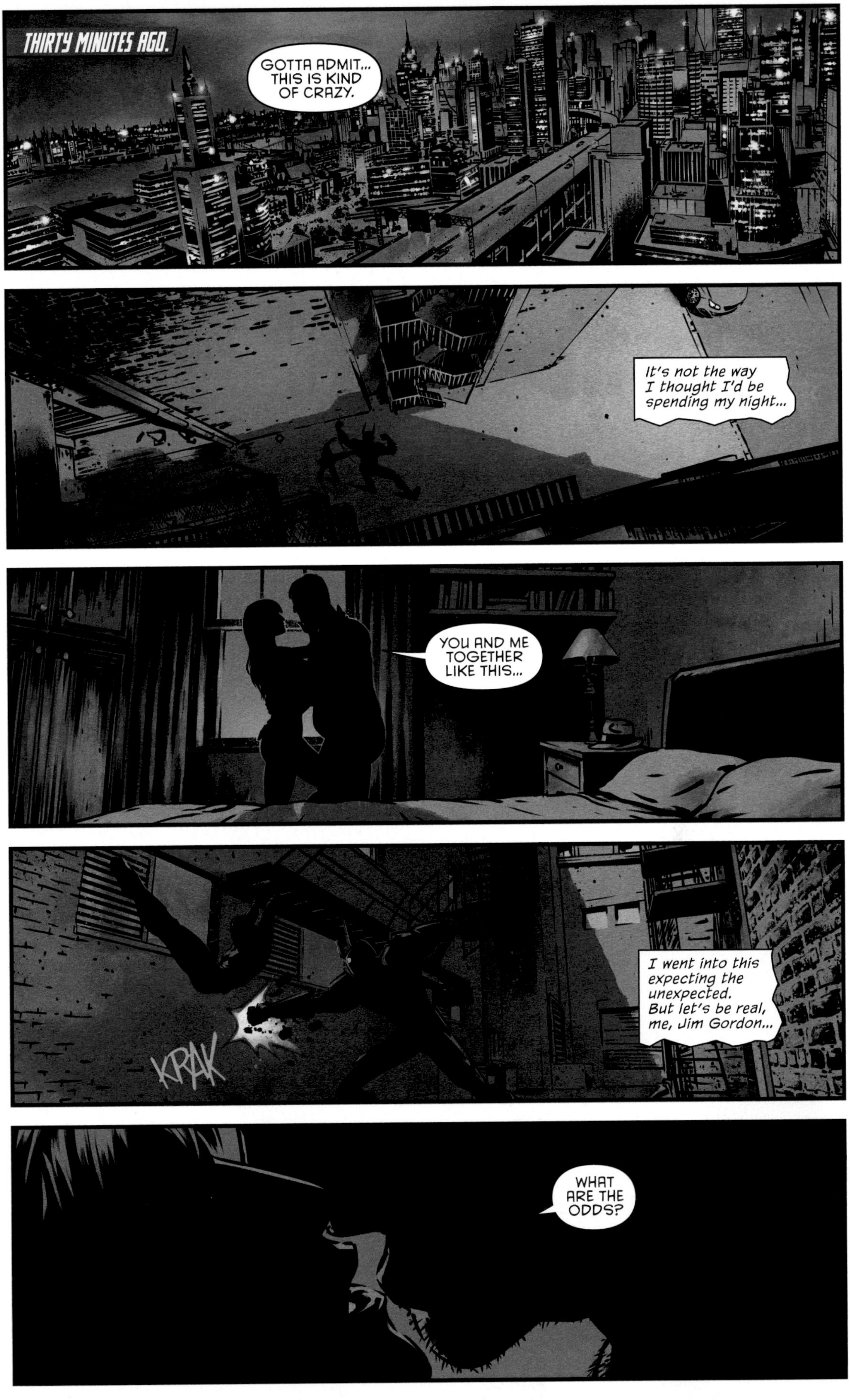
THIRTY MINUTES AGO.
GOTTA ADMIT... THIS IS KIND OF CRAZY.
It's not the way I thought I'd be spending my night...
YOU AND ME TOGETHER LIKE THIS...
KRAK
I went into this expecting the unexpected. But let's be real, me, Jim Gordon...
WHAT ARE THE ODDS?

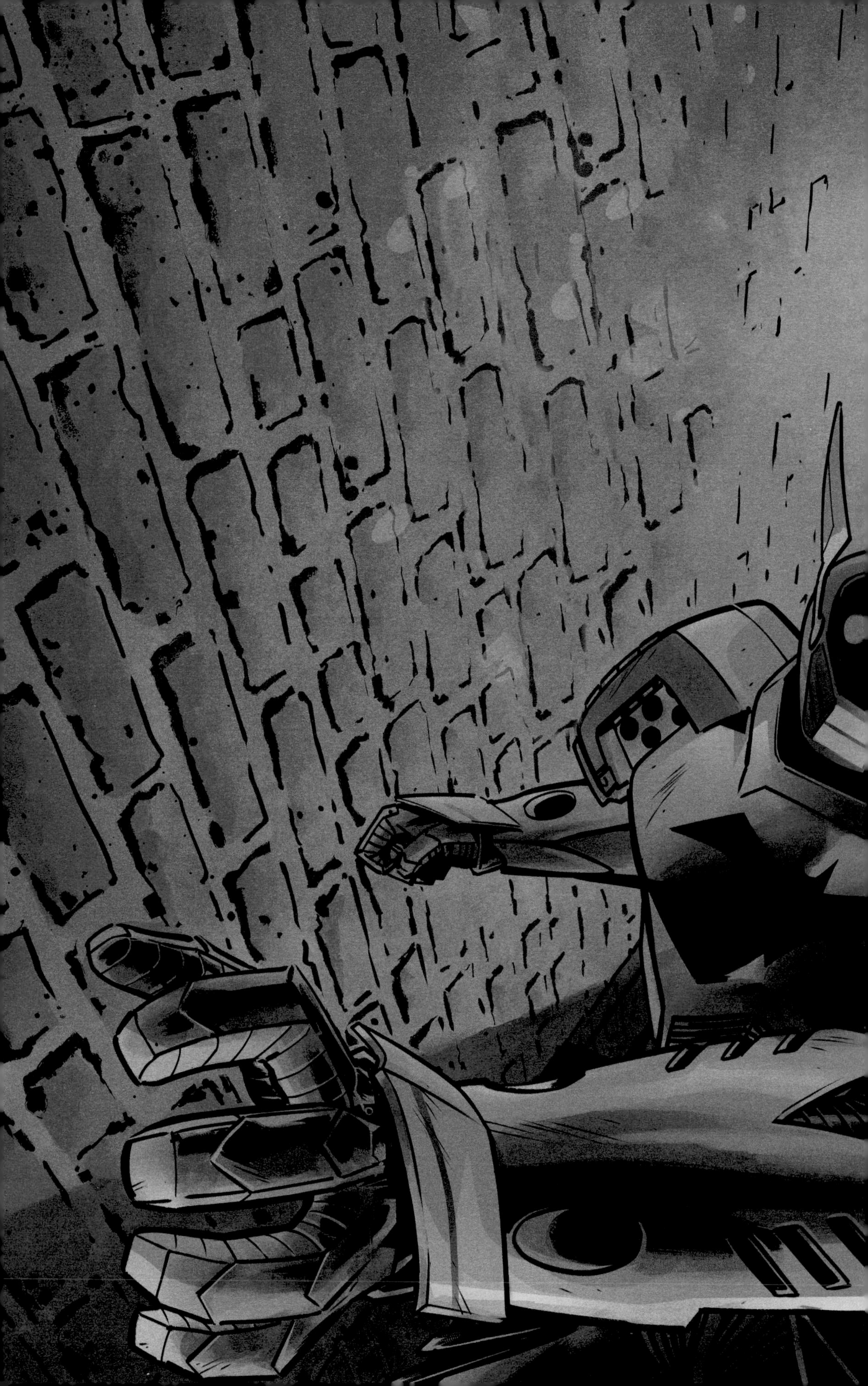

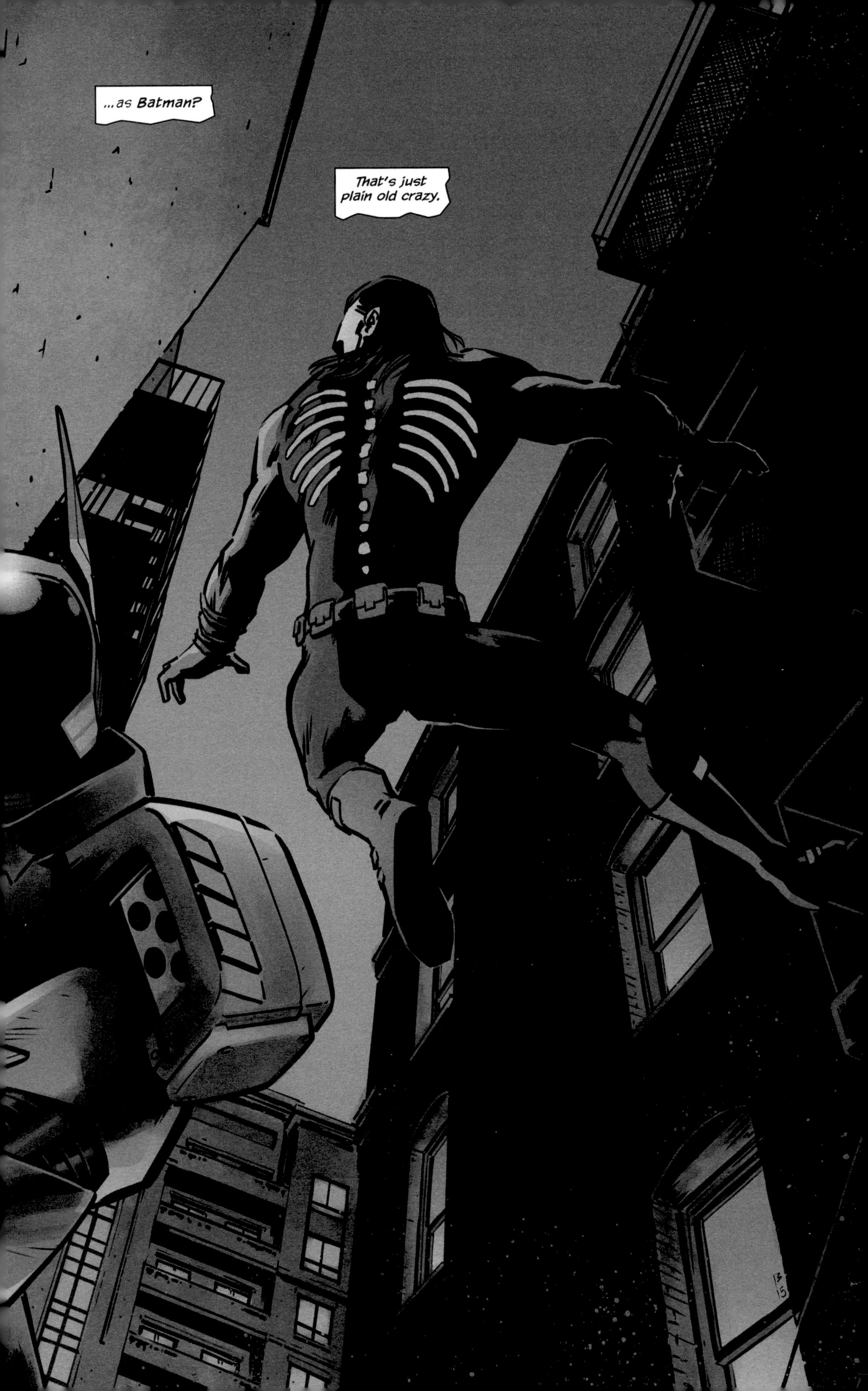
...as Batman?
That's just plain old crazy.

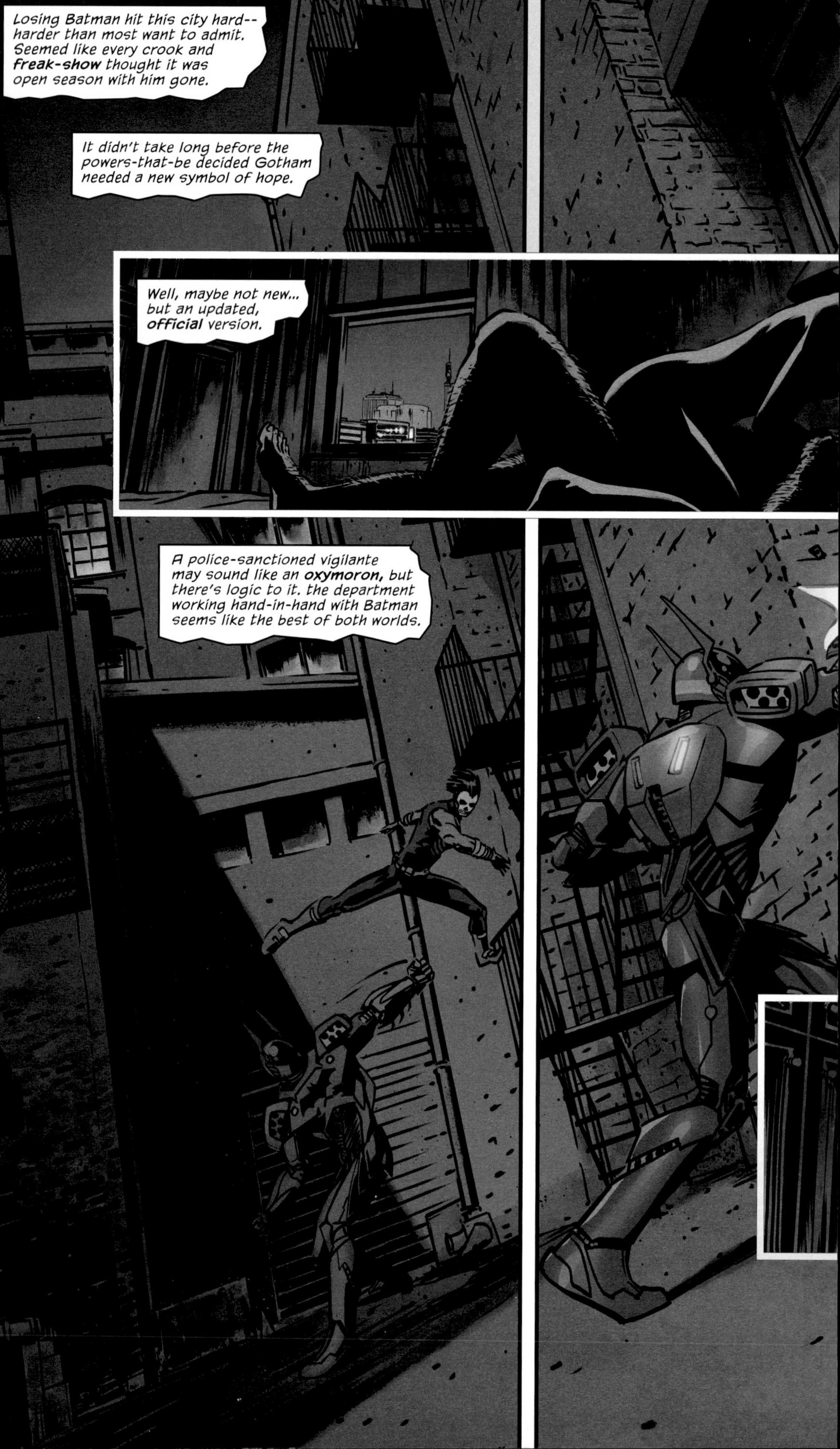
Losing **Batman** hit this city hard--harder than most want to admit. Seemed like every crook and ***freak-show*** thought it was open season with him gone.
It didn't take long before the powers-that-be decided Gotham needed a new symbol of hope.
Well, maybe not new... but an updated, ***official*** version.
A police-sanctioned vigilante may sound like an **oxymoron,** but there's logic to it. the department working hand-in-hand with Batman seems like the best of both worlds.

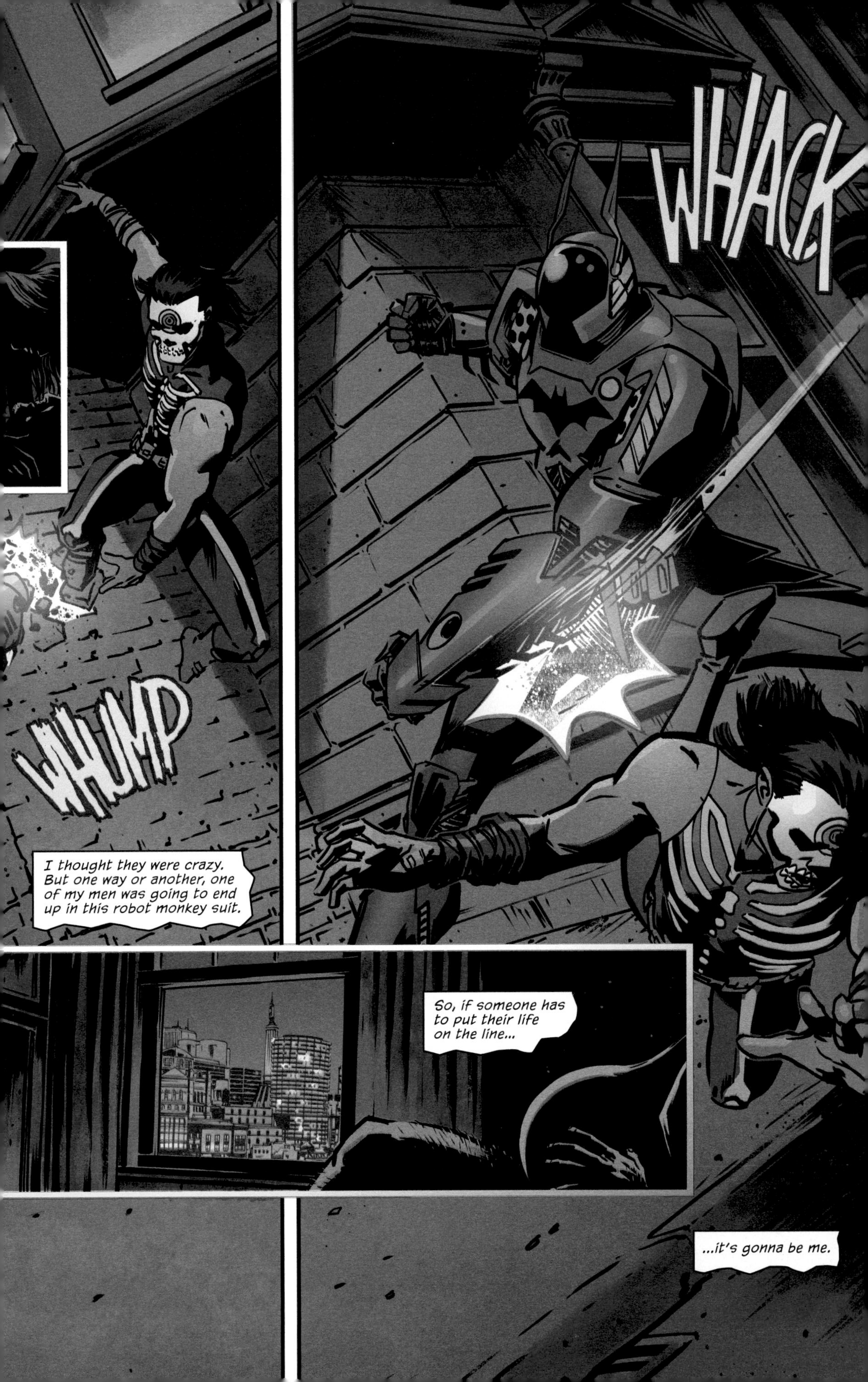
WHACK
WHUMP
I thought they were crazy. But one way or another, one of my men was going to end up in this robot monkey suit.
So, if someone has to put their life on the line...
...it's gonna be me.

I may be the one in the suit... but I'm not going at this alone. I've got a whole support team backing me up.

And I'm not foolish enough to think I'm going to replace the **real deal.** But we owe it to the man who wore the mask to do our best to honor his legacy.

If that means taking down this Day of the Dead-looking chump who had the stones to try a bank job--so be it.

I'm just hoping I don't get myself **killed** by one of these nut jobs.

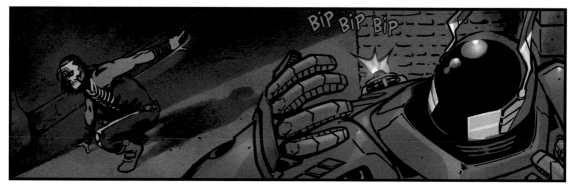

BIP BIP BIP

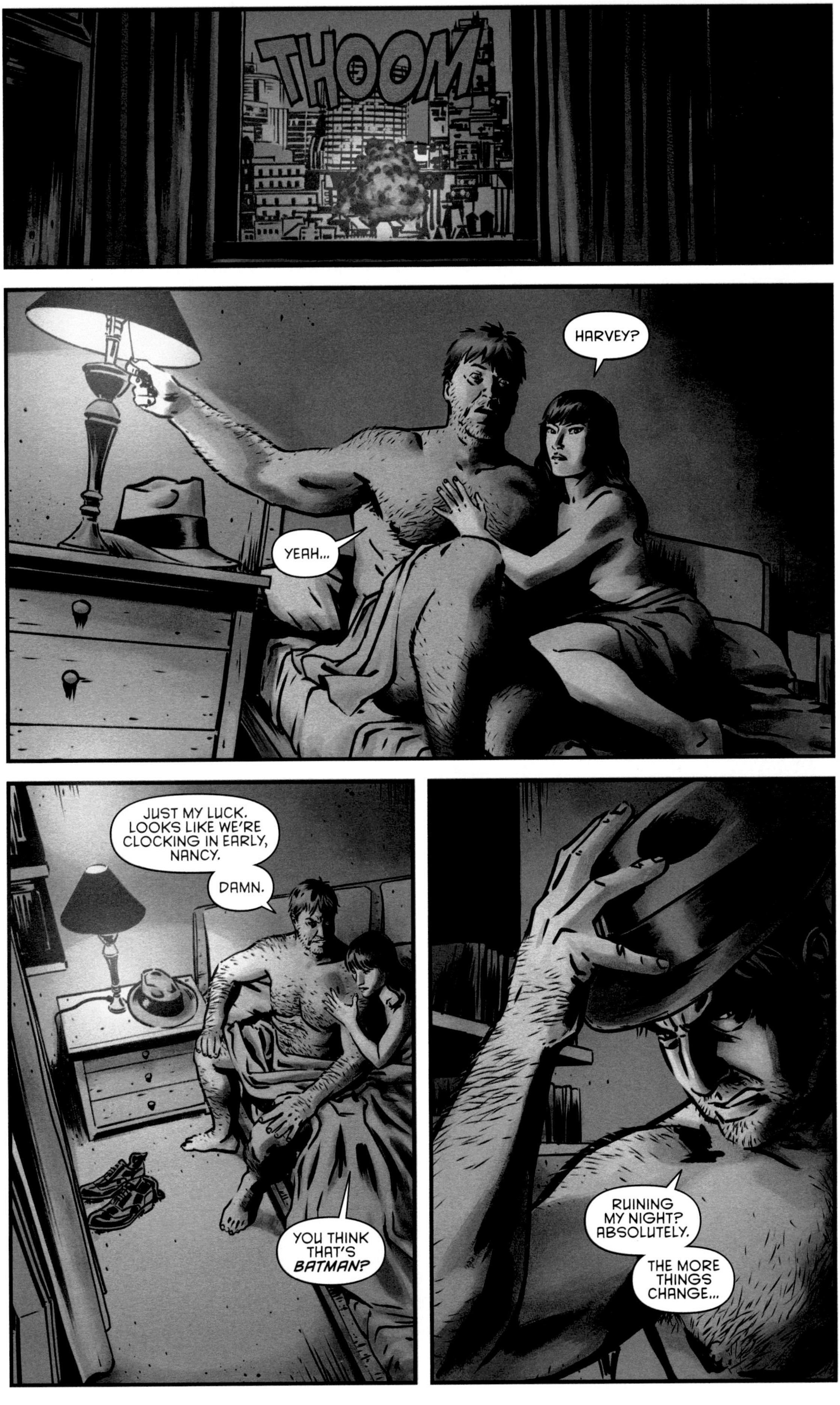
THOOM
HARVEY?
YEAH...
JUST MY LUCK. LOOKS LIKE WE'RE CLOCKING IN EARLY, NANCY.
DAMN.
YOU THINK THAT'S *BATMAN?*
RUINING MY NIGHT? ABSOLUTELY.
THE MORE THINGS CHANGE...

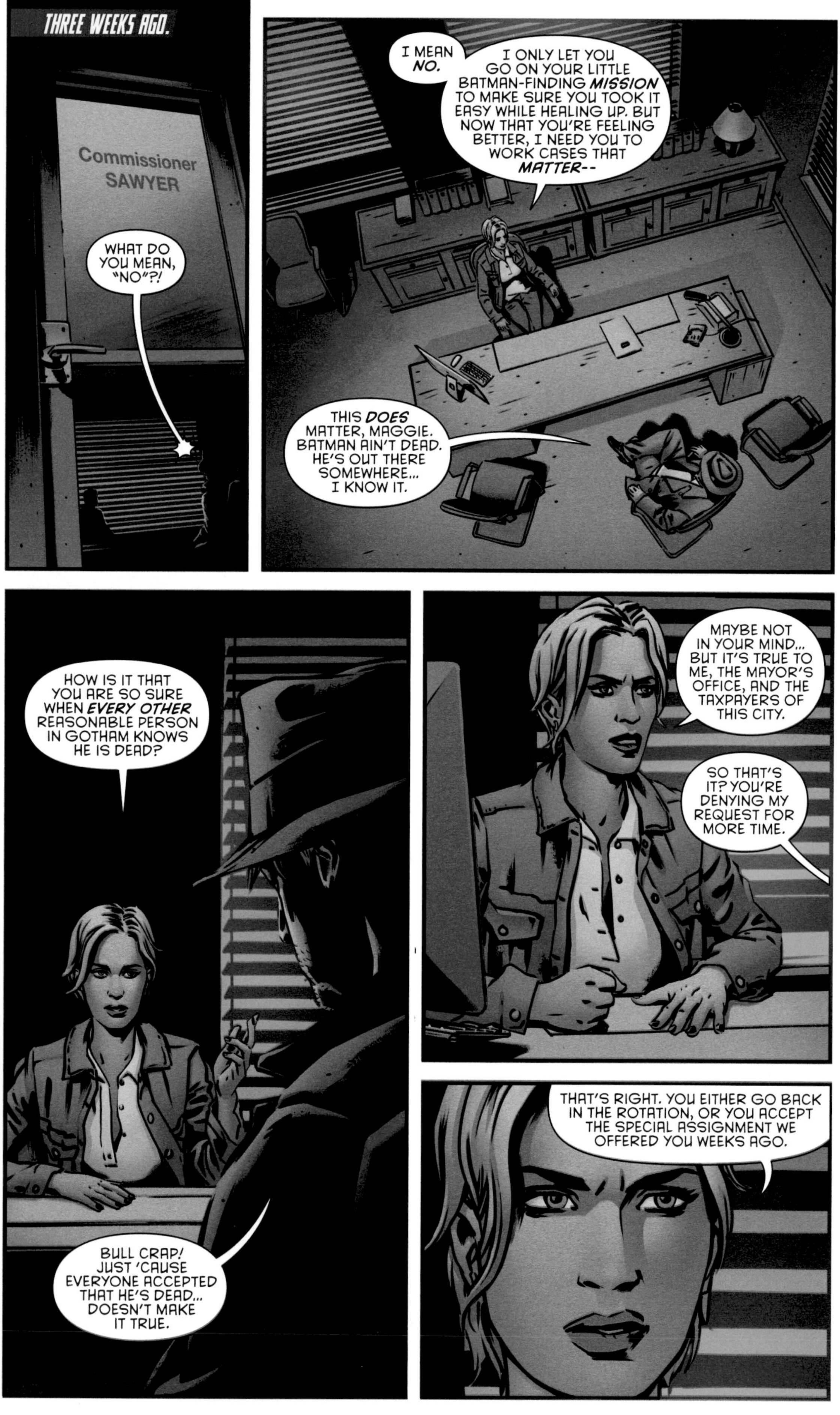
THREE WEEKS AGO.
Commissioner SAWYER
WHAT DO YOU MEAN, "NO"?!
I MEAN NO.
I ONLY LET YOU GO ON YOUR LITTLE BATMAN-FINDING MISSION TO MAKE SURE YOU TOOK IT EASY WHILE HEALING UP. BUT NOW THAT YOU'RE FEELING BETTER, I NEED YOU TO WORK CASES THAT MATTER--
THIS DOES MATTER, MAGGIE. BATMAN AIN'T DEAD. HE'S OUT THERE SOMEWHERE... I KNOW IT.
HOW IS IT THAT YOU ARE SO SURE WHEN EVERY OTHER REASONABLE PERSON IN GOTHAM KNOWS HE IS DEAD?
BULL CRAP! JUST 'CAUSE EVERYONE ACCEPTED THAT HE'S DEAD... DOESN'T MAKE IT TRUE.
MAYBE NOT IN YOUR MIND... BUT IT'S TRUE TO ME, THE MAYOR'S OFFICE, AND THE TAXPAYERS OF THIS CITY.
SO THAT'S IT? YOU'RE DENYING MY REQUEST FOR MORE TIME.
THAT'S RIGHT. YOU EITHER GO BACK IN THE ROTATION, OR YOU ACCEPT THE SPECIAL ASSIGNMENT WE OFFERED YOU WEEKS AGO.

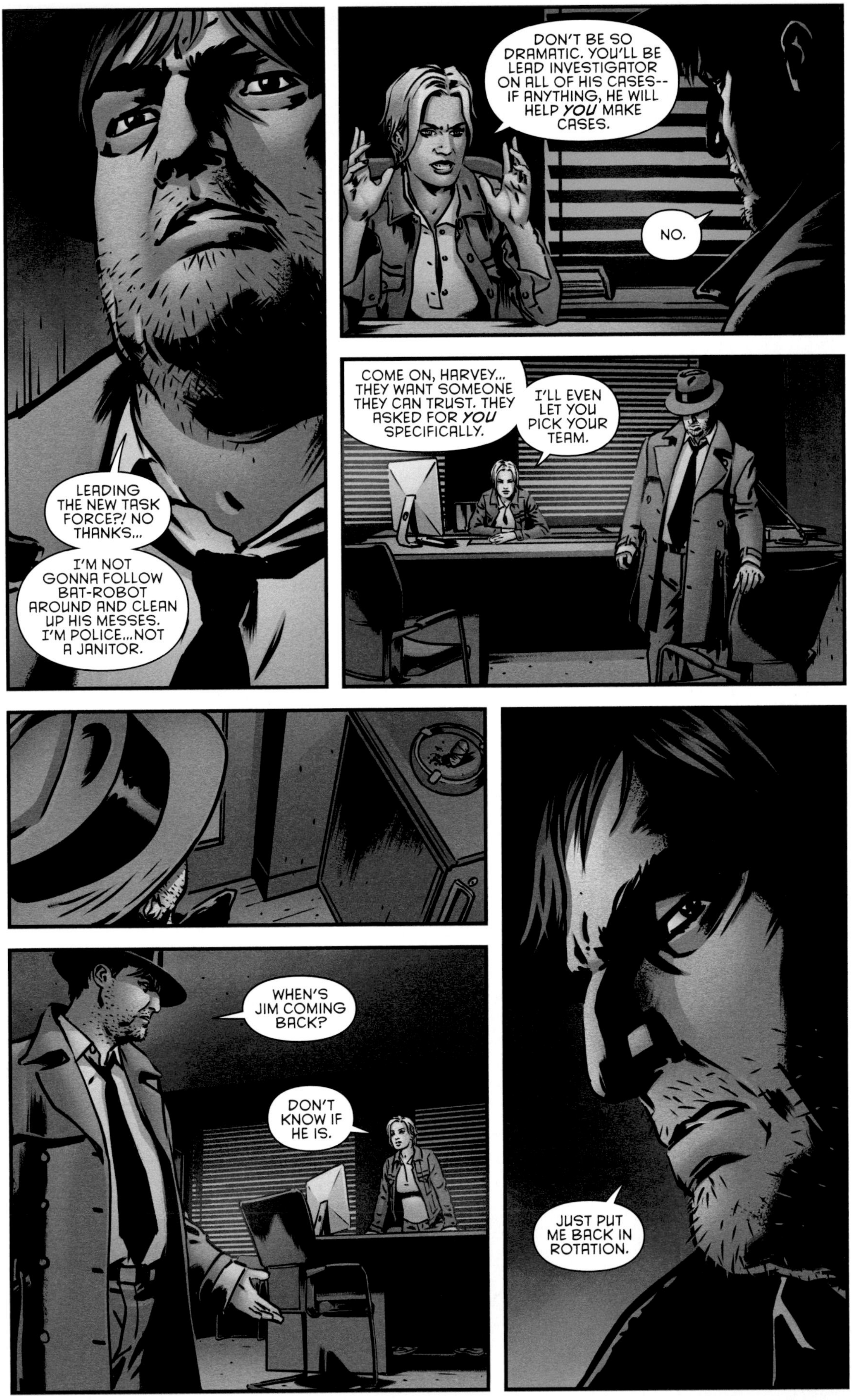
LEADING THE NEW TASK FORCE?! NO THANKS...
I'M NOT GONNA FOLLOW BAT-ROBOT AROUND AND CLEAN UP HIS MESSES. I'M POLICE...NOT A JANITOR.
DON'T BE SO DRAMATIC. YOU'LL BE LEAD INVESTIGATOR ON ALL OF HIS CASES--IF ANYTHING, HE WILL HELP *YOU* MAKE CASES.
NO.
COME ON, HARVEY... THEY WANT SOMEONE THEY CAN TRUST. THEY ASKED FOR *YOU* SPECIFICALLY.
I'LL EVEN LET YOU PICK YOUR TEAM.
WHEN'S JIM COMING BACK?
DON'T KNOW IF HE IS.
JUST PUT ME BACK IN ROTATION.

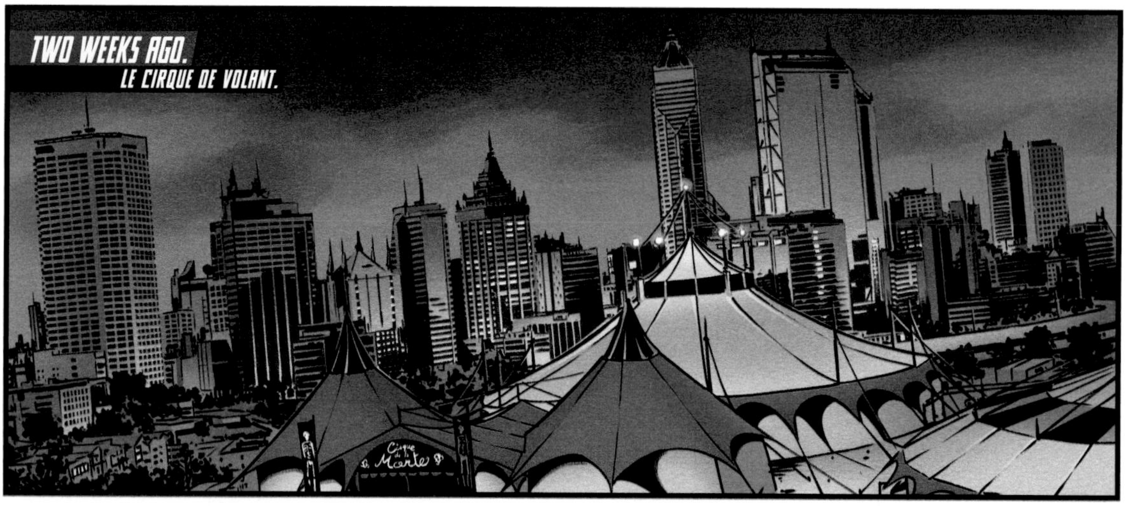
TWO WEEKS AGO.
LE CIRQUE DE VOLANT.

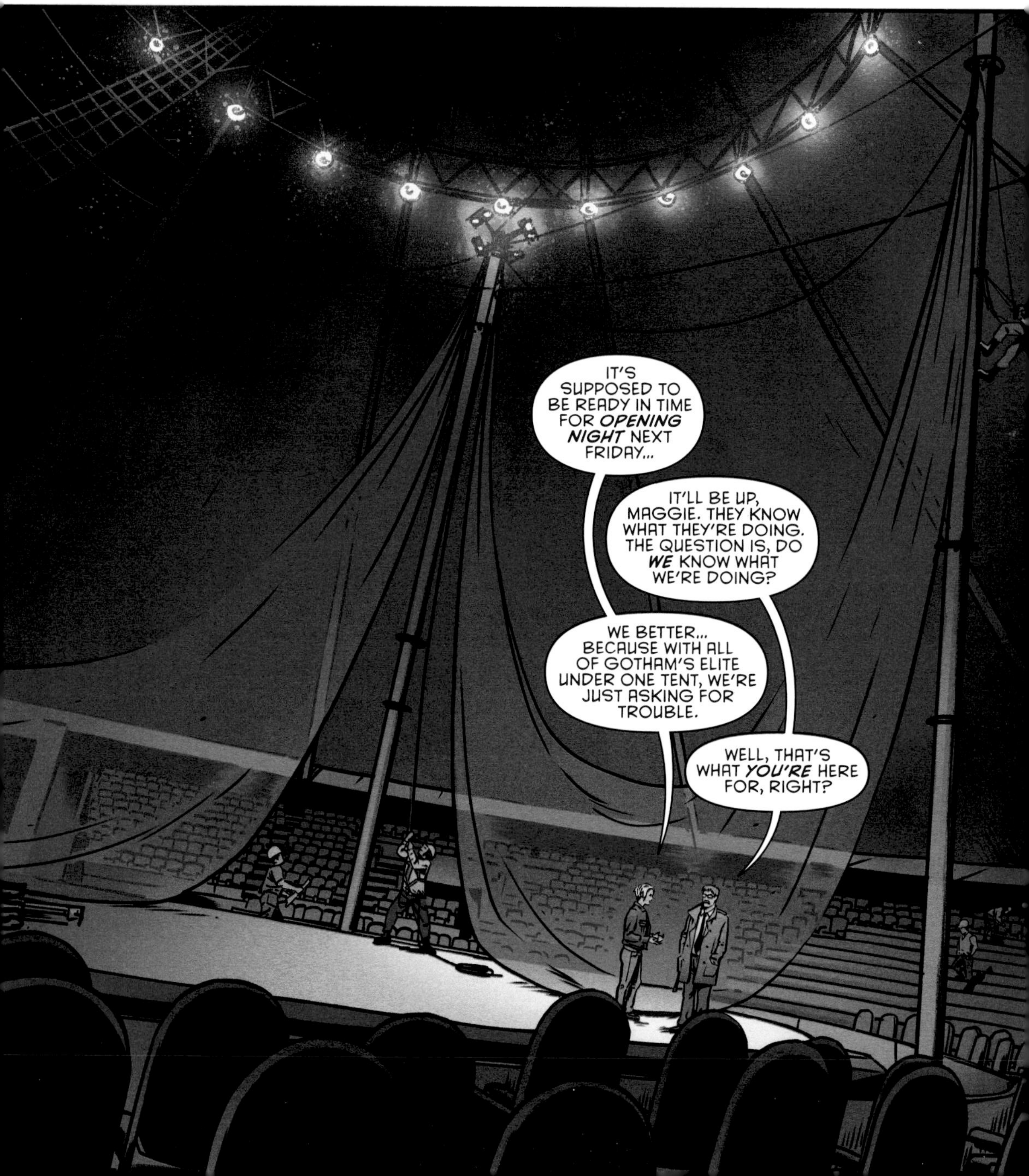
IT'S SUPPOSED TO BE READY IN TIME FOR OPENING NIGHT NEXT FRIDAY...
IT'LL BE UP, MAGGIE. THEY KNOW WHAT THEY'RE DOING. THE QUESTION IS, DO WE KNOW WHAT WE'RE DOING?
WE BETTER... BECAUSE WITH ALL OF GOTHAM'S ELITE UNDER ONE TENT, WE'RE JUST ASKING FOR TROUBLE.
WELL, THAT'S WHAT YOU'RE HERE FOR, RIGHT?

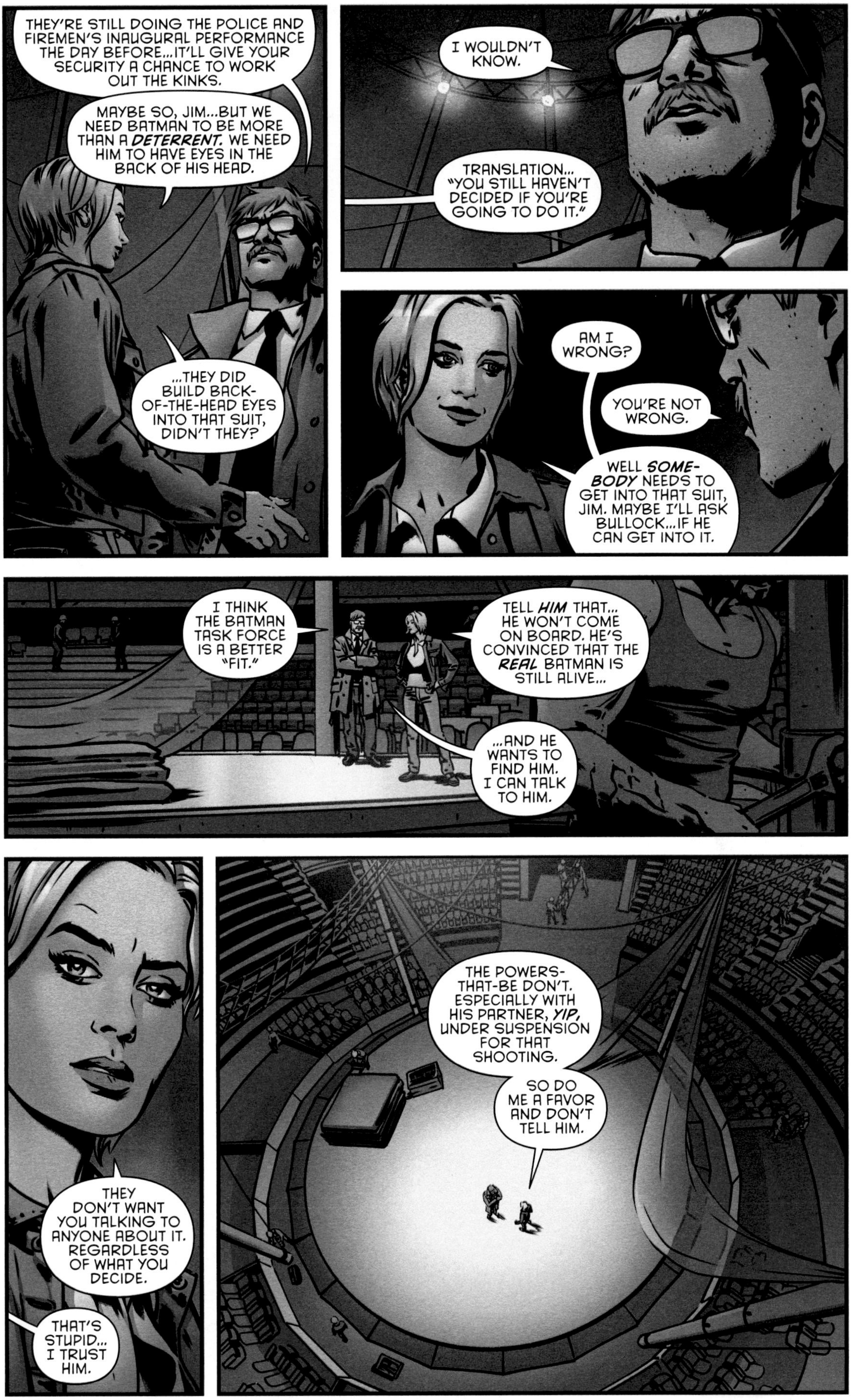
THEY'RE STILL DOING THE POLICE AND FIREMEN'S INAUGURAL PERFORMANCE THE DAY BEFORE...IT'LL GIVE YOUR SECURITY A CHANCE TO WORK OUT THE KINKS.
MAYBE SO, JIM...BUT WE NEED BATMAN TO BE MORE THAN A DETERRENT. WE NEED HIM TO HAVE EYES IN THE BACK OF HIS HEAD.
...THEY DID BUILD BACK-OF-THE-HEAD EYES INTO THAT SUIT, DIDN'T THEY?
I WOULDN'T KNOW.
TRANSLATION... "YOU STILL HAVEN'T DECIDED IF YOU'RE GOING TO DO IT."
AM I WRONG?
YOU'RE NOT WRONG.
WELL SOME-BODY NEEDS TO GET INTO THAT SUIT, JIM. MAYBE I'LL ASK BULLOCK...IF HE CAN GET INTO IT.
I THINK THE BATMAN TASK FORCE IS A BETTER "FIT."
TELL HIM THAT... HE WON'T COME ON BOARD. HE'S CONVINCED THAT THE REAL BATMAN IS STILL ALIVE...
...AND HE WANTS TO FIND HIM. I CAN TALK TO HIM.
THEY DON'T WANT YOU TALKING TO ANYONE ABOUT IT. REGARDLESS OF WHAT YOU DECIDE.
THAT'S STUPID... I TRUST HIM.
THE POWERS-THAT-BE DON'T. ESPECIALLY WITH HIS PARTNER, YIP, UNDER SUSPENSION FOR THAT SHOOTING.
SO DO ME A FAVOR AND DON'T TELL HIM.

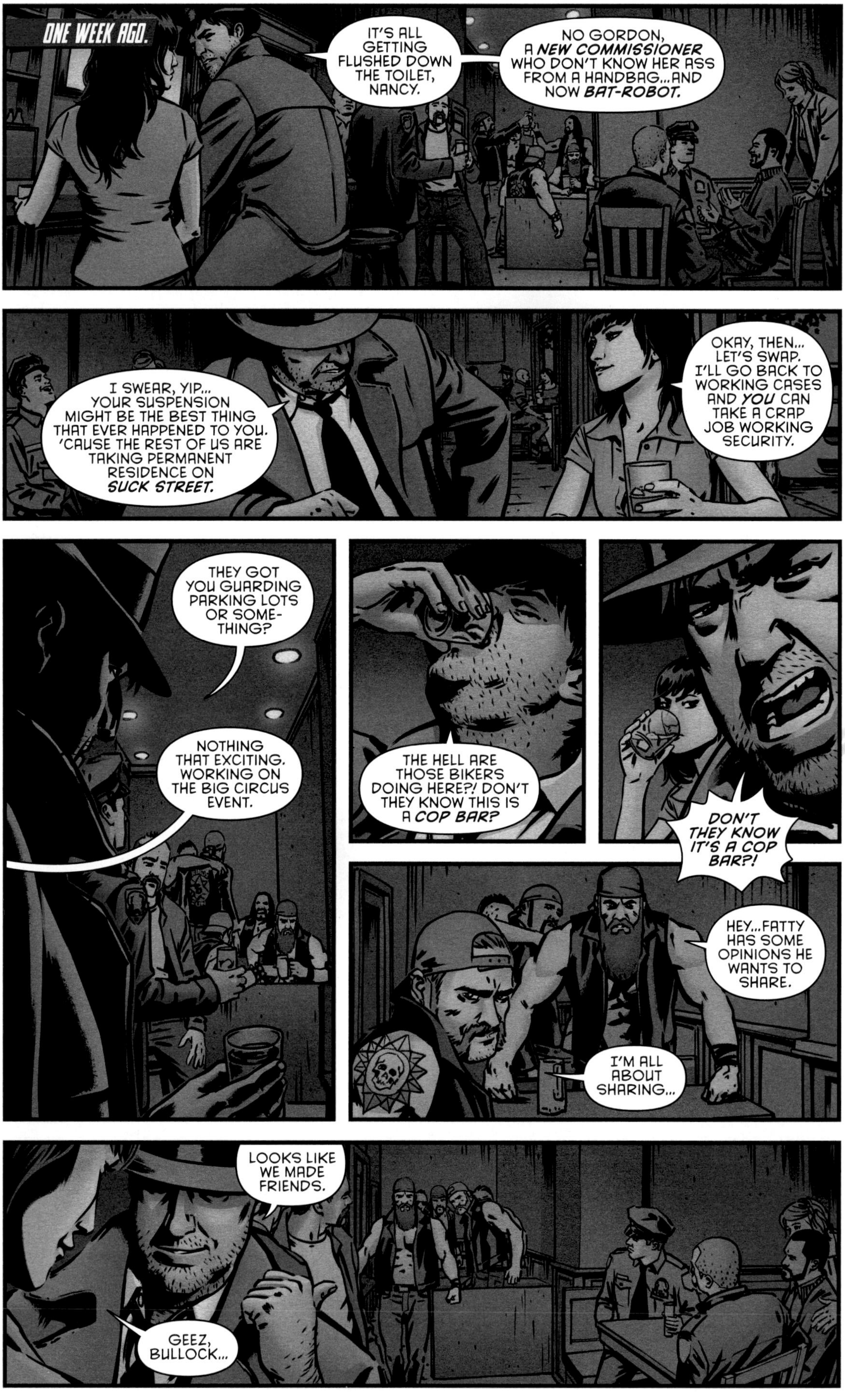
ONE WEEK AGO.
IT'S ALL GETTING FLUSHED DOWN THE TOILET, NANCY.
NO GORDON, A NEW COMMISSIONER WHO DON'T KNOW HER ASS FROM A HANDBAG...AND NOW BAT-ROBOT.
I SWEAR, YIP... YOUR SUSPENSION MIGHT BE THE BEST THING THAT EVER HAPPENED TO YOU. 'CAUSE THE REST OF US ARE TAKING PERMANENT RESIDENCE ON SUCK STREET.
OKAY, THEN... LET'S SWAP. I'LL GO BACK TO WORKING CASES AND YOU CAN TAKE A CRAP JOB WORKING SECURITY.
THEY GOT YOU GUARDING PARKING LOTS OR SOME-THING?
NOTHING THAT EXCITING. WORKING ON THE BIG CIRCUS EVENT.
THE HELL ARE THOSE BIKERS DOING HERE?! DON'T THEY KNOW THIS IS A COP BAR?
DON'T THEY KNOW IT'S A COP BAR?!
HEY...FATTY HAS SOME OPINIONS HE WANTS TO SHARE.
I'M ALL ABOUT SHARING...
LOOKS LIKE WE MADE FRIENDS.
GEEZ, BULLOCK...

WHY DON'T YOU SHARE WITH US?

YOU GOT IT!

YEAH, A COUPLE COPS IN A COP BAR.

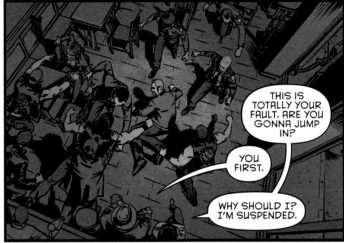

THIS IS TOTALLY YOUR FAULT. ARE YOU GONNA JUMP IN?

YOU FIRST.

WHY SHOULD I? I'M SUSPENDED.

LOOKS LIKE GILES COULD USE A HAND.

HE'S ON THE REVIEW BOARD...SAVE HIS BACON AND MAYBE HE REINSTATES YOU.

WHY DIDN'T YOU SAY SO...

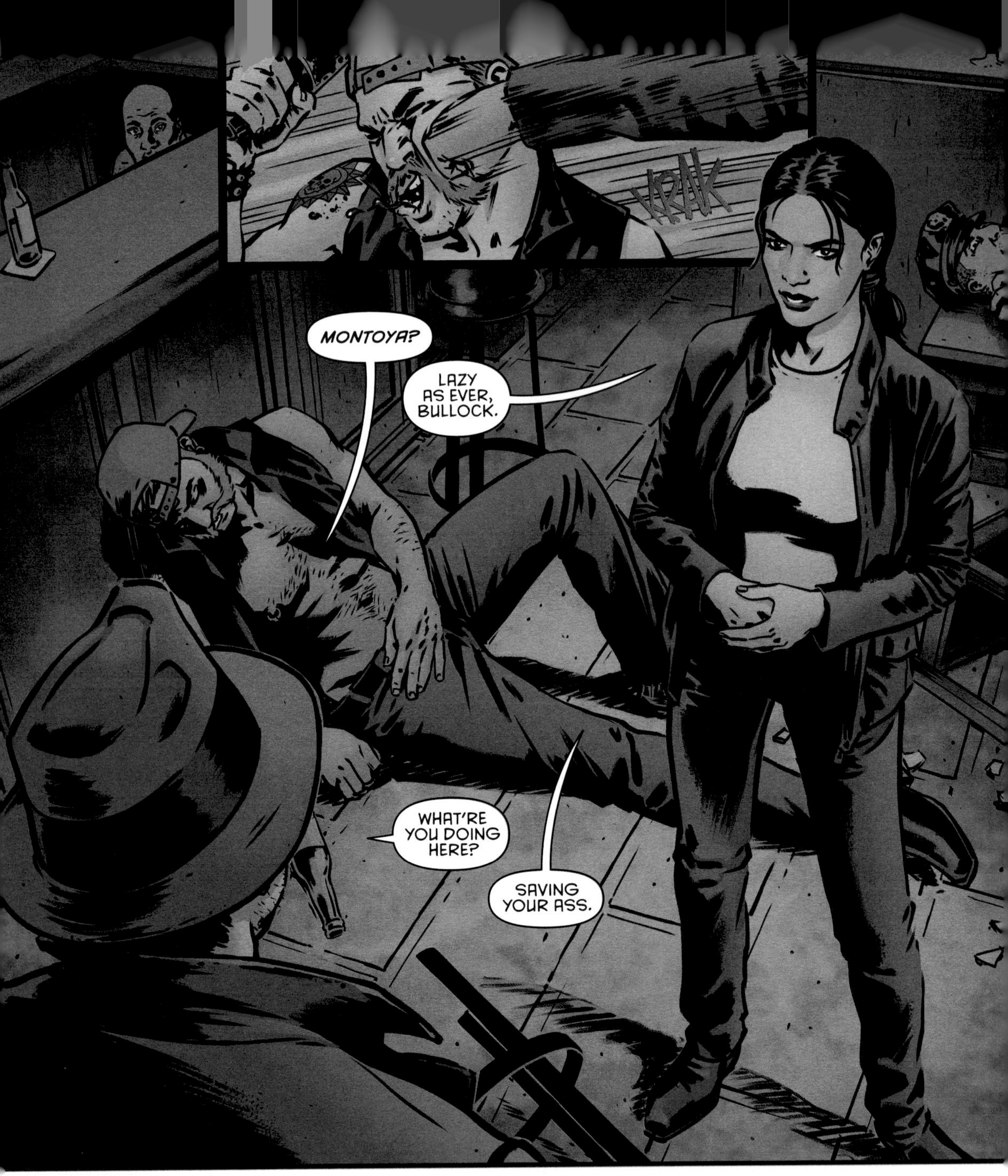
VRAK
MONTOYA?
LAZY AS EVER, BULLOCK.
WHAT'RE YOU DOING HERE?
SAVING YOUR ASS.
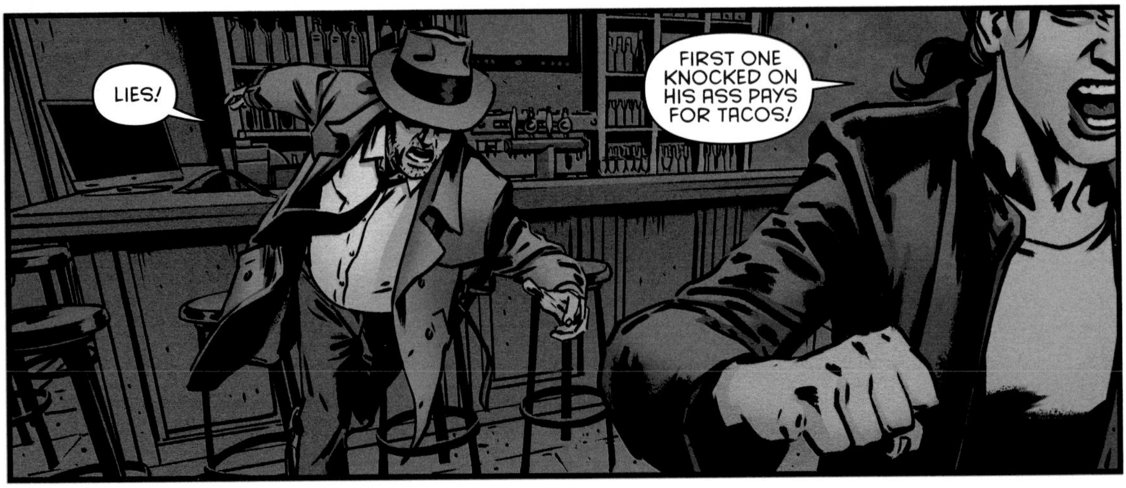
LIES!
FIRST ONE KNOCKED ON HIS ASS PAYS FOR TACOS!

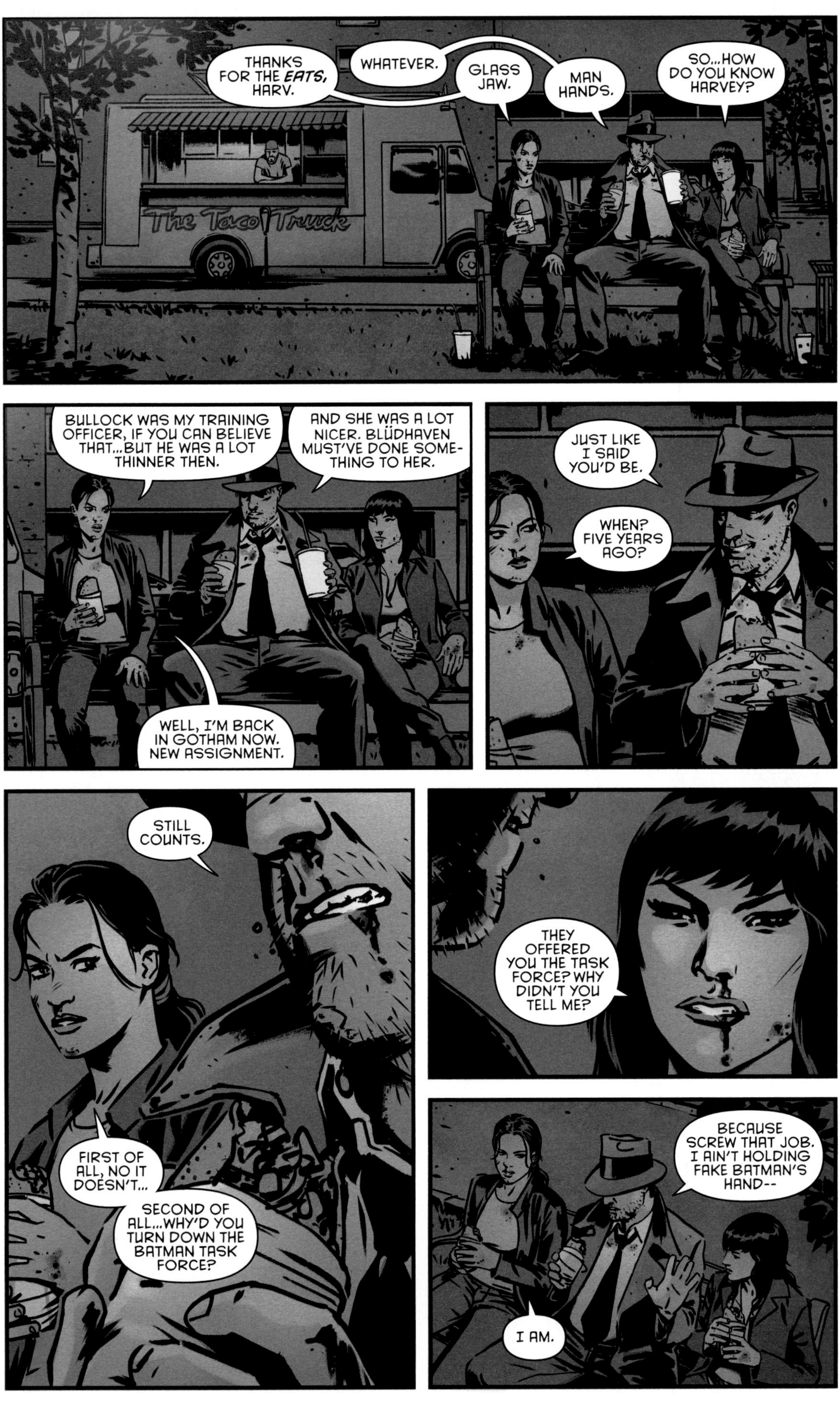
THANKS FOR THE EATS, HARV.
WHATEVER.
GLASS JAW.
MAN HANDS.
SO...HOW DO YOU KNOW HARVEY?
The Taco Truck
BULLOCK WAS MY TRAINING OFFICER, IF YOU CAN BELIEVE THAT...BUT HE WAS A LOT THINNER THEN.
AND SHE WAS A LOT NICER. BLÜDHAVEN MUST'VE DONE SOME-THING TO HER.
WELL, I'M BACK IN GOTHAM NOW. NEW ASSIGNMENT.
JUST LIKE I SAID YOU'D BE.
WHEN? FIVE YEARS AGO?
STILL COUNTS.
FIRST OF ALL, NO IT DOESN'T...
SECOND OF ALL...WHY'D YOU TURN DOWN THE BATMAN TASK FORCE?
THEY OFFERED YOU THE TASK FORCE? WHY DIDN'T YOU TELL ME?
BECAUSE SCREW THAT JOB. I AIN'T HOLDING FAKE BATMAN'S HAND--
I AM.

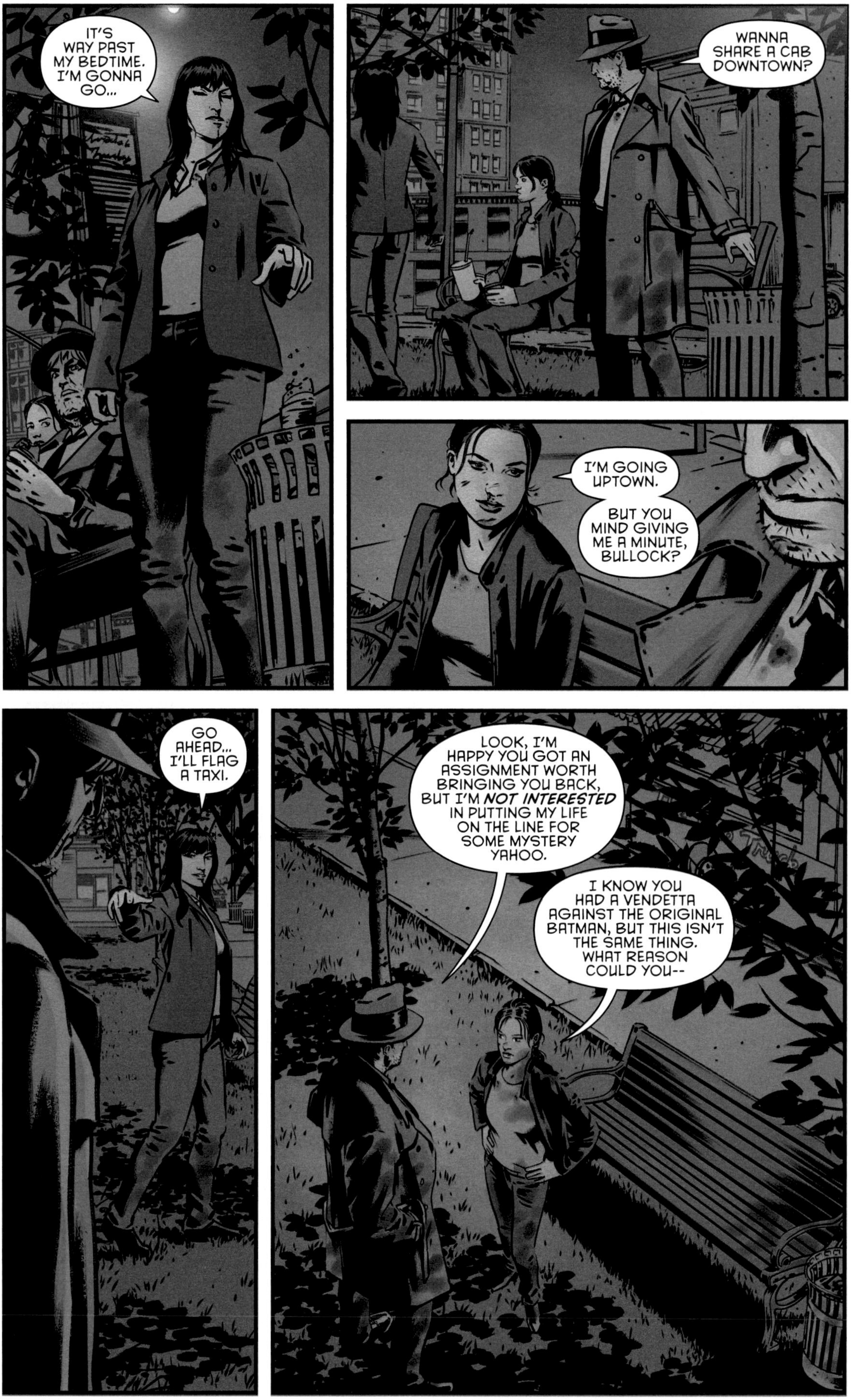
IT'S WAY PAST MY BEDTIME. I'M GONNA GO...
WANNA SHARE A CAB DOWNTOWN?
I'M GOING UPTOWN.
BUT YOU MIND GIVING ME A MINUTE, BULLOCK?
GO AHEAD... I'LL FLAG A TAXI.
LOOK, I'M HAPPY YOU GOT AN ASSIGNMENT WORTH BRINGING YOU BACK, BUT I'M ***NOT INTERESTED*** IN PUTTING MY LIFE ON THE LINE FOR SOME MYSTERY YAHOO.
I KNOW YOU HAD A VENDETTA AGAINST THE ORIGINAL BATMAN, BUT THIS ISN'T THE SAME THING. WHAT REASON COULD YOU--

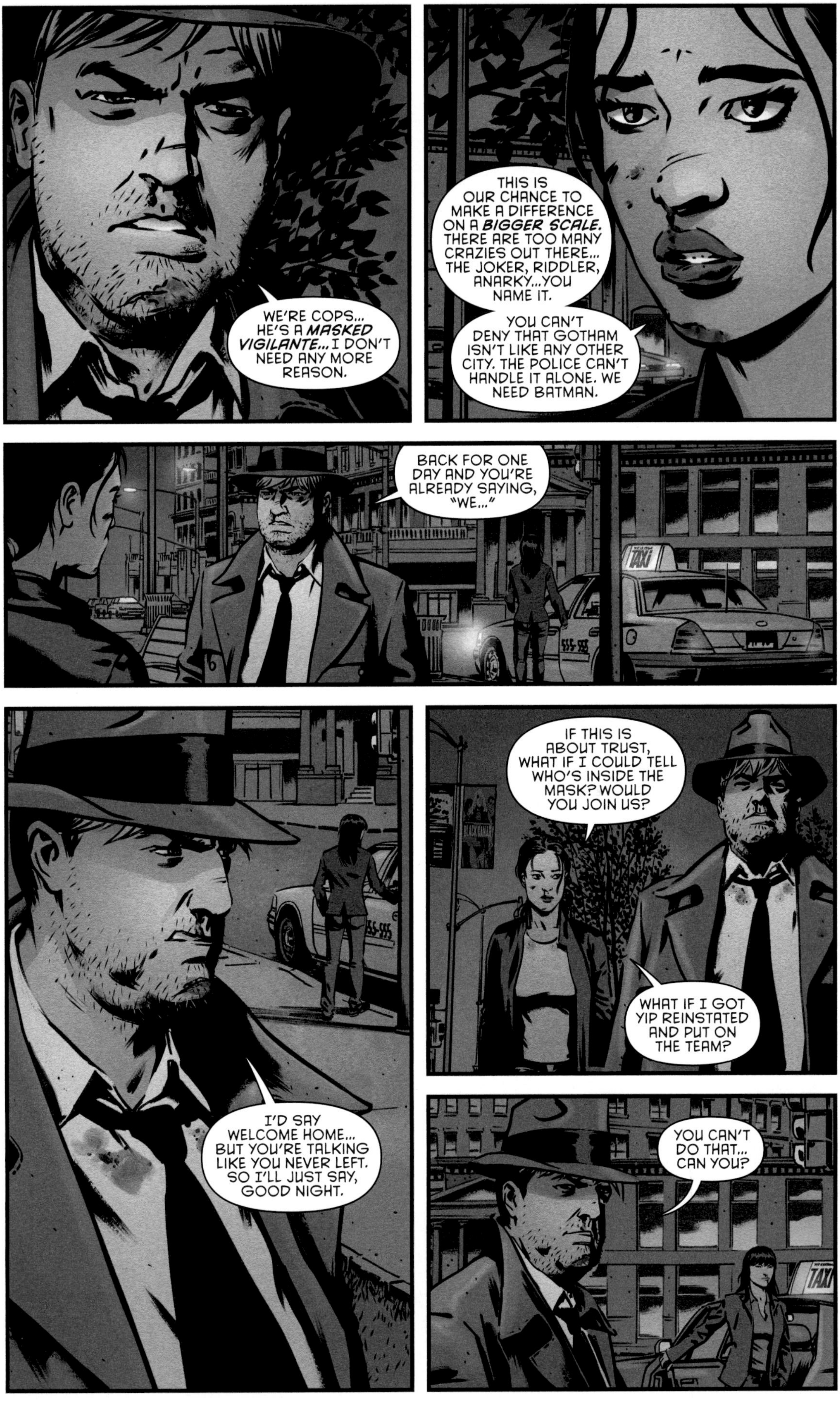
WE'RE COPS... HE'S A *MASKED VIGILANTE...* I DON'T NEED ANY MORE REASON.
THIS IS OUR CHANCE TO MAKE A DIFFERENCE ON A *BIGGER SCALE.* THERE ARE TOO MANY CRAZIES OUT THERE... THE JOKER, RIDDLER, ANARKY...YOU NAME IT.
YOU CAN'T DENY THAT GOTHAM ISN'T LIKE ANY OTHER CITY. THE POLICE CAN'T HANDLE IT ALONE. WE NEED BATMAN.
BACK FOR ONE DAY AND YOU'RE ALREADY SAYING, "WE..."
TAXI
I'D SAY WELCOME HOME... BUT YOU'RE TALKING LIKE YOU NEVER LEFT. SO I'LL JUST SAY, GOOD NIGHT.
IF THIS IS ABOUT TRUST, WHAT IF I COULD TELL WHO'S INSIDE THE MASK? WOULD YOU JOIN US?
WHAT IF I GOT YIP REINSTATED AND PUT ON THE TEAM?
YOU CAN'T DO THAT... CAN YOU?
TAXI

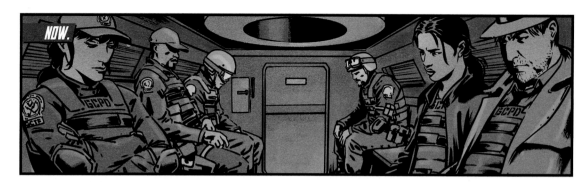

NOW.

DAMN...

WHERE THE HELL IS HE?

I DON'T KNOW. THERE COULD BE A SLIGHT VARIANCE...BUT HE SHOULD BE HERE.

WHAT DO YOU MEAN, *HERE*?

LIKE RIGHT HERE. *GROUND ZERO.*

ARE YOU SAYING THIS MESS COULD BE *HIM?*

I'M NOT SAYING ANYTHING...EXCEPT HE SHOULD BE HERE!

OF COURSE HE SHOULD BE. BUT HE'S NOT.

UM...

YES HE IS.

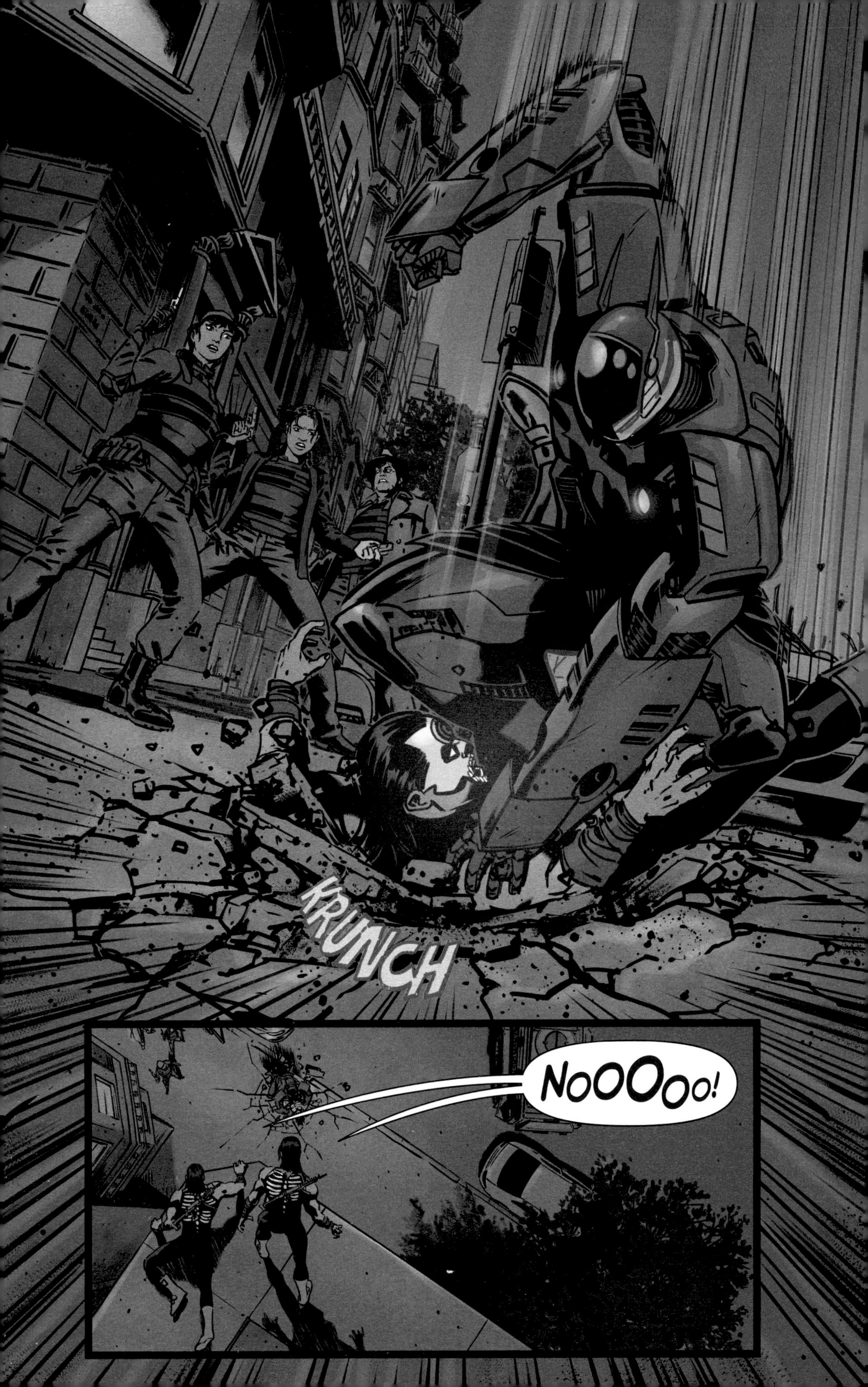
KRUNCH
NOOOoo!

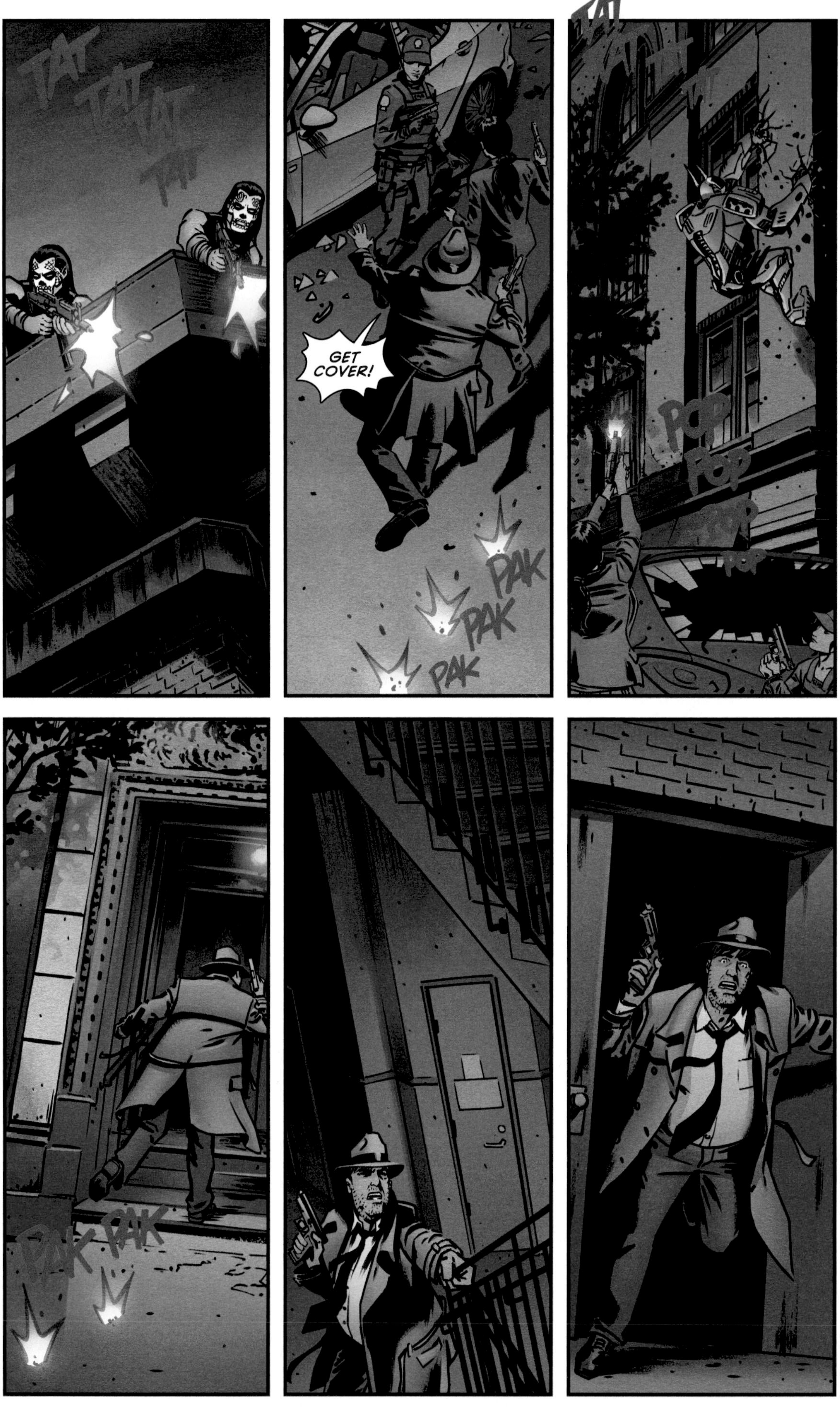
TAT
TAT
TAT
TAT
GET COVER!
PAK
PAK
PAK
TAT
TAT
TAT
POP
POP
POP
POP
PAK
PAK

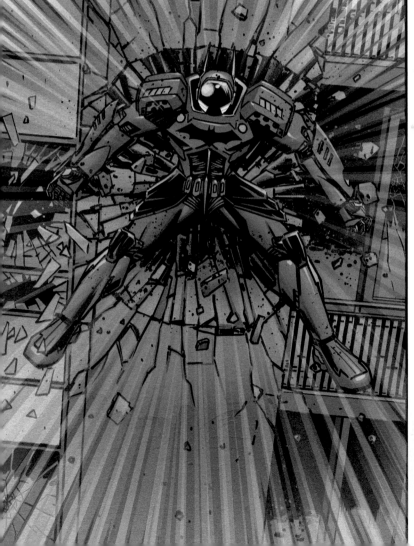

NO!

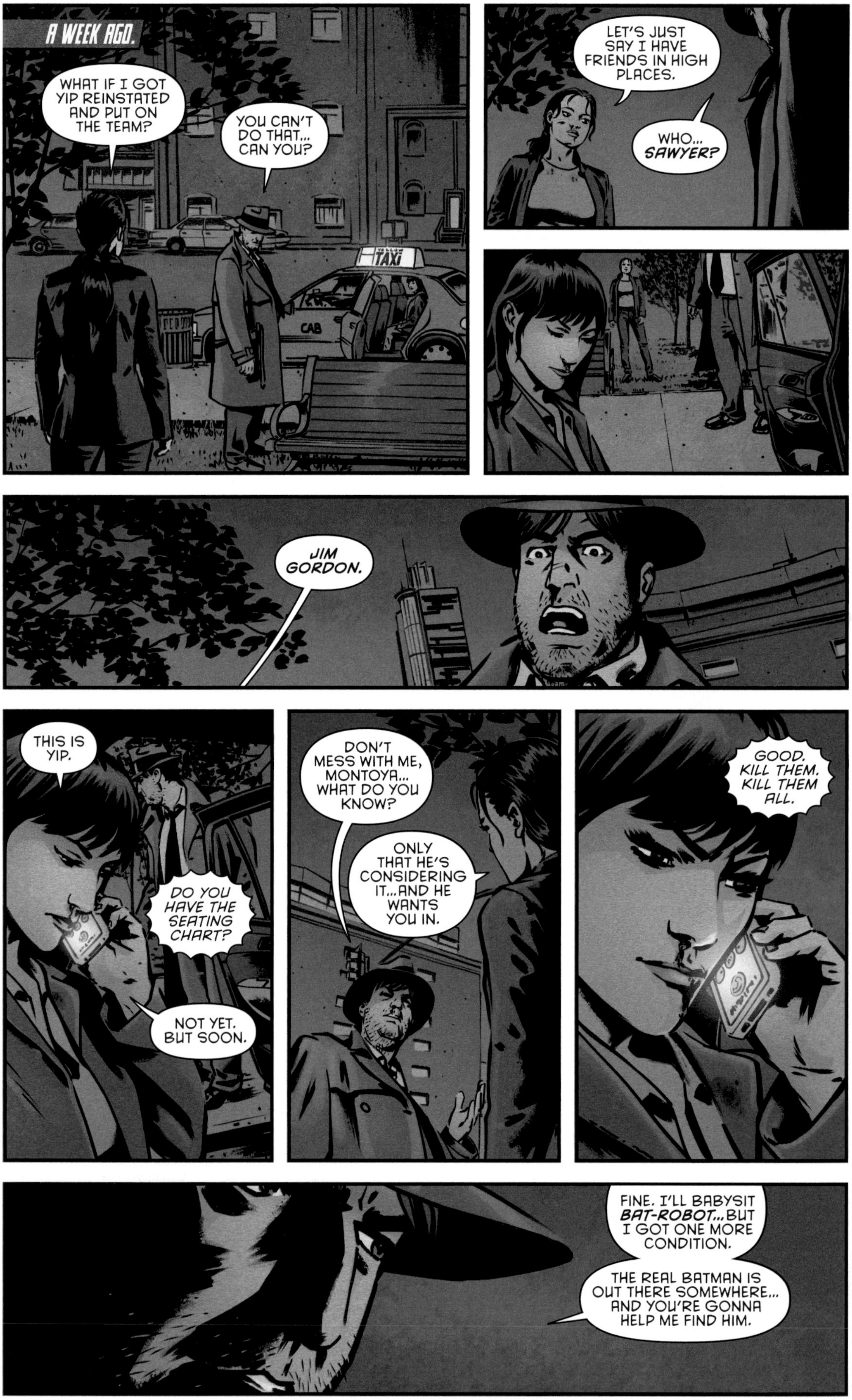
A WEEK AGO.
WHAT IF I GOT YIP REINSTATED AND PUT ON THE TEAM?
YOU CAN'T DO THAT... CAN YOU?
TAXI
CAB
LET'S JUST SAY I HAVE FRIENDS IN HIGH PLACES.
WHO... SAWYER?
JIM GORDON.
THIS IS YIP.
DO YOU HAVE THE SEATING CHART?
NOT YET. BUT SOON.
DON'T MESS WITH ME, MONTOYA... WHAT DO YOU KNOW?
ONLY THAT HE'S CONSIDERING IT...AND HE WANTS YOU IN.
GOOD. KILL THEM. KILL THEM ALL.
FINE. I'LL BABYSIT BAT-ROBOT...BUT I GOT ONE MORE CONDITION.
THE REAL BATMAN IS OUT THERE SOMEWHERE... AND YOU'RE GONNA HELP ME FIND HIM.

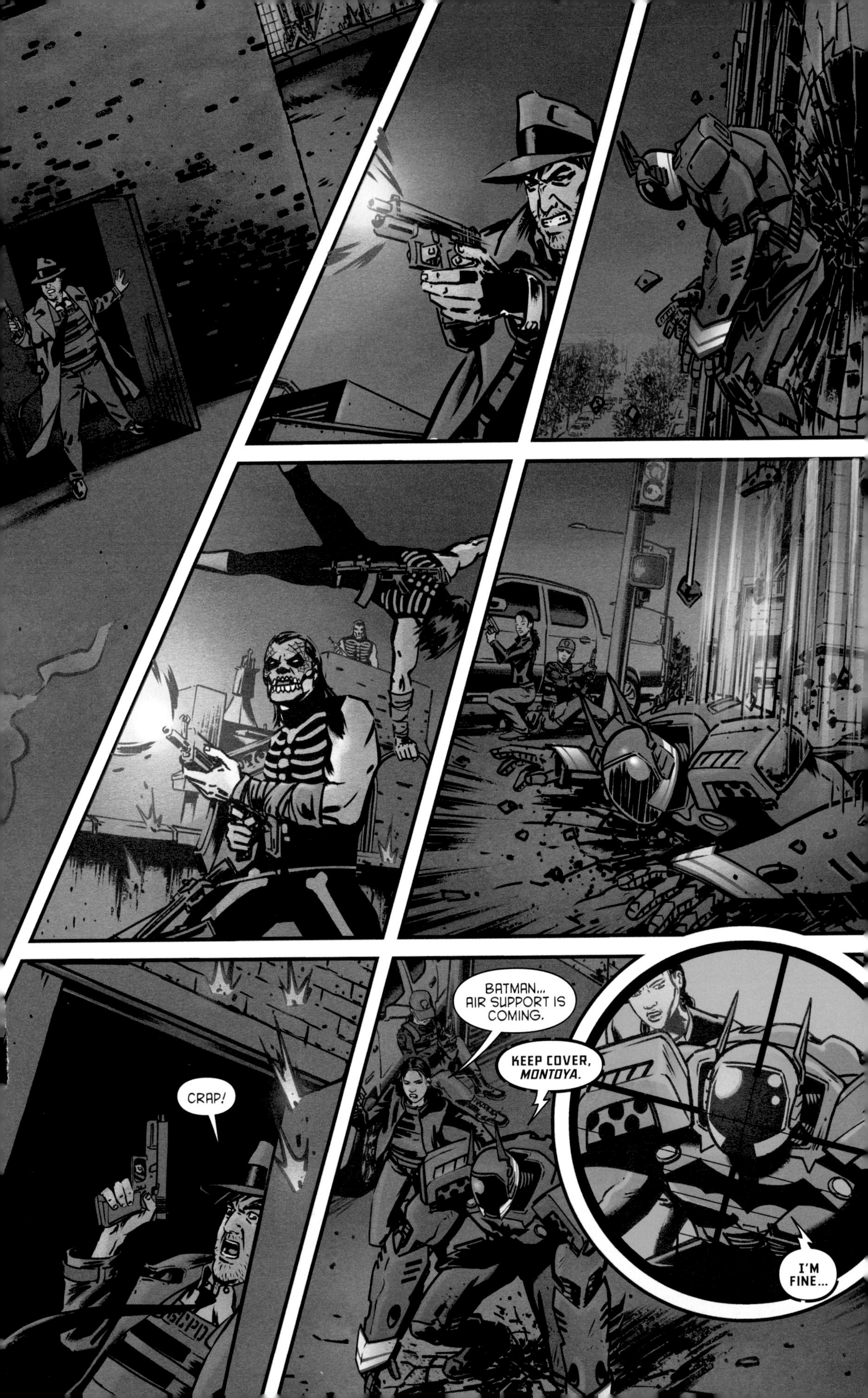
CRAP!
BATMAN... AIR SUPPORT IS COMING.
KEEP COVER, MONTOYA.
I'M FINE...

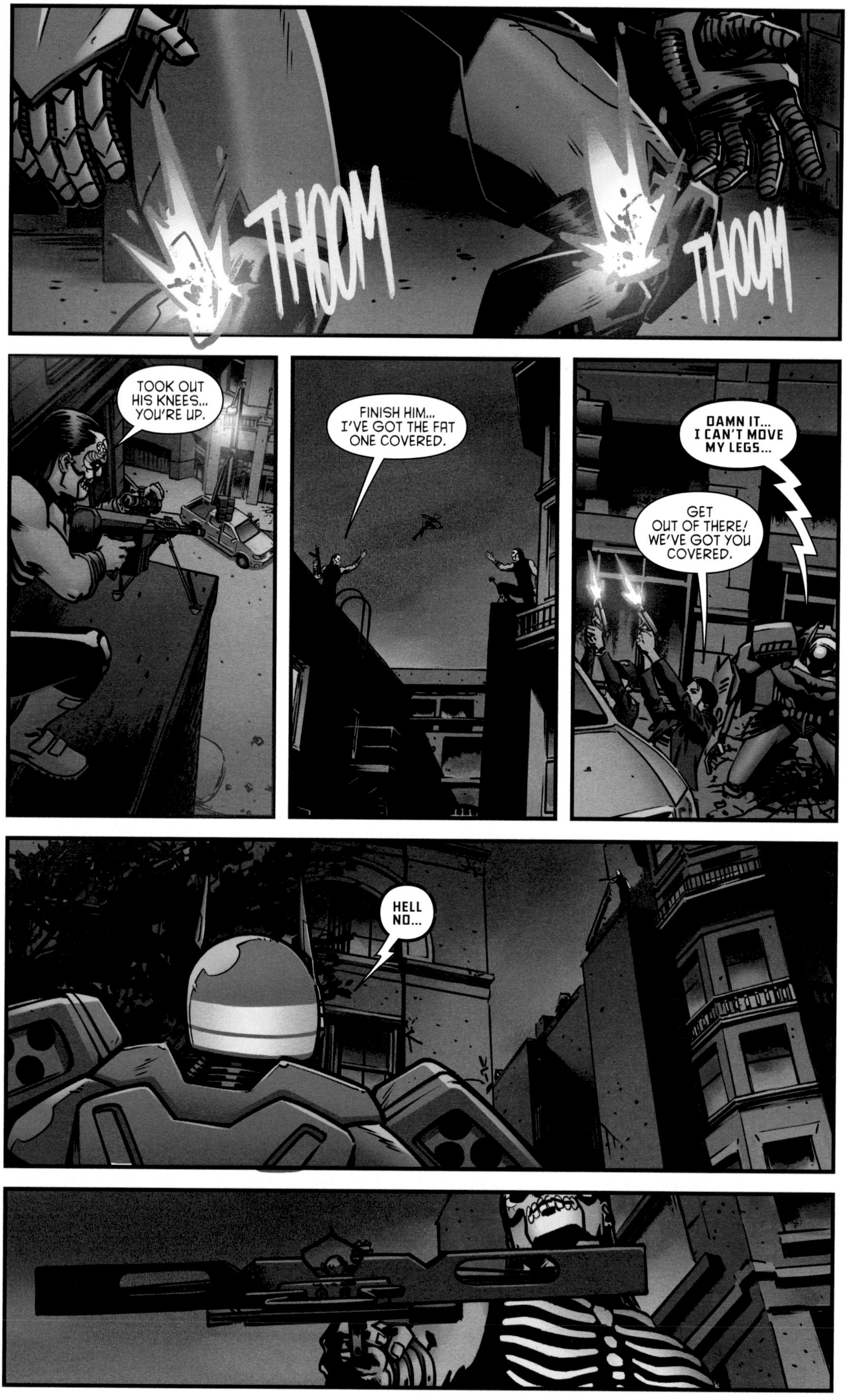
THOOM
THOOM
TOOK OUT HIS KNEES... YOU'RE UP.
FINISH HIM... I'VE GOT THE FAT ONE COVERED.
DAMN IT... I CAN'T MOVE MY LEGS...
GET OUT OF THERE! WE'VE GOT YOU COVERED.
HELL NO...

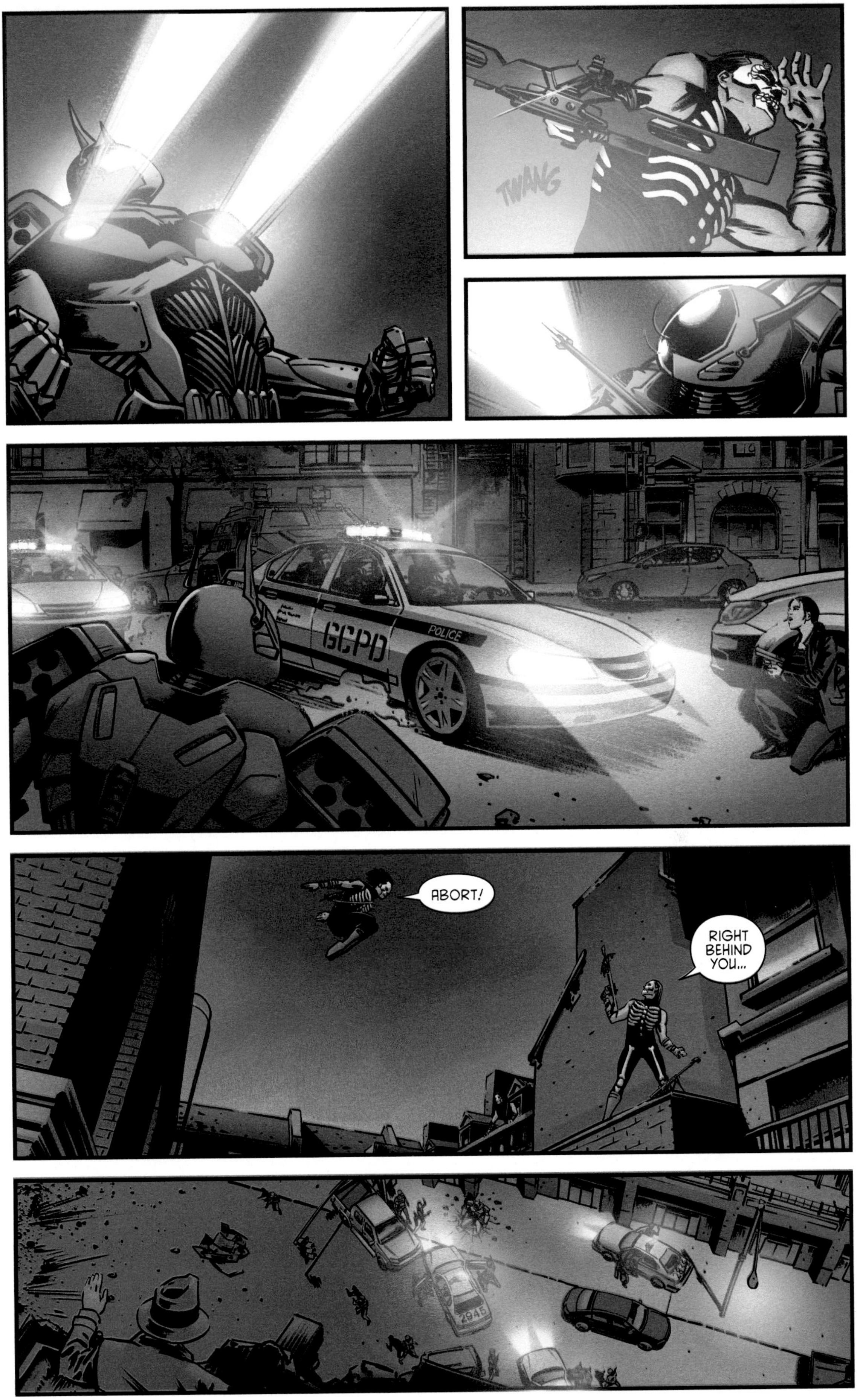
TWANG
GCPD
POLICE
ABORT!
RIGHT BEHIND YOU...
2945

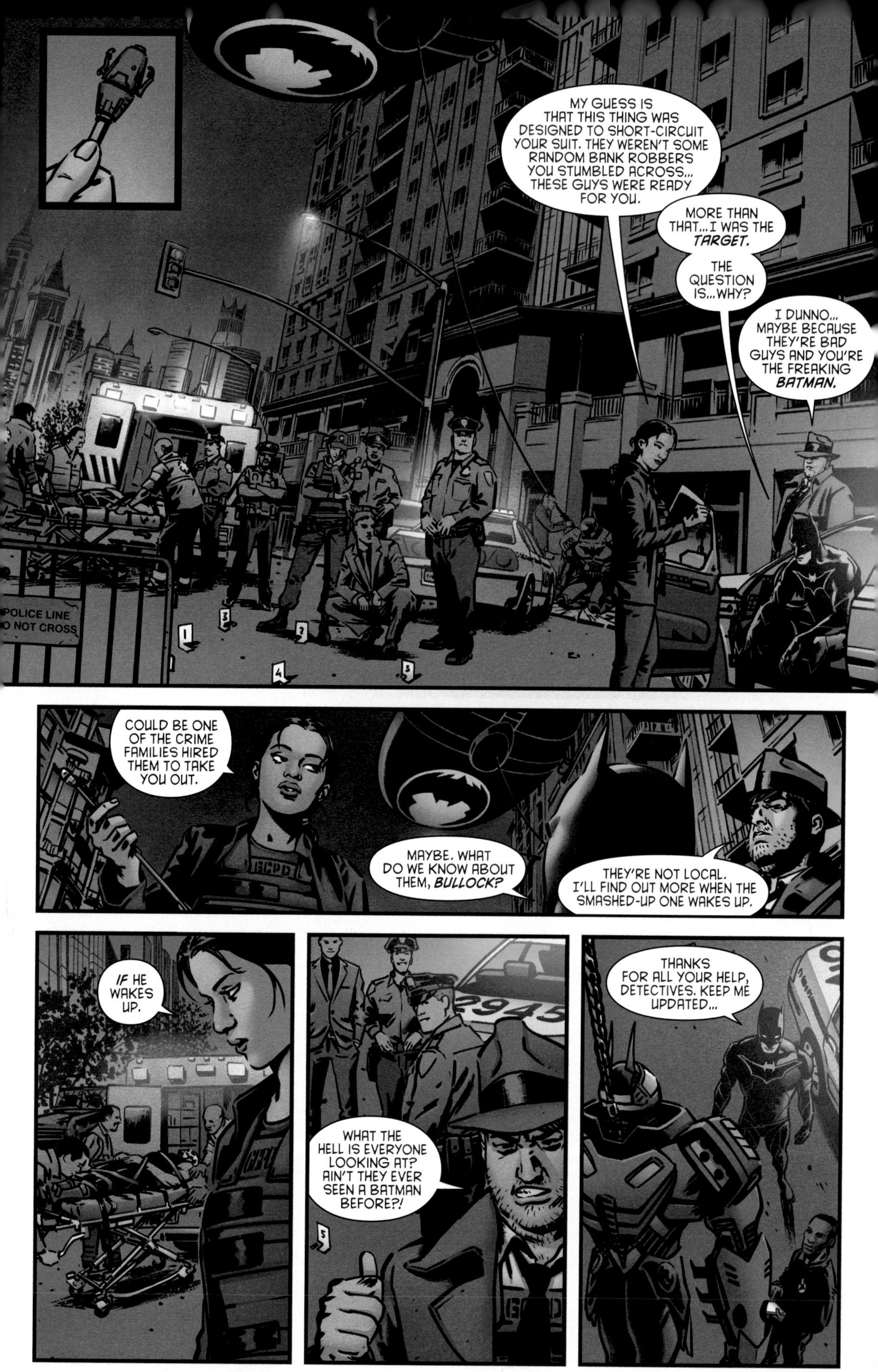
MY GUESS IS THAT THIS THING WAS DESIGNED TO SHORT-CIRCUIT YOUR SUIT. THEY WEREN'T SOME RANDOM BANK ROBBERS YOU STUMBLED ACROSS... THESE GUYS WERE READY FOR YOU.
MORE THAN THAT...I WAS THE *TARGET.*
THE QUESTION IS...WHY?
I DUNNO... MAYBE BECAUSE THEY'RE BAD GUYS AND YOU'RE THE FREAKING *BATMAN.*
POLICE LINE
O NOT CROSS
COULD BE ONE OF THE CRIME FAMILIES HIRED THEM TO TAKE YOU OUT.
MAYBE. WHAT DO WE KNOW ABOUT THEM, *BULLOCK?*
THEY'RE NOT LOCAL. I'LL FIND OUT MORE WHEN THE SMASHED-UP ONE WAKES UP.
IF HE WAKES UP.
WHAT THE HELL IS EVERYONE LOOKING AT? AIN'T THEY EVER SEEN A BATMAN BEFORE?!
THANKS FOR ALL YOUR HELP, DETECTIVES. KEEP ME UPDATED...

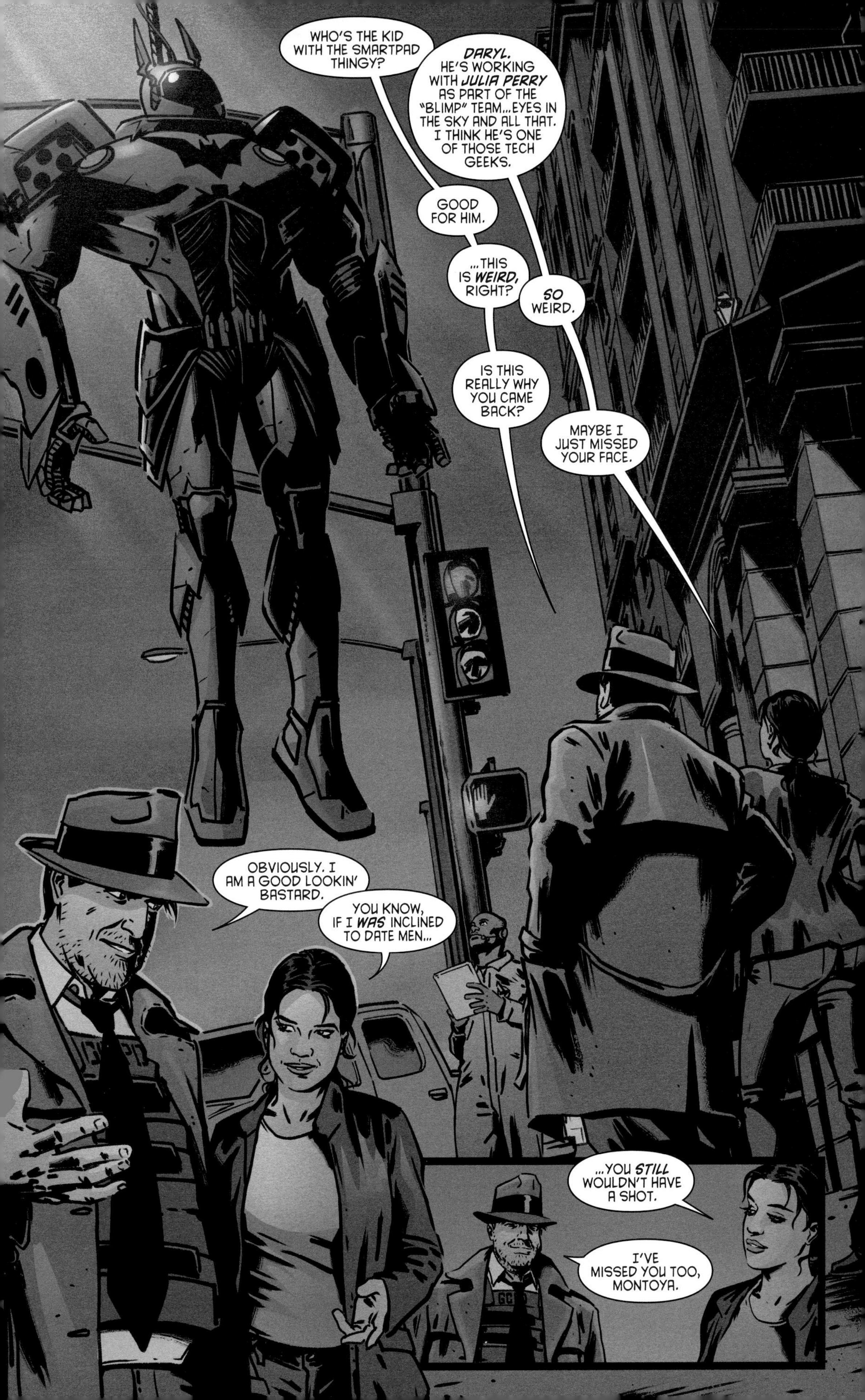
WHO'S THE KID WITH THE SMARTPAD THINGY?
DARYL. HE'S WORKING WITH JULIA PERRY AS PART OF THE "BLIMP" TEAM...EYES IN THE SKY AND ALL THAT. I THINK HE'S ONE OF THOSE TECH GEEKS.
GOOD FOR HIM.
...THIS IS WEIRD, RIGHT?
SO WEIRD.
IS THIS REALLY WHY YOU CAME BACK?
MAYBE I JUST MISSED YOUR FACE.
OBVIOUSLY. I AM A GOOD LOOKIN' BASTARD.
YOU KNOW, IF I WAS INCLINED TO DATE MEN...
...YOU STILL WOULDN'T HAVE A SHOT.
I'VE MISSED YOU TOO, MONTOYA.

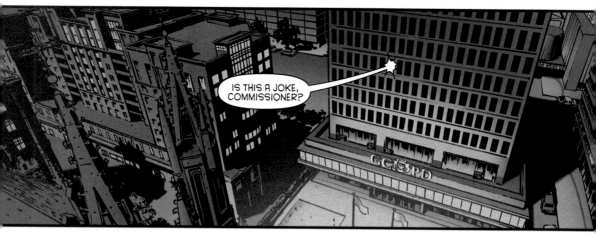

IS THIS A JOKE, COMMISSIONER?

YOU'RE TELLING US WE **HAVE TO** GO THIS STUPID CIRCUS THING TOMORROW?

YES, **DETECTIVE KEYES**... THAT'S WHAT MANDATORY MEANS. AND THERE WILL BE ASSIGNED SEATING.

EVEN MAJOR CRIMES?

YES.

WHY?

THOSE SEAT ASSIGNMENTS WILL BELONG TO **VIPs** THE FOLLOWING NIGHT.

TAKE NOTE OF YOUR SEAT NUMBER... AFTER THE SHOW, WE ARE GOING TO RUN EMERGENCY DRILLS...WHERE YOU GET TO PRETEND TO BE PEOPLE WORTH SAVING.

MAJOR CRIMES IS ALREADY UP TO ITS GILLS IN CASES. WE STILL GOTTA FIND THAT MISSING EGGHEAD WHO WORKS FOR **POWERS**.

WELL, **ALVAREZ**, HE'S BEEN MISSING FOR WEEKS. **NOW** HE'S A PRIORITY FOR YOU?!

HE'S STILL MISSING, AIN'T HE?

WITH RESPECT TO HIM AND HIS FAMILY, FOR THE NEXT SEVENTY-TWO HOURS, WE NEED TO FOCUS ON MAKING SURE SECURITY IS LOCKED DOWN FOR THE EVENT.

WE'VE HAD CREDIBLE THREATS THAT WE JUST CAN'T IGNORE.

CLIK

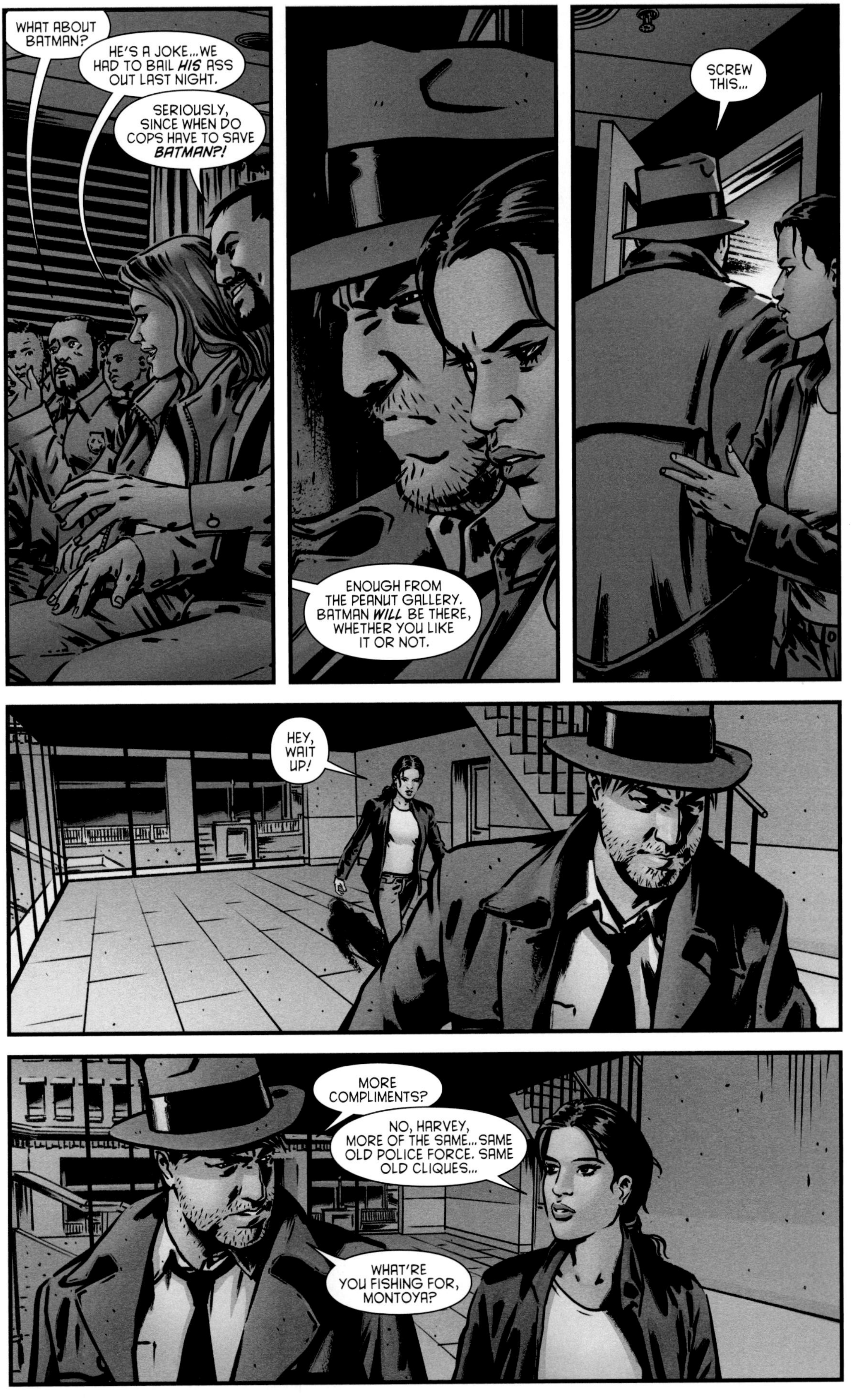
WHAT ABOUT BATMAN?
HE'S A JOKE...WE HAD TO BAIL HIS ASS OUT LAST NIGHT.
SERIOUSLY, SINCE WHEN DO COPS HAVE TO SAVE BATMAN?!
ENOUGH FROM THE PEANUT GALLERY. BATMAN WILL BE THERE, WHETHER YOU LIKE IT OR NOT.
SCREW THIS...
HEY, WAIT UP!
MORE COMPLIMENTS?
NO, HARVEY, MORE OF THE SAME...SAME OLD POLICE FORCE. SAME OLD CLIQUES...
WHAT'RE YOU FISHING FOR, MONTOYA?

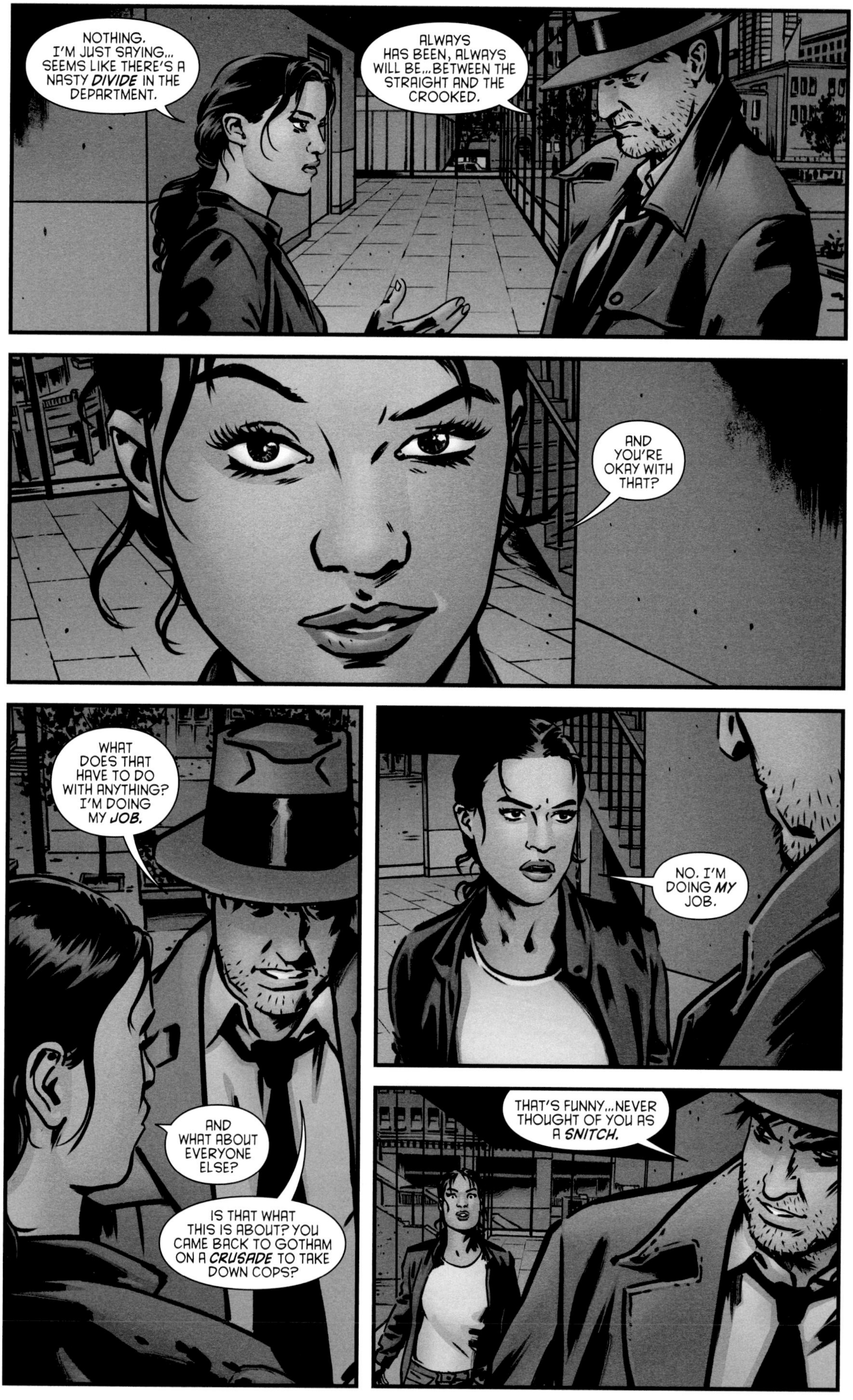
NOTHING. I'M JUST SAYING... SEEMS LIKE THERE'S A NASTY *DIVIDE* IN THE DEPARTMENT.
ALWAYS HAS BEEN, ALWAYS WILL BE...BETWEEN THE STRAIGHT AND THE CROOKED.
AND YOU'RE OKAY WITH THAT?
WHAT DOES THAT HAVE TO DO WITH ANYTHING? I'M DOING MY *JOB.*
AND WHAT ABOUT EVERYONE ELSE?
IS THAT WHAT THIS IS ABOUT? YOU CAME BACK TO GOTHAM ON A *CRUSADE* TO TAKE DOWN COPS?
NO. I'M DOING *MY* JOB.
THAT'S FUNNY...NEVER THOUGHT OF YOU AS A *SNITCH.*

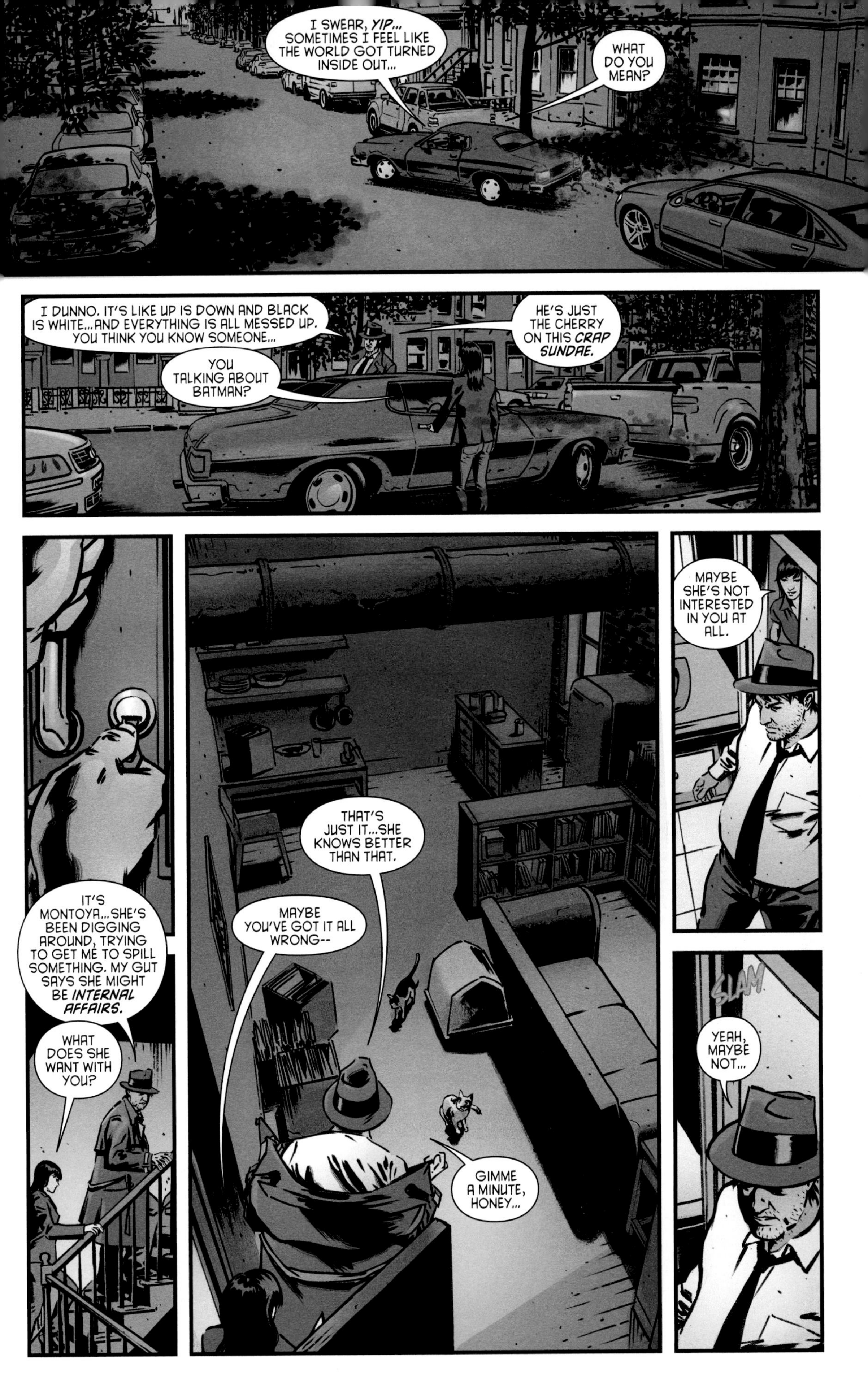
I SWEAR, *YIP*... SOMETIMES I FEEL LIKE THE WORLD GOT TURNED INSIDE OUT...
WHAT DO YOU MEAN?
I DUNNO. IT'S LIKE UP IS DOWN AND BLACK IS WHITE... AND EVERYTHING IS ALL MESSED UP. YOU THINK YOU KNOW SOMEONE...
YOU TALKING ABOUT BATMAN?
HE'S JUST THE CHERRY ON THIS *CRAP SUNDAE.*
IT'S MONTOYA... SHE'S BEEN DIGGING AROUND, TRYING TO GET ME TO SPILL SOMETHING. MY GUT SAYS SHE MIGHT BE *INTERNAL AFFAIRS.*
WHAT DOES SHE WANT WITH YOU?
THAT'S JUST IT... SHE KNOWS BETTER THAN THAT.
MAYBE YOU'VE GOT IT ALL WRONG--
GIMME A MINUTE, HONEY...
MAYBE SHE'S NOT INTERESTED IN YOU AT ALL.
SLAM
YEAH, MAYBE NOT...

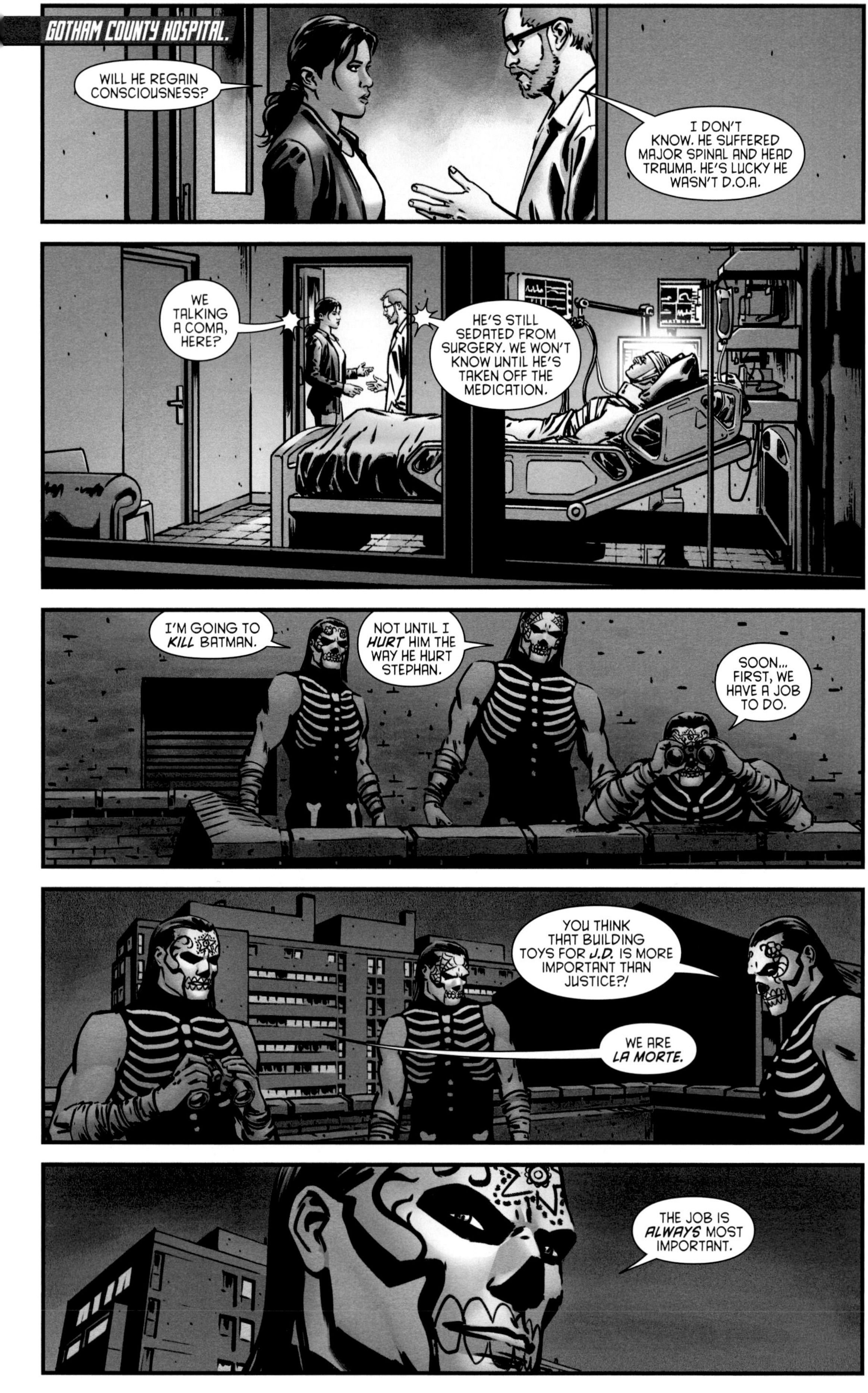
GOTHAM COUNTY HOSPITAL.
WILL HE REGAIN CONSCIOUSNESS?
I DON'T KNOW. HE SUFFERED MAJOR SPINAL AND HEAD TRAUMA. HE'S LUCKY HE WASN'T D.O.A.
WE TALKING A COMA, HERE?
HE'S STILL SEDATED FROM SURGERY. WE WON'T KNOW UNTIL HE'S TAKEN OFF THE MEDICATION.
I'M GOING TO *KILL* BATMAN.
NOT UNTIL I *HURT* HIM THE WAY HE HURT STEPHAN.
SOON... FIRST, WE HAVE A JOB TO DO.
YOU THINK THAT BUILDING TOYS FOR *J.D.* IS MORE IMPORTANT THAN JUSTICE?!
WE ARE *LA MORTE.*
THE JOB IS *ALWAYS* MOST IMPORTANT.

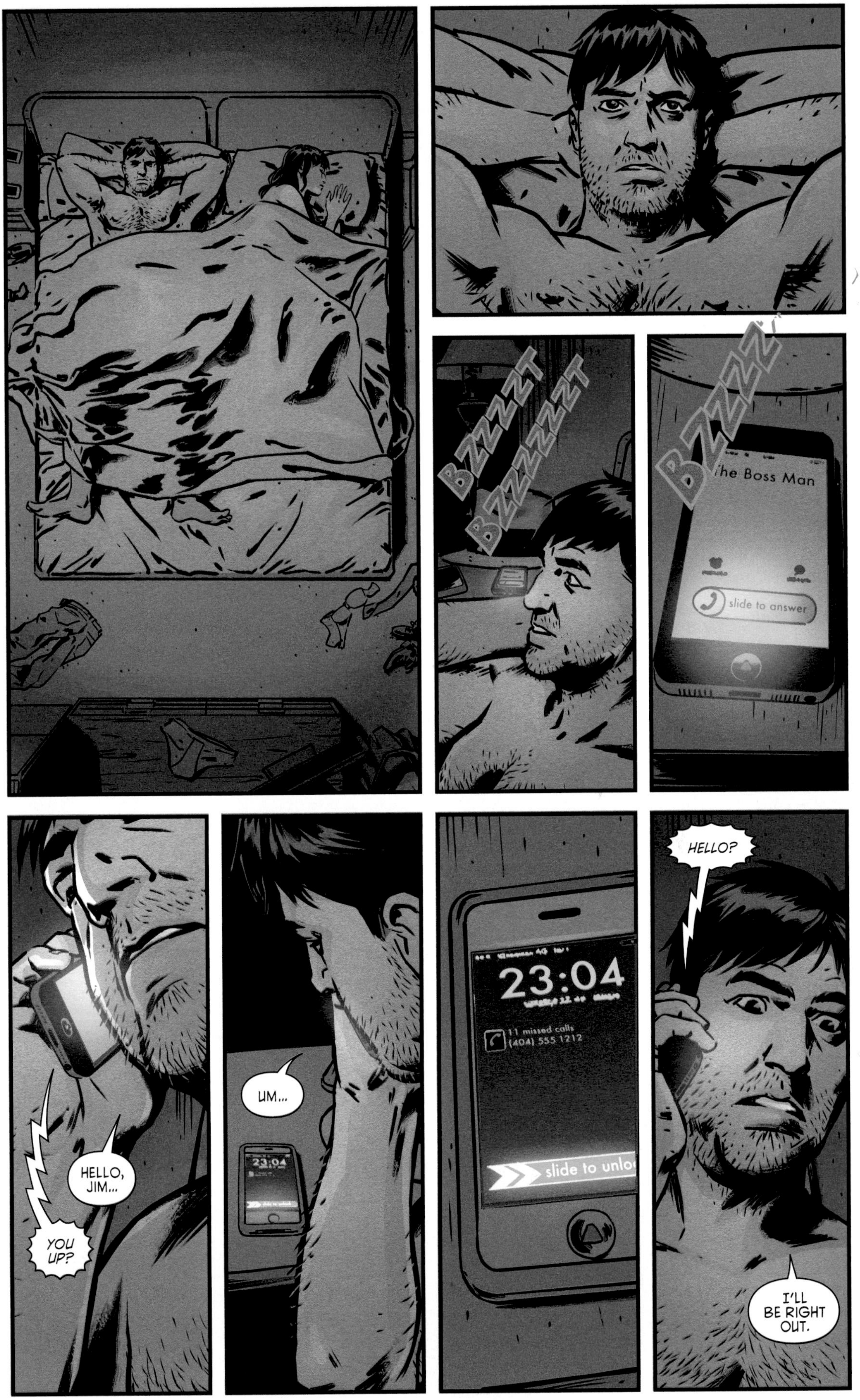
BZZZZZT
BZZZZZZZT
The Boss Man
slide to answer
BZZZZ
HELLO, JIM...
YOU UP?
23:04
slide to unlock
UM...
23:04
11 missed calls
(404) 555 1212
slide to unlo
HELLO?
I'LL BE RIGHT OUT.

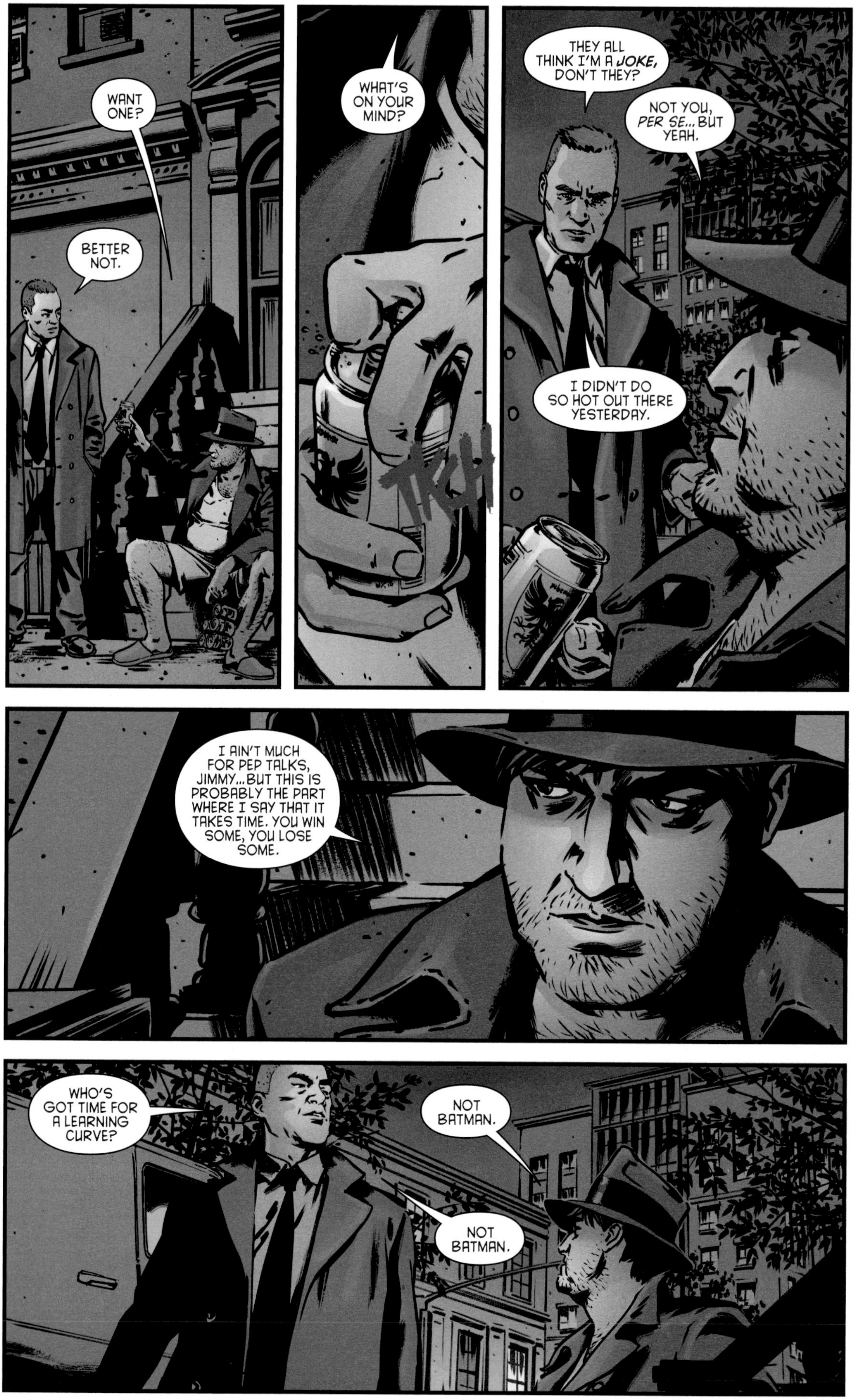
WANT ONE?
BETTER NOT.
WHAT'S ON YOUR MIND?
TKCH
THEY ALL THINK I'M A *JOKE,* DON'T THEY?
NOT YOU, *PER SE*... BUT YEAH.
I DIDN'T DO SO HOT OUT THERE YESTERDAY.
I AIN'T MUCH FOR PEP TALKS, JIMMY... BUT THIS IS PROBABLY THE PART WHERE I SAY THAT IT TAKES TIME. YOU WIN SOME, YOU LOSE SOME.
WHO'S GOT TIME FOR A LEARNING CURVE?
NOT BATMAN.
NOT BATMAN.

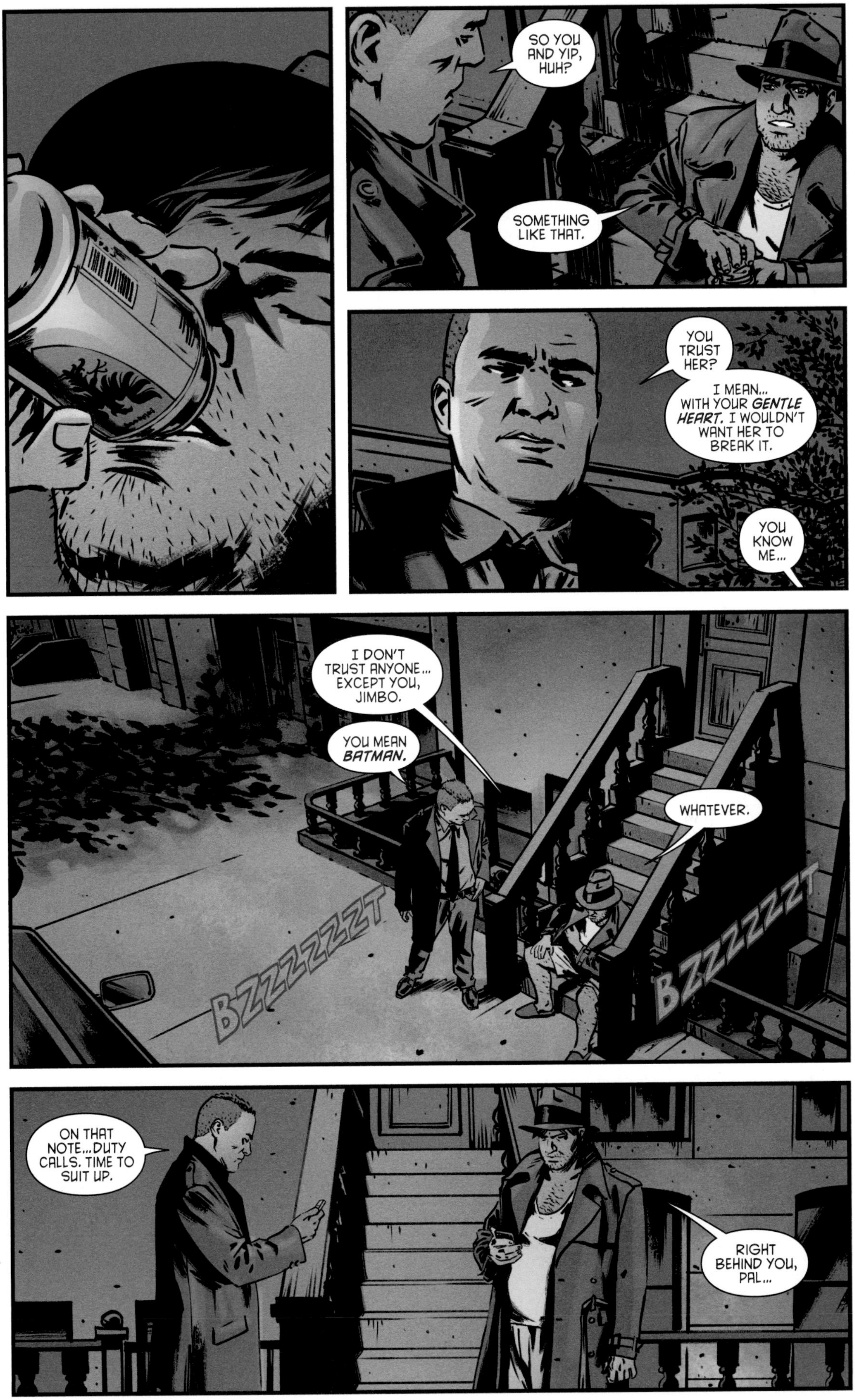
SO YOU AND YIP, HUH?
SOMETHING LIKE THAT.
YOU TRUST HER?
I MEAN... WITH YOUR *GENTLE HEART*. I WOULDN'T WANT HER TO BREAK IT.
YOU KNOW ME...
I DON'T TRUST ANYONE... EXCEPT YOU, JIMBO.
YOU MEAN *BATMAN*.
WHATEVER.
BZZZZZZT
BZZZZZZT
ON THAT NOTE...DUTY CALLS. TIME TO SUIT UP.
RIGHT BEHIND YOU, PAL...

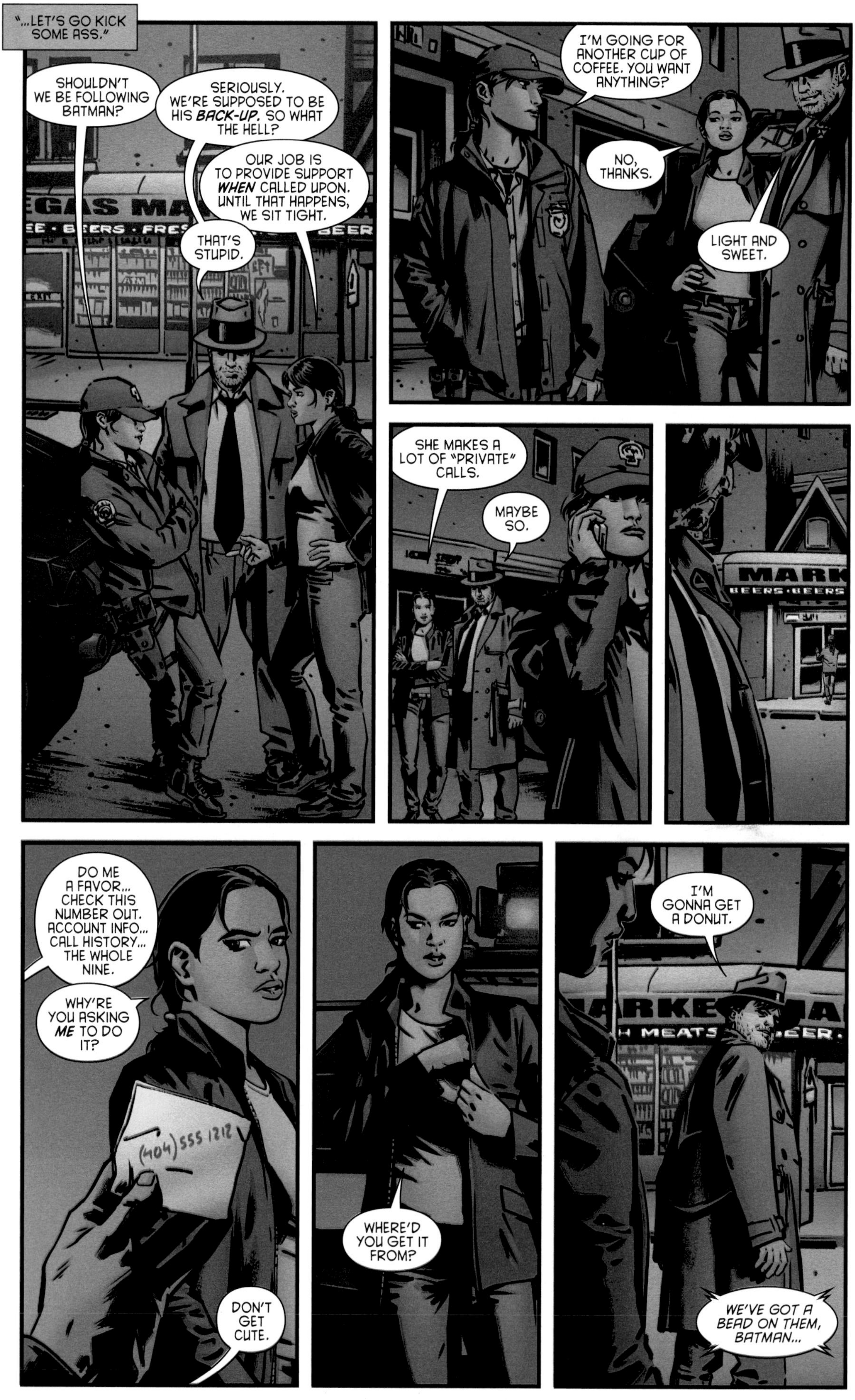
"...LET'S GO KICK SOME ASS."
SHOULDN'T WE BE FOLLOWING BATMAN?
SERIOUSLY. WE'RE SUPPOSED TO BE HIS BACK-UP. SO WHAT THE HELL?
OUR JOB IS TO PROVIDE SUPPORT WHEN CALLED UPON. UNTIL THAT HAPPENS, WE SIT TIGHT.
THAT'S STUPID.
I'M GOING FOR ANOTHER CUP OF COFFEE. YOU WANT ANYTHING?
NO, THANKS.
LIGHT AND SWEET.
SHE MAKES A LOT OF "PRIVATE" CALLS.
MAYBE SO.
MARK
BEERS · BEERS
DO ME A FAVOR... CHECK THIS NUMBER OUT. ACCOUNT INFO... CALL HISTORY... THE WHOLE NINE.
WHY'RE YOU ASKING ME TO DO IT?
(404) 555 1212
DON'T GET CUTE.
WHERE'D YOU GET IT FROM?
I'M GONNA GET A DONUT.
WE'VE GOT A BEAD ON THEM, BATMAN...

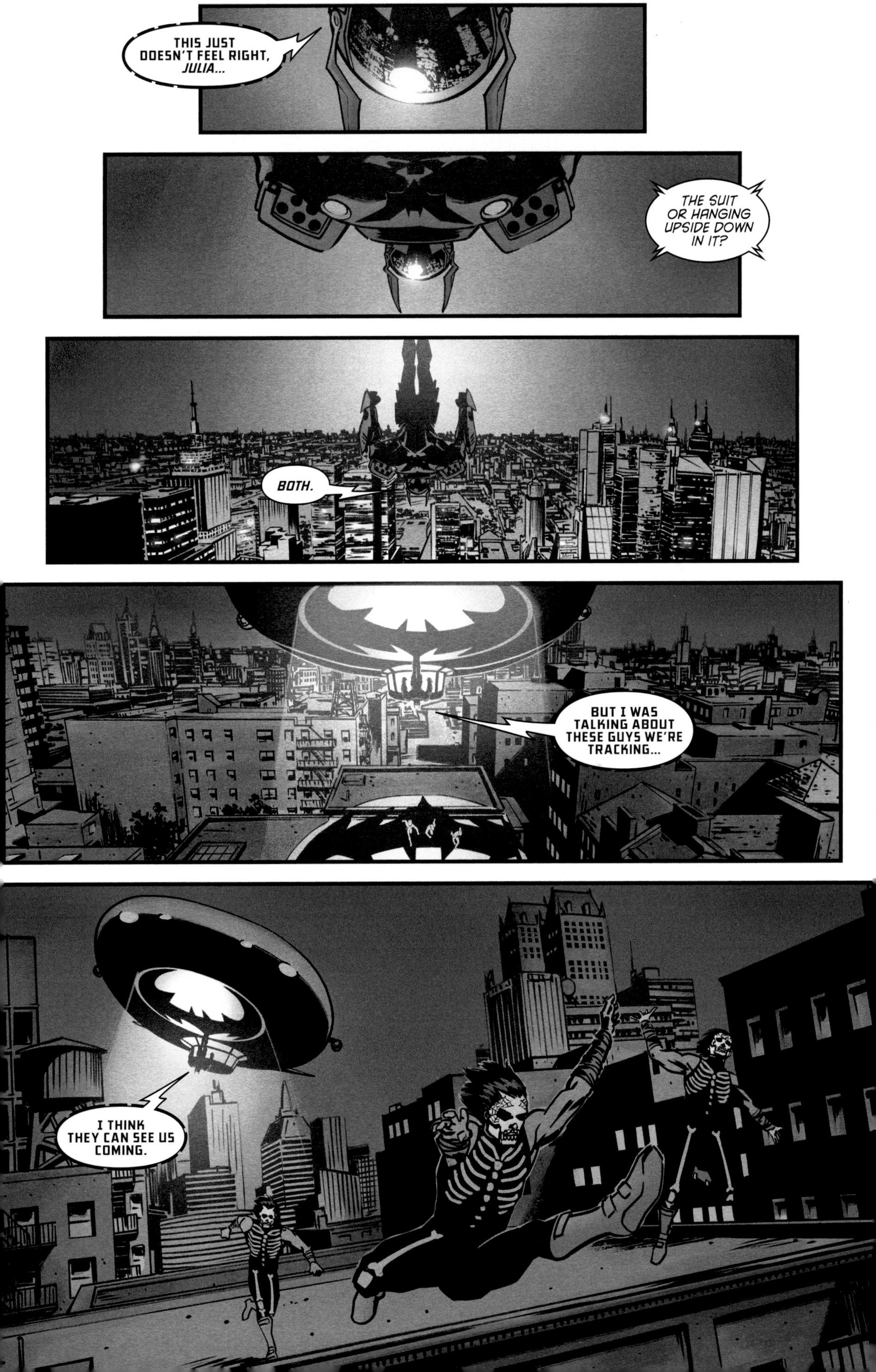
THIS JUST DOESN'T FEEL RIGHT, *JULIA*...
THE SUIT OR HANGING UPSIDE DOWN IN IT?
BOTH.
BUT I WAS TALKING ABOUT THESE GUYS WE'RE TRACKING...
I THINK THEY CAN SEE US COMING.

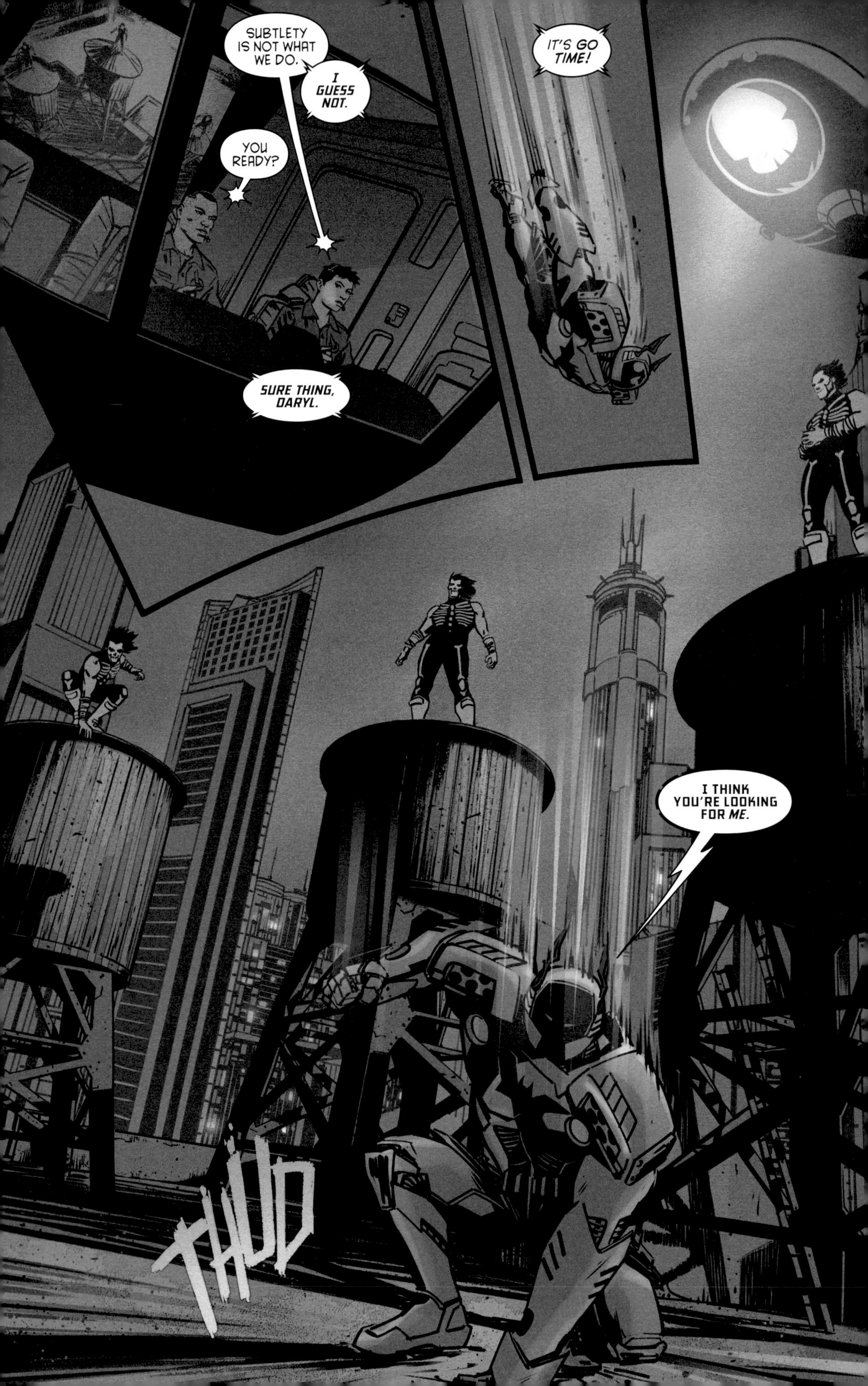
SUBTLETY IS NOT WHAT WE DO.
I GUESS NOT.
YOU READY?
SURE THING, DARYL.
IT'S GO TIME!
I THINK YOU'RE LOOKING FOR ME.
THUD

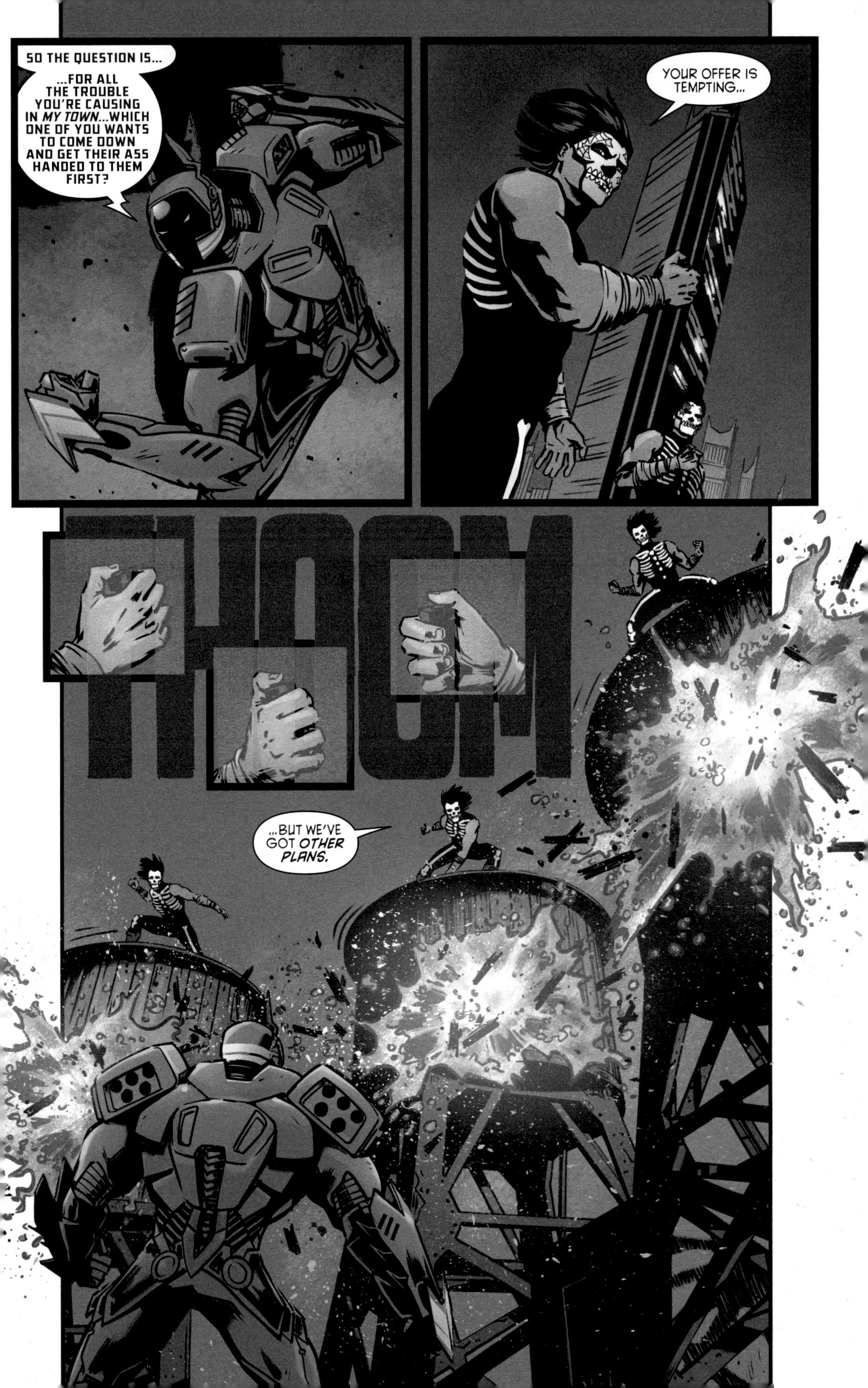
SO THE QUESTION IS...
...FOR ALL THE TROUBLE YOU'RE CAUSING IN *MY TOWN*...WHICH ONE OF YOU WANTS TO COME DOWN AND GET THEIR ASS HANDED TO THEM FIRST?
YOUR OFFER IS TEMPTING...
THOOM
...BUT WE'VE GOT *OTHER PLANS.*

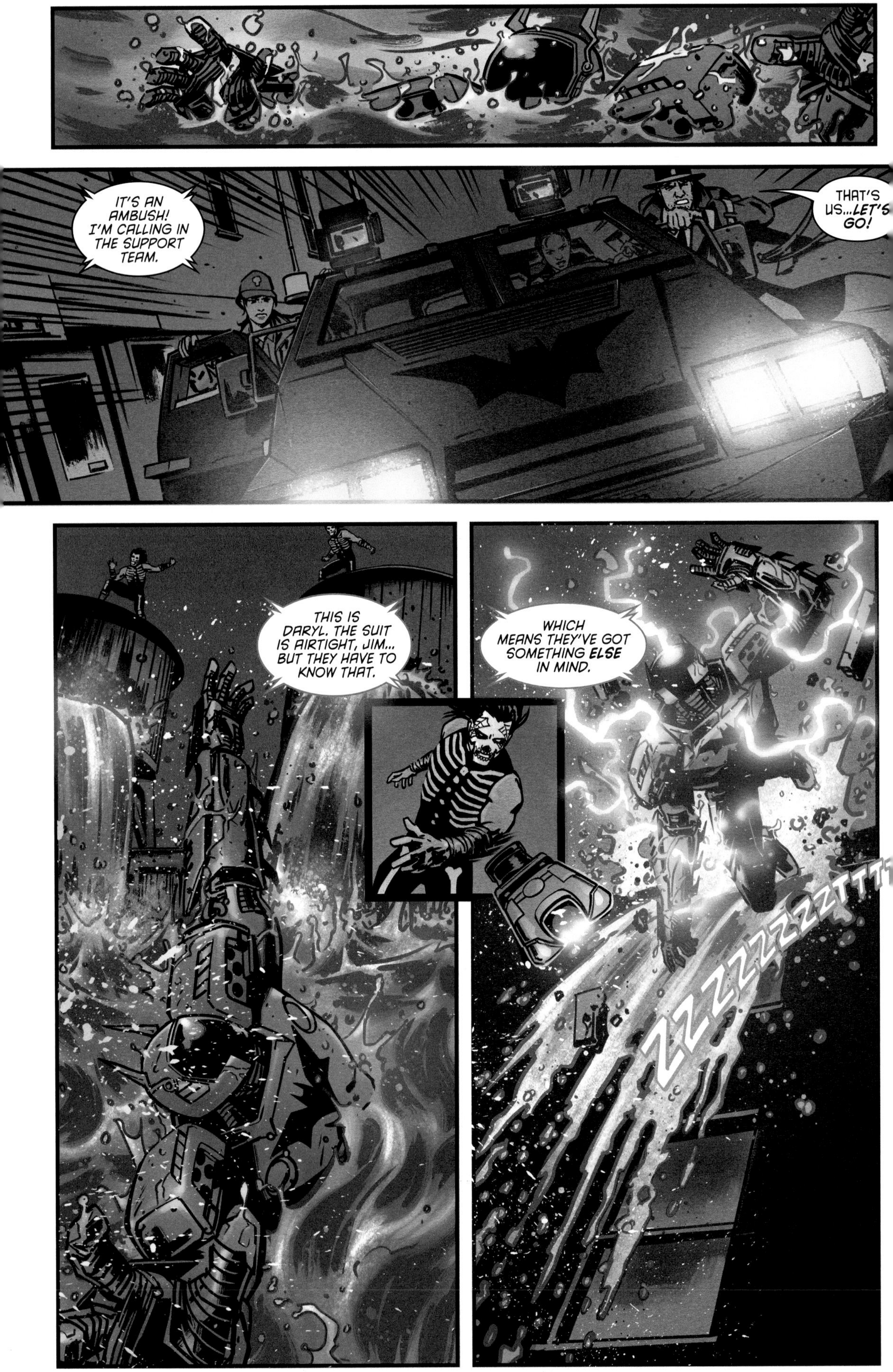
IT'S AN AMBUSH! I'M CALLING IN THE SUPPORT TEAM.
THAT'S US...LET'S GO!
THIS IS DARYL. THE SUIT IS AIRTIGHT, JIM... BUT THEY HAVE TO KNOW THAT.
WHICH MEANS THEY'VE GOT SOMETHING ELSE IN MIND.
ZZZZZZZZZTTTT

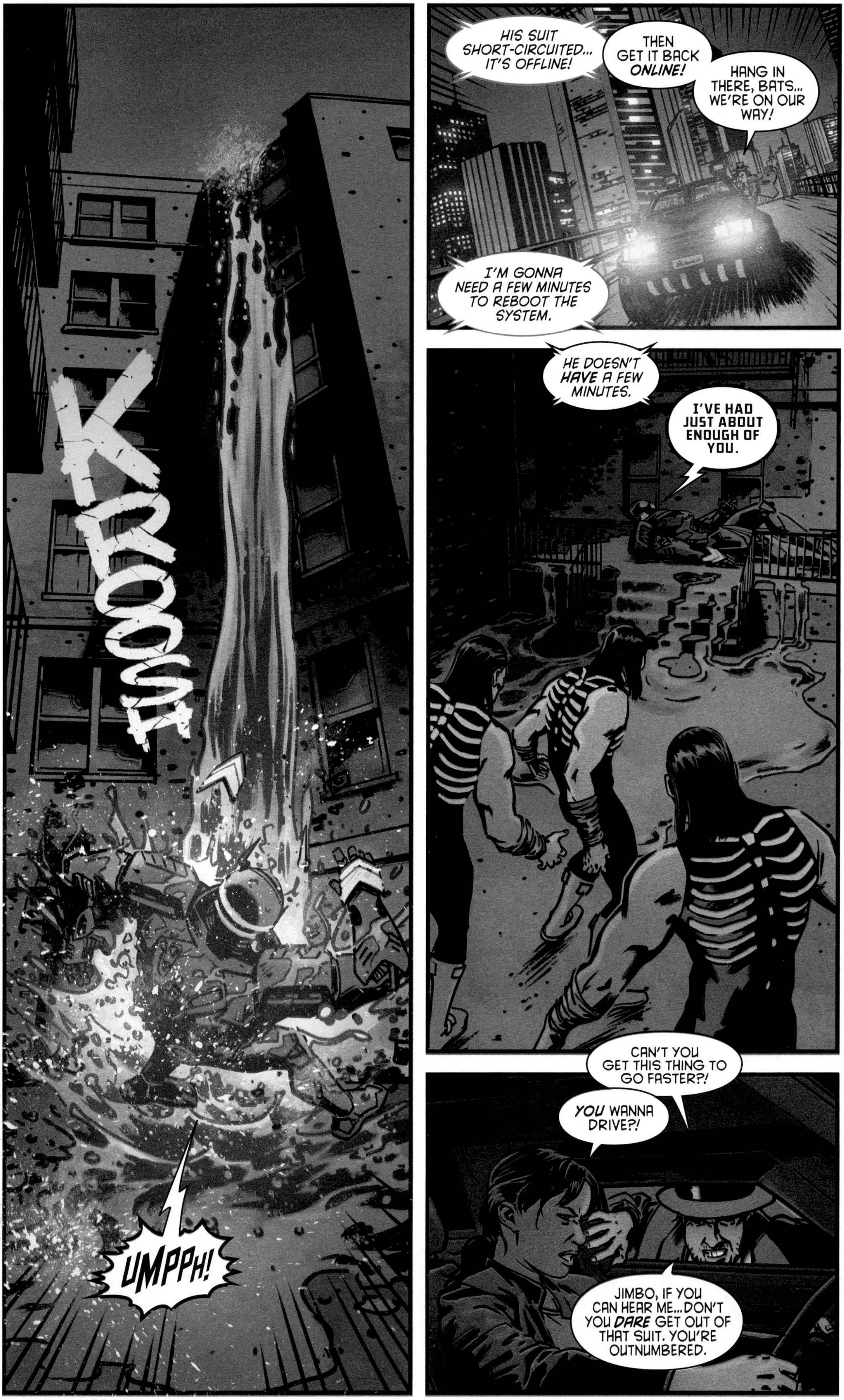
KROOSH
UMPPH!
HIS SUIT SHORT-CIRCUITED... IT'S OFFLINE!
THEN GET IT BACK ONLINE!
HANG IN THERE, BATS... WE'RE ON OUR WAY!
I'M GONNA NEED A FEW MINUTES TO REBOOT THE SYSTEM.
HE DOESN'T HAVE A FEW MINUTES.
I'VE HAD JUST ABOUT ENOUGH OF YOU.
CAN'T YOU GET THIS THING TO GO FASTER?!
YOU WANNA DRIVE?!
JIMBO, IF YOU CAN HEAR ME...DON'T YOU DARE GET OUT OF THAT SUIT. YOU'RE OUTNUMBERED.

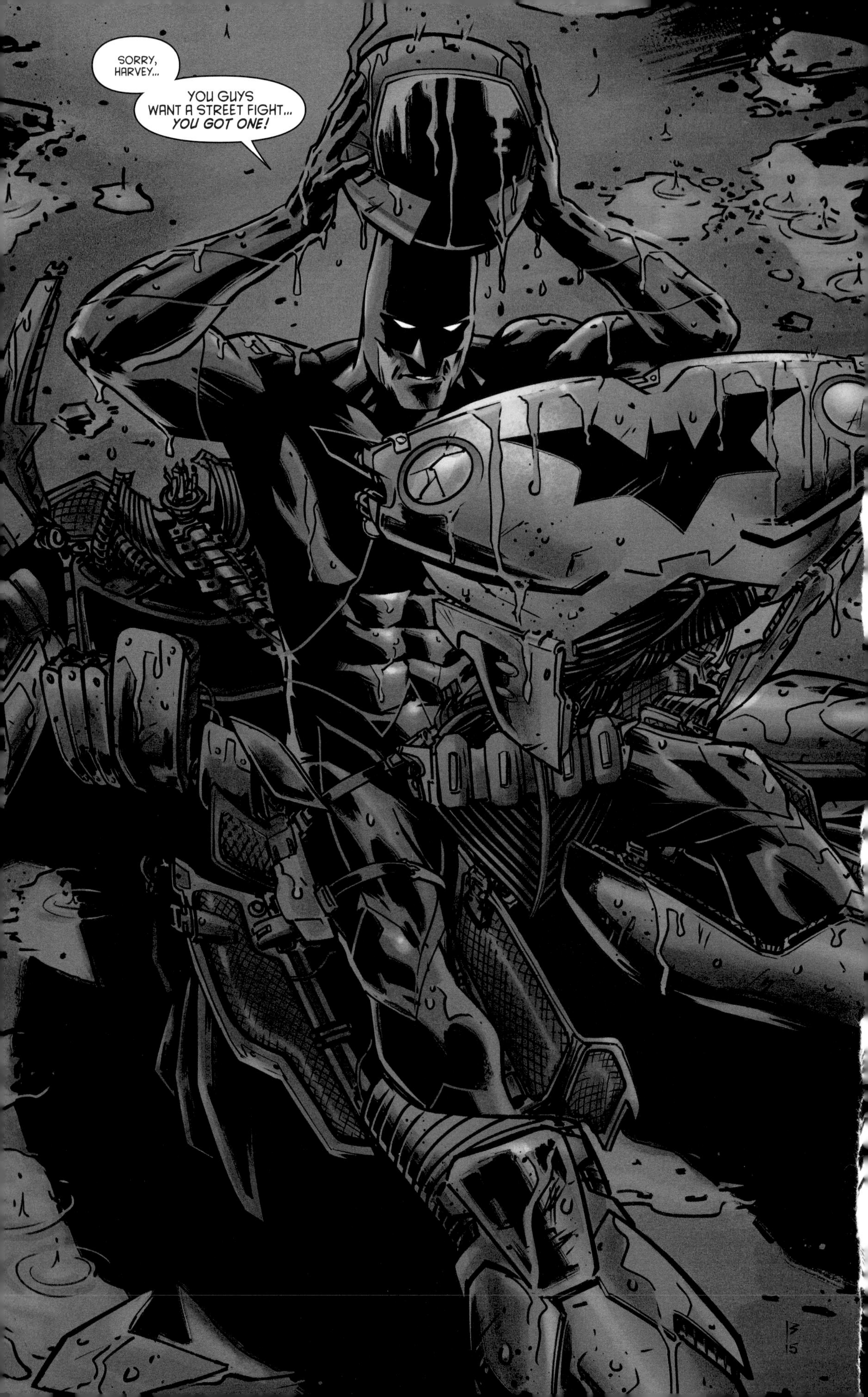
SORRY, HARVEY...
YOU GUYS WANT A STREET FIGHT... YOU GOT ONE!

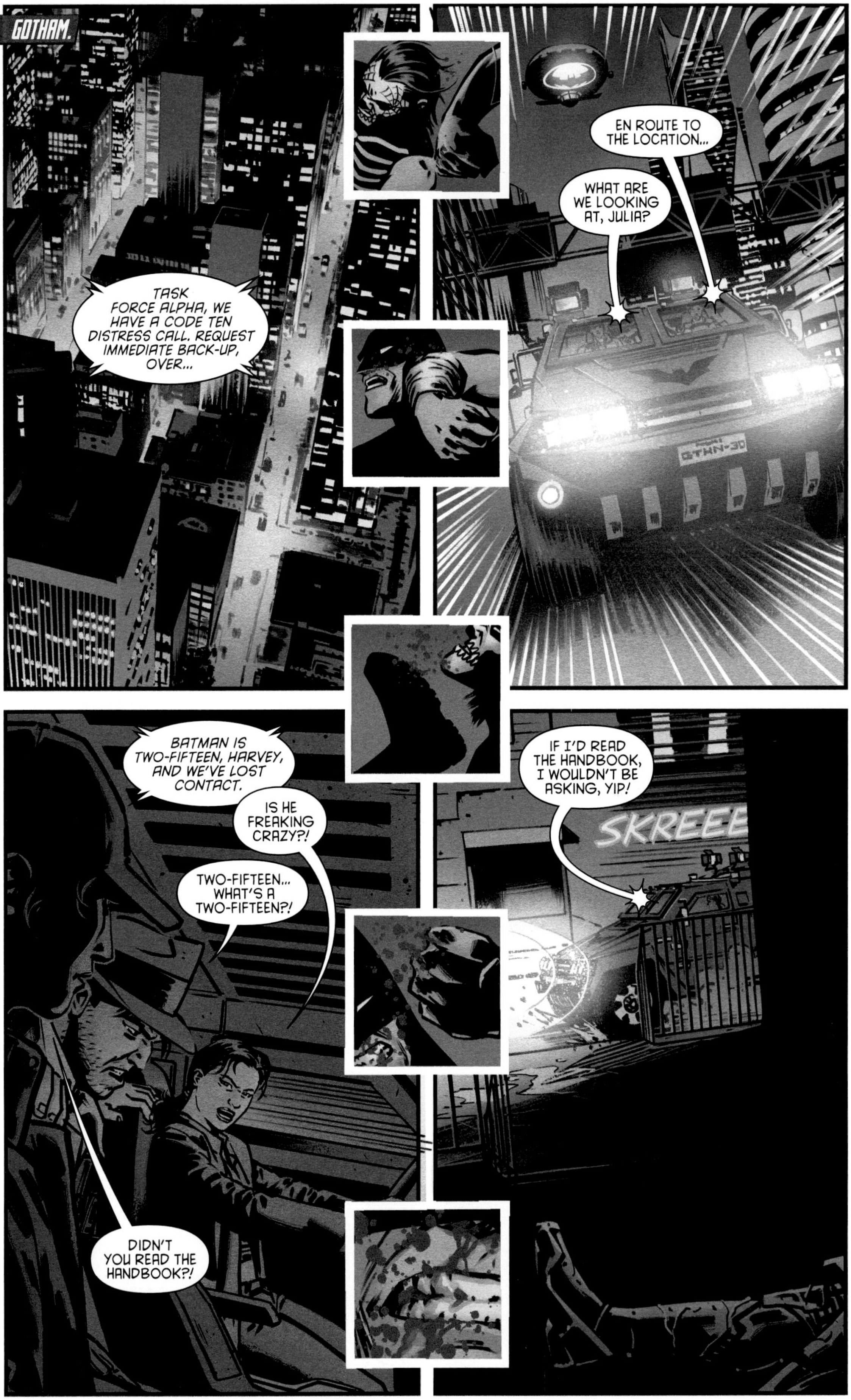
GOTHAM.
TASK FORCE ALPHA, WE HAVE A CODE TEN DISTRESS CALL. REQUEST IMMEDIATE BACK-UP, OVER...
EN ROUTE TO THE LOCATION...
WHAT ARE WE LOOKING AT, JULIA?
GTHN-30
BATMAN IS TWO-FIFTEEN, HARVEY, AND WE'VE LOST CONTACT.
IS HE FREAKING CRAZY?!
TWO-FIFTEEN... WHAT'S A TWO-FIFTEEN?!
DIDN'T YOU READ THE HANDBOOK?!
IF I'D READ THE HANDBOOK, I WOULDN'T BE ASKING, YIP!
SKREEE

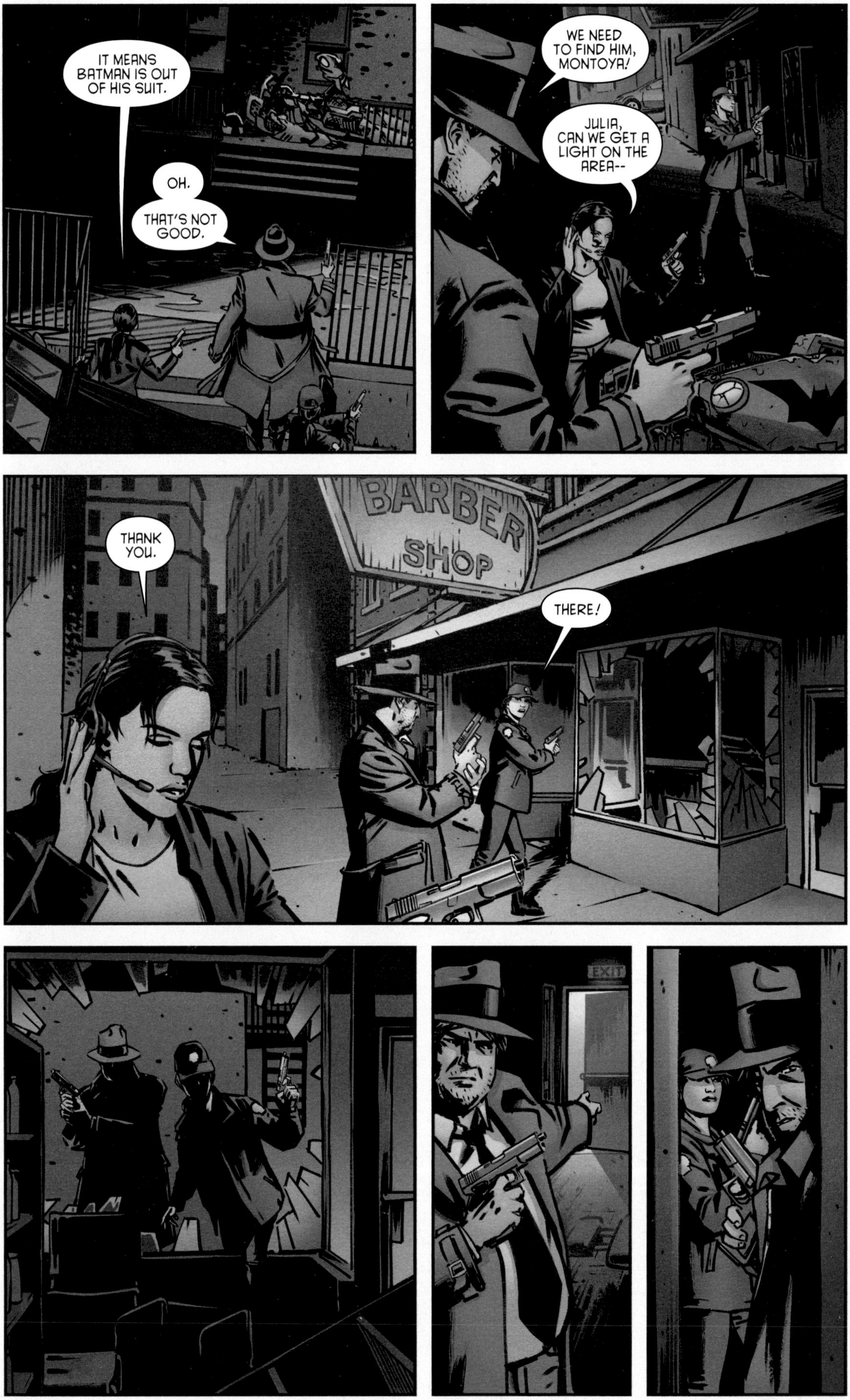
IT MEANS BATMAN IS OUT OF HIS SUIT.
OH.
THAT'S NOT GOOD.
WE NEED TO FIND HIM, MONTOYA!
JULIA, CAN WE GET A LIGHT ON THE AREA--
BARBER SHOP
THANK YOU.
THERE!
EXIT

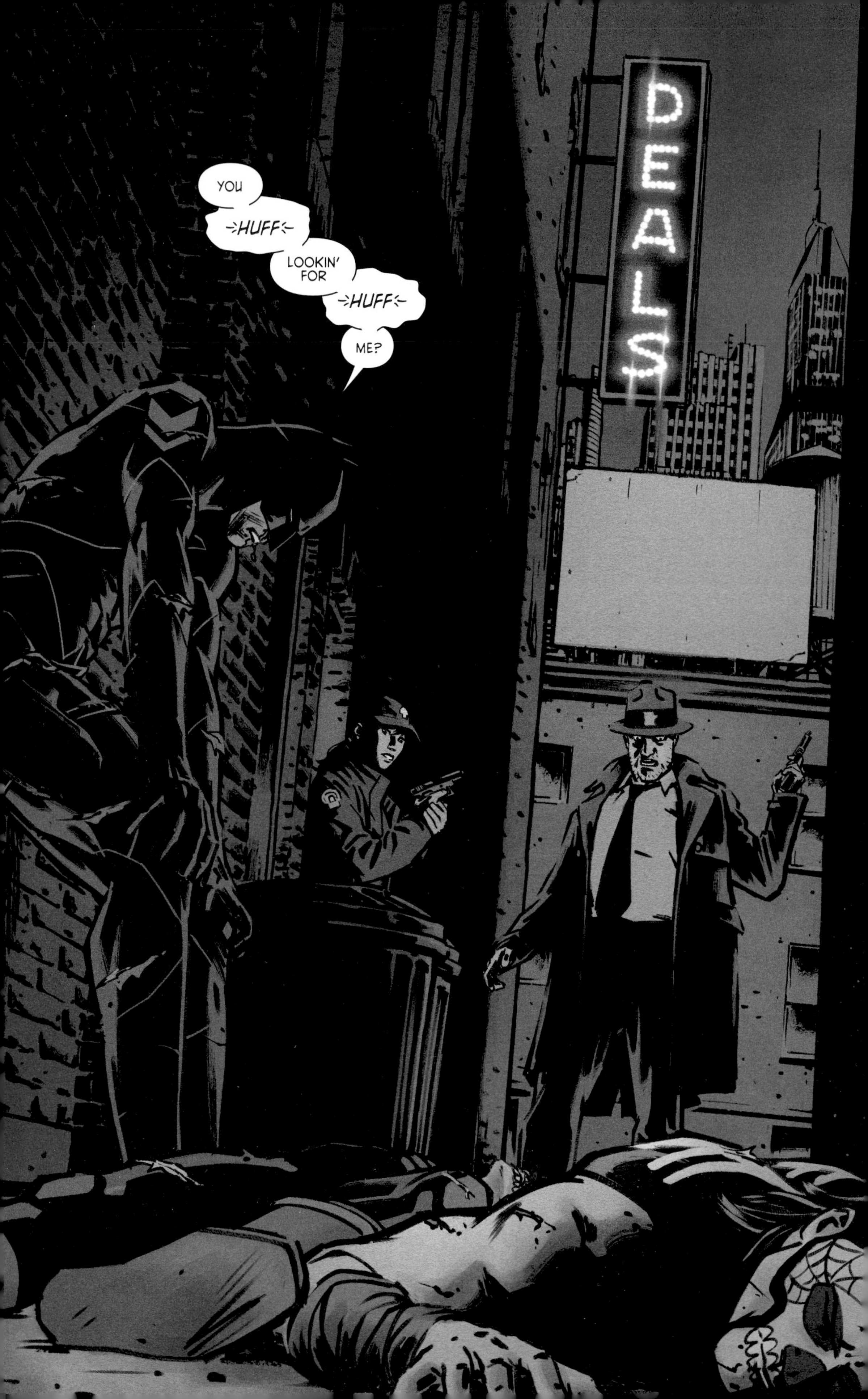
YOU
-HUFF-
LOOKIN' FOR
-HUFF-
ME?
DEALS

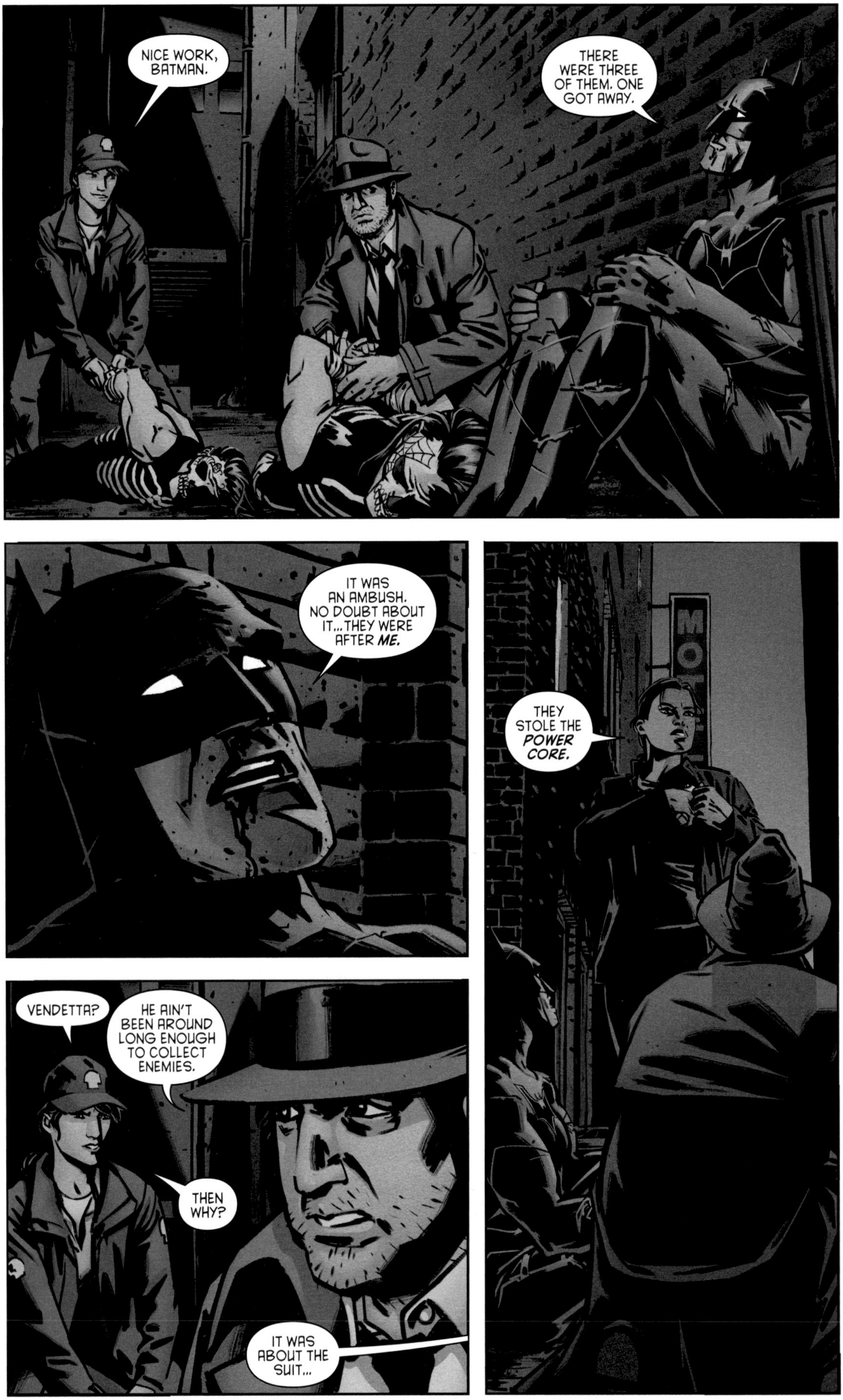
NICE WORK, BATMAN.
THERE WERE THREE OF THEM. ONE GOT AWAY.
IT WAS AN AMBUSH. NO DOUBT ABOUT IT... THEY WERE AFTER *ME.*
VENDETTA?
HE AIN'T BEEN AROUND LONG ENOUGH TO COLLECT ENEMIES.
THEN WHY?
IT WAS ABOUT THE SUIT...
THEY STOLE THE *POWER CORE.*
MO

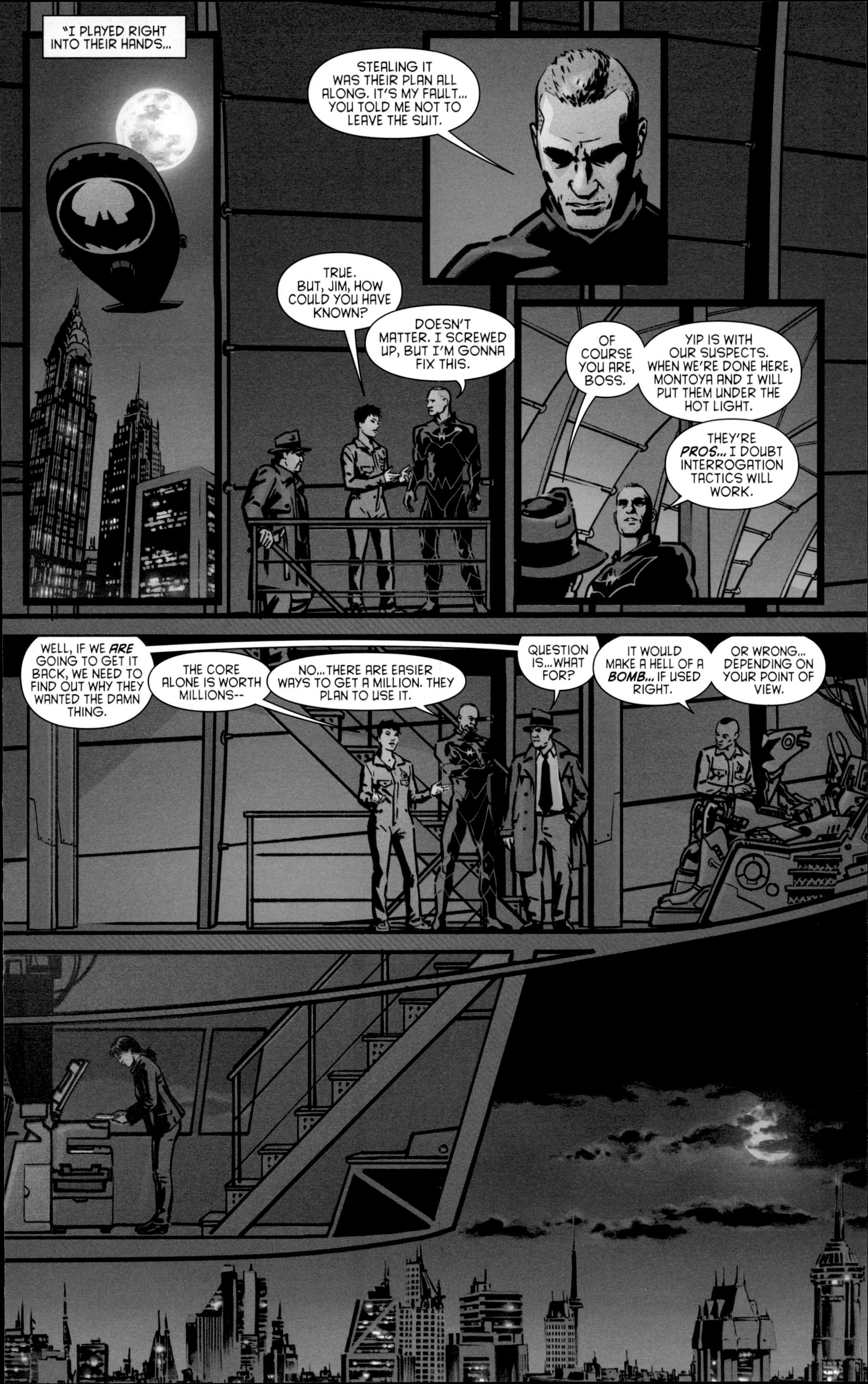

"I PLAYED RIGHT INTO THEIR HANDS...
STEALING IT WAS THEIR PLAN ALL ALONG. IT'S MY FAULT... YOU TOLD ME NOT TO LEAVE THE SUIT.
TRUE. BUT, JIM, HOW COULD YOU HAVE KNOWN?
DOESN'T MATTER. I SCREWED UP, BUT I'M GONNA FIX THIS.
OF COURSE YOU ARE, BOSS.
YIP IS WITH OUR SUSPECTS. WHEN WE'RE DONE HERE, MONTOYA AND I WILL PUT THEM UNDER THE HOT LIGHT.
THEY'RE ***PROS...*** I DOUBT INTERROGATION TACTICS WILL WORK.
WELL, IF WE ***ARE*** GOING TO GET IT BACK, WE NEED TO FIND OUT WHY THEY WANTED THE DAMN THING.
THE CORE ALONE IS WORTH MILLIONS--
NO...THERE ARE EASIER WAYS TO GET A MILLION. THEY PLAN TO USE IT.
QUESTION IS...WHAT FOR?
IT WOULD MAKE A HELL OF A ***BOMB...*** IF USED RIGHT.
OR WRONG... DEPENDING ON YOUR POINT OF VIEW.

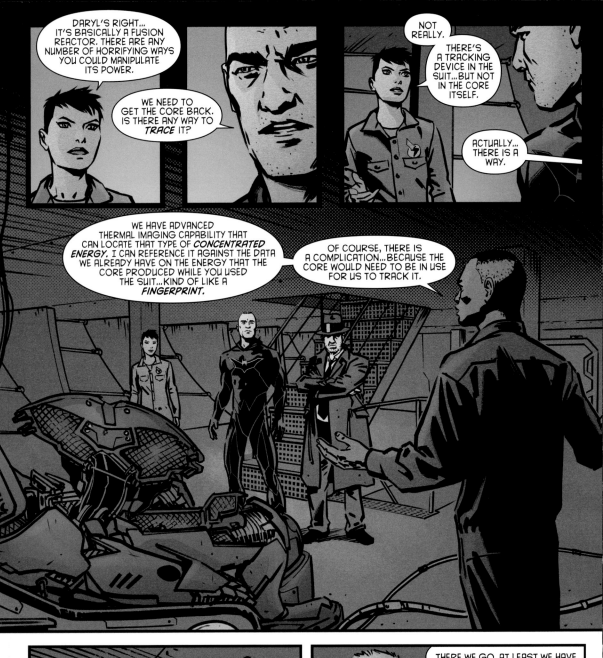

DARYL'S RIGHT... IT'S BASICALLY A FUSION REACTOR. THERE ARE ANY NUMBER OF HORRIFYING WAYS YOU COULD MANIPULATE ITS POWER.

WE NEED TO GET THE CORE BACK. IS THERE ANY WAY TO *TRACE* IT?

NOT REALLY. THERE'S A TRACKING DEVICE IN THE SUIT...BUT NOT IN THE CORE ITSELF.

ACTUALLY... THERE IS A WAY.

WE HAVE ADVANCED THERMAL IMAGING CAPABILITY THAT CAN LOCATE THAT TYPE OF *CONCENTRATED ENERGY*. I CAN REFERENCE IT AGAINST THE DATA WE ALREADY HAVE ON THE ENERGY THAT THE CORE PRODUCED WHILE YOU USED THE SUIT...KIND OF LIKE A *FINGERPRINT*.

OF COURSE, THERE IS A COMPLICATION...BECAUSE THE CORE WOULD NEED TO BE IN USE FOR US TO TRACK IT.

THERE WE GO. AT LEAST WE HAVE SOMEPLACE WE CAN START.

LET'S SEE IF WE CAN MAKE SOME HEADWAY ASAP. TOMORROW THERE WILL BE A *LOT* OF VERY IMPORTANT PEOPLE AT THE CIRCUS, AND WE NEED TO MAKE SURE THEY ARE SAFE.

SPEAKING OF WHICH...

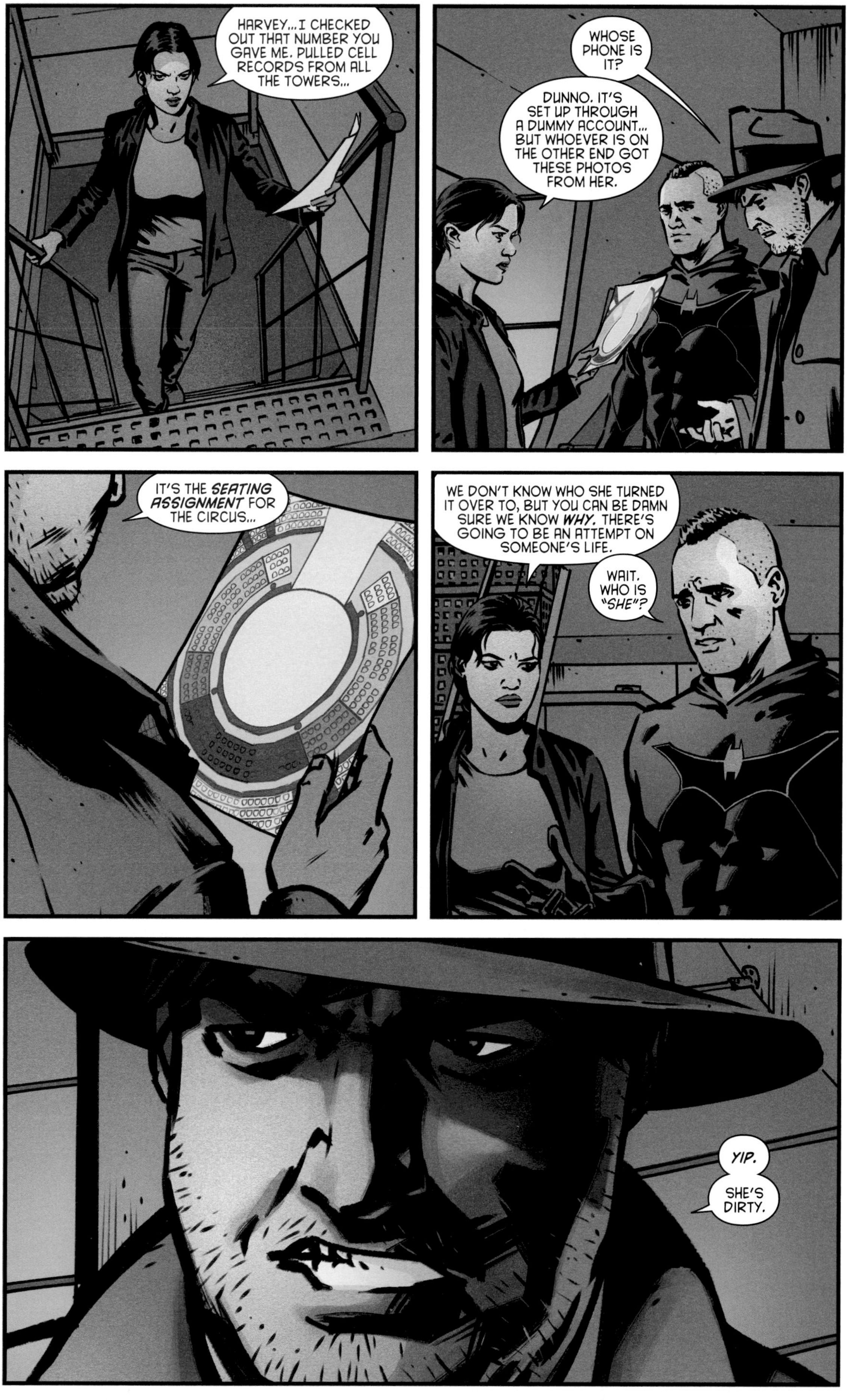
HARVEY...I CHECKED OUT THAT NUMBER YOU GAVE ME. PULLED CELL RECORDS FROM ALL THE TOWERS...
WHOSE PHONE IS IT?
DUNNO. IT'S SET UP THROUGH A DUMMY ACCOUNT... BUT WHOEVER IS ON THE OTHER END GOT THESE PHOTOS FROM HER.
IT'S THE *SEATING ASSIGNMENT* FOR THE CIRCUS...
WE DON'T KNOW WHO SHE TURNED IT OVER TO, BUT YOU CAN BE DAMN SURE WE KNOW *WHY.* THERE'S GOING TO BE AN ATTEMPT ON SOMEONE'S LIFE.
WAIT. WHO IS *"SHE"*?
YIP.
SHE'S DIRTY.

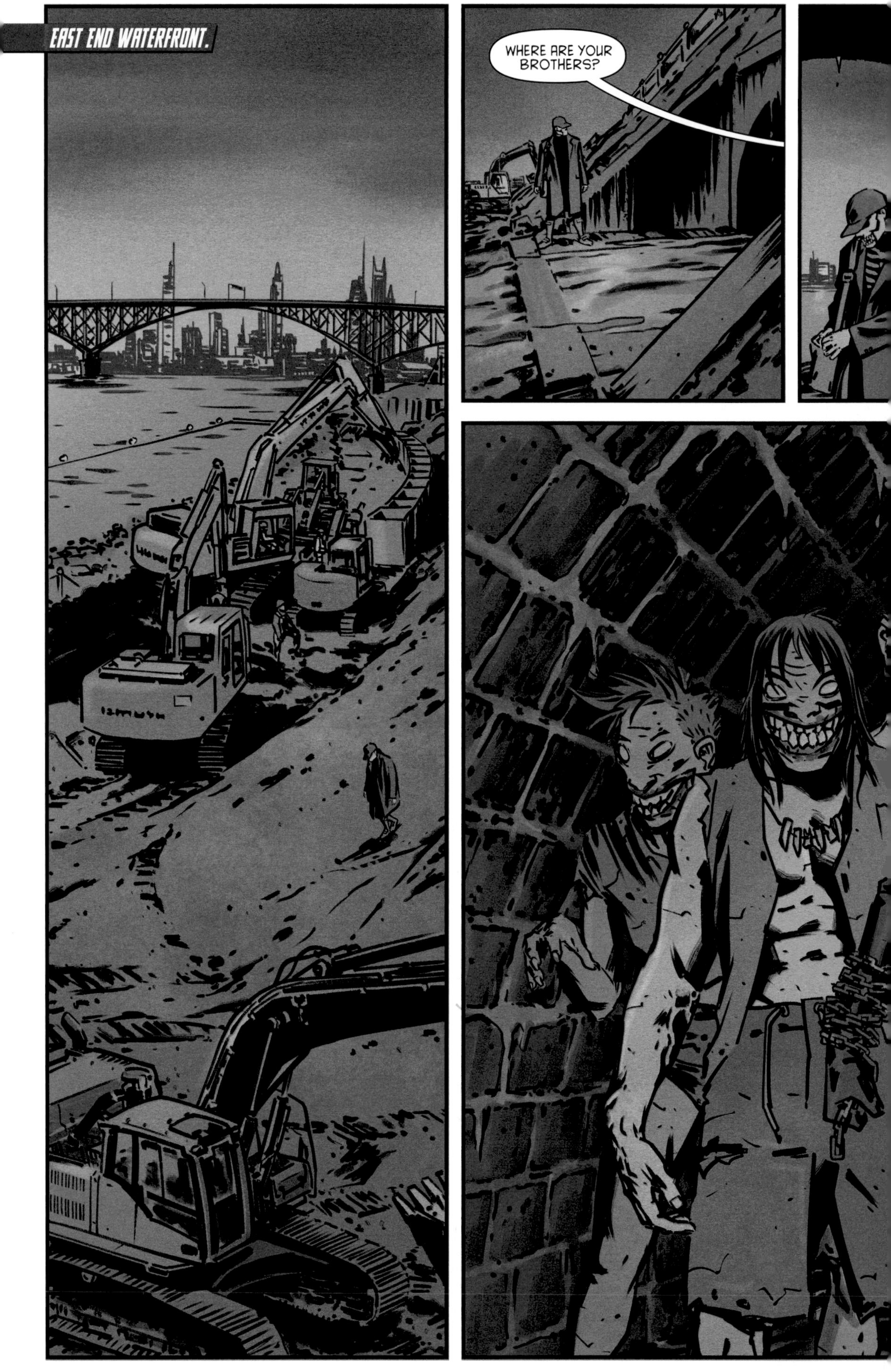
EAST END WATERFRONT.
WHERE ARE YOUR BROTHERS?

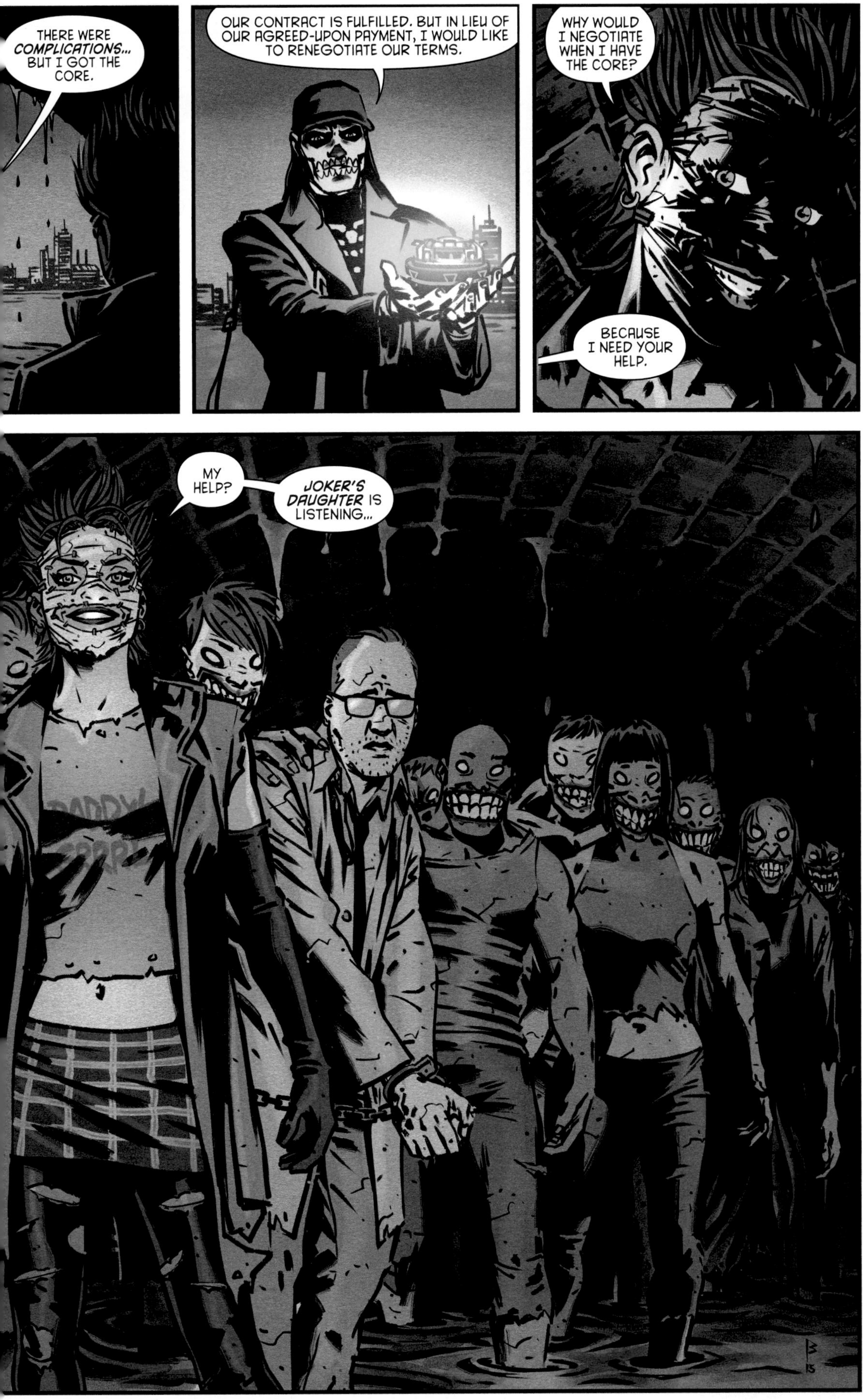
THERE WERE *COMPLICATIONS*... BUT I GOT THE CORE.
OUR CONTRACT IS FULFILLED. BUT IN LIEU OF OUR AGREED-UPON PAYMENT, I WOULD LIKE TO RENEGOTIATE OUR TERMS.
WHY WOULD I NEGOTIATE WHEN I HAVE THE CORE?
BECAUSE I NEED YOUR HELP.
MY HELP?
JOKER'S DAUGHTER IS LISTENING...

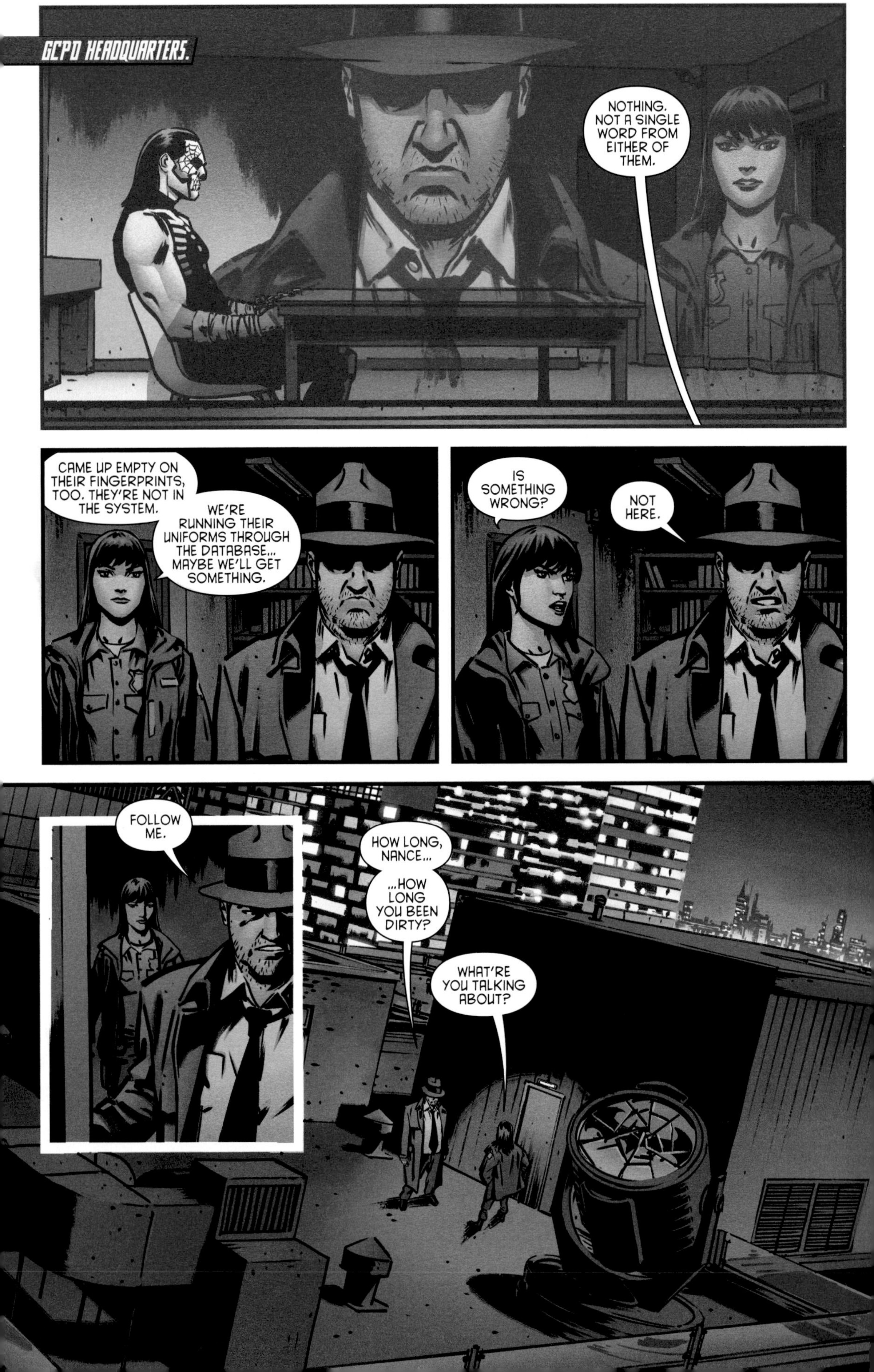
GCPD HEADQUARTERS.
NOTHING. NOT A SINGLE WORD FROM EITHER OF THEM.
CAME UP EMPTY ON THEIR FINGERPRINTS, TOO. THEY'RE NOT IN THE SYSTEM.
WE'RE RUNNING THEIR UNIFORMS THROUGH THE DATABASE... MAYBE WE'LL GET SOMETHING.
IS SOMETHING WRONG?
NOT HERE.
FOLLOW ME.
HOW LONG, NANCE...
...HOW LONG YOU BEEN DIRTY?
WHAT'RE YOU TALKING ABOUT?

YOU'VE BEEN FEEDING SENSITIVE INFORMATION TO SOMEONE. I'VE SEEN THE *TEXTS,* BUT I CAN BARELY BELIEVE IT...

WHY'D YOU BREAK BAD?

DOES IT MATTER?

TO ME IT DOES.

YOU GOING TO TURN ME IN?

IT'S NOT UP TO ME. I'M NOT THE ONLY ONE WHO KNOWS.

MONTOYA. SO YOU WERE RIGHT ABOUT HER? SHE'S INTERNAL AFFAIRS.

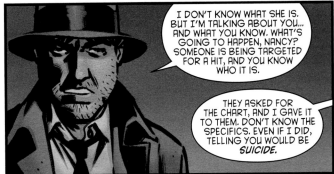

I DON'T KNOW WHAT SHE IS. BUT I'M TALKING ABOUT YOU... AND WHAT YOU KNOW. WHAT'S GOING TO HAPPEN, NANCY? SOMEONE IS BEING TARGETED FOR A HIT, AND YOU KNOW WHO IT IS.

THEY ASKED FOR THE CHART, AND I GAVE IT TO THEM. DON'T KNOW THE SPECIFICS. EVEN IF I DID, TELLING YOU WOULD BE *SUICIDE.*

YOU'RE A *COP.* YOU HAVE BROTHERS WHO WILL PROTECT YOU.

NOT AFTER WHAT I DID.

YOU AIN'T DONE IT YET. WE CAN STOP THIS...

IT'S TOO LATE. WHEN YOU SEE WHAT HAPPENS, YOU'LL KNOW.

I'M DEAD ALREADY.

HEY...

THOK

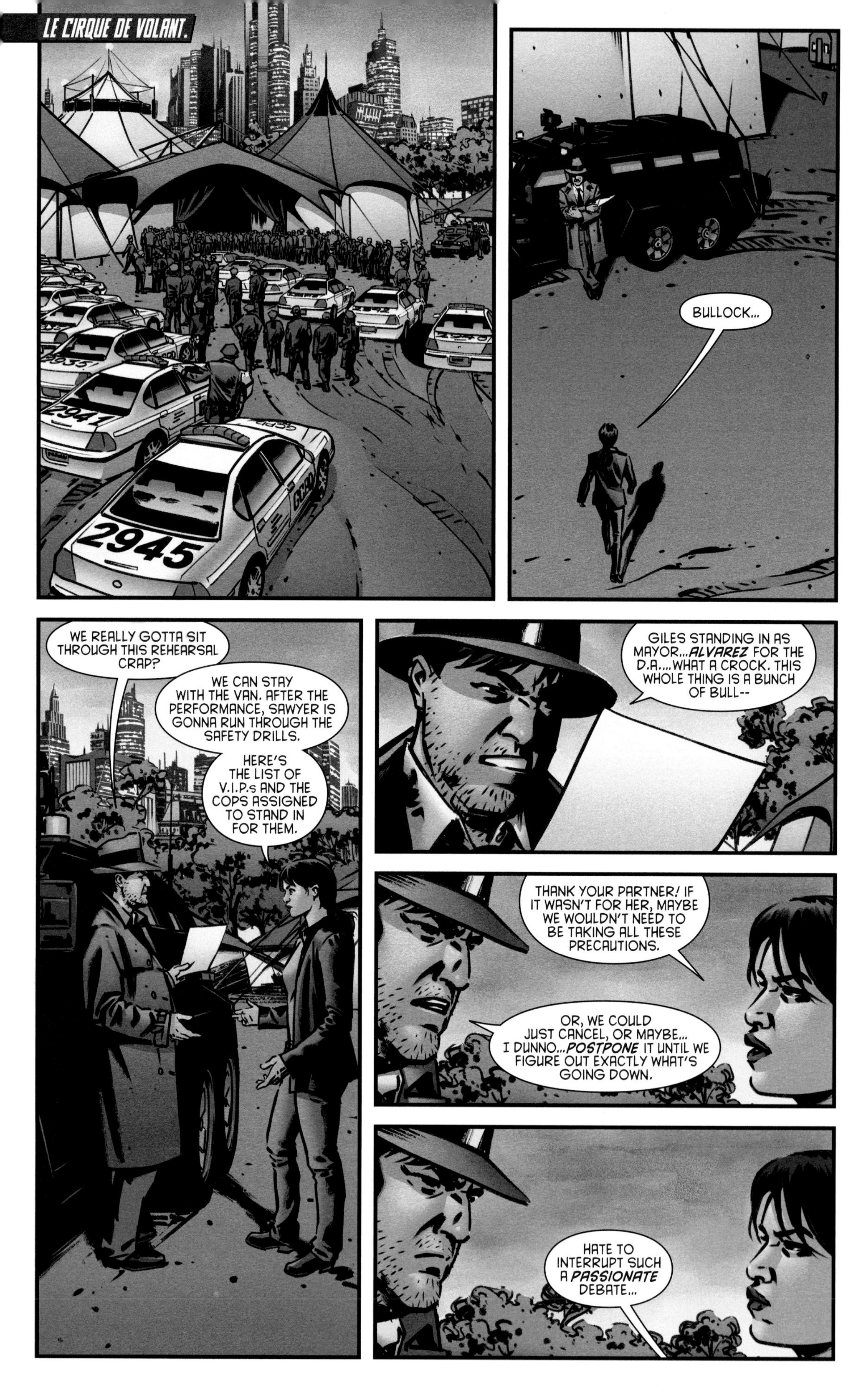
LE CIRQUE DE VOLANT.
2945
2941
BULLOCK...
WE REALLY GOTTA SIT THROUGH THIS REHEARSAL CRAP?
WE CAN STAY WITH THE VAN. AFTER THE PERFORMANCE, SAWYER IS GONNA RUN THROUGH THE SAFETY DRILLS.
HERE'S THE LIST OF V.I.P.s AND THE COPS ASSIGNED TO STAND IN FOR THEM.
GILES STANDING IN AS MAYOR...*ALVAREZ* FOR THE D.A....WHAT A CROCK. THIS WHOLE THING IS A BUNCH OF BULL--
THANK YOUR PARTNER! IF IT WASN'T FOR HER, MAYBE WE WOULDN'T NEED TO BE TAKING ALL THESE PRECAUTIONS.
OR, WE COULD JUST CANCEL, OR MAYBE... I DUNNO...*POSTPONE* IT UNTIL WE FIGURE OUT EXACTLY WHAT'S GOING DOWN.
HATE TO INTERRUPT SUCH A *PASSIONATE* DEBATE...

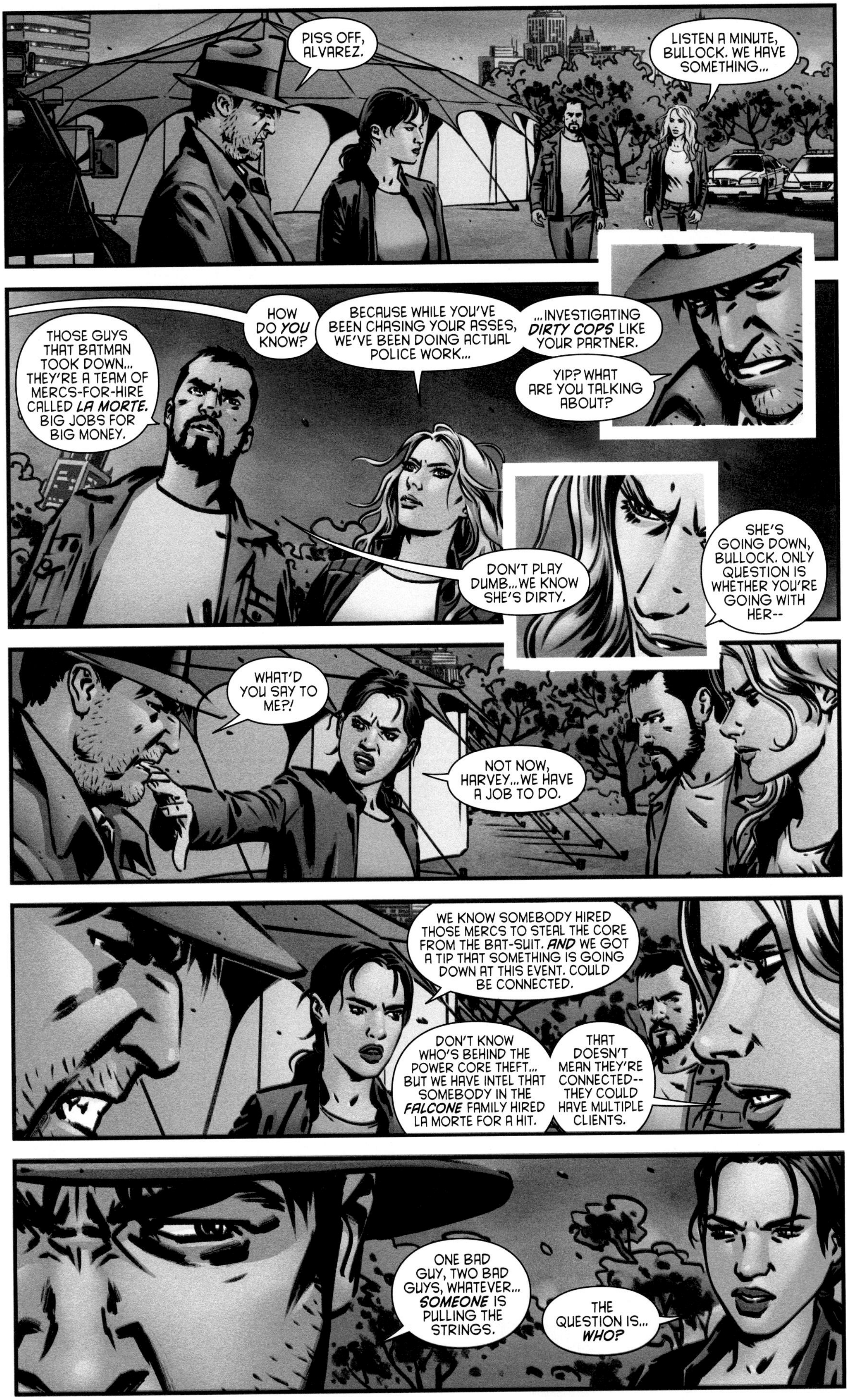
PISS OFF, ALVAREZ.
LISTEN A MINUTE, BULLOCK. WE HAVE SOMETHING...
THOSE GUYS THAT BATMAN TOOK DOWN... THEY'RE A TEAM OF MERCS-FOR-HIRE CALLED *LA MORTE.* BIG JOBS FOR BIG MONEY.
HOW DO *YOU* KNOW?
BECAUSE WHILE YOU'VE BEEN CHASING YOUR ASSES, WE'VE BEEN DOING ACTUAL POLICE WORK...
...INVESTIGATING *DIRTY COPS* LIKE YOUR PARTNER.
YIP? WHAT ARE YOU TALKING ABOUT?
DON'T PLAY DUMB...WE KNOW SHE'S DIRTY.
SHE'S GOING DOWN, BULLOCK. ONLY QUESTION IS WHETHER YOU'RE GOING WITH HER--
WHAT'D YOU SAY TO ME?!
NOT NOW, HARVEY...WE HAVE A JOB TO DO.
WE KNOW SOMEBODY HIRED THOSE MERCS TO STEAL THE CORE FROM THE BAT-SUIT. *AND* WE GOT A TIP THAT SOMETHING IS GOING DOWN AT THIS EVENT. COULD BE CONNECTED.
DON'T KNOW WHO'S BEHIND THE POWER CORE THEFT... BUT WE HAVE INTEL THAT SOMEBODY IN THE *FALCONE* FAMILY HIRED LA MORTE FOR A HIT.
THAT DOESN'T MEAN THEY'RE CONNECTED-- THEY COULD HAVE MULTIPLE CLIENTS.
ONE BAD GUY, TWO BAD GUYS, WHATEVER... *SOMEONE* IS PULLING THE STRINGS.
THE QUESTION IS... *WHO?*

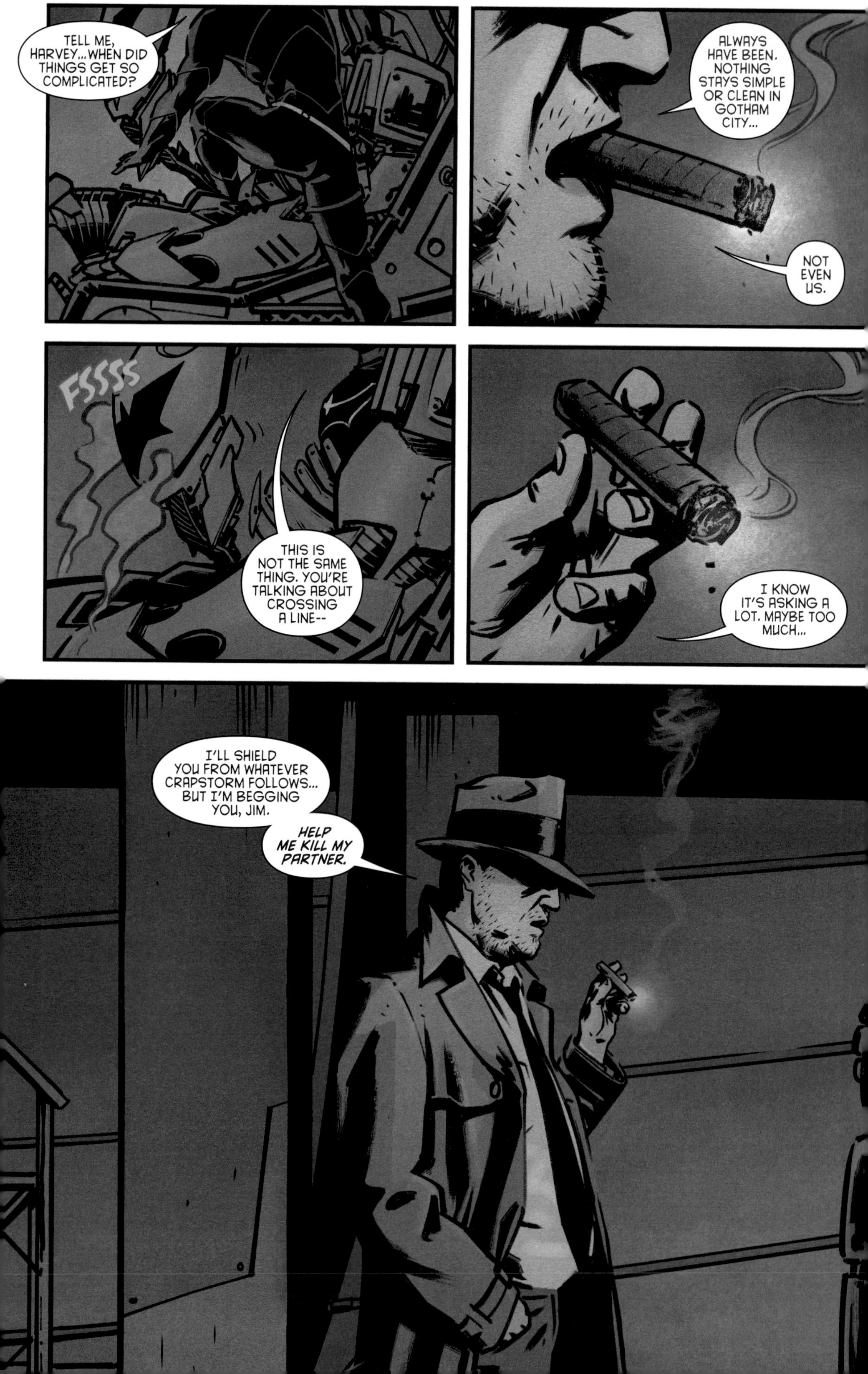
TELL ME, HARVEY...WHEN DID THINGS GET SO COMPLICATED?
ALWAYS HAVE BEEN. NOTHING STAYS SIMPLE OR CLEAN IN GOTHAM CITY...
NOT EVEN US.
FSSSS
THIS IS NOT THE SAME THING. YOU'RE TALKING ABOUT CROSSING A LINE--
I KNOW IT'S ASKING A LOT. MAYBE TOO MUCH...
I'LL SHIELD YOU FROM WHATEVER CRAPSTORM FOLLOWS... BUT I'M BEGGING YOU, JIM.
HELP ME KILL MY PARTNER.

LISTEN, WHAT YOU'RE ASKING ME TO DO--

I'M ASKING YOU TO TRUST ME. I *NEED* YOU TO HAVE MY BACK...

...LIKE I'VE ALWAYS HAD *YOURS.*

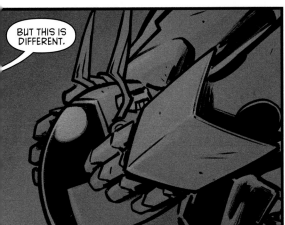

BUT THIS IS DIFFERENT.

SHE COULD BRING THE WHOLE DAMN DEPARTMENT DOWN.

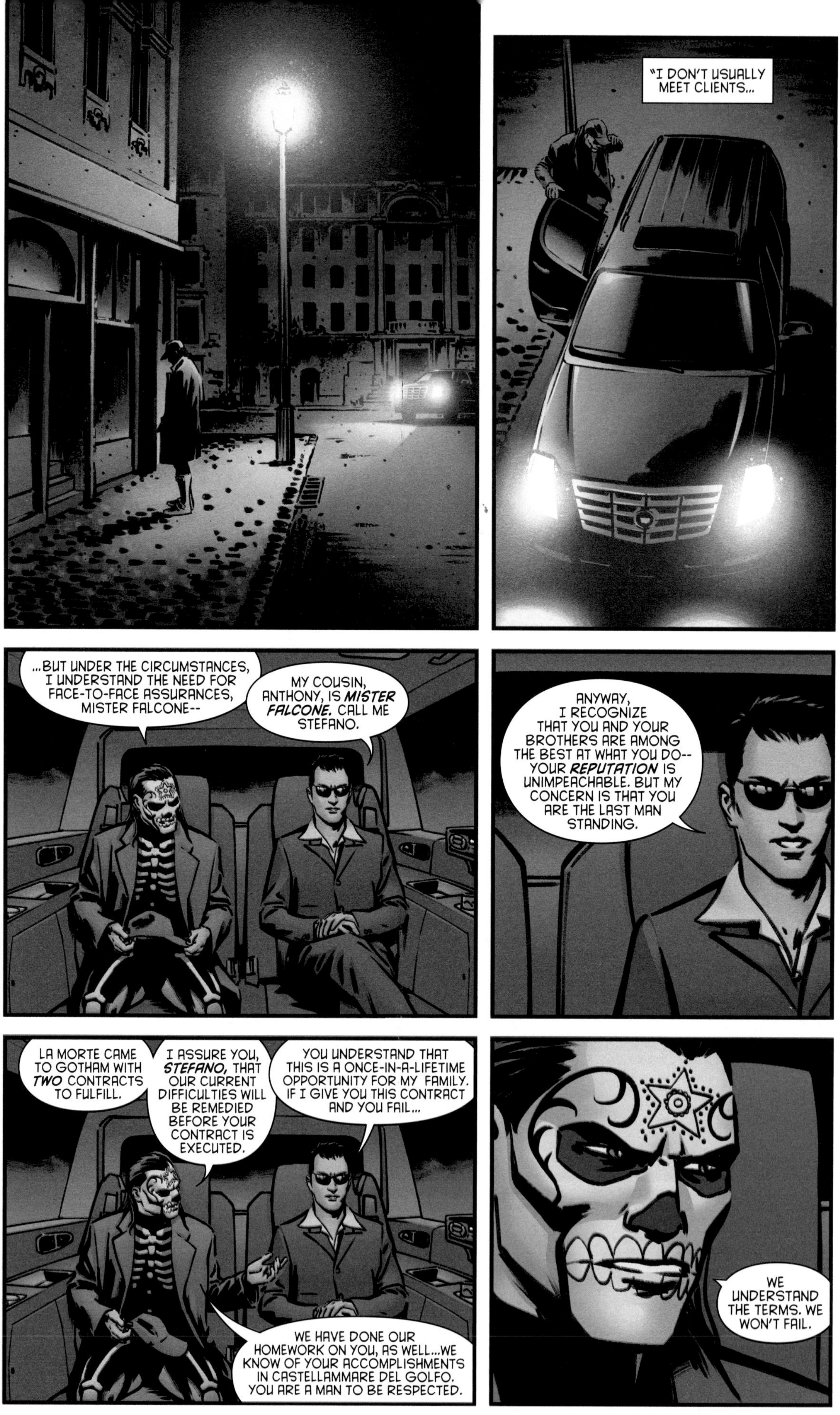
"I DON'T USUALLY MEET CLIENTS...
...BUT UNDER THE CIRCUMSTANCES, I UNDERSTAND THE NEED FOR FACE-TO-FACE ASSURANCES, MISTER FALCONE--
MY COUSIN, ANTHONY, IS MISTER FALCONE. CALL ME STEFANO.
ANYWAY, I RECOGNIZE THAT YOU AND YOUR BROTHERS ARE AMONG THE BEST AT WHAT YOU DO--YOUR REPUTATION IS UNIMPEACHABLE. BUT MY CONCERN IS THAT YOU ARE THE LAST MAN STANDING.
LA MORTE CAME TO GOTHAM WITH TWO CONTRACTS TO FULFILL.
I ASSURE YOU, STEFANO, THAT OUR CURRENT DIFFICULTIES WILL BE REMEDIED BEFORE YOUR CONTRACT IS EXECUTED.
YOU UNDERSTAND THAT THIS IS A ONCE-IN-A-LIFETIME OPPORTUNITY FOR MY FAMILY. IF I GIVE YOU THIS CONTRACT AND YOU FAIL...
WE HAVE DONE OUR HOMEWORK ON YOU, AS WELL...WE KNOW OF YOUR ACCOMPLISHMENTS IN CASTELLAMMARE DEL GOLFO. YOU ARE A MAN TO BE RESPECTED.
WE UNDERSTAND THE TERMS. WE WON'T FAIL.

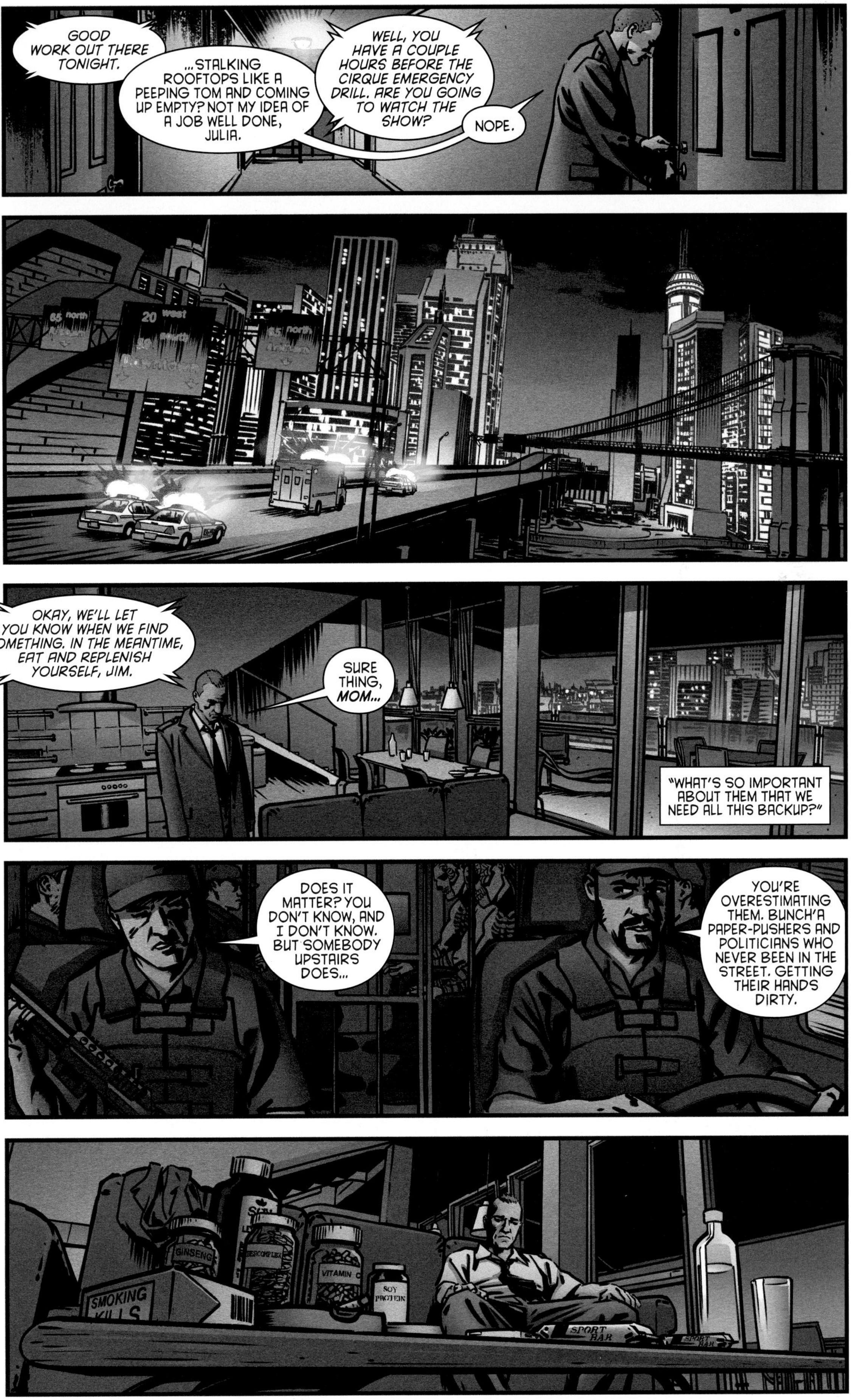
GOOD WORK OUT THERE TONIGHT.
...STALKING ROOFTOPS LIKE A PEEPING TOM AND COMING UP EMPTY? NOT MY IDEA OF A JOB WELL DONE, JULIA.
WELL, YOU HAVE A COUPLE HOURS BEFORE THE CIRQUE EMERGENCY DRILL. ARE YOU GOING TO WATCH THE SHOW?
NOPE.
65 north
20 west
65 north
OKAY, WE'LL LET YOU KNOW WHEN WE FIND SOMETHING. IN THE MEANTIME, EAT AND REPLENISH YOURSELF, JIM.
SURE THING, *MOM*...
"WHAT'S SO IMPORTANT ABOUT THEM THAT WE NEED ALL THIS BACKUP?"
DOES IT MATTER? YOU DON'T KNOW, AND I DON'T KNOW. BUT SOMEBODY UPSTAIRS DOES...
YOU'RE OVERESTIMATING THEM. BUNCH'A PAPER-PUSHERS AND POLITICIANS WHO NEVER BEEN IN THE STREET. GETTING THEIR HANDS DIRTY.
GINSENG
VITAMIN C
SOY PROTEIN
SMOKING KILLS
SPORT BAR
SPORT BAR

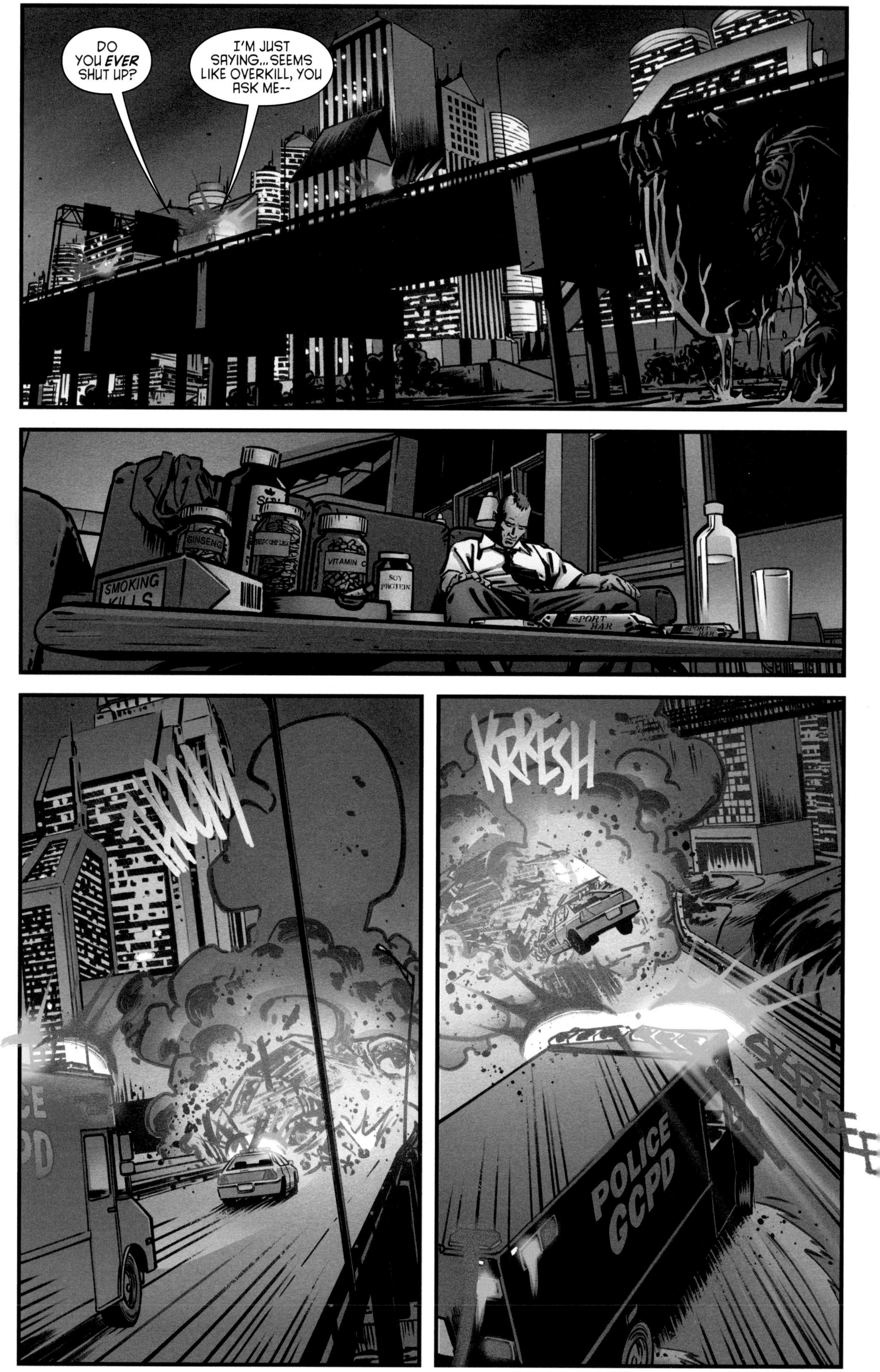
DO YOU *EVER* SHUT UP?
I'M JUST SAYING... SEEMS LIKE OVERKILL, YOU ASK ME--
GINSENG
VITAMIN C
SOY PROTEIN
SMOKING KILLS
SPORT BAR
KRRESH
POLICE GCPD
SKREEEE

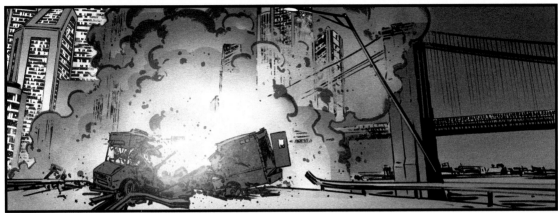

YOU'VE REACHED DETECTIVE YIP OF THE GCPD... LEAVE A MESSAGE AFTER THE BEEP, AND I'LL CALL YOU BACK...

BEEEP

DAMMIT, NANCE...PICK UP YOUR PHONE. WE NEED TO TALK.

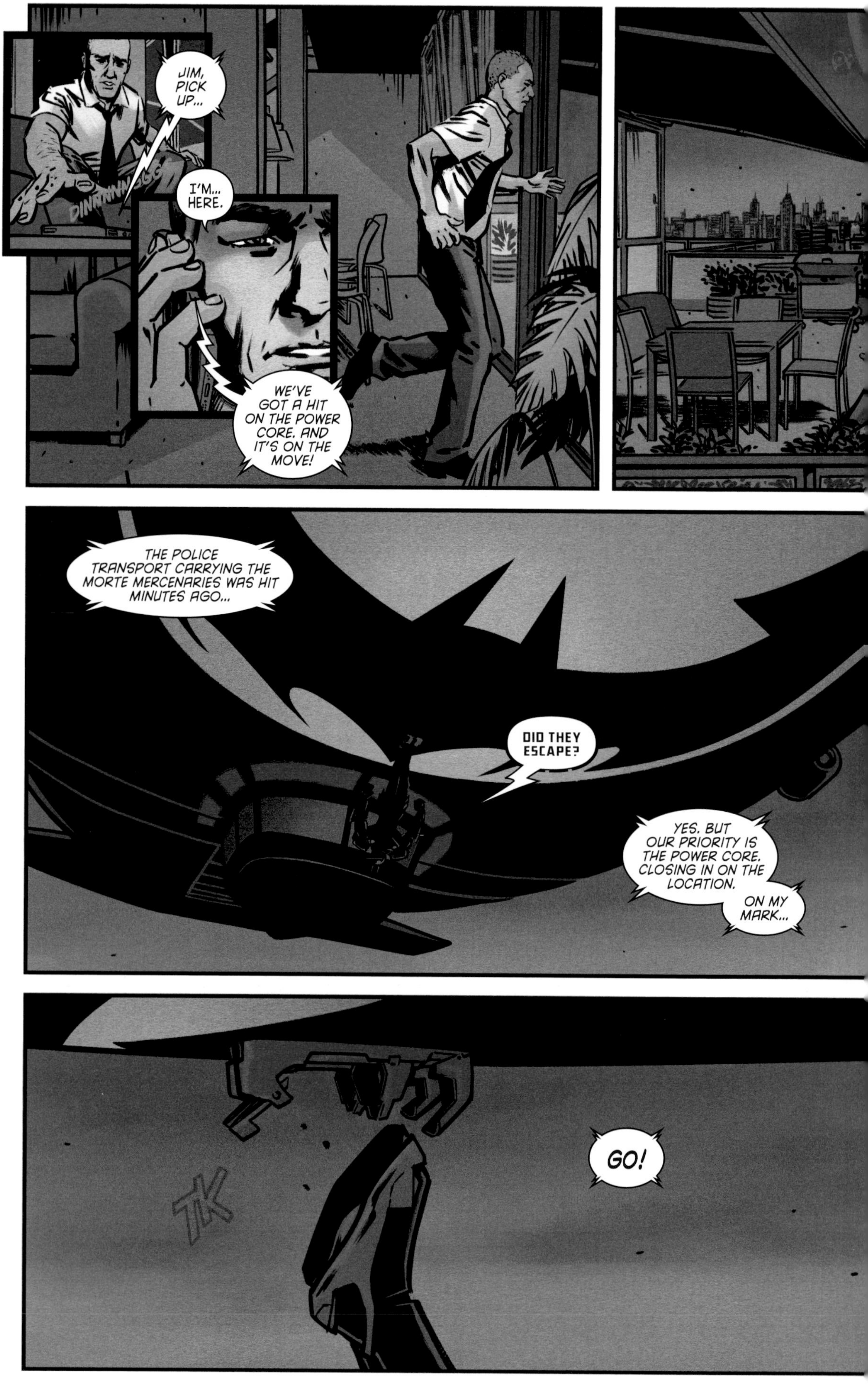
JIM, PICK UP...
DINRRNNNGGG
I'M... HERE.
WE'VE GOT A HIT ON THE POWER CORE. AND IT'S ON THE MOVE!
THE POLICE TRANSPORT CARRYING THE MORTE MERCENARIES WAS HIT MINUTES AGO...
DID THEY ESCAPE?
YES. BUT OUR PRIORITY IS THE POWER CORE. CLOSING IN ON THE LOCATION.
ON MY MARK...
TK
GO!

YOU READY?

DOES IT MATTER?

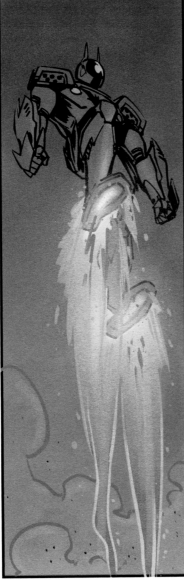

WHEN YOU LAND, THE TARGET SHOULD BE RIGHT THERE AT YOUR TWELVE.

YOU'RE RIGHT ON TOP OF IT.

DO YOU HAVE A VISUAL?

KA-THUNK

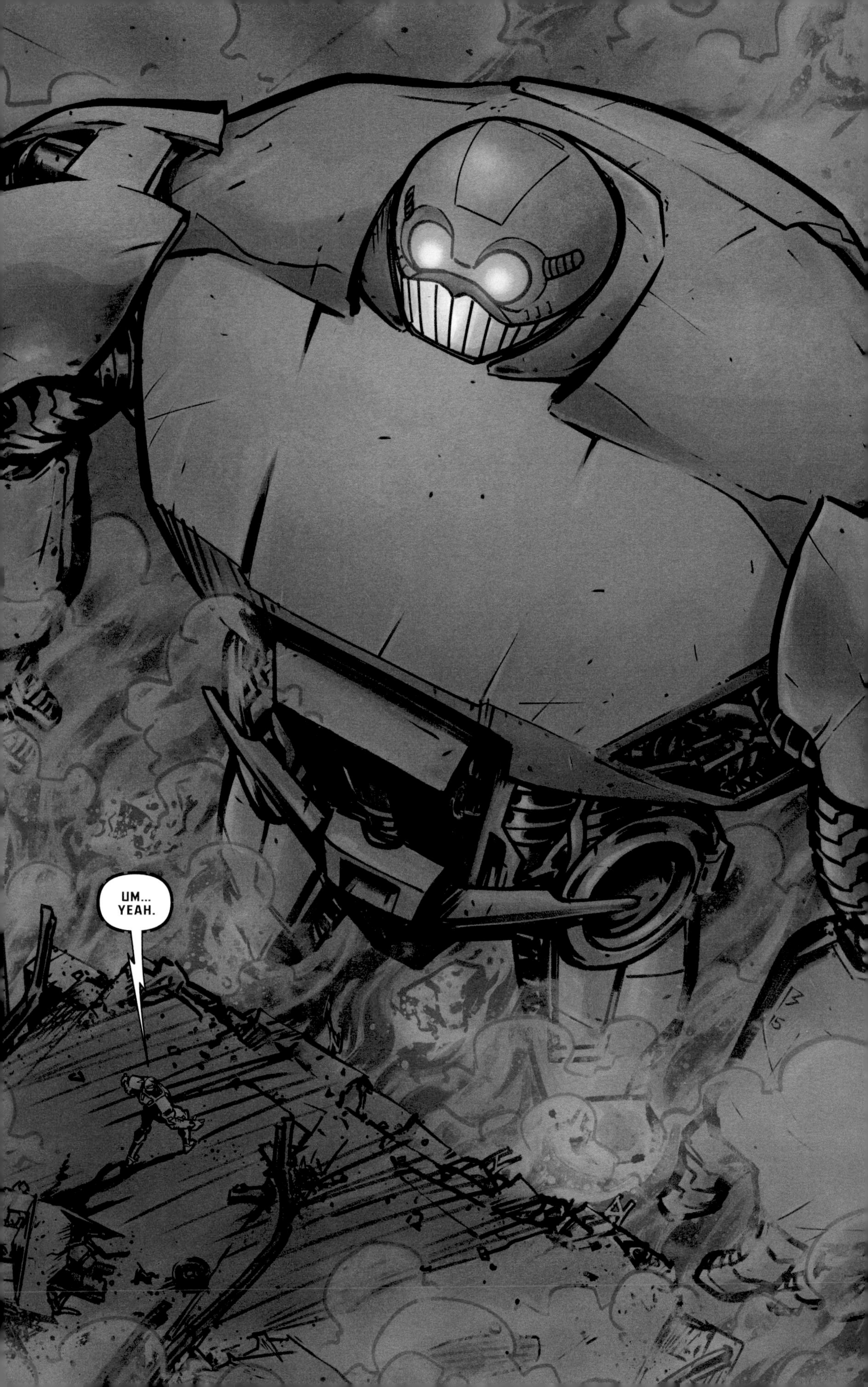
UM... YEAH.

YOU'VE REACHED *DETECTIVE YIP* OF THE GCPD... LEAVE A MESSAGE AFTER THE BEEP, AND I'LL CALL YOU BACK...

BEEP

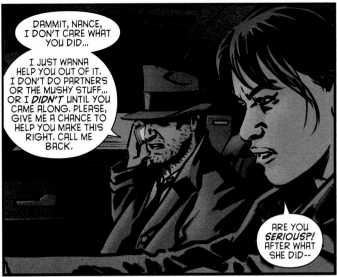

DAMMIT, NANCE, I DON'T CARE WHAT YOU DID...

I JUST WANNA HELP YOU OUT OF IT. I DON'T DO PARTNERS OR THE MUSHY STUFF... OR I *DIDN'T* UNTIL YOU CAME ALONG. PLEASE, GIVE ME A CHANCE TO HELP YOU MAKE THIS RIGHT. CALL ME BACK.

ARE YOU *SERIOUS?!* AFTER WHAT SHE DID--

LEAVE IT ALONE, *RENEE...*

"...I'M GONNA TAKE CARE OF EVERYTHING."

PLEASE, GIVE ME A CHANCE TO HELP YOU MAKE THIS RIGHT. CALL ME BACK.

SORRY. MESSAGE FROM MY PARTNER...

DOES HE KNOW?

IF HE DID, I WOULDN'T BE HERE RIGHT NOW.

WHAT HAPPENS WHEN HE DOES?

DOESN'T MATTER. AFTER WHAT I DID, MY LIFE IS OVER, *MISTER FALCONE.* THERE'S NO GOING BACK. NO FORGIVENESS...

AND YET, IT DIDN'T TAKE MUCH FOR YOU TO FLIP.

MAYBE BECAUSE I KNOW YOU ALREADY HAVE THE DEPARTMENT IN YOUR POCKET.

AND IF IT'S GONNA BE RUN BY *SCUMBAGS* LIKE YOU...I MIGHT AS WELL GET OUT NOW.

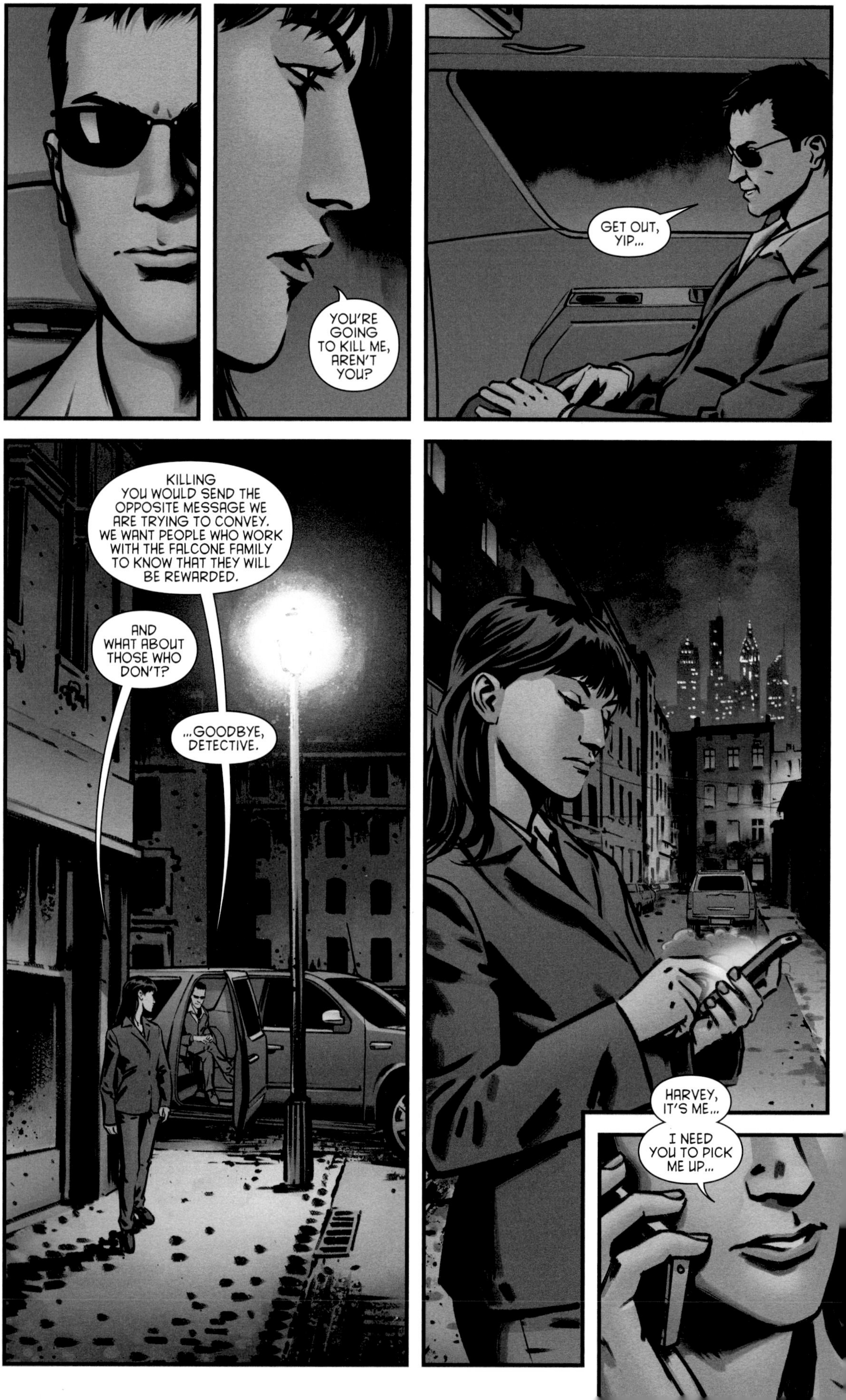
YOU'RE GOING TO KILL ME, AREN'T YOU?
GET OUT, YIP...
KILLING YOU WOULD SEND THE OPPOSITE MESSAGE WE ARE TRYING TO CONVEY. WE WANT PEOPLE WHO WORK WITH THE FALCONE FAMILY TO KNOW THAT THEY WILL BE REWARDED.
AND WHAT ABOUT THOSE WHO DON'T?
...GOODBYE, DETECTIVE.
HARVEY, IT'S ME...
I NEED YOU TO PICK ME UP...

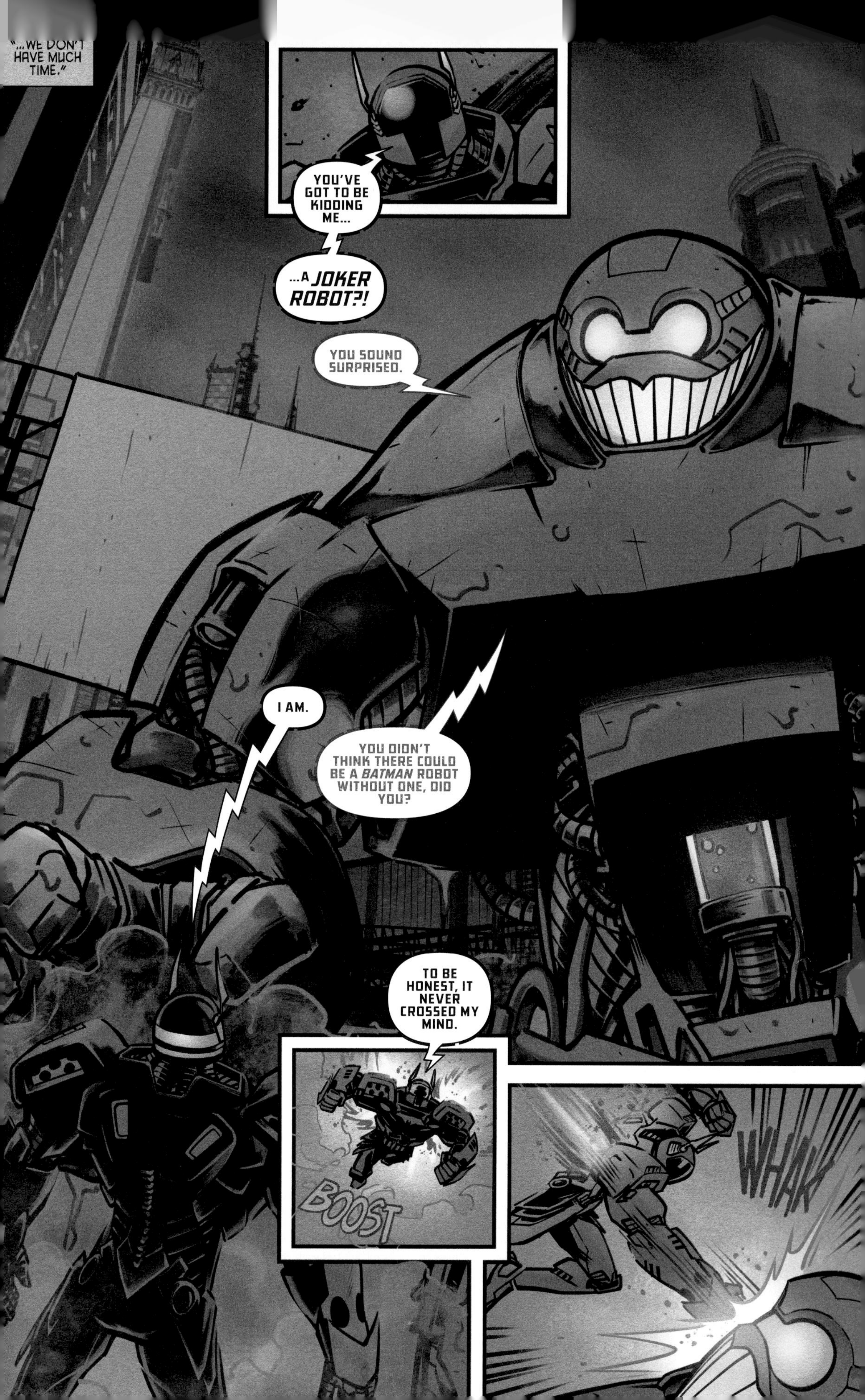
"...WE DON'T HAVE MUCH TIME."
YOU'VE GOT TO BE KIDDING ME...
...A *JOKER ROBOT?!*
YOU SOUND SURPRISED.
I AM.
YOU DIDN'T THINK THERE COULD BE A *BATMAN* ROBOT WITHOUT ONE, DID YOU?
TO BE HONEST, IT NEVER CROSSED MY MIND.
BOOST
WHAK

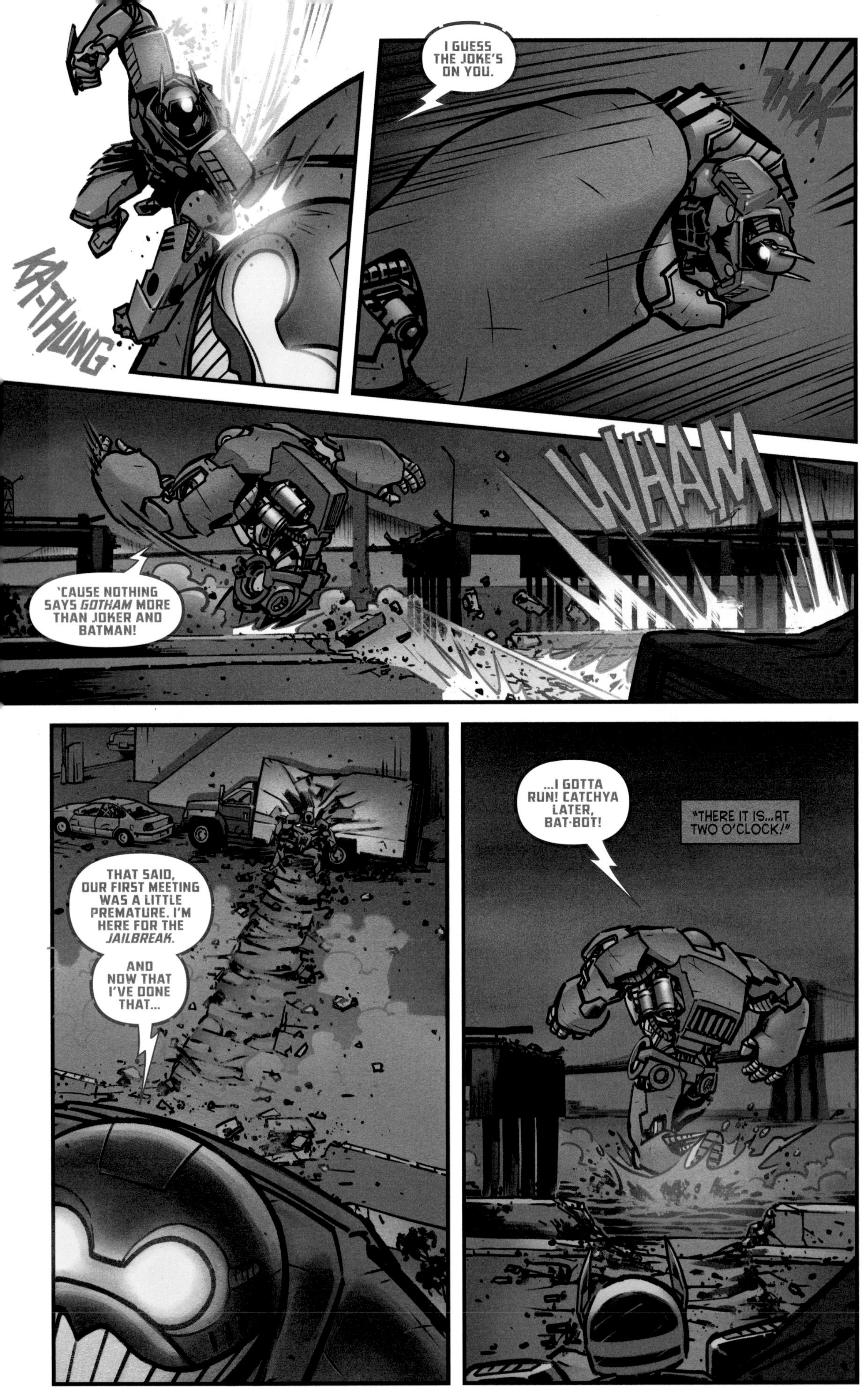
KA-THUNG
I GUESS THE JOKE'S ON YOU.
THOK
'CAUSE NOTHING SAYS *GOTHAM* MORE THAN JOKER AND BATMAN!
WHAM
THAT SAID, OUR FIRST MEETING WAS A LITTLE PREMATURE. I'M HERE FOR THE *JAILBREAK*.
AND NOW THAT I'VE DONE THAT...
...I GOTTA RUN! CATCHYA LATER, BAT-BOT!
"THERE IT IS...AT TWO O'CLOCK!"

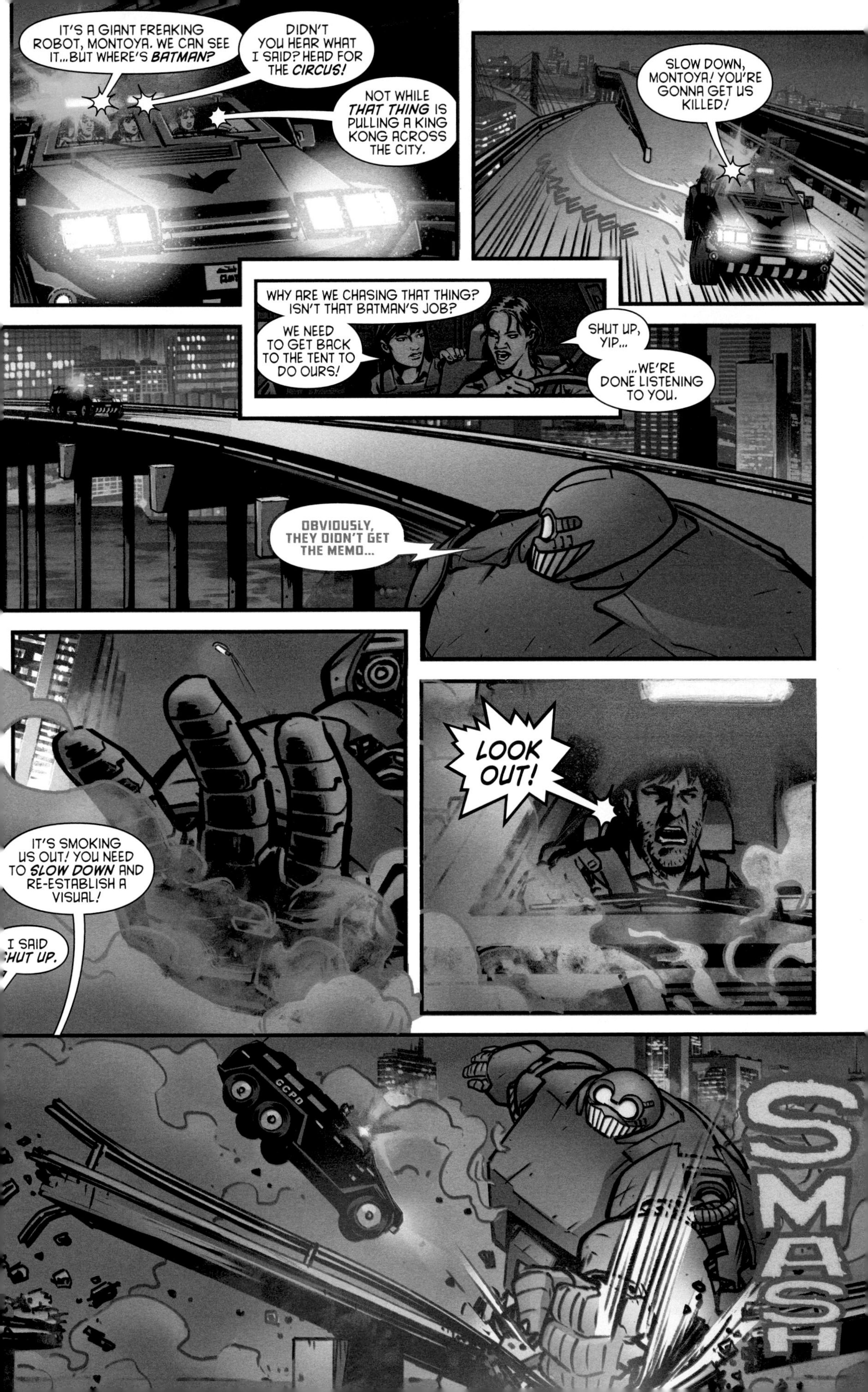
IT'S A GIANT FREAKING ROBOT, MONTOYA. WE CAN SEE IT...BUT WHERE'S *BATMAN?*
DIDN'T YOU HEAR WHAT I SAID? HEAD FOR THE *CIRCUS!*
NOT WHILE *THAT THING* IS PULLING A KING KONG ACROSS THE CITY.
SLOW DOWN, MONTOYA! YOU'RE GONNA GET US KILLED!
SKREEEEEE
WHY ARE WE CHASING THAT THING? ISN'T THAT BATMAN'S JOB?
WE NEED TO GET BACK TO THE TENT TO DO OURS!
SHUT UP, YIP...
...WE'RE DONE LISTENING TO YOU.
OBVIOUSLY, THEY DIDN'T GET THE MEMO...
IT'S SMOKING US OUT! YOU NEED TO *SLOW DOWN* AND RE-ESTABLISH A VISUAL!
I SAID *HUT UP.*
LOOK OUT!
GCPD
SMASH

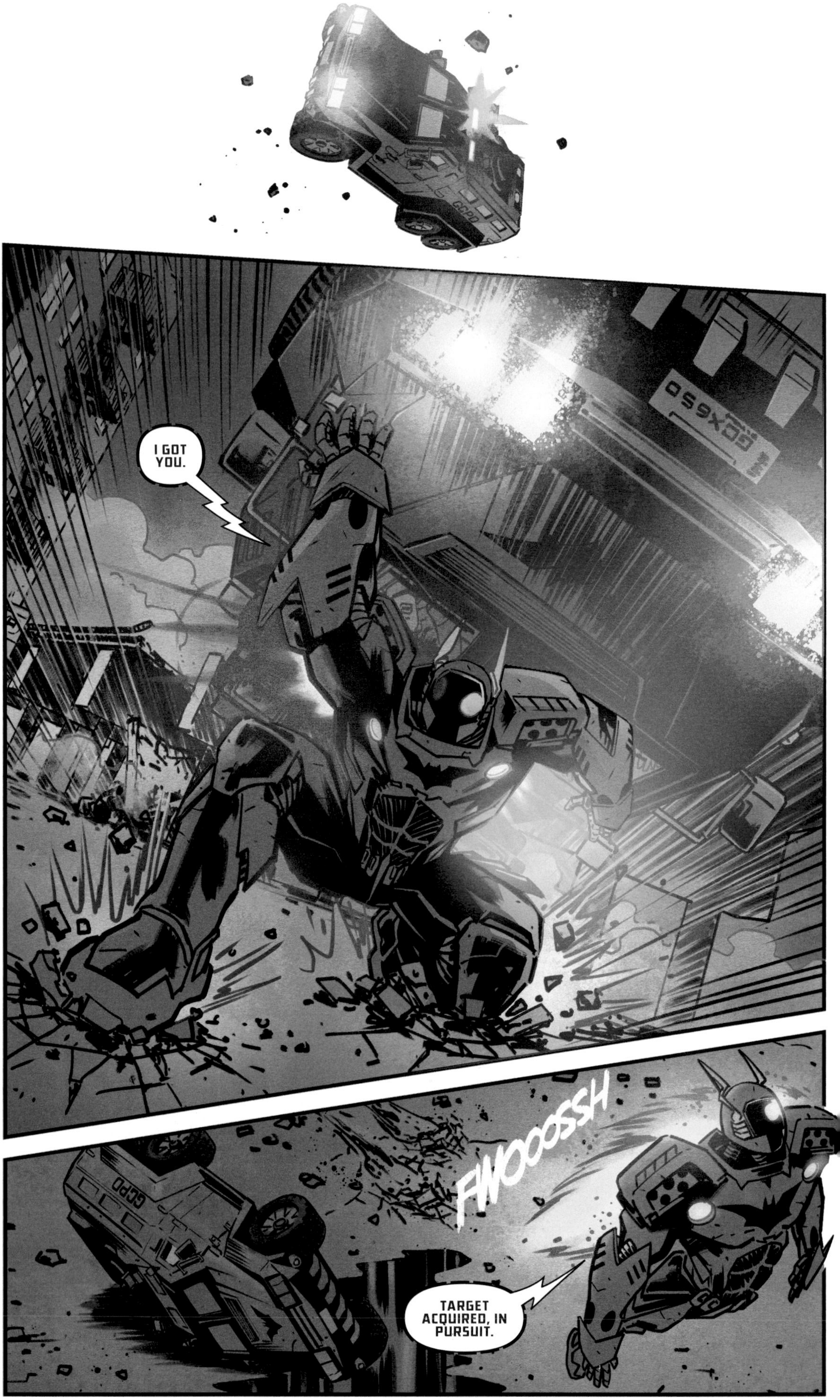
I GOT YOU.
FWOOOSSH
TARGET ACQUIRED, IN PURSUIT.

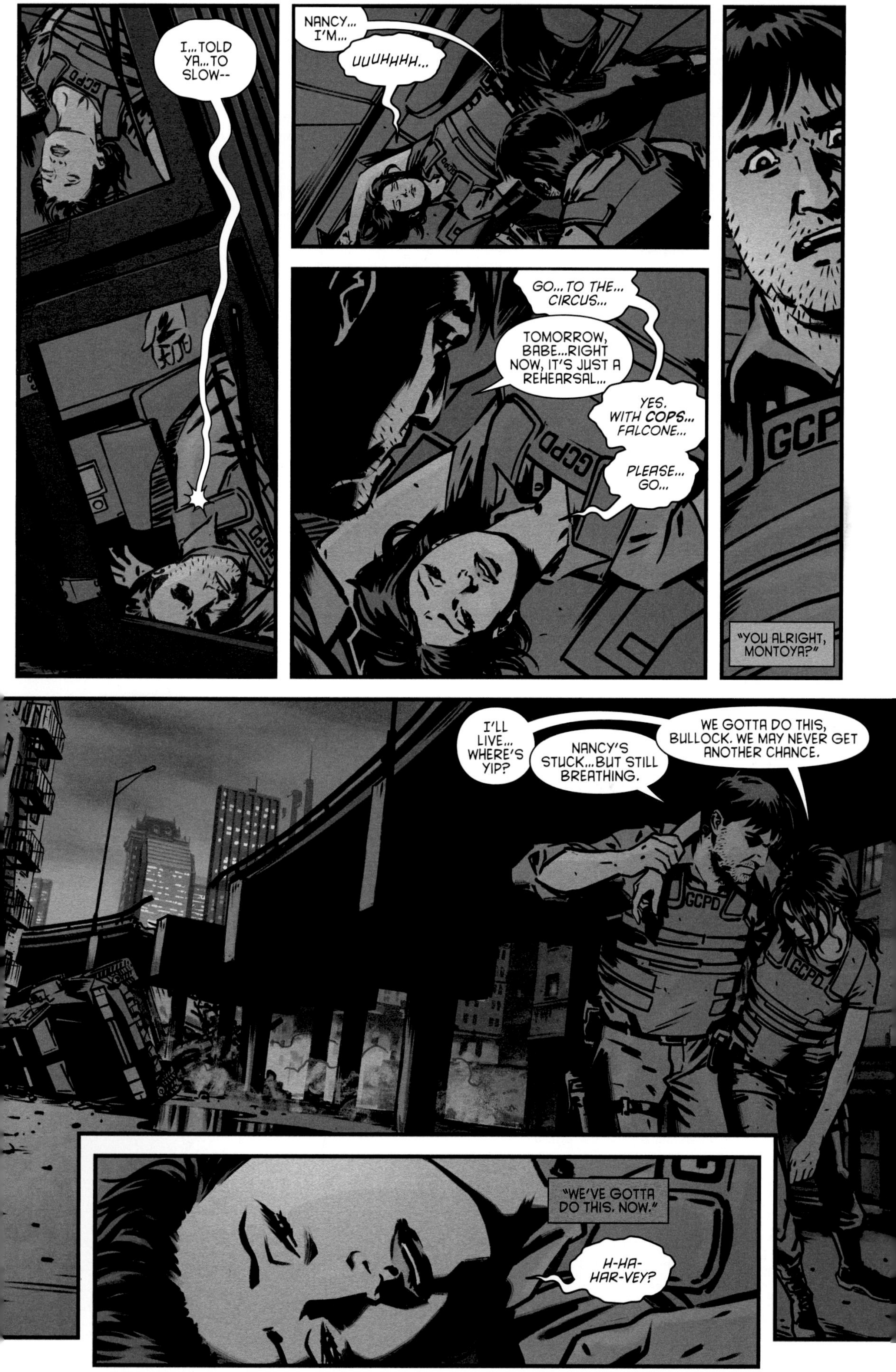
I...TOLD YA...TO SLOW--
NANCY... I'M...
UUUHHHH...
GO...TO THE... CIRCUS...
TOMORROW, BABE...RIGHT NOW, IT'S JUST A REHEARSAL...
YES. WITH COPS... FALCONE...
PLEASE... GO...
"YOU ALRIGHT, MONTOYA?"
I'LL LIVE... WHERE'S YIP?
NANCY'S STUCK...BUT STILL BREATHING.
WE GOTTA DO THIS, BULLOCK. WE MAY NEVER GET ANOTHER CHANCE.
"WE'VE GOTTA DO THIS. NOW."
H-HA-HAR-VEY?

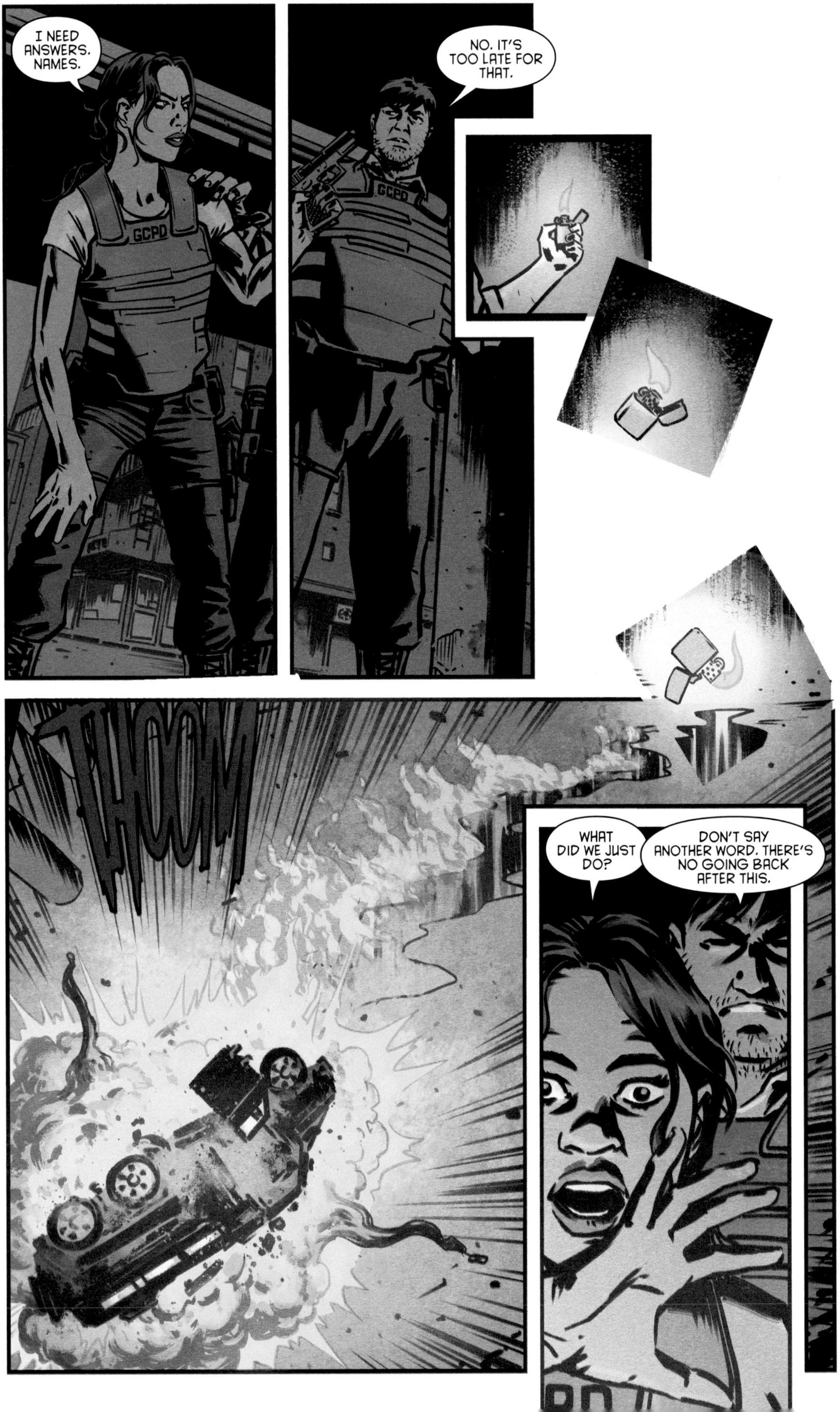
I NEED ANSWERS. NAMES.
NO. IT'S TOO LATE FOR THAT.
THOOM
WHAT DID WE JUST DO?
DON'T SAY ANOTHER WORD. THERE'S NO GOING BACK AFTER THIS.

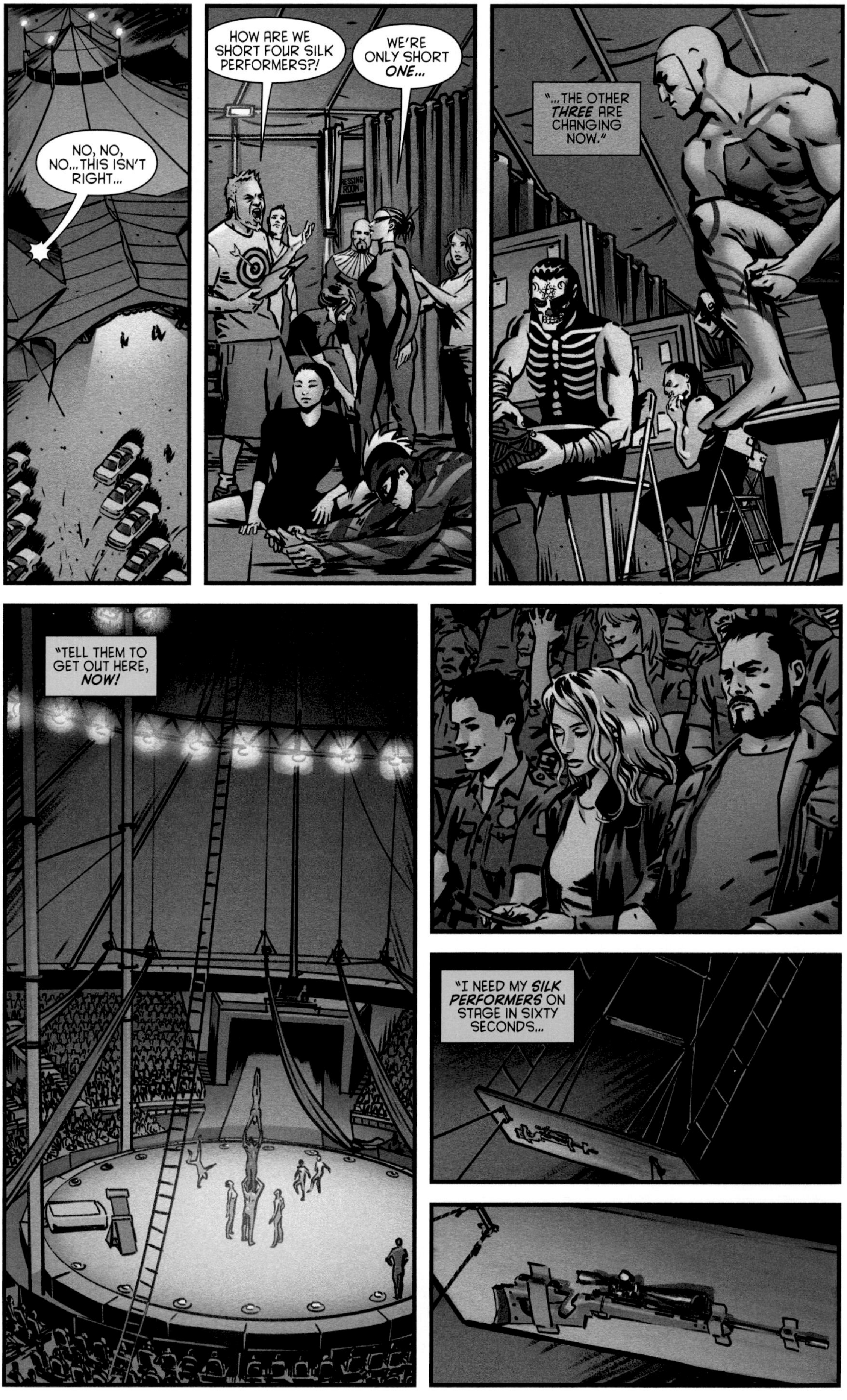
NO, NO, NO...THIS ISN'T RIGHT...
HOW ARE WE SHORT FOUR SILK PERFORMERS?!
WE'RE ONLY SHORT *ONE*...
"...THE OTHER *THREE* ARE CHANGING NOW."
DRESSING ROOM
"TELL THEM TO GET OUT HERE, *NOW!*
"I NEED MY *SILK PERFORMERS* ON STAGE IN SIXTY SECONDS...

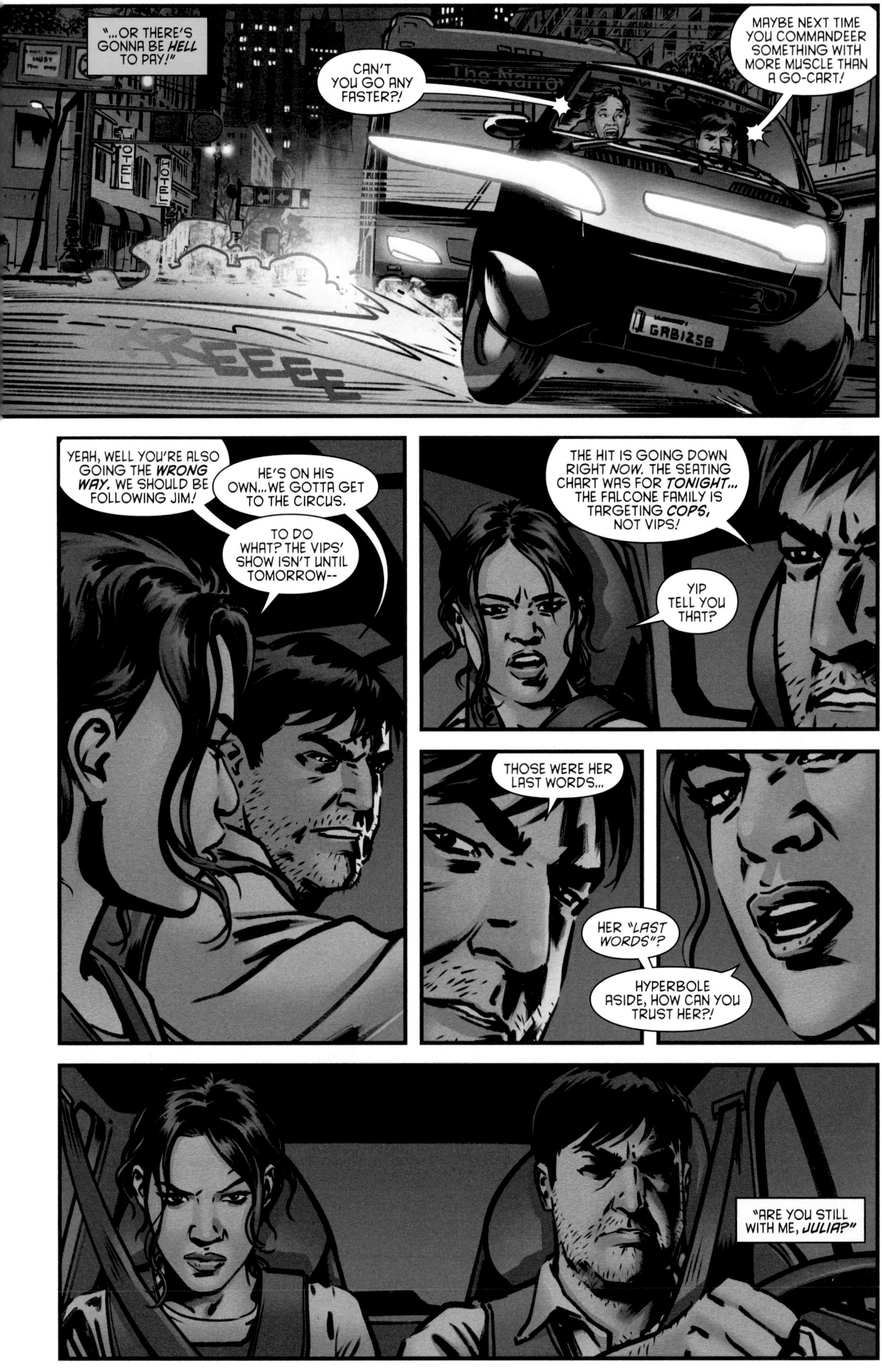
"...OR THERE'S GONNA BE HELL TO PAY!"
CAN'T YOU GO ANY FASTER?!
MAYBE NEXT TIME YOU COMMANDEER SOMETHING WITH MORE MUSCLE THAN A GO-CART!
HOTEL
HOTEL
GRB1258
RREEEE
YEAH, WELL YOU'RE ALSO GOING THE WRONG WAY. WE SHOULD BE FOLLOWING JIM!
HE'S ON HIS OWN...WE GOTTA GET TO THE CIRCUS.
TO DO WHAT? THE VIPS' SHOW ISN'T UNTIL TOMORROW--
THE HIT IS GOING DOWN RIGHT NOW. THE SEATING CHART WAS FOR TONIGHT... THE FALCONE FAMILY IS TARGETING COPS, NOT VIPS!
YIP TELL YOU THAT?
THOSE WERE HER LAST WORDS...
HER "LAST WORDS"?
HYPERBOLE ASIDE, HOW CAN YOU TRUST HER?!
"ARE YOU STILL WITH ME, JULIA?"

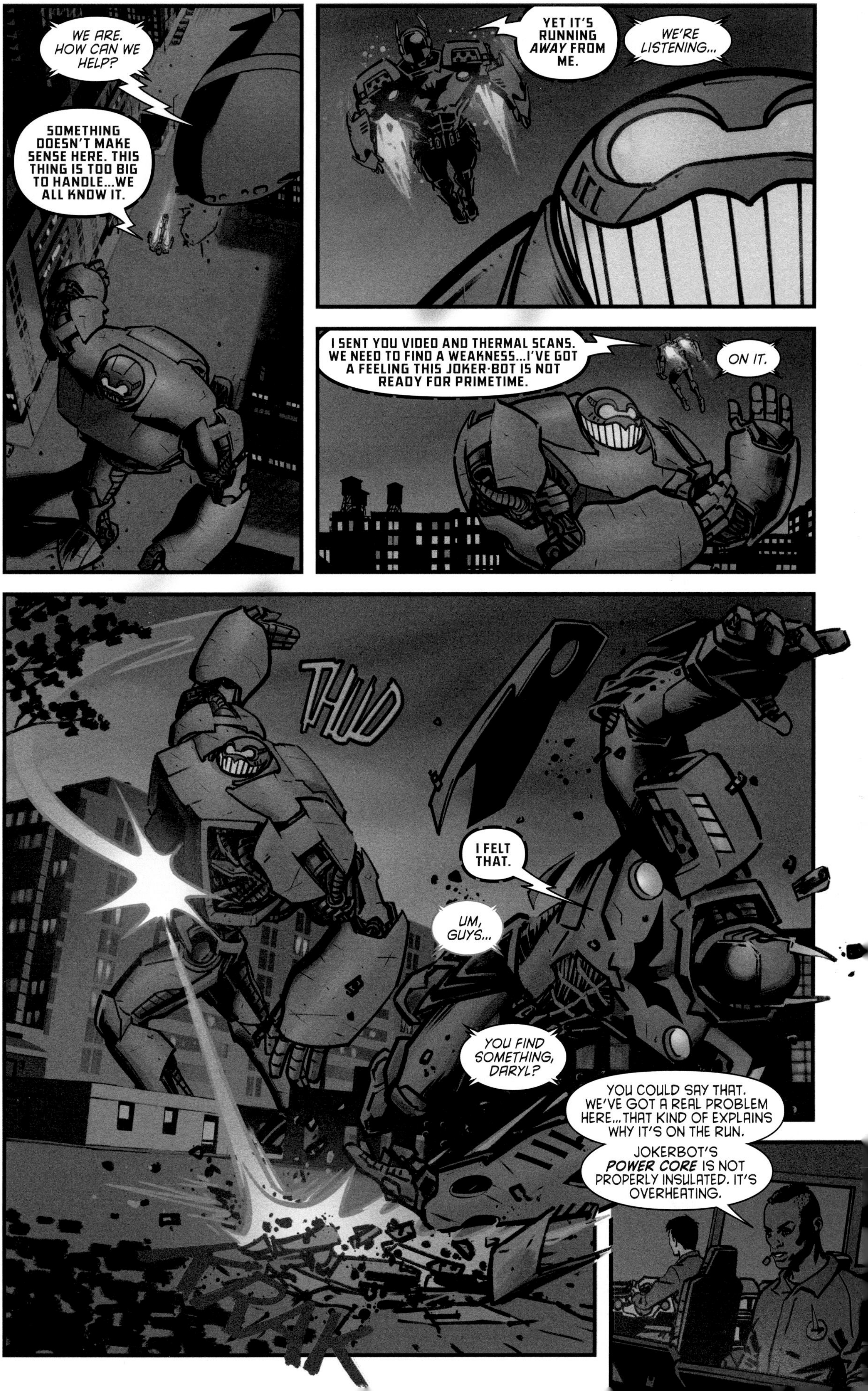
WE ARE. HOW CAN WE HELP?
SOMETHING DOESN'T MAKE SENSE HERE. THIS THING IS TOO BIG TO HANDLE...WE ALL KNOW IT.
YET IT'S RUNNING *AWAY* FROM ME.
WE'RE LISTENING...
I SENT YOU VIDEO AND THERMAL SCANS. WE NEED TO FIND A WEAKNESS...I'VE GOT A FEELING THIS JOKER-BOT IS NOT READY FOR PRIMETIME.
ON IT.
THUD
I FELT THAT.
UM, GUYS...
YOU FIND SOMETHING, DARYL?
YOU COULD SAY THAT. WE'VE GOT A REAL PROBLEM HERE...THAT KIND OF EXPLAINS WHY IT'S ON THE RUN.
JOKERBOT'S ***POWER CORE*** IS NOT PROPERLY INSULATED. IT'S OVERHEATING.
KRAK

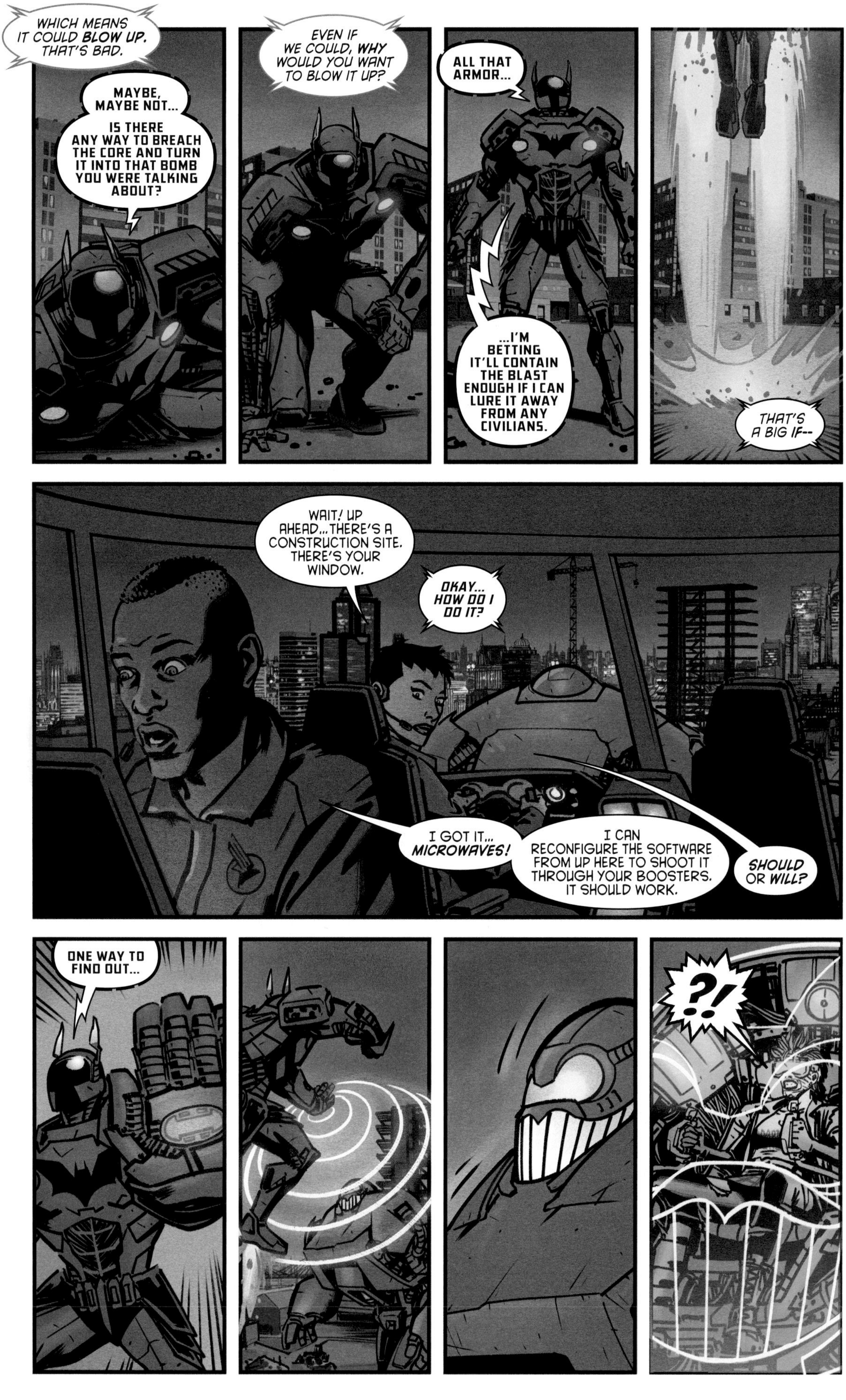
WHICH MEANS IT COULD **BLOW UP.** THAT'S BAD.
MAYBE, MAYBE NOT...
IS THERE ANY WAY TO BREACH THE CORE AND TURN IT INTO THAT BOMB YOU WERE TALKING ABOUT?
EVEN IF WE COULD, **WHY** WOULD YOU WANT TO BLOW IT UP?
ALL THAT ARMOR...
...I'M BETTING IT'LL CONTAIN THE BLAST ENOUGH IF I CAN LURE IT AWAY FROM ANY CIVILIANS.
THAT'S A BIG ***IF***--
WAIT! UP AHEAD...THERE'S A CONSTRUCTION SITE. THERE'S YOUR WINDOW.
OKAY... HOW DO I DO IT?
I GOT IT... ***MICROWAVES!***
I CAN RECONFIGURE THE SOFTWARE FROM UP HERE TO SHOOT IT THROUGH YOUR BOOSTERS. IT SHOULD WORK.
SHOULD OR ***WILL?***
ONE WAY TO FIND OUT...
?!

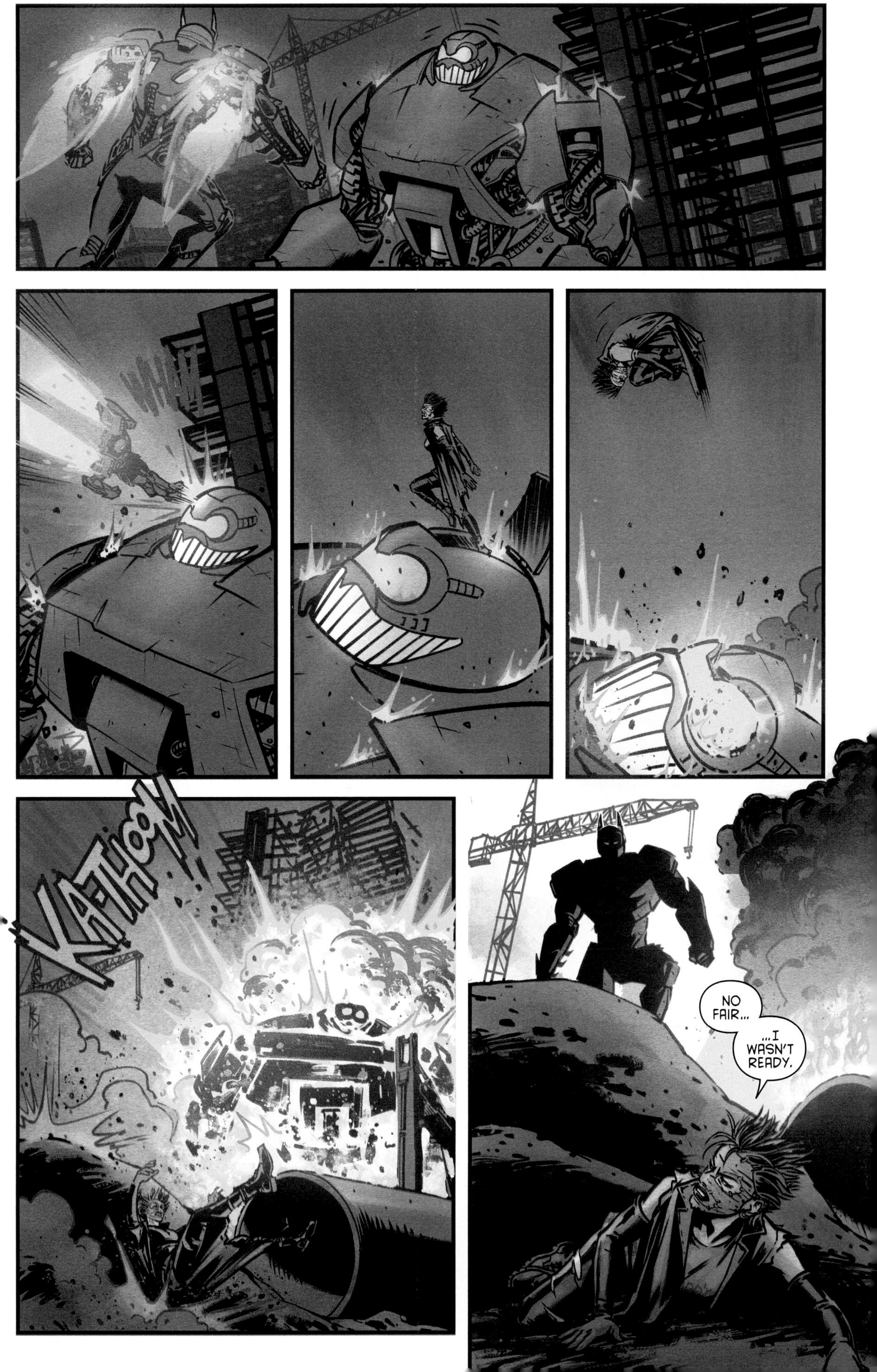
WHAM
KATHOOM
NO FAIR...
...I WASN'T READY.

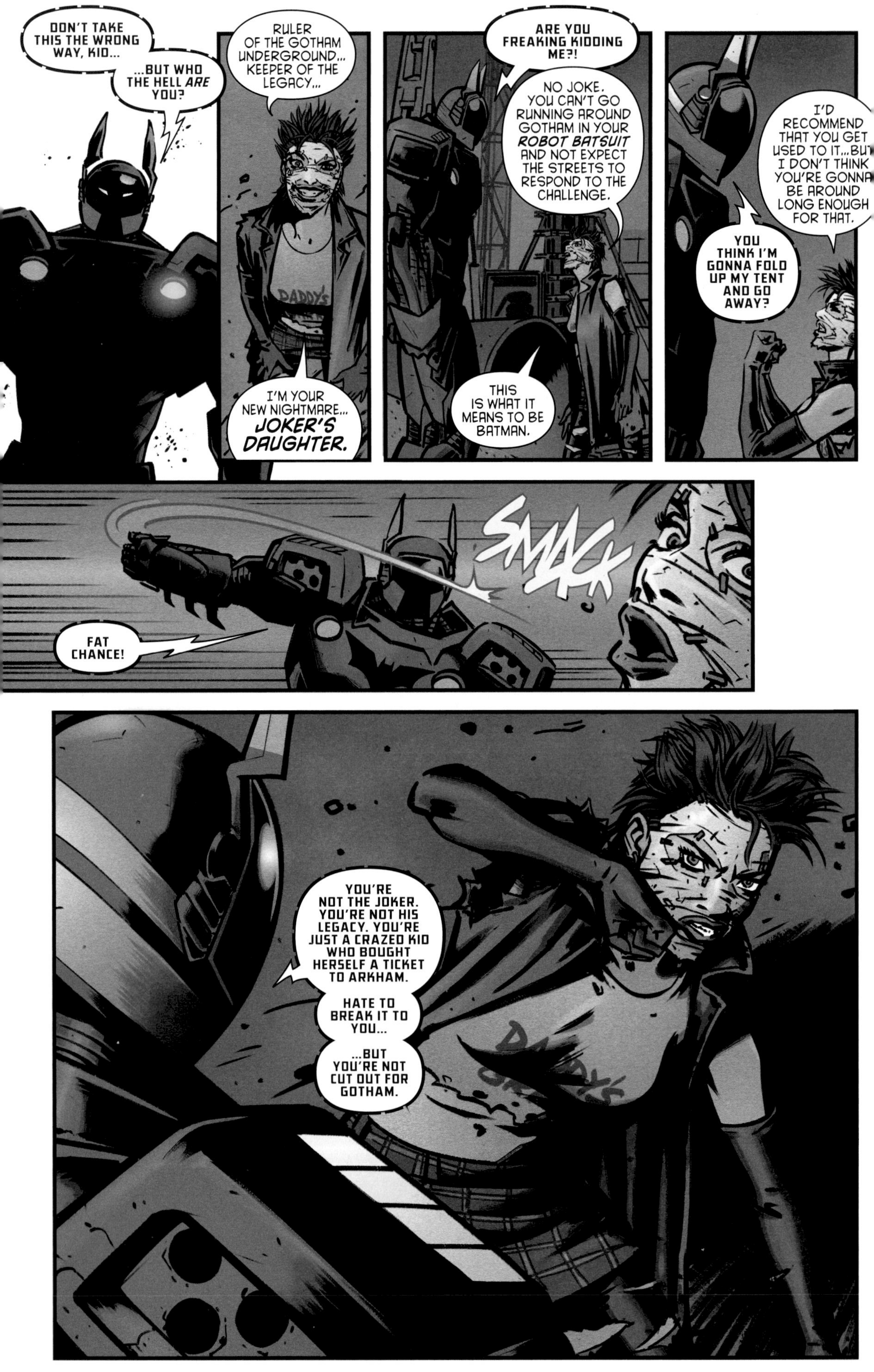
DON'T TAKE THIS THE WRONG WAY, KID...
...BUT WHO THE HELL *ARE* YOU?
RULER OF THE GOTHAM UNDERGROUND... KEEPER OF THE LEGACY...
DADDY'S
I'M YOUR NEW NIGHTMARE... ***JOKER'S DAUGHTER.***
ARE YOU FREAKING KIDDING ME?!
NO JOKE. YOU CAN'T GO RUNNING AROUND GOTHAM IN YOUR ***ROBOT BATSUIT*** AND NOT EXPECT THE STREETS TO RESPOND TO THE CHALLENGE.
THIS IS WHAT IT MEANS TO BE BATMAN.
I'D RECOMMEND THAT YOU GET USED TO IT...BUT I DON'T THINK YOU'RE GONNA BE AROUND LONG ENOUGH FOR THAT.
YOU THINK I'M GONNA FOLD UP MY TENT AND GO AWAY?
SMACK
FAT CHANCE!
YOU'RE NOT THE JOKER. YOU'RE NOT HIS LEGACY. YOU'RE JUST A CRAZED KID WHO BOUGHT HERSELF A TICKET TO ARKHAM.
HATE TO BREAK IT TO YOU...
...BUT YOU'RE NOT CUT OUT FOR GOTHAM.

Losing Batman hit this city harder than most want to admit.

YOU BORED?

Every crook and freak-show thought it was open season with him gone.

TO TEARS.

I'm Batman now, and I've got some whack-jobs of my own to deal with.

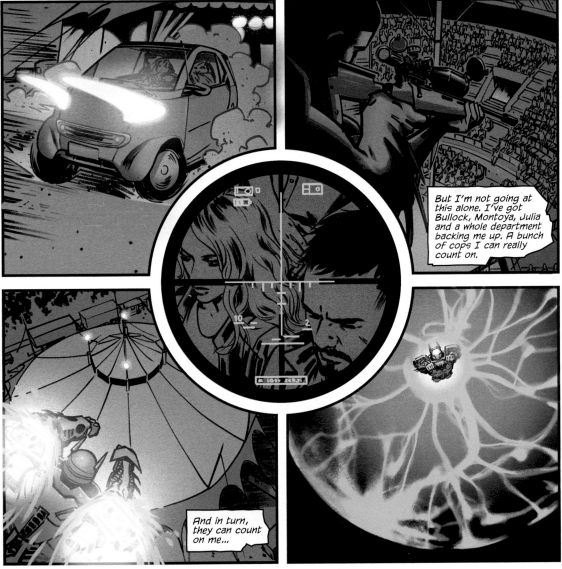

But I'm not going at this alone. I've got Bullock, Montoya, Julia and a whole department backing me up. A bunch of cops I can really count on.

And in turn, they can count on me...

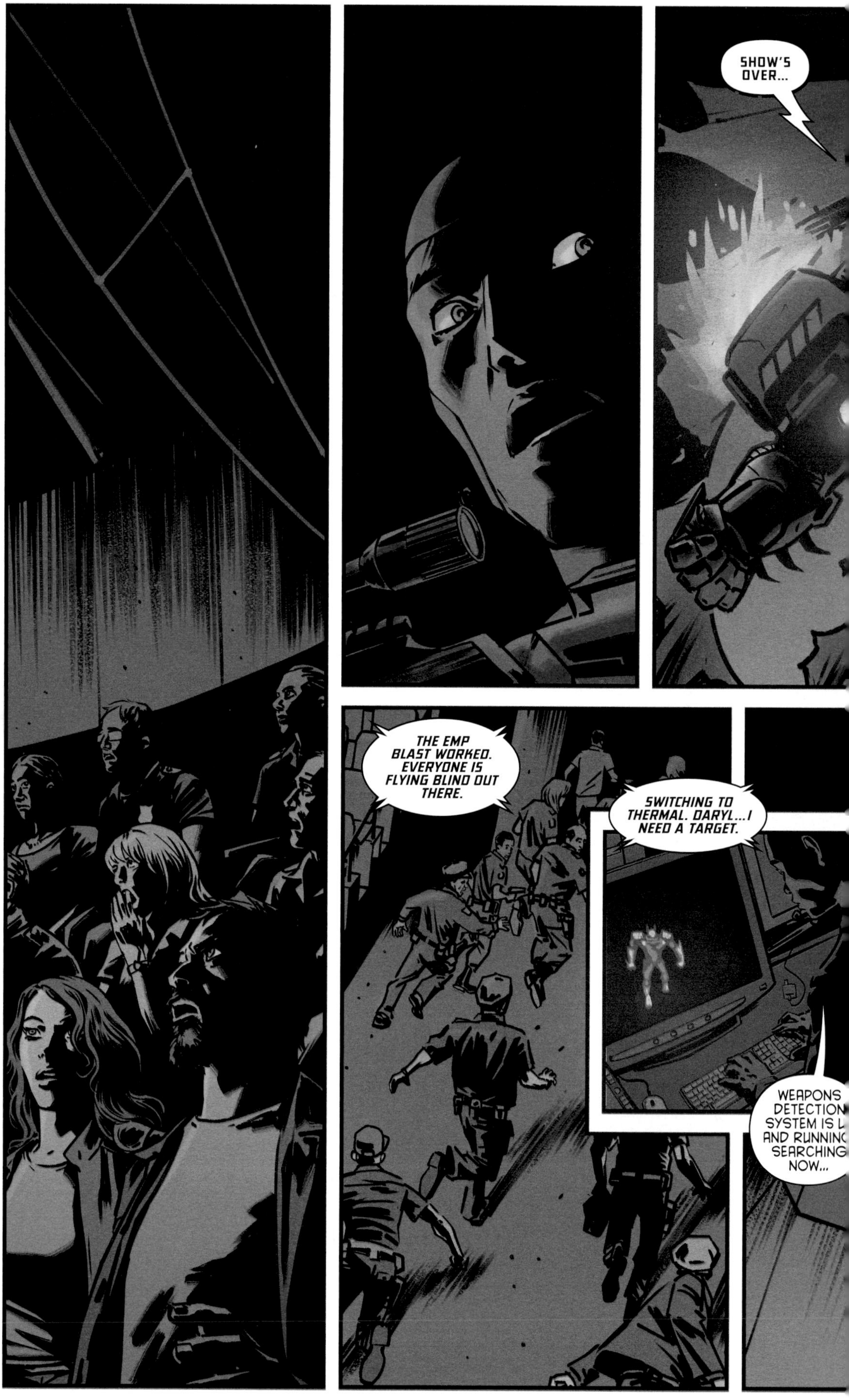
SHOW'S OVER...
THE EMP BLAST WORKED. EVERYONE IS FLYING BLIND OUT THERE.
SWITCHING TO THERMAL. DARYL...I NEED A TARGET.
WEAPONS DETECTION SYSTEM IS L AND RUNNIN SEARCHING NOW...

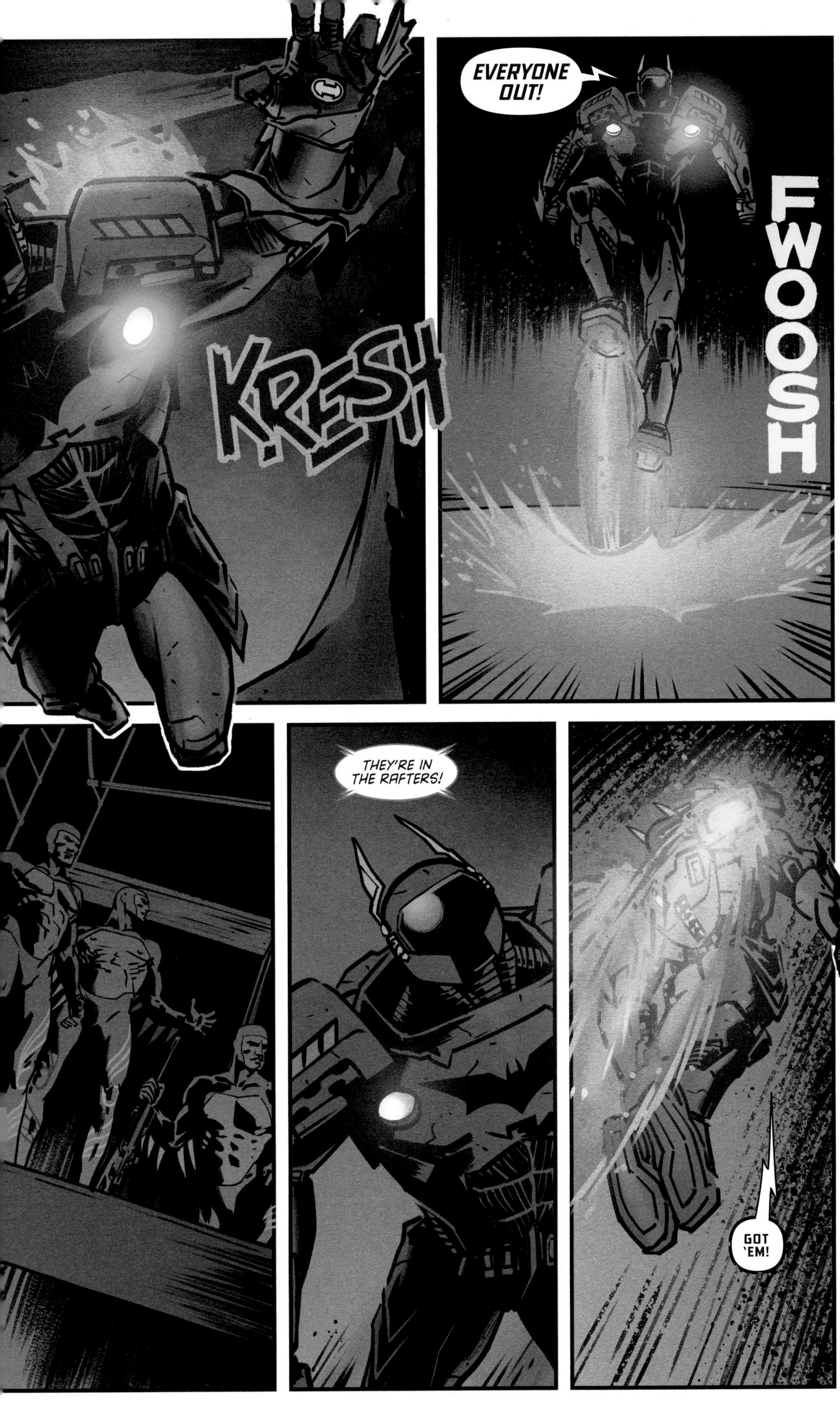
KRESH
EVERYONE OUT!
FWOOSH
THEY'RE IN THE RAFTERS!
GOT 'EM!

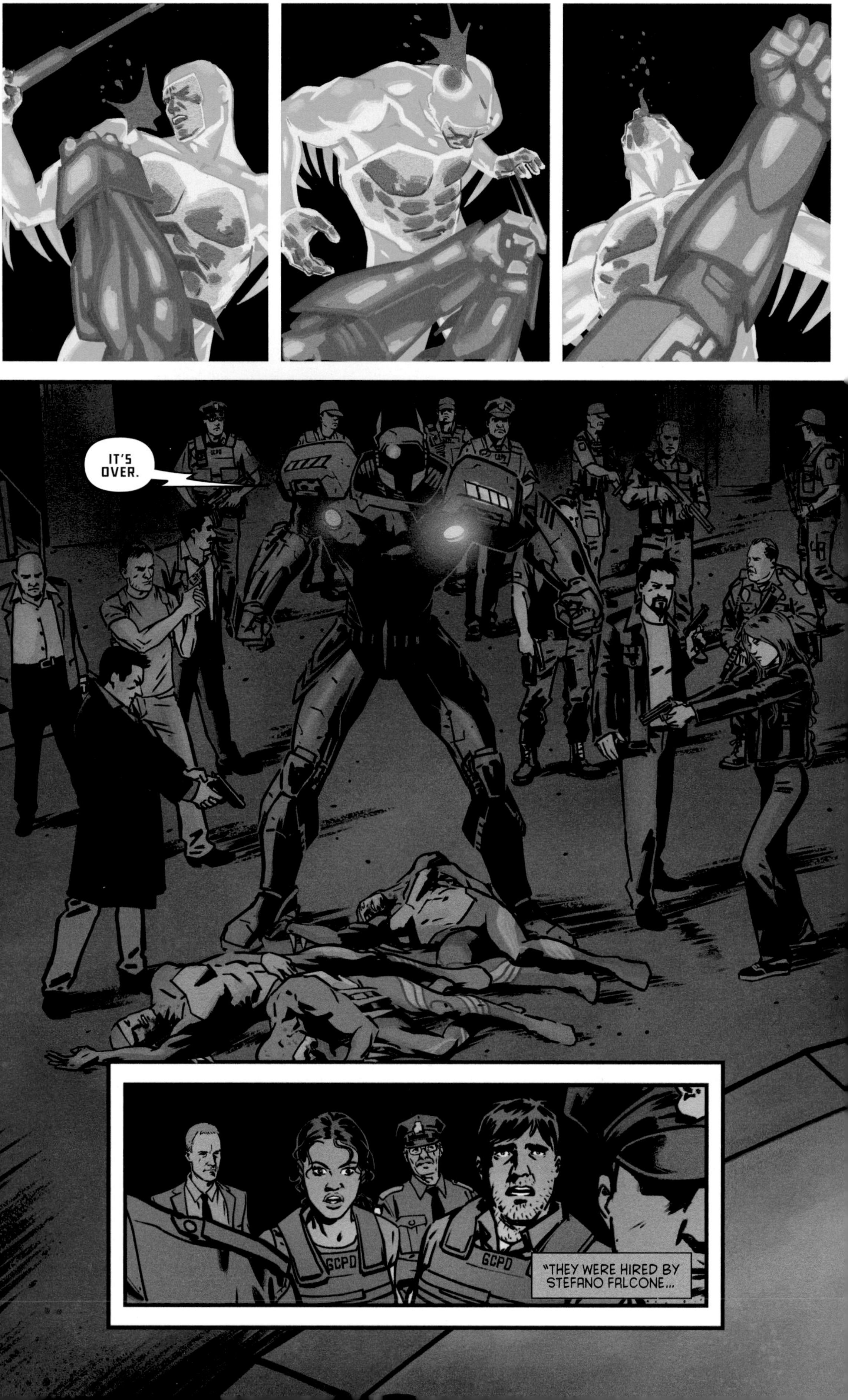
IT'S OVER.
"THEY WERE HIRED BY STEFANO FALCONE...

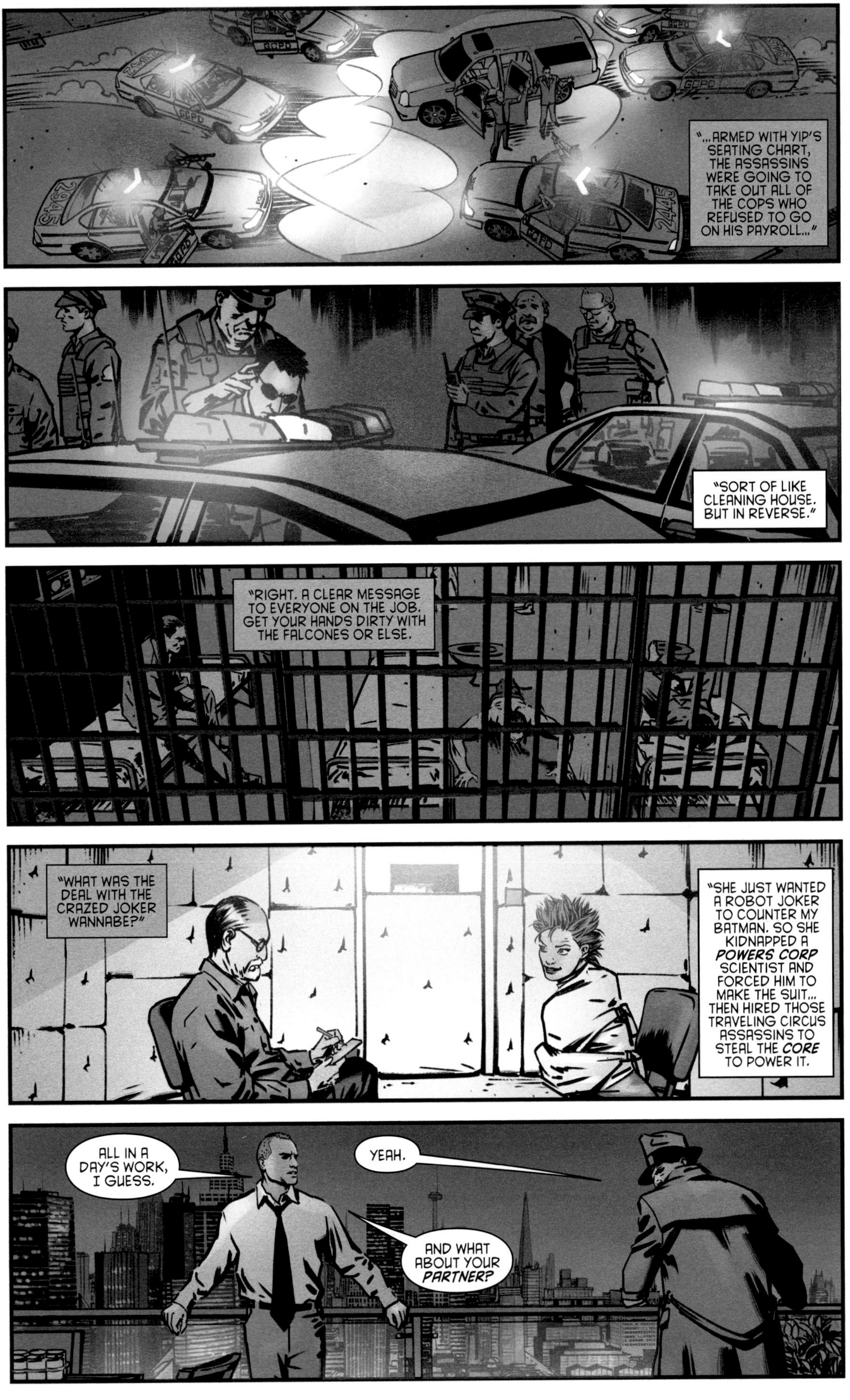

"...ARMED WITH YIP'S SEATING CHART, THE ASSASSINS WERE GOING TO TAKE OUT ALL OF THE COPS WHO REFUSED TO GO ON HIS PAYROLL..."
"SORT OF LIKE CLEANING HOUSE. BUT IN REVERSE."
"RIGHT. A CLEAR MESSAGE TO EVERYONE ON THE JOB. GET YOUR HANDS DIRTY WITH THE FALCONES OR ELSE.
"WHAT WAS THE DEAL WITH THE CRAZED JOKER WANNABE?"
"SHE JUST WANTED A ROBOT JOKER TO COUNTER MY BATMAN. SO SHE KIDNAPPED A *POWERS CORP* SCIENTIST AND FORCED HIM TO MAKE THE SUIT... THEN HIRED THOSE TRAVELING CIRCUS ASSASSINS TO STEAL THE *CORE* TO POWER IT.
ALL IN A DAY'S WORK, I GUESS.
YEAH.
AND WHAT ABOUT YOUR *PARTNER?*

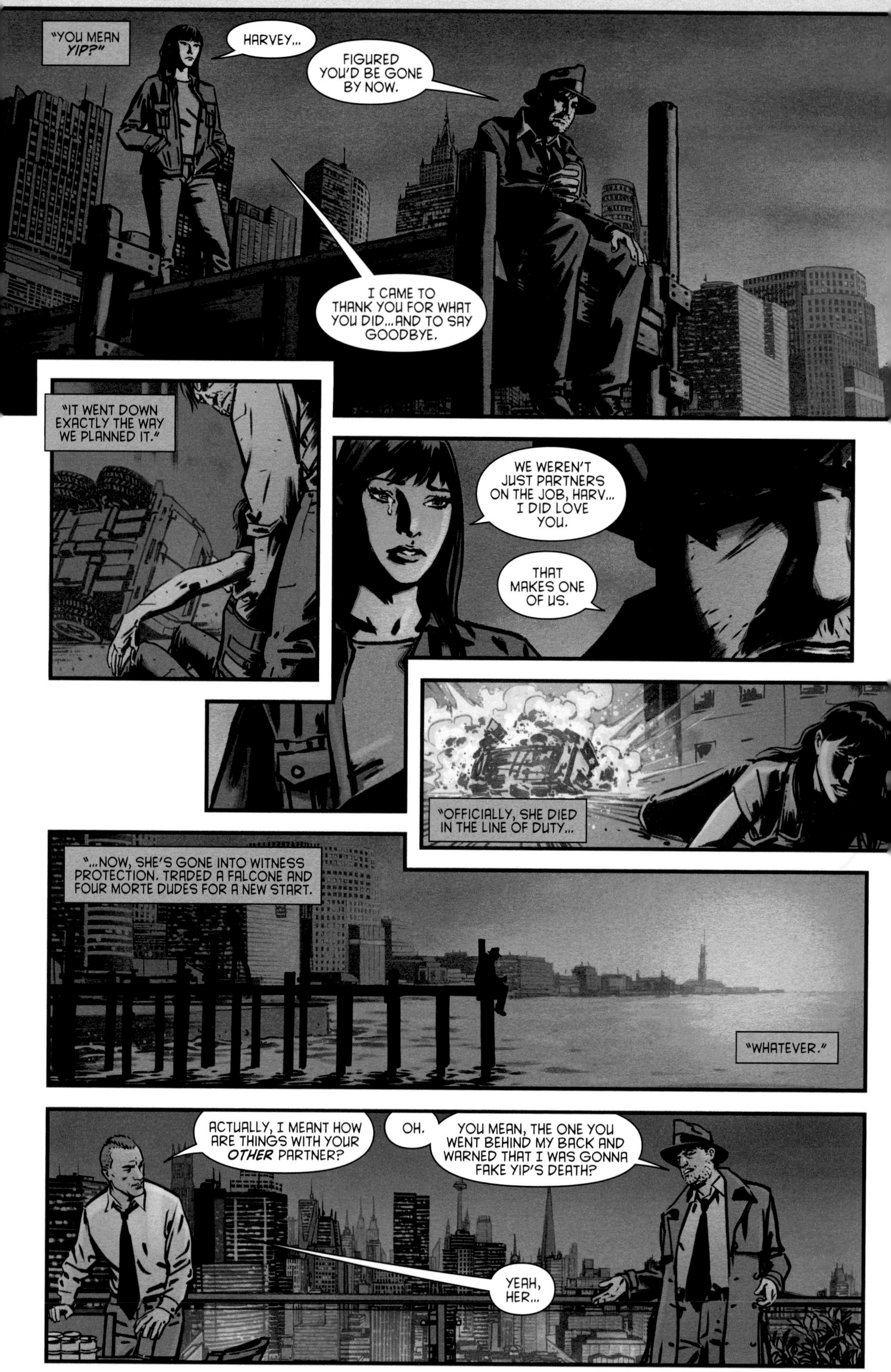

"YOU MEAN *YIP?*"
HARVEY...
FIGURED YOU'D BE GONE BY NOW.
I CAME TO THANK YOU FOR WHAT YOU DID...AND TO SAY GOODBYE.
"IT WENT DOWN EXACTLY THE WAY WE PLANNED IT."
WE WEREN'T JUST PARTNERS ON THE JOB, HARV... I DID LOVE YOU.
THAT MAKES ONE OF US.
"OFFICIALLY, SHE DIED IN THE LINE OF DUTY...
"...NOW, SHE'S GONE INTO WITNESS PROTECTION. TRADED A FALCONE AND FOUR MORTE DUDES FOR A NEW START.
"WHATEVER."
ACTUALLY, I MEANT HOW ARE THINGS WITH YOUR *OTHER* PARTNER?
OH.
YOU MEAN, THE ONE YOU WENT BEHIND MY BACK AND WARNED THAT I WAS GONNA FAKE YIP'S DEATH?
YEAH, HER...

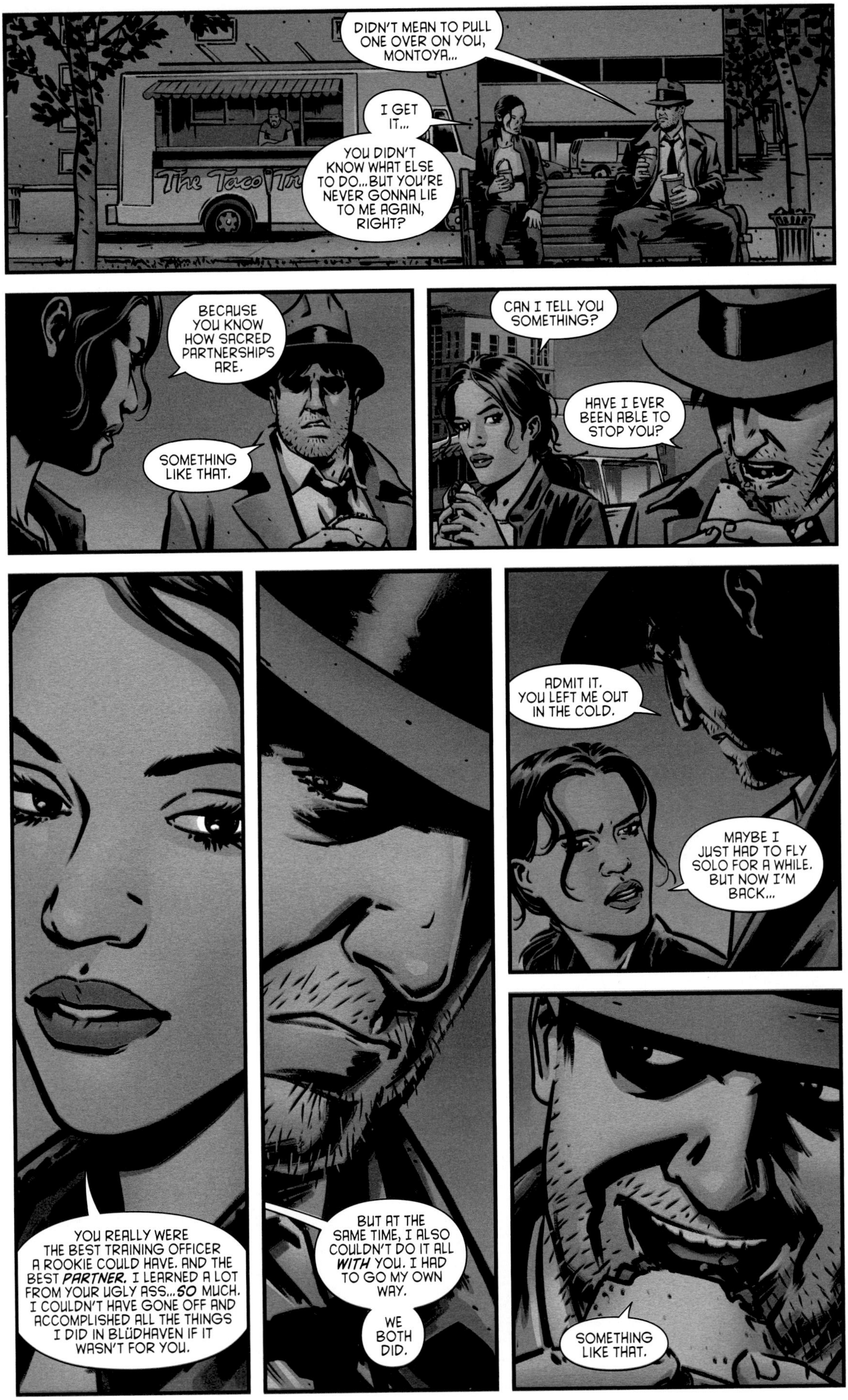

The Taco Tr
DIDN'T MEAN TO PULL ONE OVER ON YOU, MONTOYA...
I GET IT...
YOU DIDN'T KNOW WHAT ELSE TO DO...BUT YOU'RE NEVER GONNA LIE TO ME AGAIN, RIGHT?
BECAUSE YOU KNOW HOW SACRED PARTNERSHIPS ARE.
SOMETHING LIKE THAT.
CAN I TELL YOU SOMETHING?
HAVE I EVER BEEN ABLE TO STOP YOU?
YOU REALLY WERE THE BEST TRAINING OFFICER A ROOKIE COULD HAVE. AND THE BEST *PARTNER.* I LEARNED A LOT FROM YOUR UGLY ASS...*SO* MUCH. I COULDN'T HAVE GONE OFF AND ACCOMPLISHED ALL THE THINGS I DID IN BLÜDHAVEN IF IT WASN'T FOR YOU.
BUT AT THE SAME TIME, I ALSO COULDN'T DO IT ALL *WITH* YOU. I HAD TO GO MY OWN WAY.
WE BOTH DID.
ADMIT IT. YOU LEFT ME OUT IN THE COLD.
MAYBE I JUST HAD TO FLY SOLO FOR A WHILE. BUT NOW I'M BACK...
SOMETHING LIKE THAT.

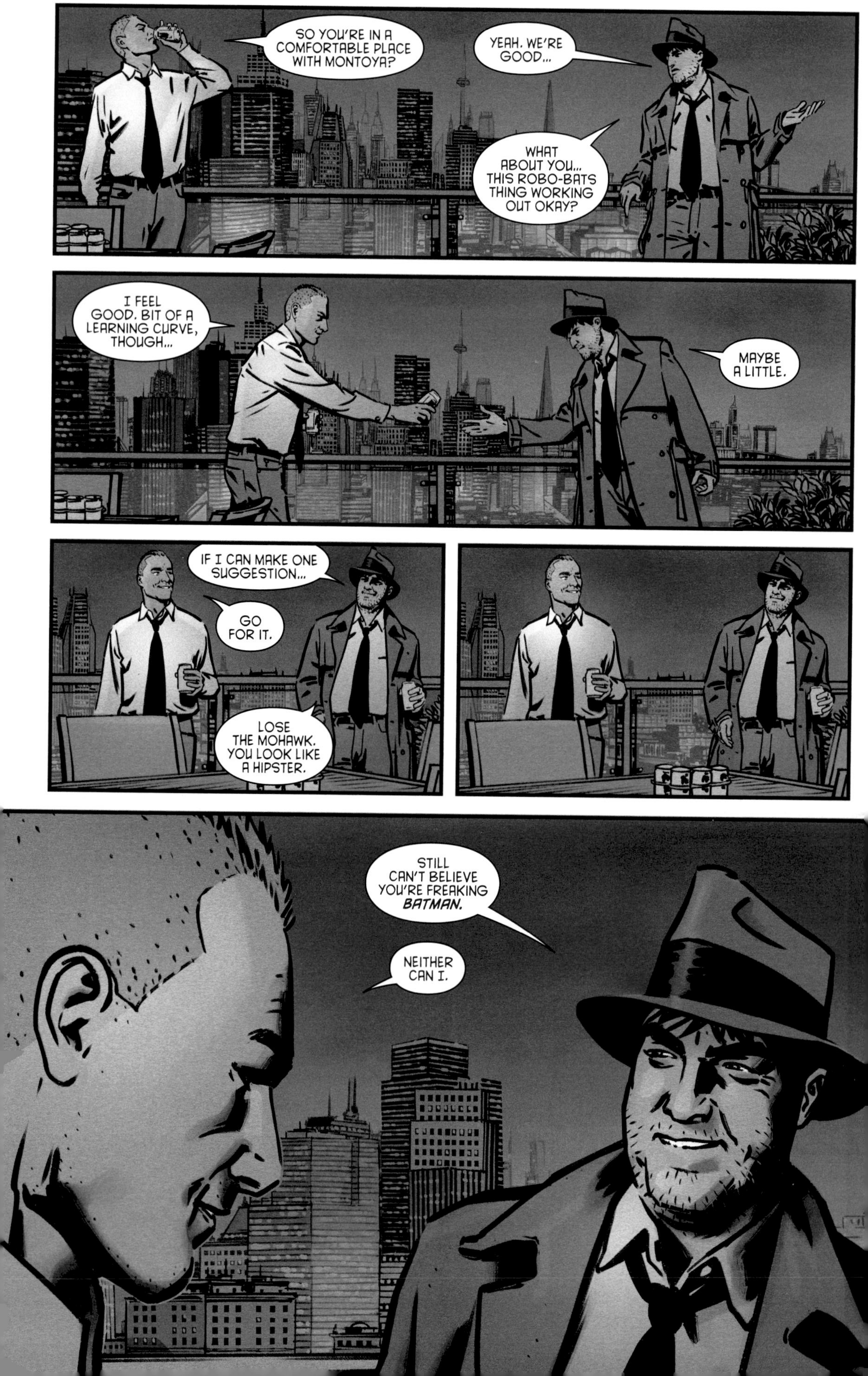
SO YOU'RE IN A COMFORTABLE PLACE WITH MONTOYA?
YEAH. WE'RE GOOD...
WHAT ABOUT YOU... THIS ROBO-BATS THING WORKING OUT OKAY?
I FEEL GOOD. BIT OF A LEARNING CURVE, THOUGH...
MAYBE A LITTLE.
IF I CAN MAKE ONE SUGGESTION...
GO FOR IT.
LOSE THE MOHAWK. YOU LOOK LIKE A HIPSTER.
STILL CAN'T BELIEVE YOU'RE FREAKING *BATMAN.*
NEITHER CAN I.

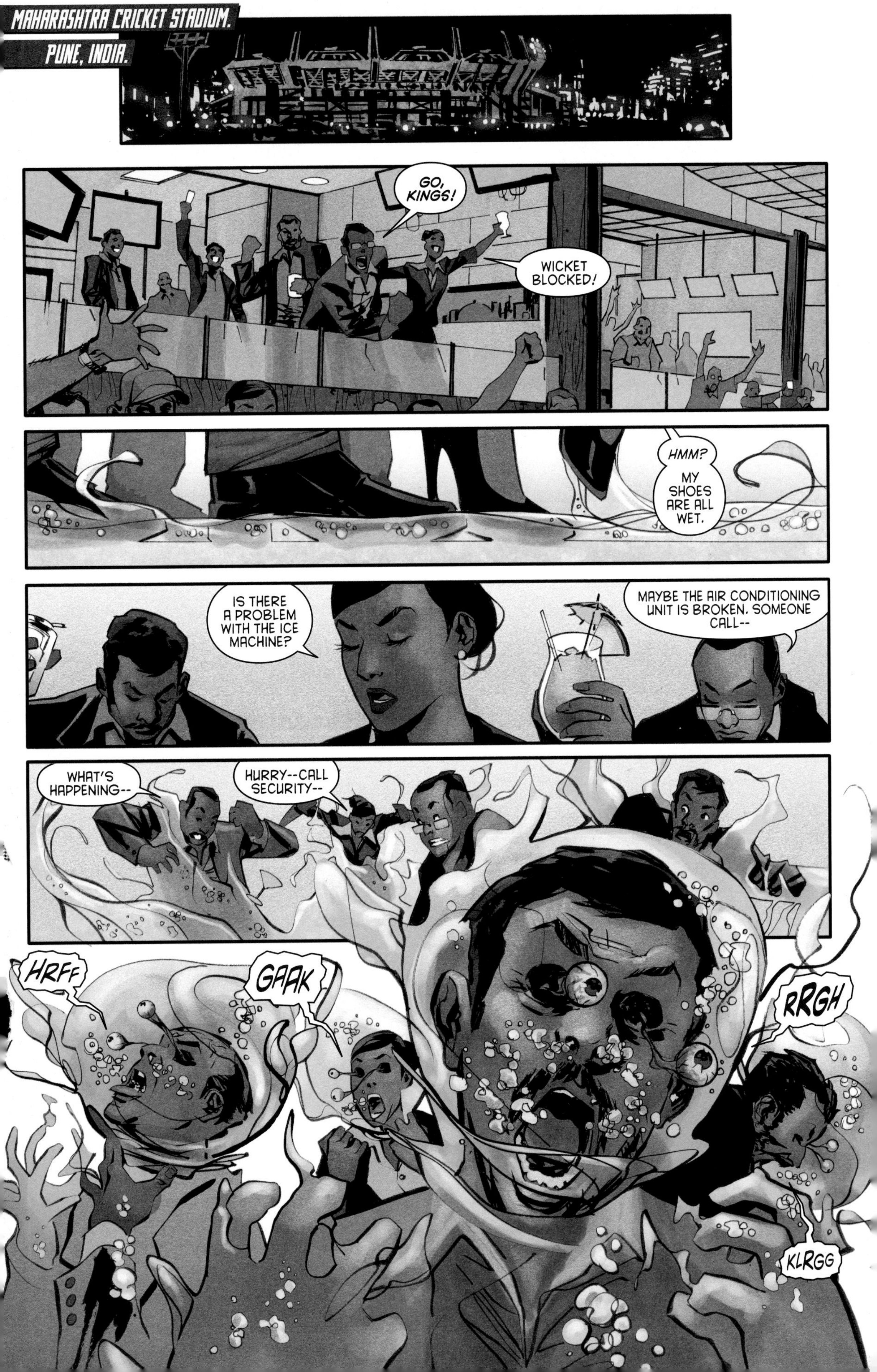
MAHARASHTRA CRICKET STADIUM.
PUNE, INDIA.
GO, KINGS!
WICKET BLOCKED!
HMM?
MY SHOES ARE ALL WET.
IS THERE A PROBLEM WITH THE ICE MACHINE?
MAYBE THE AIR CONDITIONING UNIT IS BROKEN. SOMEONE CALL--
WHAT'S HAPPENING--
HURRY--CALL SECURITY--
HRFF
GAAK
RRGH
KLRGG

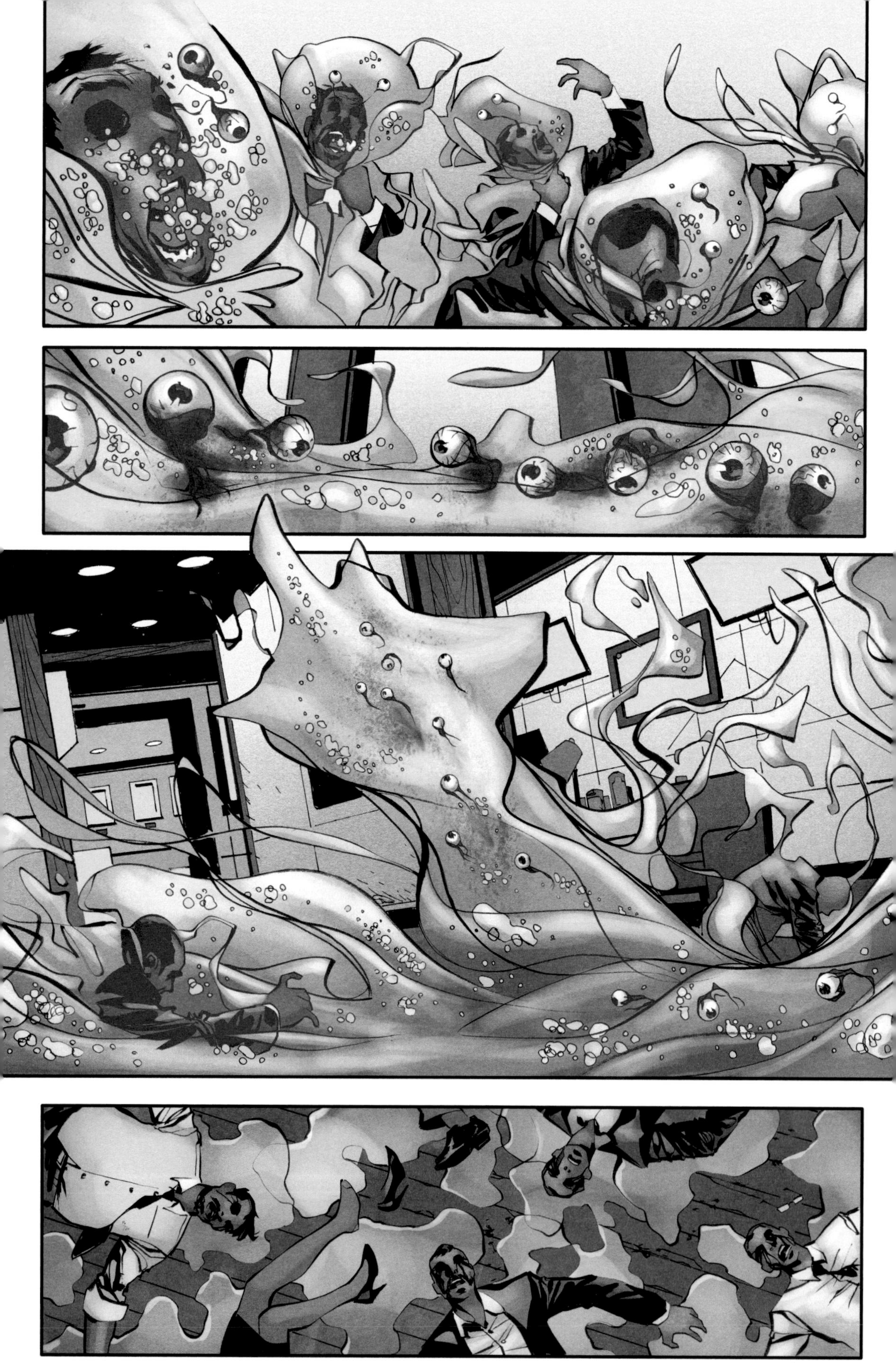

I DO NOT MEAN TO SOUND BRUSQUE, BUT AS I TOLD SUPERMAN SEVERAL DAYS AGO, THERE'S A GREAT MANY REASONS WHY MASTER BRUCE CANNOT HONOR HIS JUSTICE LEAGUE RESPONSIBILITIES ANY LONGER.

SOMETHING'S COME UP SINCE THEN, ALFRED.

A CRISIS, I ASSUME, OF EPIC PROPORTIONS?

COULD DAMN WELL BE, BUT LET'S HOPE NOT.

HATE TO ADMIT IT, BUT WE'RE STRONGER WITH BATMAN ON OUR SIDE, ESPECIALLY IN FULL-OUT DETECTIVE MODE, WHICH IS EXACTLY WHAT WE NEED RIGHT NOW.

SO GETTING HIM BACK SOONER RATHER THAN LATER IS VITAL.

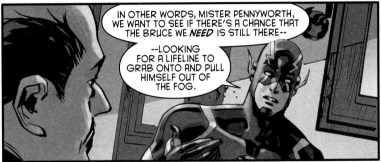

IN OTHER WORDS, MISTER PENNYWORTH, WE WANT TO SEE IF THERE'S A CHANCE THAT THE BRUCE WE NEED IS STILL THERE--

--LOOKING FOR A LIFELINE TO GRAB ONTO AND PULL HIMSELF OUT OF THE FOG.

WHAT BRUCE HAS BEEN GIVEN IS A LIFELINE OF ANONYMITY--NO HISTORY, NO BAGGAGE, NO TRAGEDY...NO ENTANGLEMENTS.

HE'S TRULY FREE TO WALK IN THE LIGHT AND START OVER.

AND AS MUCH AS YOU DON'T WANT TO FACE IT, THE BRUCE WAYNE YOU'RE LOOKING FOR IS SIMPLY NO LONGER THERE.

IF WE DIDN'T BELIEVE THE DIRE SITUATION WE'VE DISCOVERED WARRANTED KNOCKING ON YOUR FRONT DOOR, YOU KNOW WE WOULDN'T EVEN BE HERE, ALFRED.

WE'RE ASKING FOR PERMISSION TO REACH OUT TO BRUCE ONE LAST TIME TO HELP SAVE COUNTLESS LIVES.

WELL THEN MAYBE YOU SHOULD BE ASKING ME INSTEAD OF ALFRED?

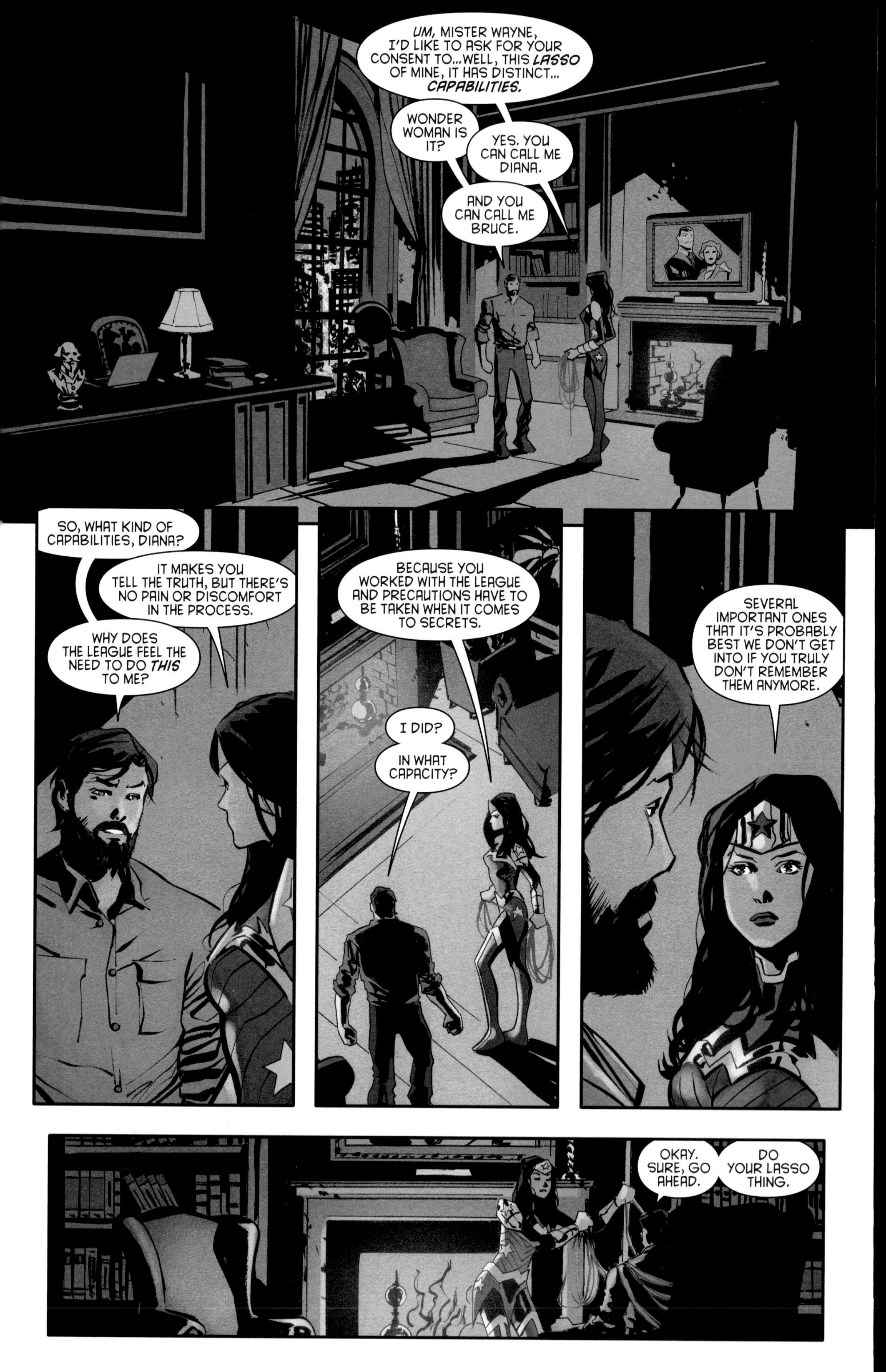
UM, MISTER WAYNE, I'D LIKE TO ASK FOR YOUR CONSENT TO...WELL, THIS LASSO OF MINE, IT HAS DISTINCT... CAPABILITIES.
WONDER WOMAN IS IT?
YES. YOU CAN CALL ME DIANA.
AND YOU CAN CALL ME BRUCE.
SO, WHAT KIND OF CAPABILITIES, DIANA?
IT MAKES YOU TELL THE TRUTH, BUT THERE'S NO PAIN OR DISCOMFORT IN THE PROCESS.
WHY DOES THE LEAGUE FEEL THE NEED TO DO THIS TO ME?
BECAUSE YOU WORKED WITH THE LEAGUE AND PRECAUTIONS HAVE TO BE TAKEN WHEN IT COMES TO SECRETS.
I DID?
IN WHAT CAPACITY?
SEVERAL IMPORTANT ONES THAT IT'S PROBABLY BEST WE DON'T GET INTO IF YOU TRULY DON'T REMEMBER THEM ANYMORE.
OKAY. SURE, GO AHEAD.
DO YOUR LASSO THING.

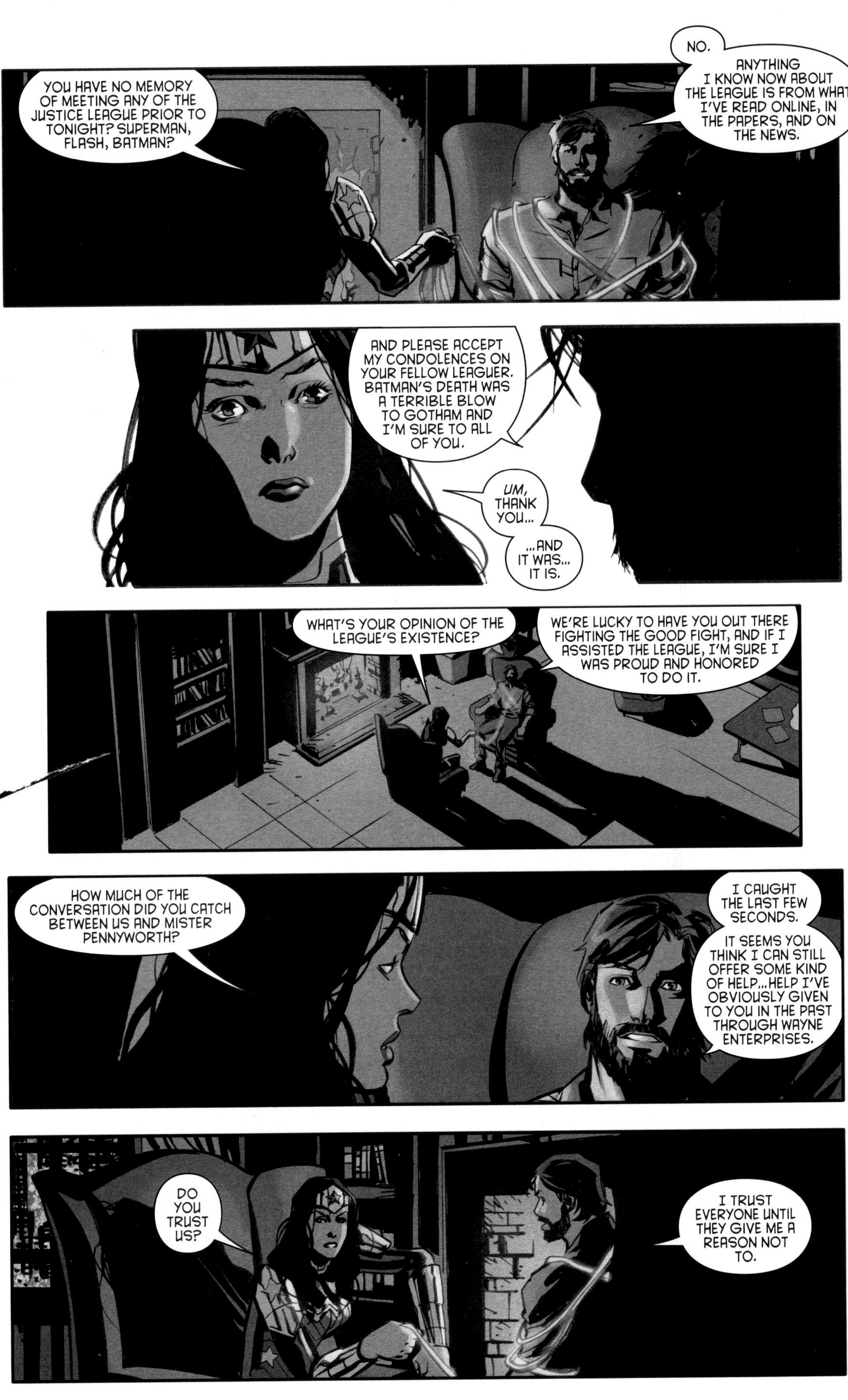
YOU HAVE NO MEMORY OF MEETING ANY OF THE JUSTICE LEAGUE PRIOR TO TONIGHT? SUPERMAN, FLASH, BATMAN?
NO.
ANYTHING I KNOW NOW ABOUT THE LEAGUE IS FROM WHAT I'VE READ ONLINE, IN THE PAPERS, AND ON THE NEWS.
AND PLEASE ACCEPT MY CONDOLENCES ON YOUR FELLOW LEAGUER. BATMAN'S DEATH WAS A TERRIBLE BLOW TO GOTHAM AND I'M SURE TO ALL OF YOU.
UM, THANK YOU...
...AND IT WAS... IT IS.
WHAT'S YOUR OPINION OF THE LEAGUE'S EXISTENCE?
WE'RE LUCKY TO HAVE YOU OUT THERE FIGHTING THE GOOD FIGHT, AND IF I ASSISTED THE LEAGUE, I'M SURE I WAS PROUD AND HONORED TO DO IT.
HOW MUCH OF THE CONVERSATION DID YOU CATCH BETWEEN US AND MISTER PENNYWORTH?
I CAUGHT THE LAST FEW SECONDS.
IT SEEMS YOU THINK I CAN STILL OFFER SOME KIND OF HELP...HELP I'VE OBVIOUSLY GIVEN TO YOU IN THE PAST THROUGH WAYNE ENTERPRISES.
DO YOU TRUST US?
I TRUST EVERYONE UNTIL THEY GIVE ME A REASON NOT TO.

SORRY FOR THE INTRUSION TONIGHT.

WHAT ABOUT THE HELP YOU BELIEVED I COULD PROVIDE?

DUE TO YOUR CURRENT CIRCUMSTANCES, I THINK IT'S BEST WE DON'T GO DOWN THAT ROAD.

I KNOW I SPEAK FOR ALL OF US WHEN I SAY THANK YOU FOR YOUR INVALUABLE PAST SERVICE TO THE LEAGUE...

...THROUGH WAYNE TECH...

...IT WAS GREATLY APPRECIATED, BRUCE.

TAKE CARE AND WE WISH YOU THE BEST.

THANKS, SUPERMAN.

SO, WHAT'S THE VERDICT?

IT'S LIKE ALFRED SAID...

...THE BRUCE WAYNE THE LEAGUE KNEW IS GONE.

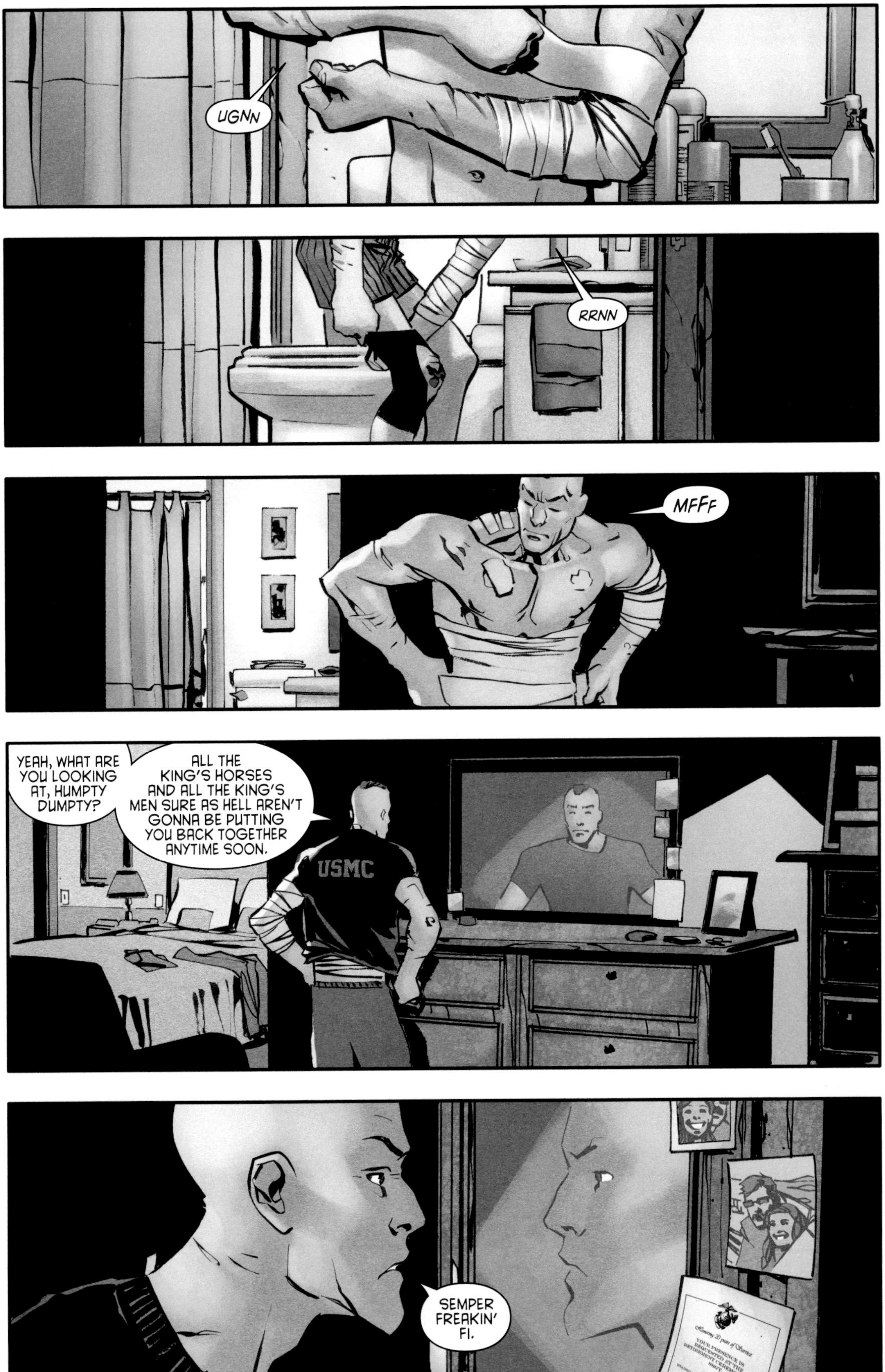
UGNN
RRNN
MFFF
YEAH, WHAT ARE YOU LOOKING AT, HUMPTY DUMPTY?
ALL THE KING'S HORSES AND ALL THE KING'S MEN SURE AS HELL AREN'T GONNA BE PUTTING YOU BACK TOGETHER ANYTIME SOON.
USMC
SEMPER FREAKIN' FI.

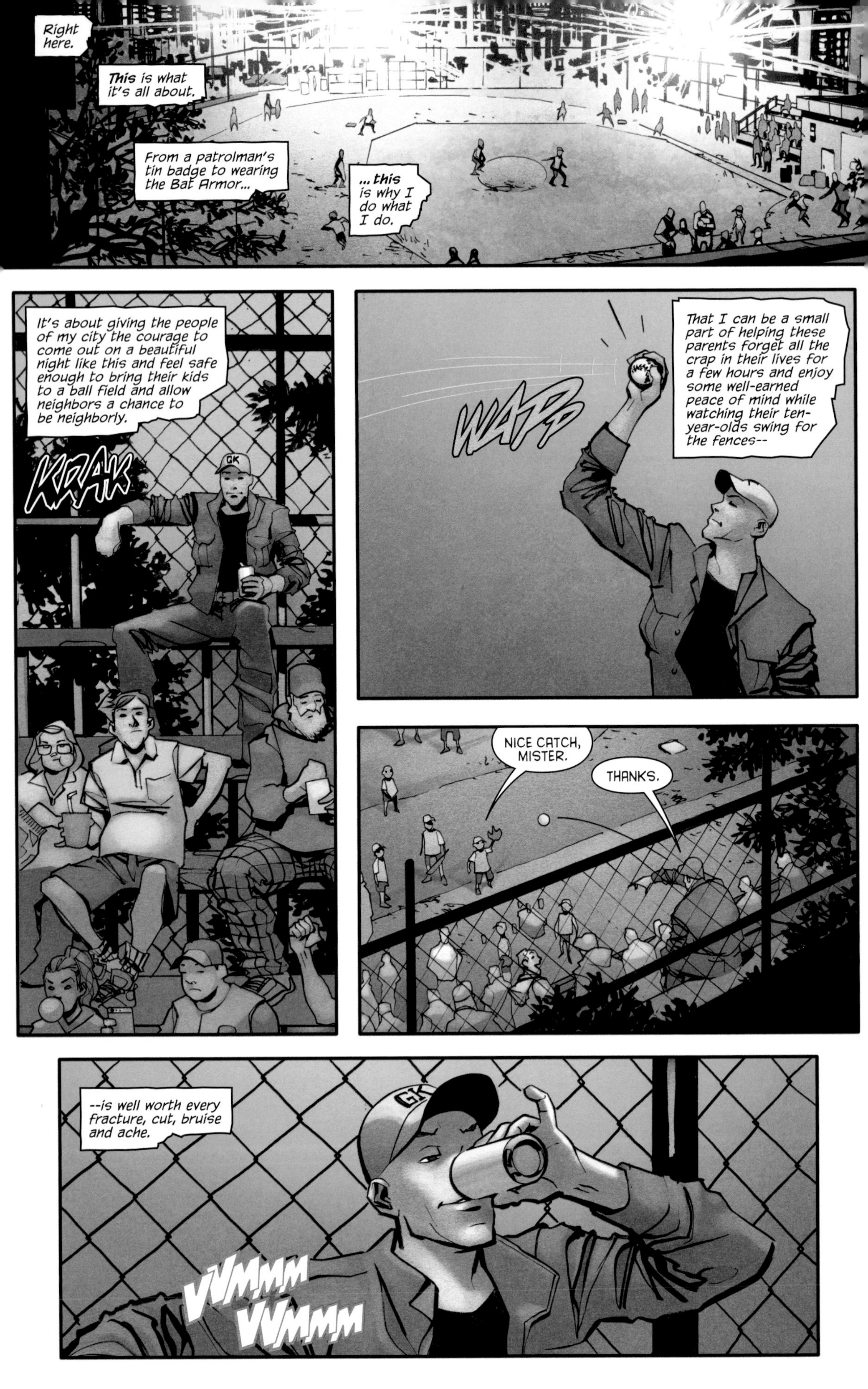

Right here.
This is what it's all about.
From a patrolman's tin badge to wearing the Bat Armor...
...this is why I do what I do.
It's about giving the people of my city the courage to come out on a beautiful night like this and feel safe enough to bring their kids to a ball field and allow neighbors a chance to be neighborly.
KRAK
GK
WAPP
That I can be a small part of helping these parents forget all the crap in their lives for a few hours and enjoy some well-earned peace of mind while watching their ten-year-olds swing for the fences--
NICE CATCH, MISTER.
THANKS.
--is well worth every fracture, cut, bruise and ache.
GK
VVMMM VVMMM

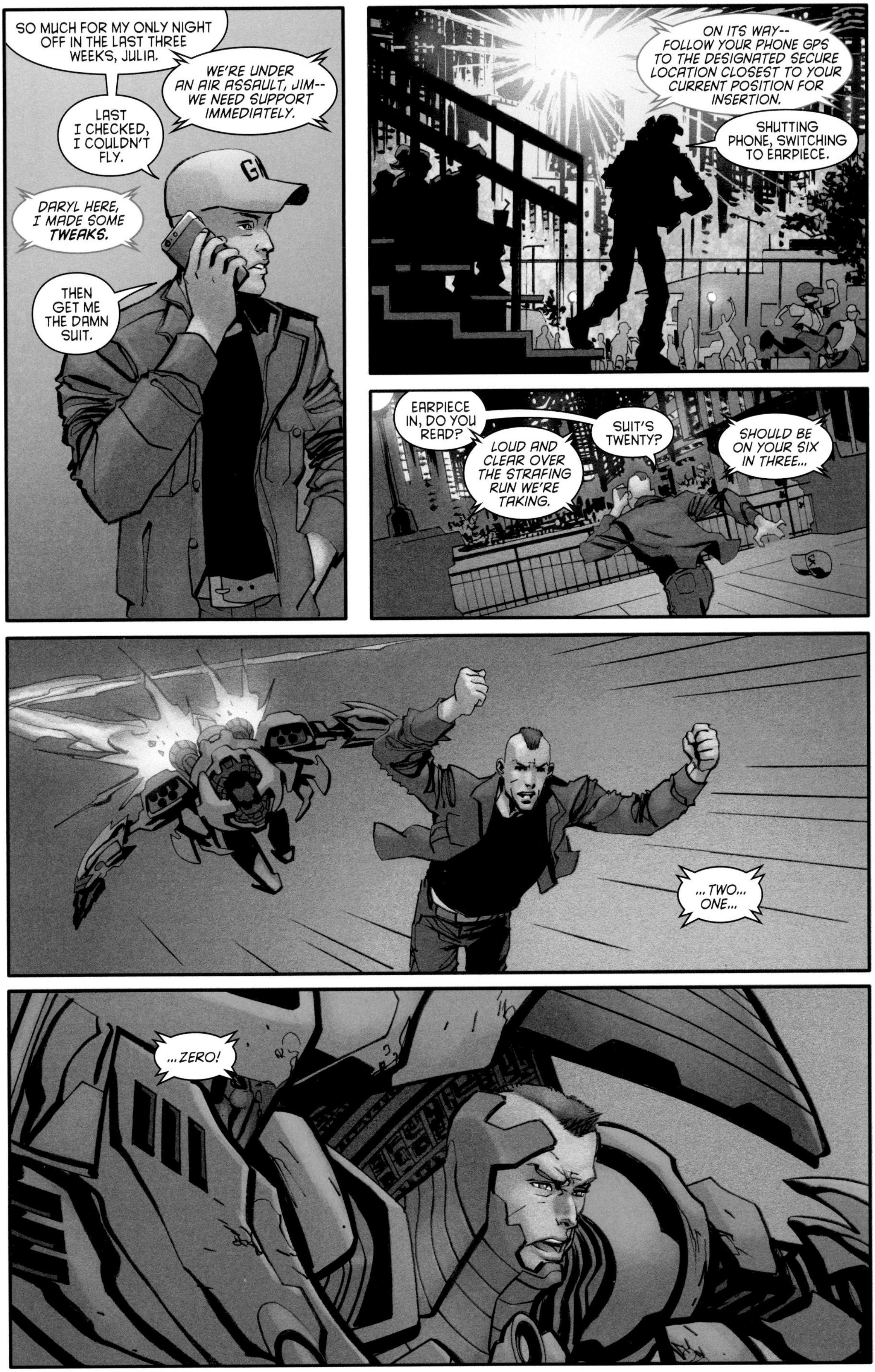
SO MUCH FOR MY ONLY NIGHT OFF IN THE LAST THREE WEEKS, JULIA.
WE'RE UNDER AN AIR ASSAULT, JIM-- WE NEED SUPPORT IMMEDIATELY.
LAST I CHECKED, I COULDN'T FLY.
DARYL HERE, I MADE SOME **TWEAKS.**
THEN GET ME THE DAMN SUIT.
ON ITS WAY-- FOLLOW YOUR PHONE GPS TO THE DESIGNATED SECURE LOCATION CLOSEST TO YOUR CURRENT POSITION FOR INSERTION.
SHUTTING PHONE, SWITCHING TO EARPIECE.
EARPIECE IN, DO YOU READ?
LOUD AND CLEAR OVER THE STRAFING RUN WE'RE TAKING.
SUIT'S TWENTY?
SHOULD BE ON YOUR SIX IN THREE...
...TWO... ONE...
...ZERO!

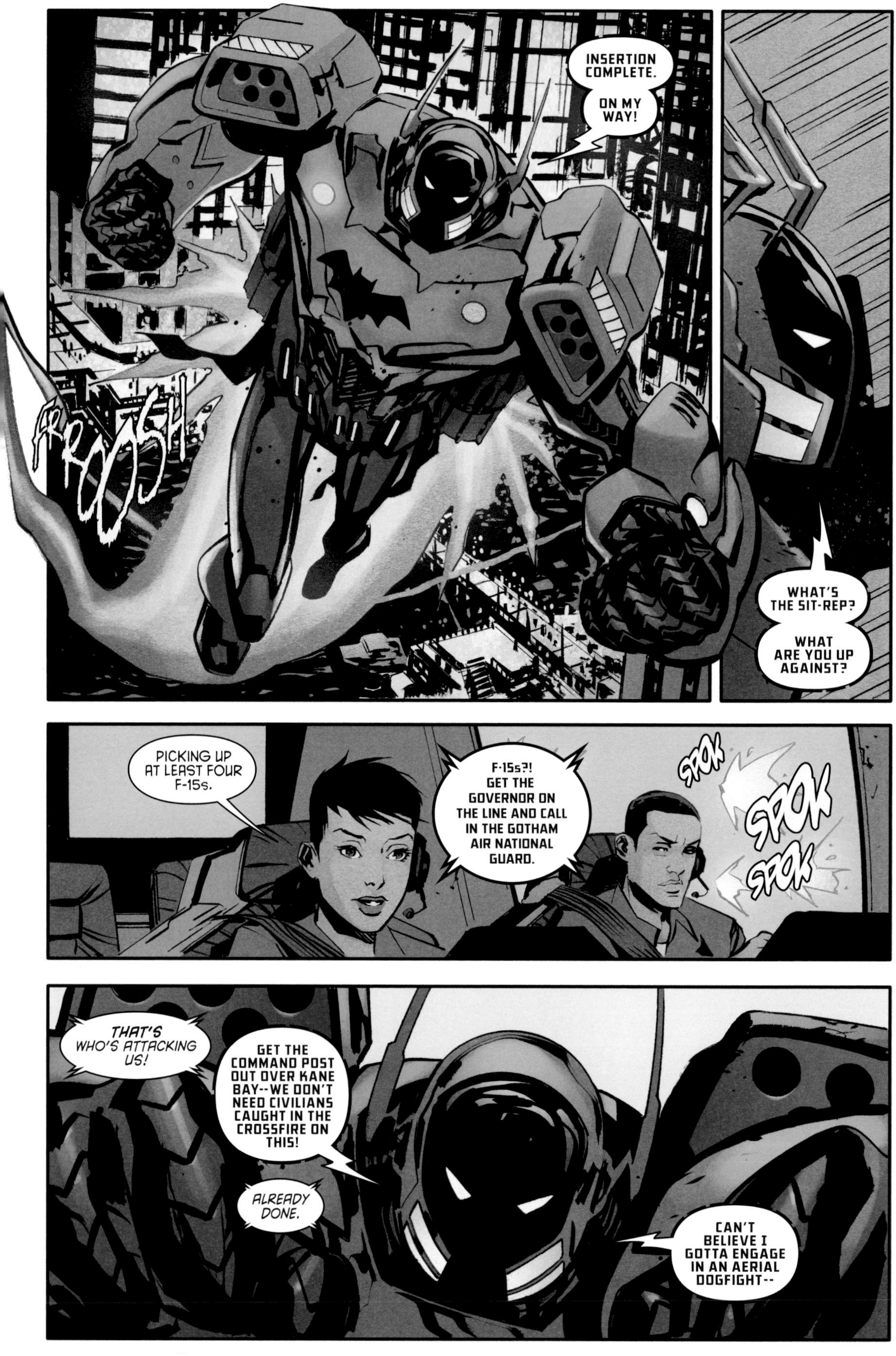
INSERTION COMPLETE.
ON MY WAY!
FRROOSH
WHAT'S THE SIT-REP?
WHAT ARE YOU UP AGAINST?
PICKING UP AT LEAST FOUR F-15s.
F-15s?! GET THE GOVERNOR ON THE LINE AND CALL IN THE GOTHAM AIR NATIONAL GUARD.
SPOK
SPOK
SPOK
THAT'S WHO'S ATTACKING US!
GET THE COMMAND POST OUT OVER KANE BAY--WE DON'T NEED CIVILIANS CAUGHT IN THE CROSSFIRE ON THIS!
ALREADY DONE.
CAN'T BELIEVE I GOTTA ENGAGE IN AN AERIAL DOGFIGHT--

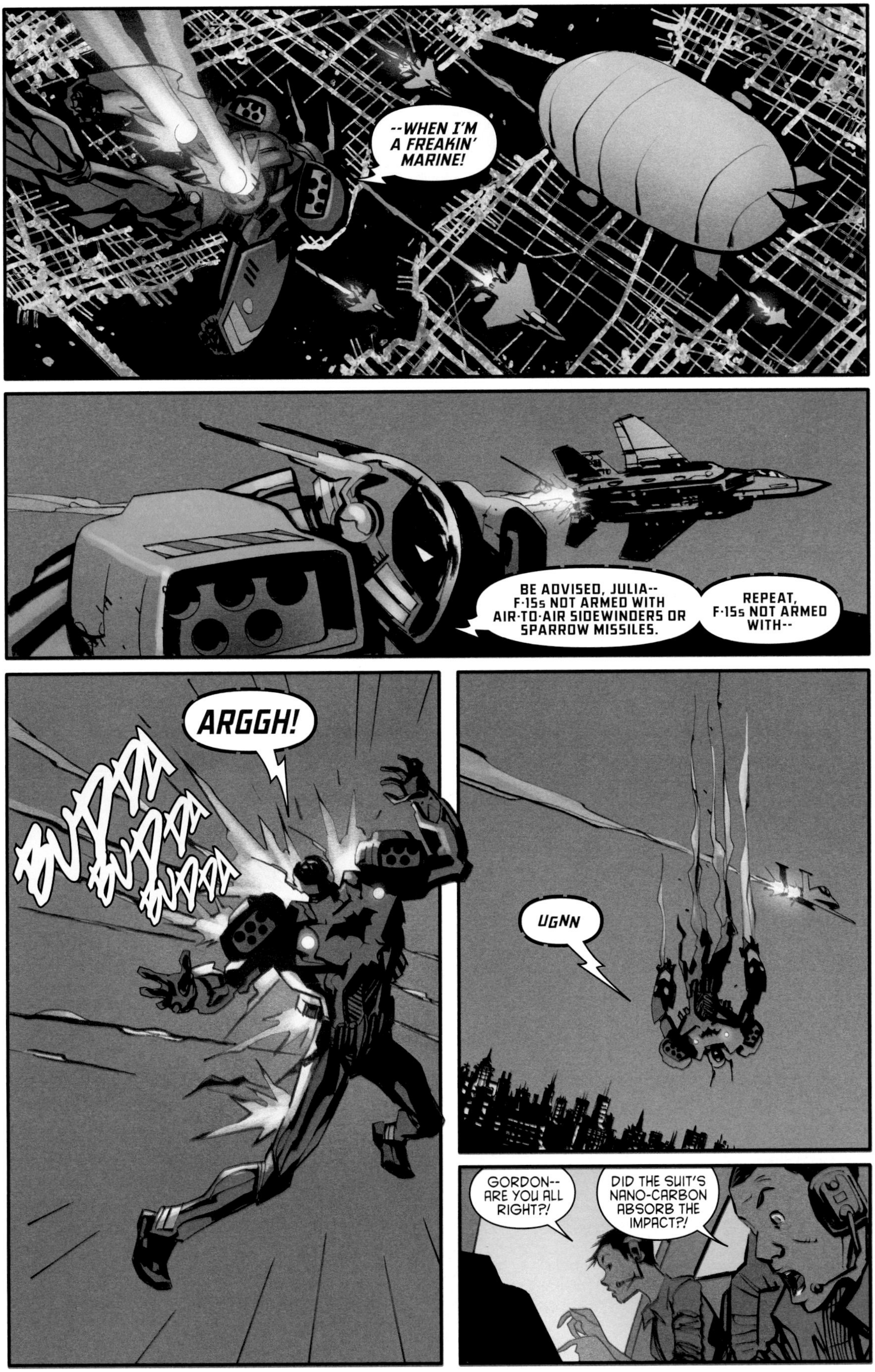
--WHEN I'M A FREAKIN' MARINE!
BE ADVISED, JULIA-- F-15s NOT ARMED WITH AIR-TO-AIR SIDEWINDERS OR SPARROW MISSILES.
REPEAT, F-15s NOT ARMED WITH--
ARGGH!
UGNN
GORDON-- ARE YOU ALL RIGHT?!
DID THE SUIT'S NANO-CARBON ABSORB THE IMPACT?!

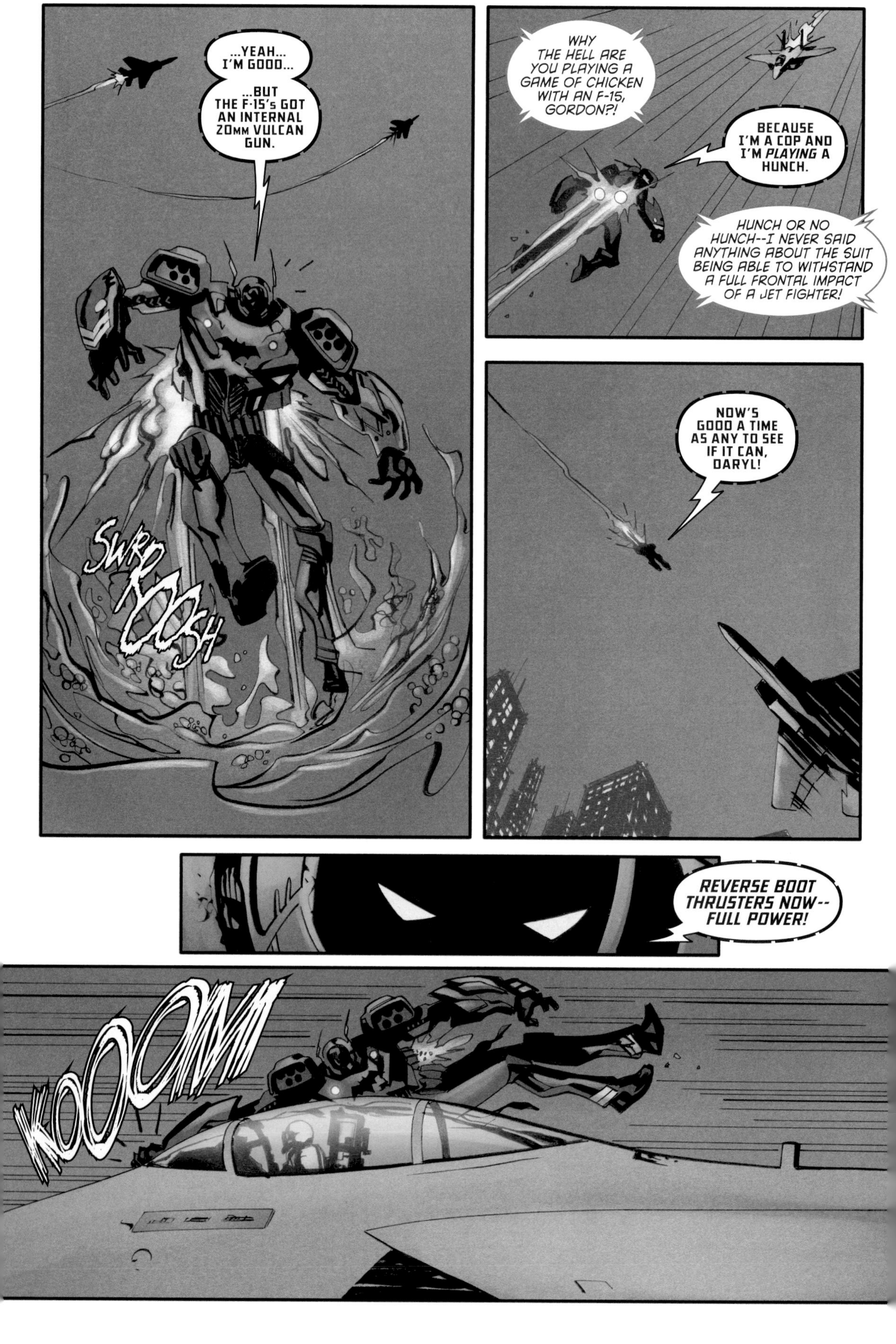
...YEAH... I'M GOOD...
...BUT THE F-15's GOT AN INTERNAL 20MM VULCAN GUN.
SWROOOSH
WHY THE HELL ARE YOU PLAYING A GAME OF CHICKEN WITH AN F-15, GORDON?!
BECAUSE I'M A COP AND I'M PLAYING A HUNCH.
HUNCH OR NO HUNCH--I NEVER SAID ANYTHING ABOUT THE SUIT BEING ABLE TO WITHSTAND A FULL FRONTAL IMPACT OF A JET FIGHTER!
NOW'S GOOD A TIME AS ANY TO SEE IF IT CAN, DARYL!
REVERSE BOOT THRUSTERS NOW--FULL POWER!
KOOOOM

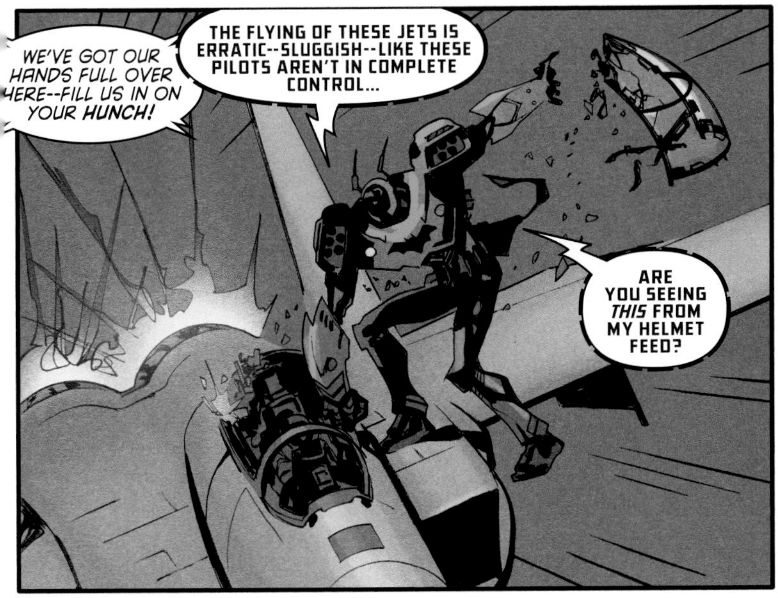
WE'VE GOT OUR HANDS FULL OVER HERE--FILL US IN ON YOUR HUNCH!
THE FLYING OF THESE JETS IS ERRATIC--SLUGGISH--LIKE THESE PILOTS AREN'T IN COMPLETE CONTROL...
ARE YOU SEEING THIS FROM MY HELMET FEED?
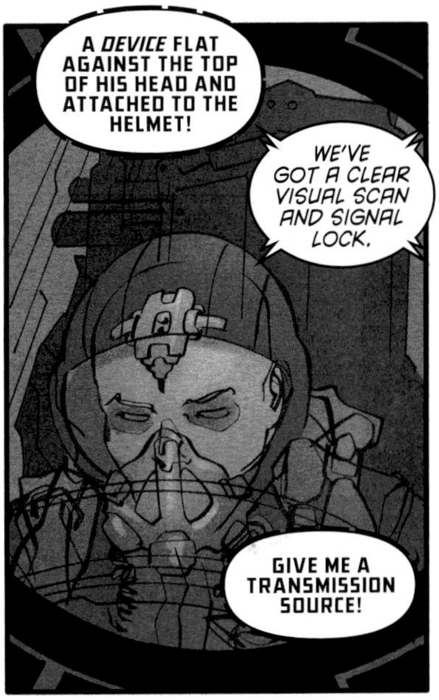
A DEVICE FLAT AGAINST THE TOP OF HIS HEAD AND ATTACHED TO THE HELMET!
WE'VE GOT A CLEAR VISUAL SCAN AND SIGNAL LOCK.
GIVE ME A TRANSMISSION SOURCE!
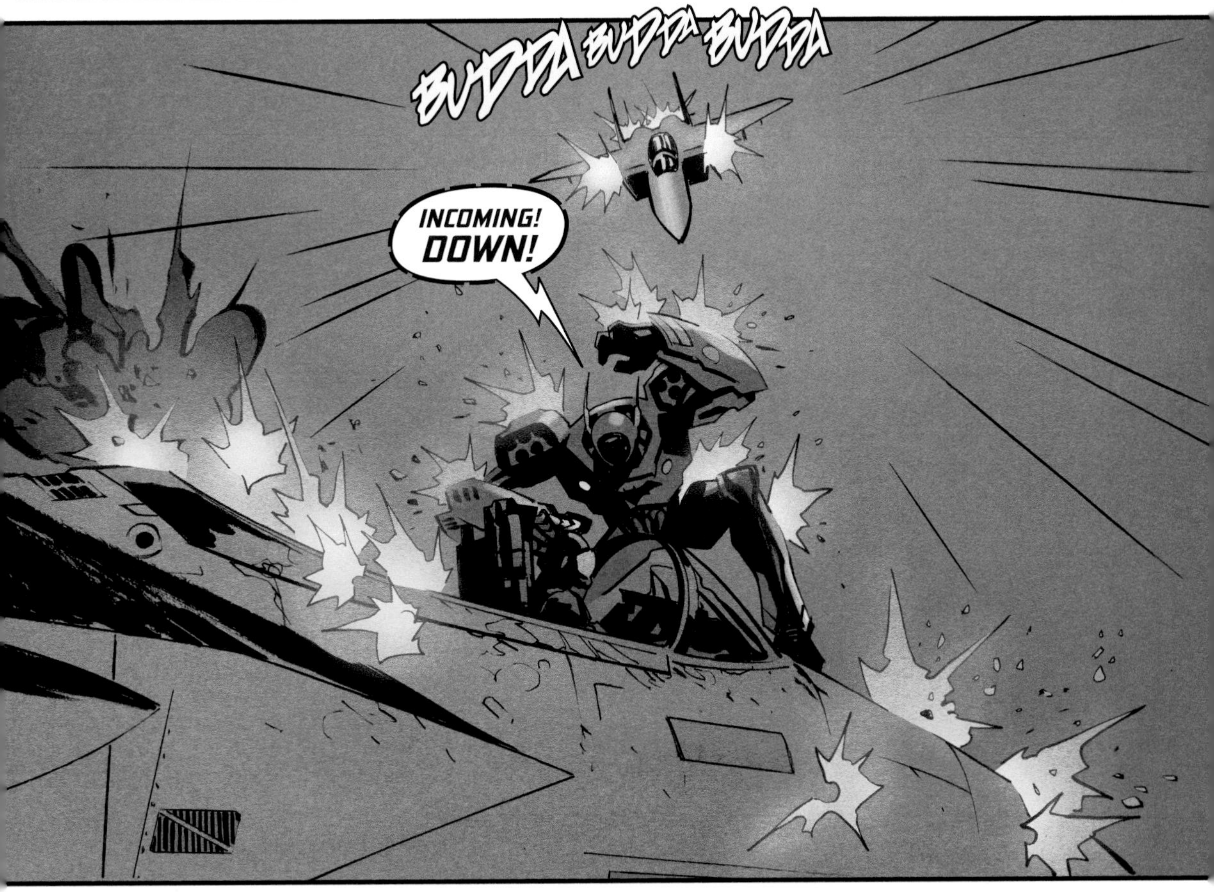
BUDDA BUDDA BUDDA
INCOMING! DOWN!
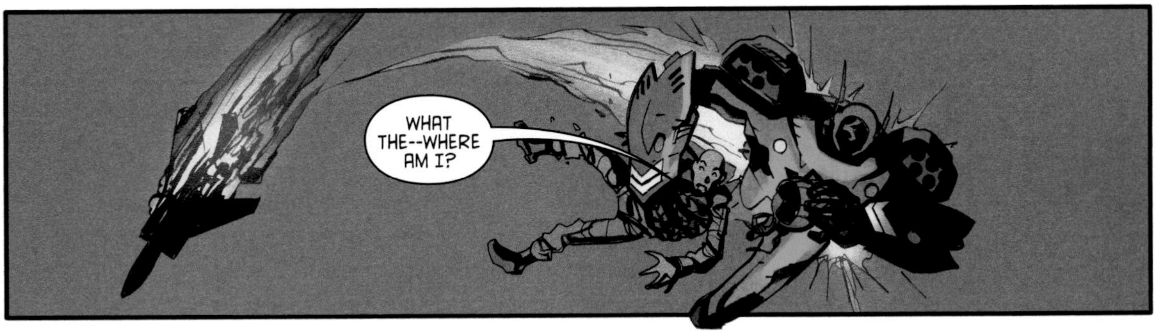
WHAT THE--WHERE AM I?

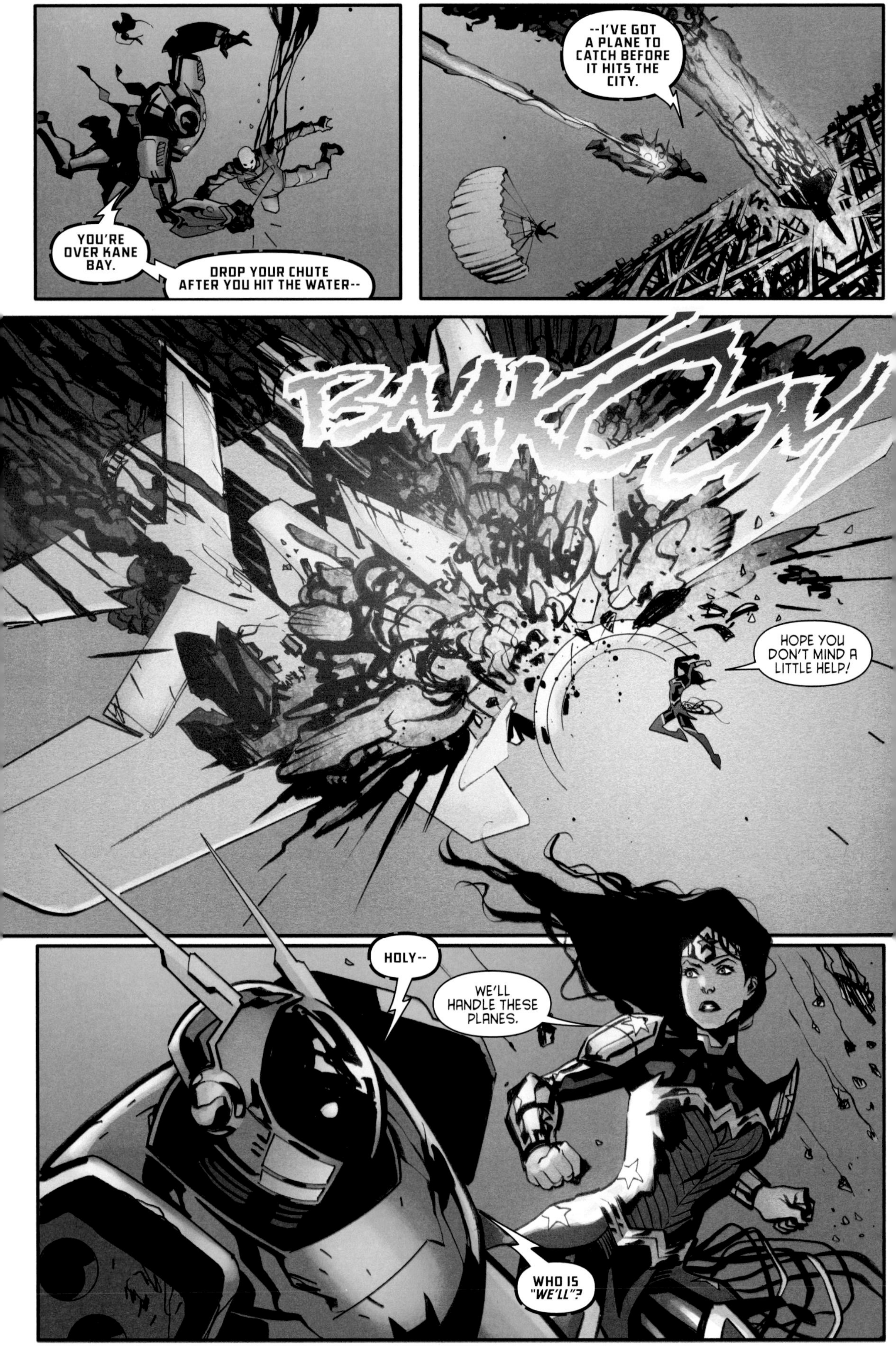
YOU'RE OVER KANE BAY.
DROP YOUR CHUTE AFTER YOU HIT THE WATER--
--I'VE GOT A PLANE TO CATCH BEFORE IT HITS THE CITY.
BAAKOOM
HOPE YOU DON'T MIND A LITTLE HELP!
HOLY--
WE'LL HANDLE THESE PLANES.
WHO IS "*WE'LL*"?

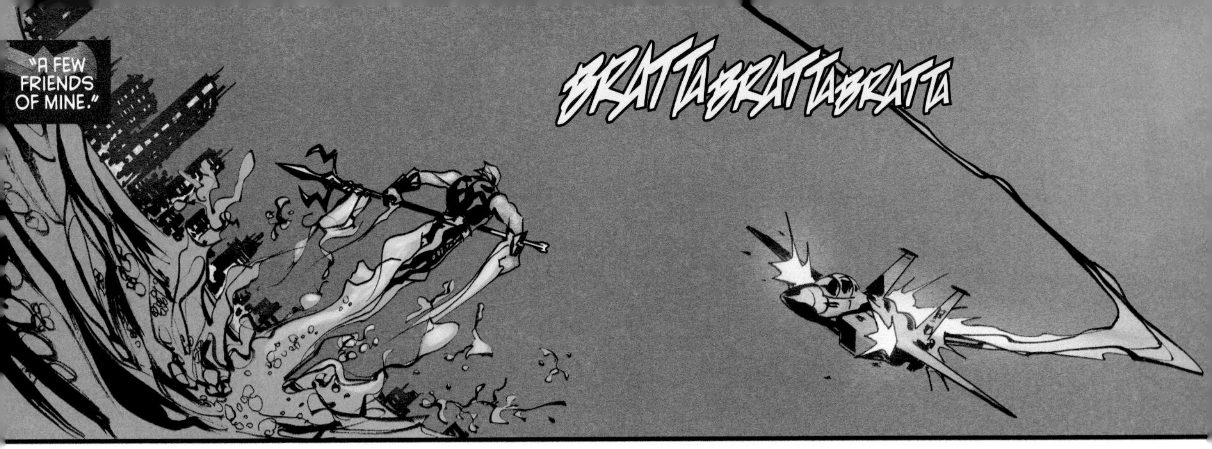
"A FEW FRIENDS OF MINE."
BRATTA BRATTA BRATTA

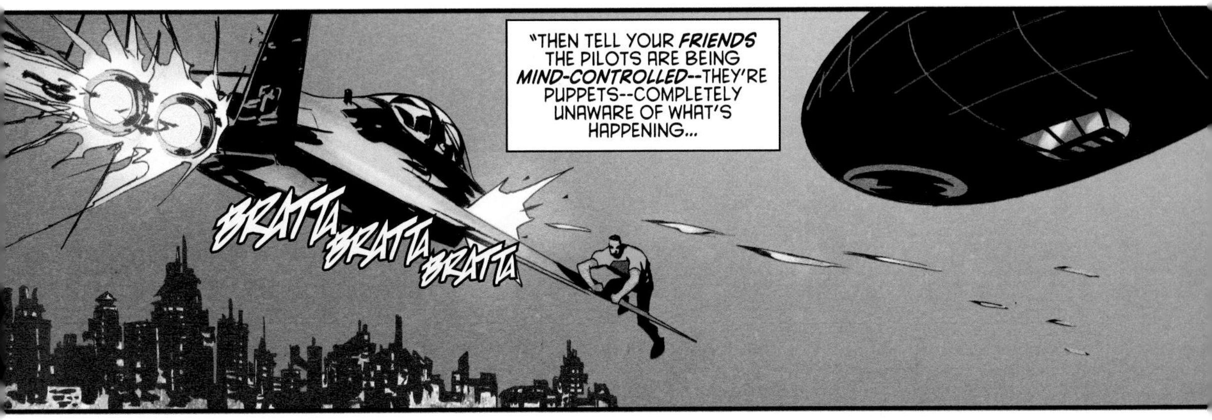
"THEN TELL YOUR *FRIENDS* THE PILOTS ARE BEING *MIND-CONTROLLED*--THEY'RE PUPPETS--COMPLETELY UNAWARE OF WHAT'S HAPPENING...
BRATTA BRATTA BRATTA

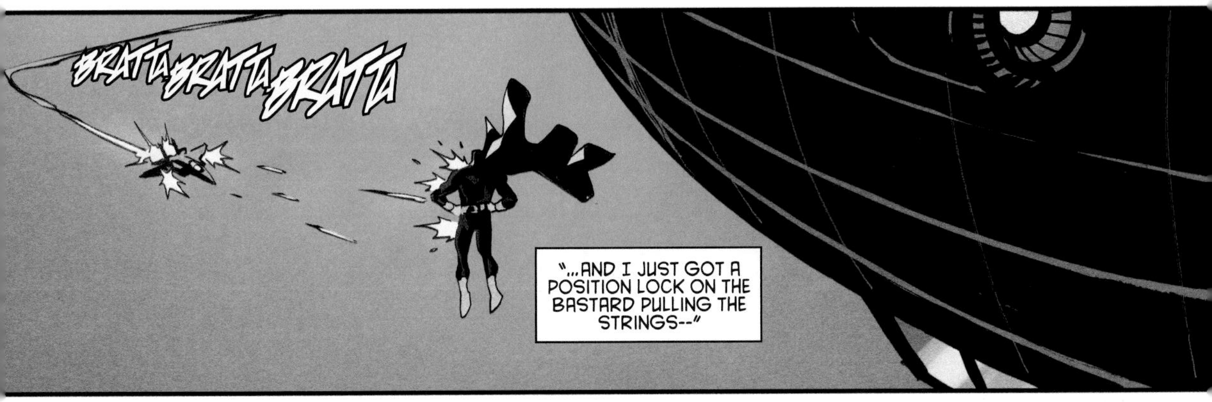
BRATTA BRATTA BRATTA
"...AND I JUST GOT A POSITION LOCK ON THE BASTARD PULLING THE STRINGS--"

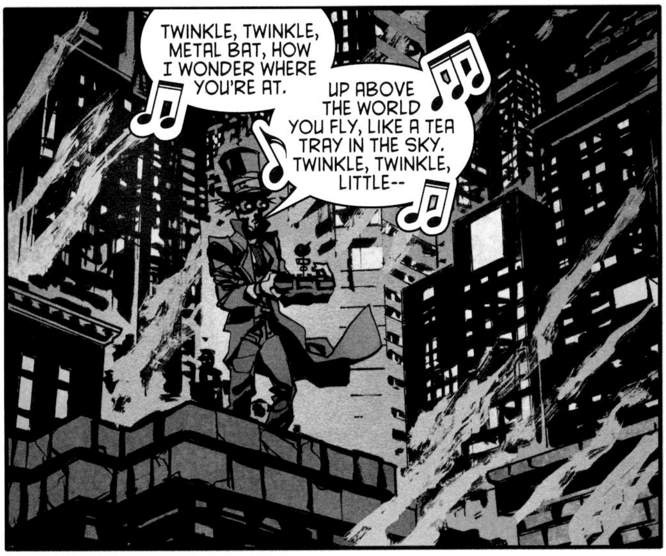
TWINKLE, TWINKLE, METAL BAT, HOW I WONDER WHERE YOU'RE AT.
UP ABOVE THE WORLD YOU FLY, LIKE A TEA TRAY IN THE SKY. TWINKLE, TWINKLE, LITTLE--

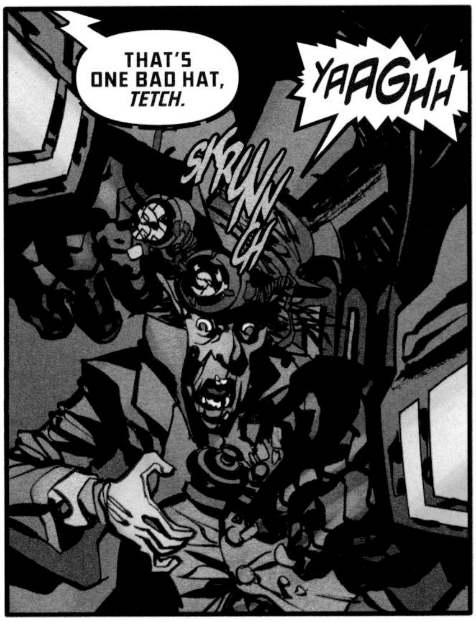
THAT'S ONE BAD HAT, *TETCH.*
YAAGHH
SKRUNCH

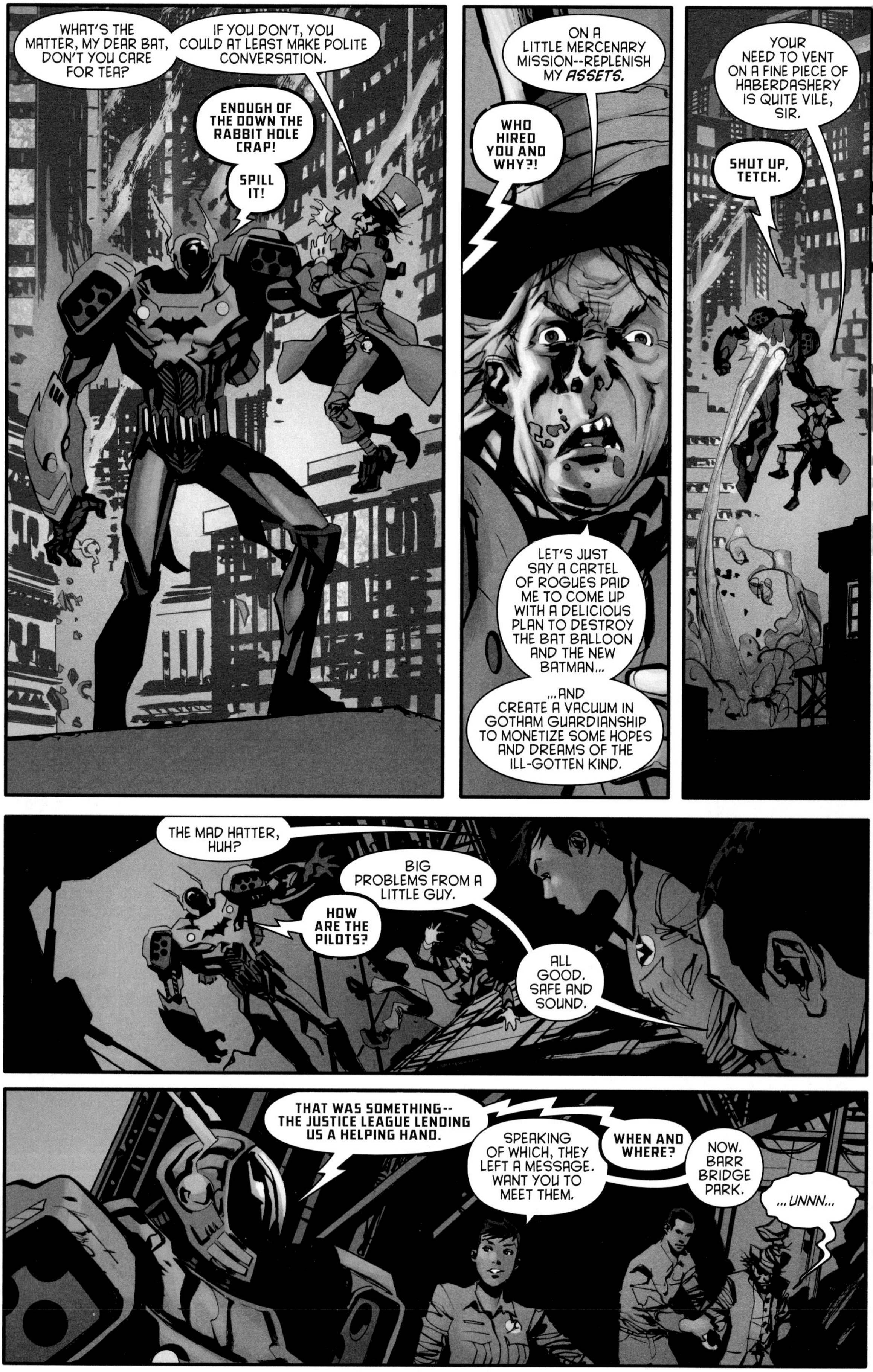
WHAT'S THE MATTER, MY DEAR BAT, DON'T YOU CARE FOR TEA?
IF YOU DON'T, YOU COULD AT LEAST MAKE POLITE CONVERSATION.
ENOUGH OF THE DOWN THE RABBIT HOLE CRAP!
SPILL IT!
ON A LITTLE MERCENARY MISSION--REPLENISH MY ASSETS.
WHO HIRED YOU AND WHY?!
LET'S JUST SAY A CARTEL OF ROGUES PAID ME TO COME UP WITH A DELICIOUS PLAN TO DESTROY THE BAT BALLOON AND THE NEW BATMAN...
...AND CREATE A VACUUM IN GOTHAM GUARDIANSHIP TO MONETIZE SOME HOPES AND DREAMS OF THE ILL-GOTTEN KIND.
YOUR NEED TO VENT ON A FINE PIECE OF HABERDASHERY IS QUITE VILE, SIR.
SHUT UP, TETCH.
THE MAD HATTER, HUH?
BIG PROBLEMS FROM A LITTLE GUY.
HOW ARE THE PILOTS?
ALL GOOD. SAFE AND SOUND.
THAT WAS SOMETHING-- THE JUSTICE LEAGUE LENDING US A HELPING HAND.
SPEAKING OF WHICH, THEY LEFT A MESSAGE. WANT YOU TO MEET THEM.
WHEN AND WHERE?
NOW. BARR BRIDGE PARK.
...UNNN...

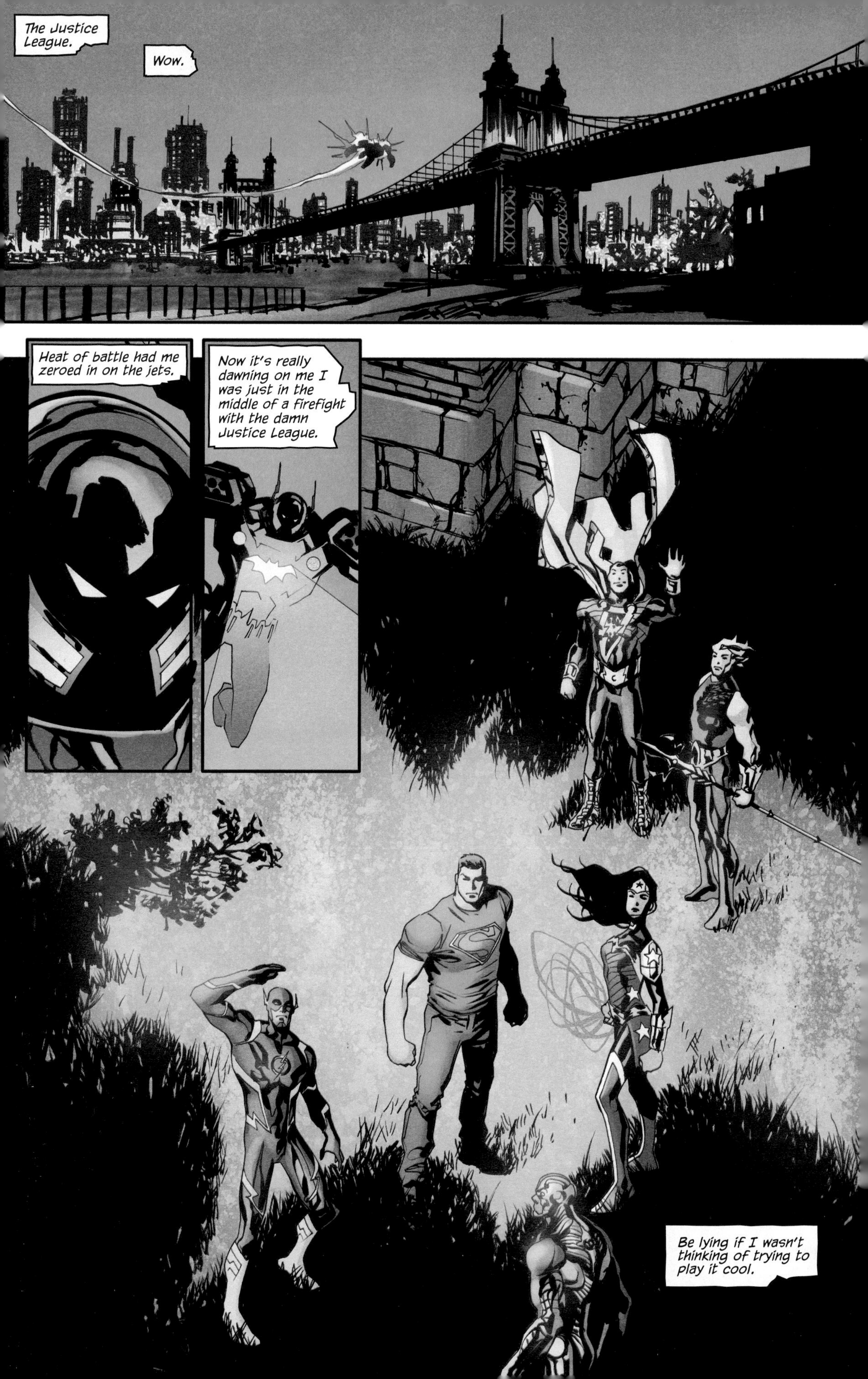
The Justice League.
Wow.
Heat of battle had me zeroed in on the jets.
Now it's really dawning on me I was just in the middle of a firefight with the damn Justice League.
Be lying if I wasn't thinking of trying to play it cool.

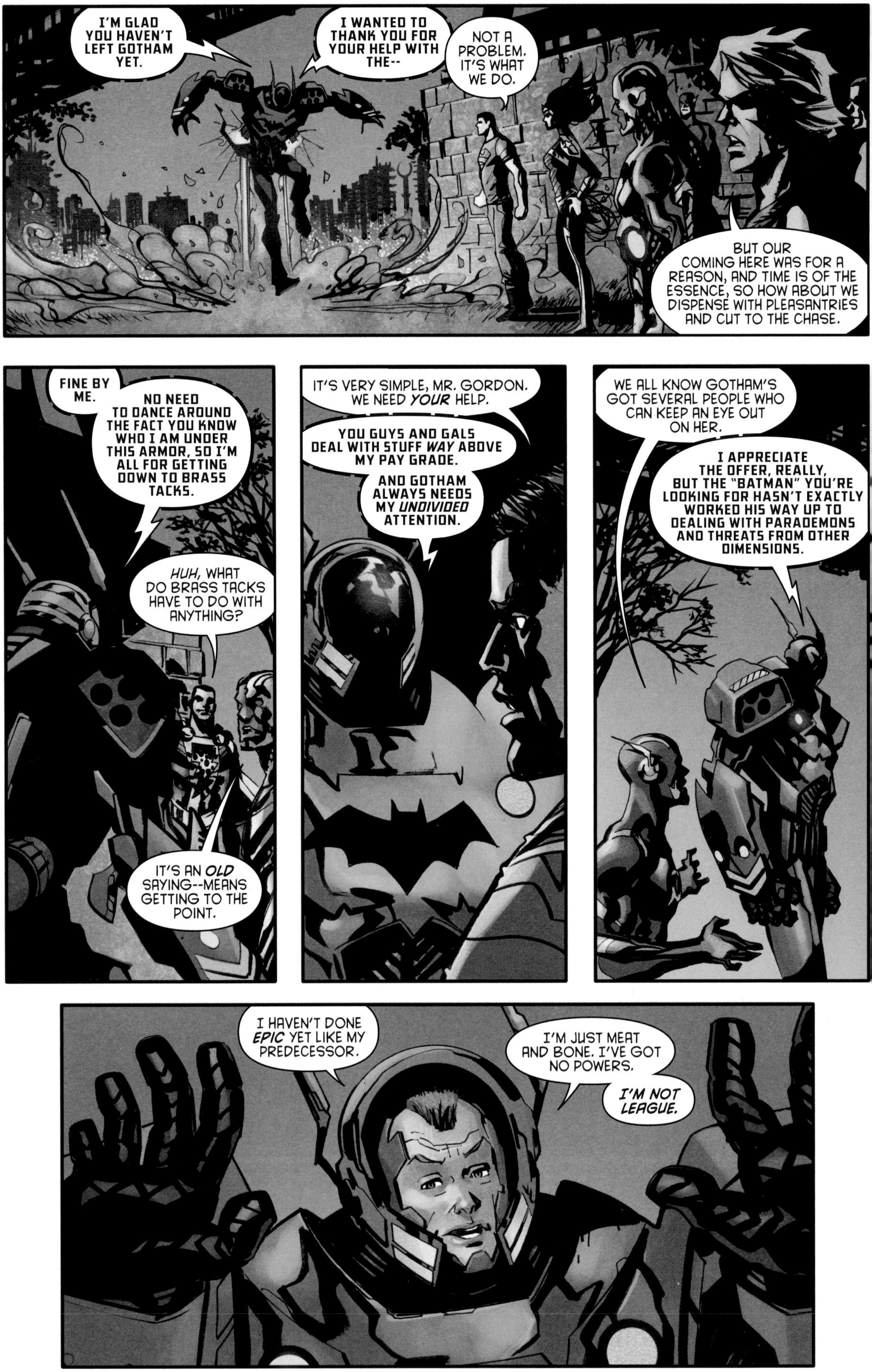
I'M GLAD YOU HAVEN'T LEFT GOTHAM YET.
I WANTED TO THANK YOU FOR YOUR HELP WITH THE--
NOT A PROBLEM. IT'S WHAT WE DO.
BUT OUR COMING HERE WAS FOR A REASON, AND TIME IS OF THE ESSENCE, SO HOW ABOUT WE DISPENSE WITH PLEASANTRIES AND CUT TO THE CHASE.
FINE BY ME.
NO NEED TO DANCE AROUND THE FACT YOU KNOW WHO I AM UNDER THIS ARMOR, SO I'M ALL FOR GETTING DOWN TO BRASS TACKS.
HUH, WHAT DO BRASS TACKS HAVE TO DO WITH ANYTHING?
IT'S AN *OLD* SAYING--MEANS GETTING TO THE POINT.
IT'S VERY SIMPLE, MR. GORDON. WE NEED *YOUR* HELP.
YOU GUYS AND GALS DEAL WITH STUFF *WAY* ABOVE MY PAY GRADE.
AND GOTHAM ALWAYS NEEDS MY *UNDIVIDED* ATTENTION.
WE ALL KNOW GOTHAM'S GOT SEVERAL PEOPLE WHO CAN KEEP AN EYE OUT ON HER.
I APPRECIATE THE OFFER, REALLY, BUT THE "BATMAN" YOU'RE LOOKING FOR HASN'T EXACTLY WORKED HIS WAY UP TO DEALING WITH PARADEMONS AND THREATS FROM OTHER DIMENSIONS.
I HAVEN'T DONE *EPIC* YET LIKE MY PREDECESSOR.
I'M JUST MEAT AND BONE. I'VE GOT NO POWERS.
I'M NOT LEAGUE.

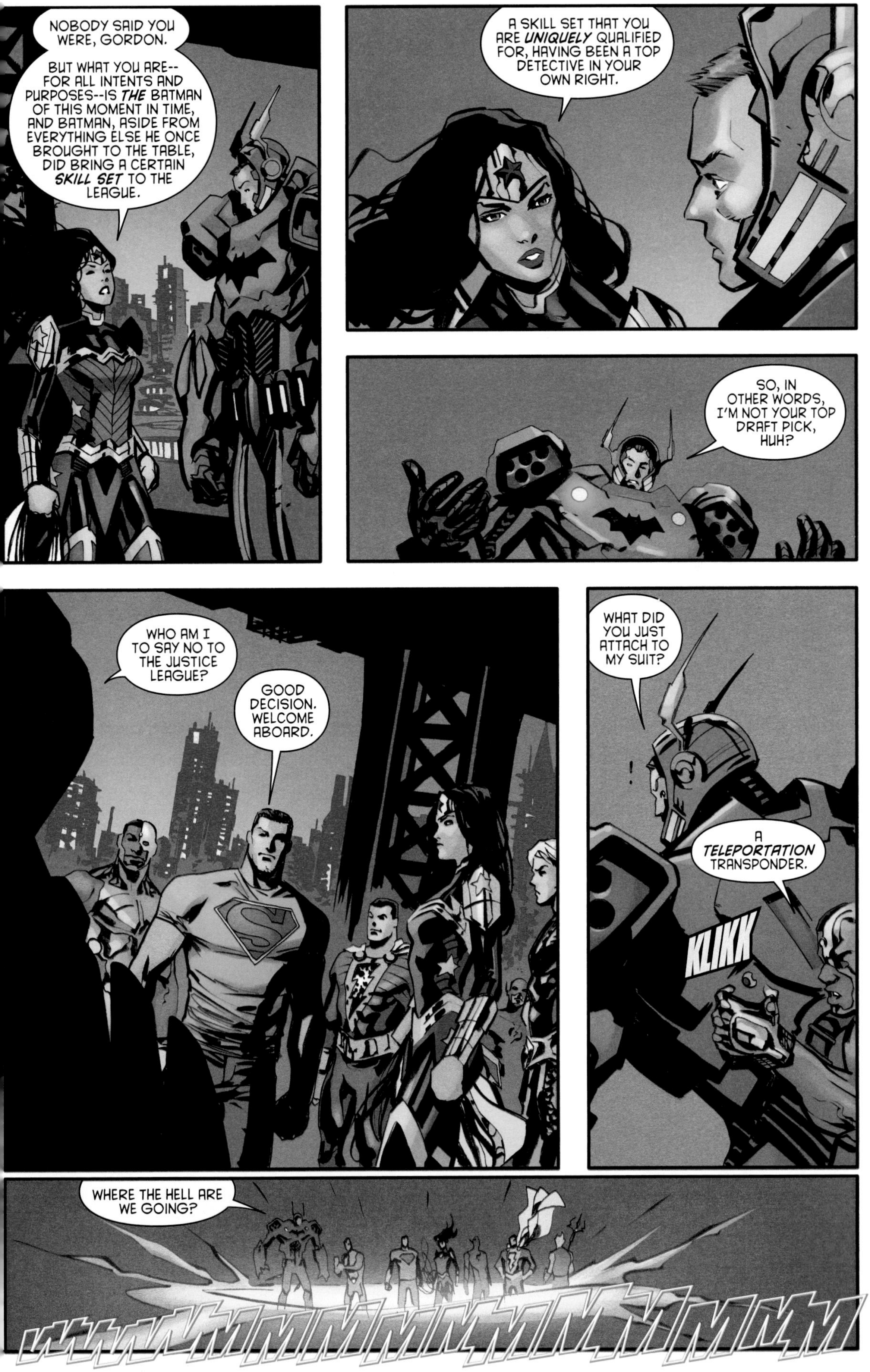
NOBODY SAID YOU WERE, GORDON.
BUT WHAT YOU ARE-- FOR ALL INTENTS AND PURPOSES--IS *THE* BATMAN OF THIS MOMENT IN TIME, AND BATMAN, ASIDE FROM EVERYTHING ELSE HE ONCE BROUGHT TO THE TABLE, DID BRING A CERTAIN *SKILL SET* TO THE LEAGUE.
A SKILL SET THAT YOU ARE *UNIQUELY* QUALIFIED FOR, HAVING BEEN A TOP DETECTIVE IN YOUR OWN RIGHT.
SO, IN OTHER WORDS, I'M NOT YOUR TOP DRAFT PICK, HUH?
WHO AM I TO SAY NO TO THE JUSTICE LEAGUE?
GOOD DECISION. WELCOME ABOARD.
WHAT DID YOU JUST ATTACH TO MY SUIT?
!
KLIKK
A *TELEPORTATION* TRANSPONDER.
WHERE THE HELL ARE WE GOING?
WWWMMMMMMMMMMMMMMMMM

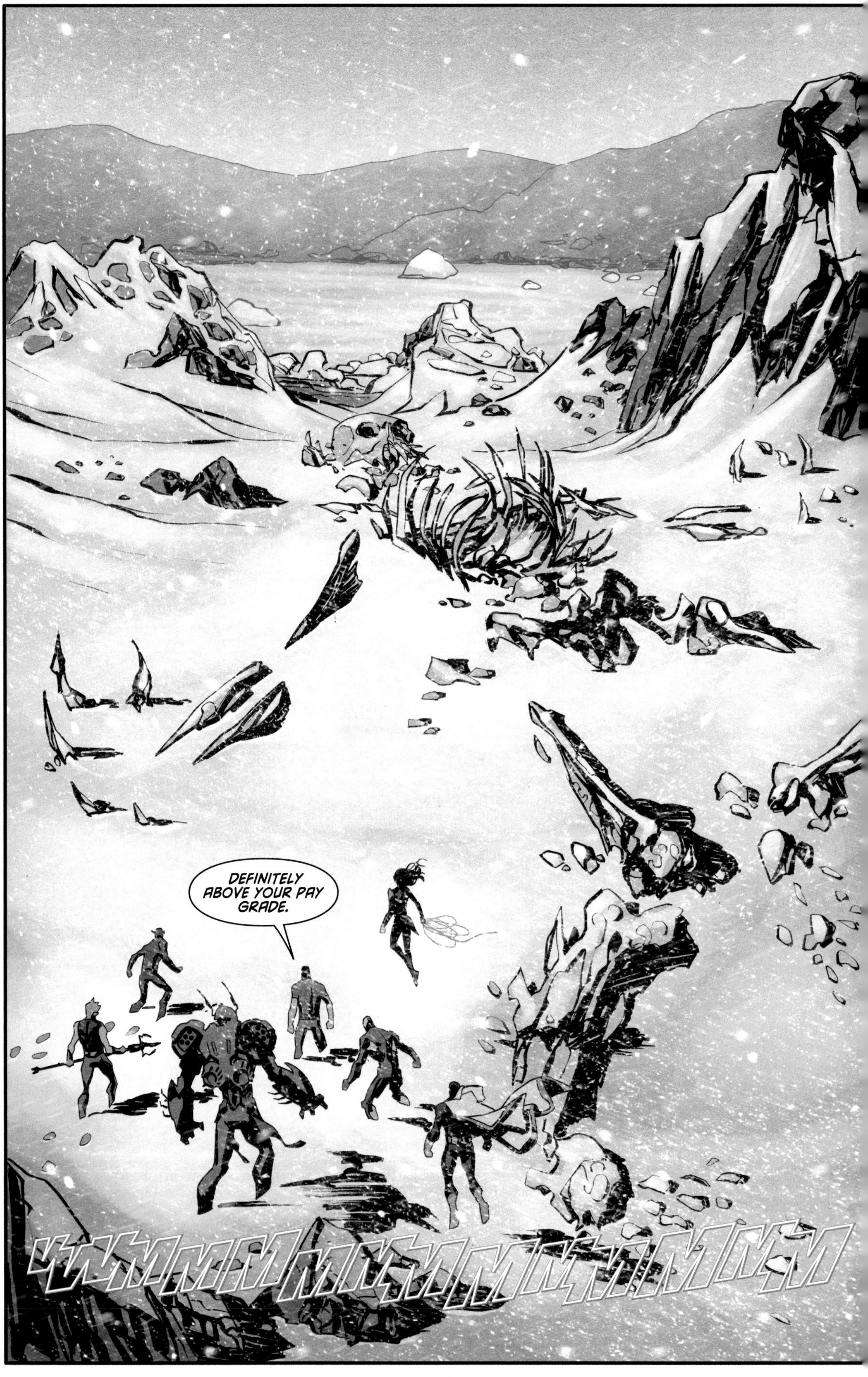
DEFINITELY ABOVE YOUR PAY GRADE.
WMMMMMMMMMMMMMMM

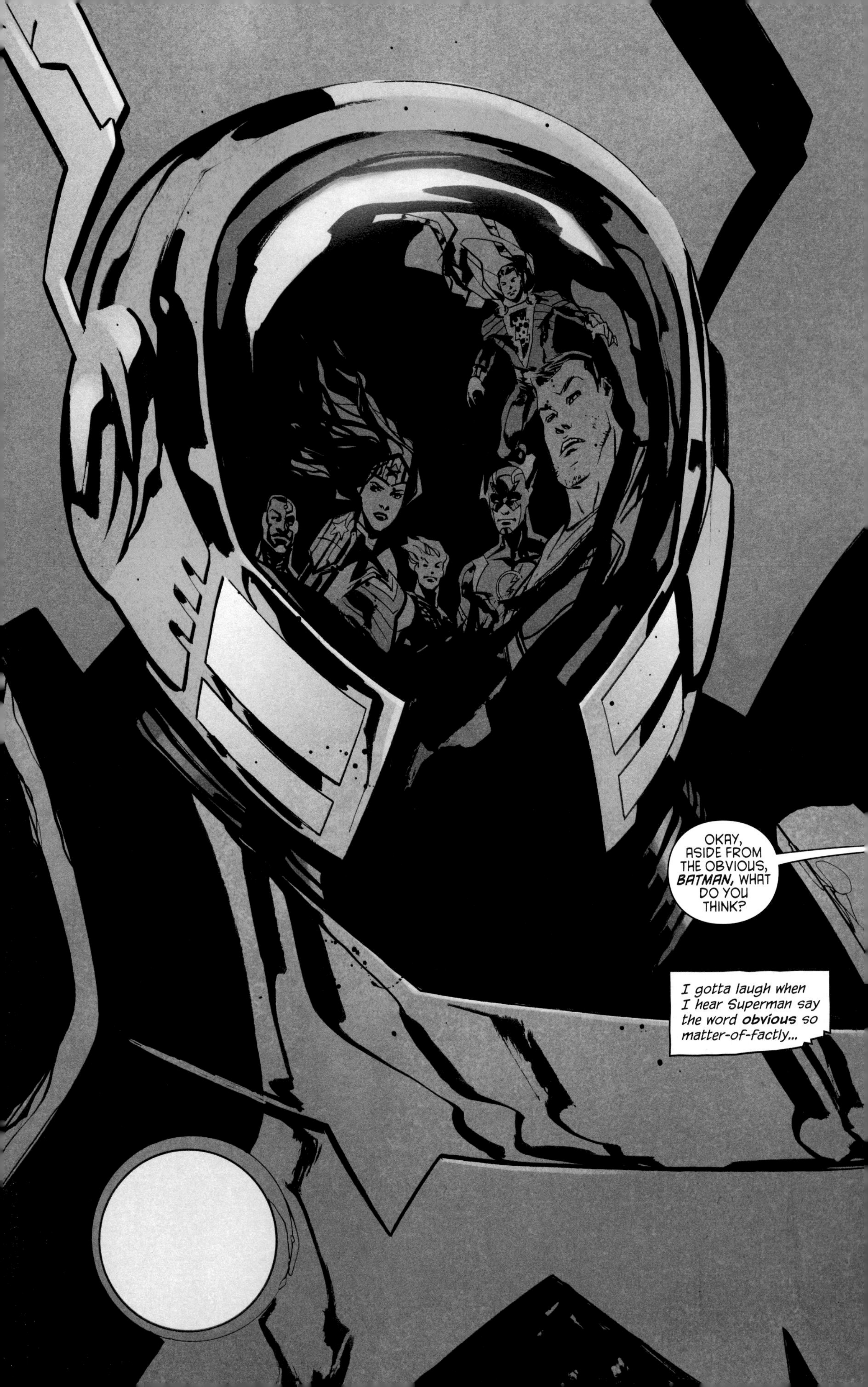
OKAY, ASIDE FROM THE OBVIOUS, **BATMAN,** WHAT DO YOU THINK?
*I gotta laugh when I hear Superman say the word **obvious** so matter-of-factly...*

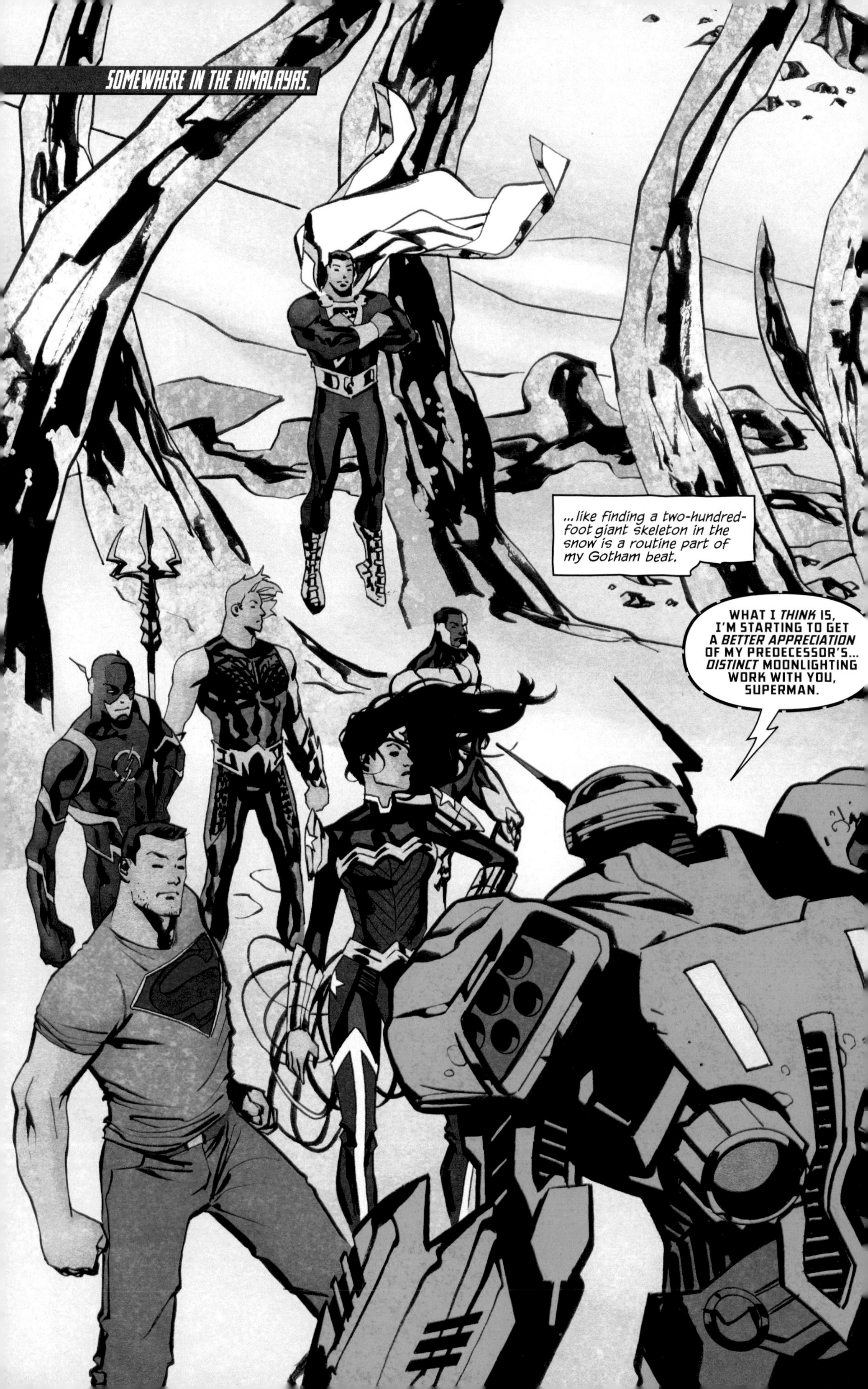
SOMEWHERE IN THE HIMALAYAS.
...like finding a two-hundred-foot giant skeleton in the snow is a routine part of my Gotham beat.
WHAT I THINK IS, I'M STARTING TO GET A BETTER APPRECIATION OF MY PREDECESSOR'S... DISTINCT MOONLIGHTING WORK WITH YOU, SUPERMAN.

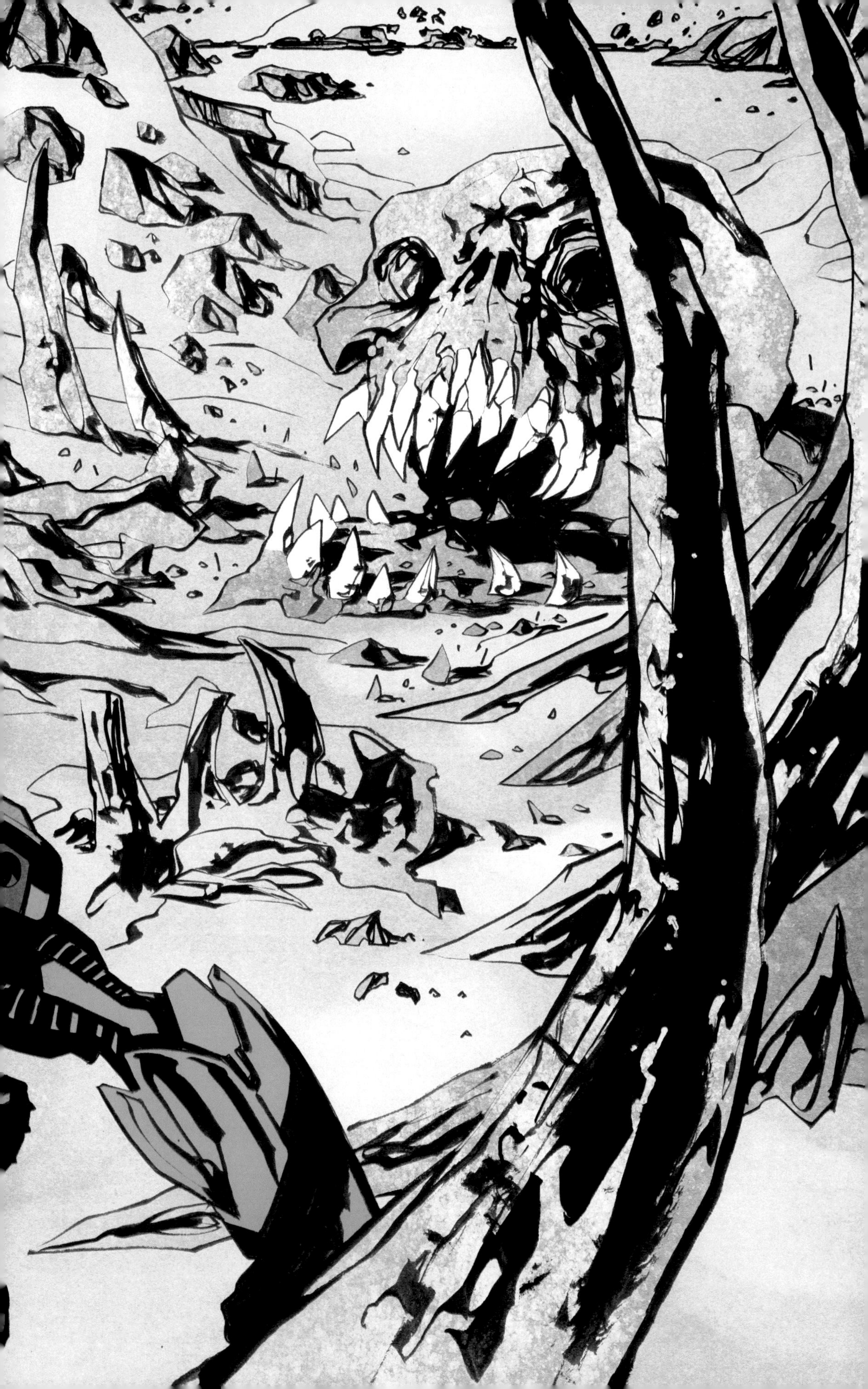

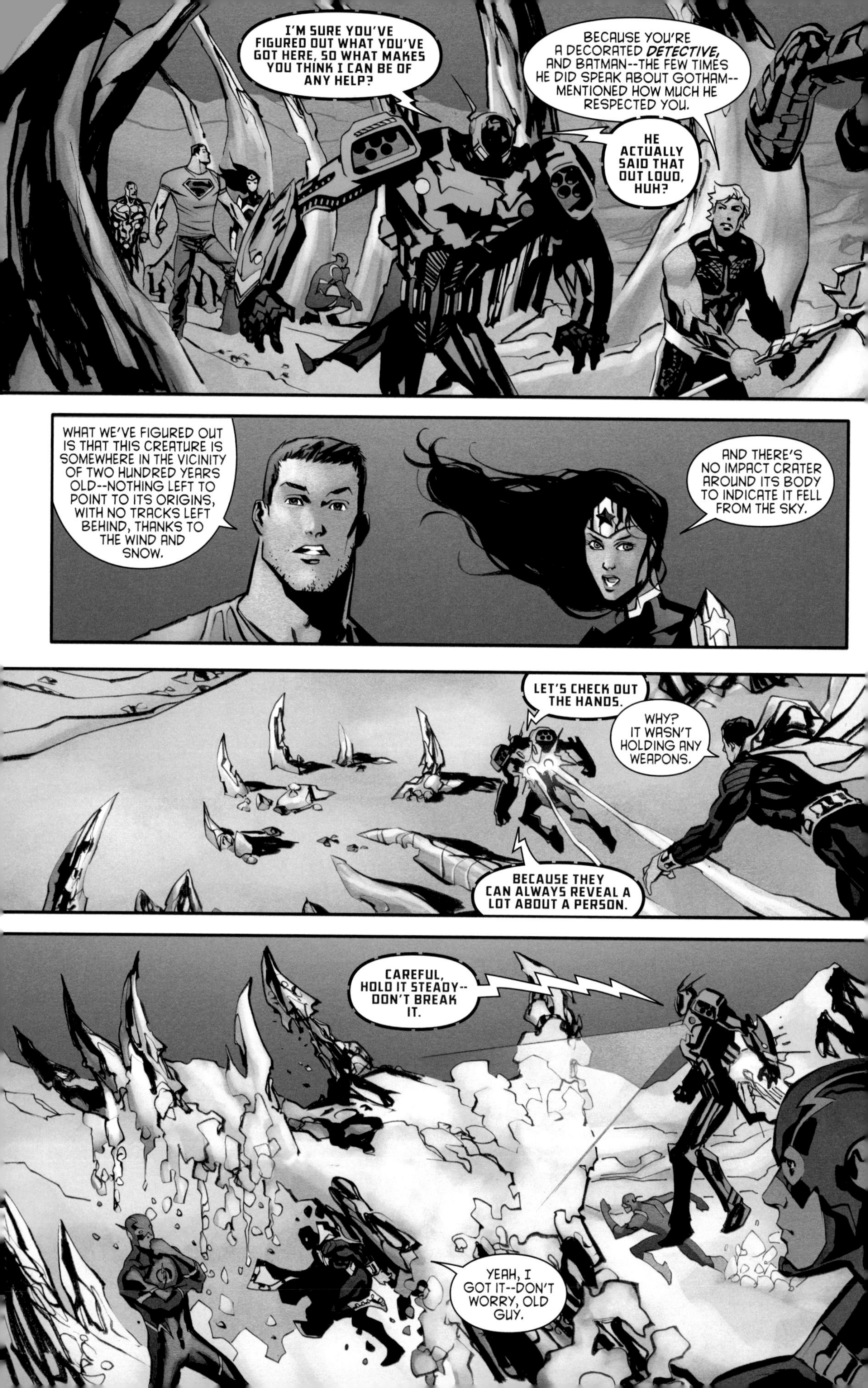
I'M SURE YOU'VE FIGURED OUT WHAT YOU'VE GOT HERE, SO WHAT MAKES YOU THINK I CAN BE OF ANY HELP?
BECAUSE YOU'RE A DECORATED *DETECTIVE,* AND BATMAN--THE FEW TIMES HE DID SPEAK ABOUT GOTHAM--MENTIONED HOW MUCH HE RESPECTED YOU.
HE ACTUALLY SAID THAT OUT LOUD, HUH?
WHAT WE'VE FIGURED OUT IS THAT THIS CREATURE IS SOMEWHERE IN THE VICINITY OF TWO HUNDRED YEARS OLD--NOTHING LEFT TO POINT TO ITS ORIGINS, WITH NO TRACKS LEFT BEHIND, THANKS TO THE WIND AND SNOW.
AND THERE'S NO IMPACT CRATER AROUND ITS BODY TO INDICATE IT FELL FROM THE SKY.
LET'S CHECK OUT THE HANDS.
WHY? IT WASN'T HOLDING ANY WEAPONS.
BECAUSE THEY CAN ALWAYS REVEAL A LOT ABOUT A PERSON.
CAREFUL, HOLD IT STEADY--DON'T BREAK IT.
YEAH, I GOT IT--DON'T WORRY, OLD GUY.

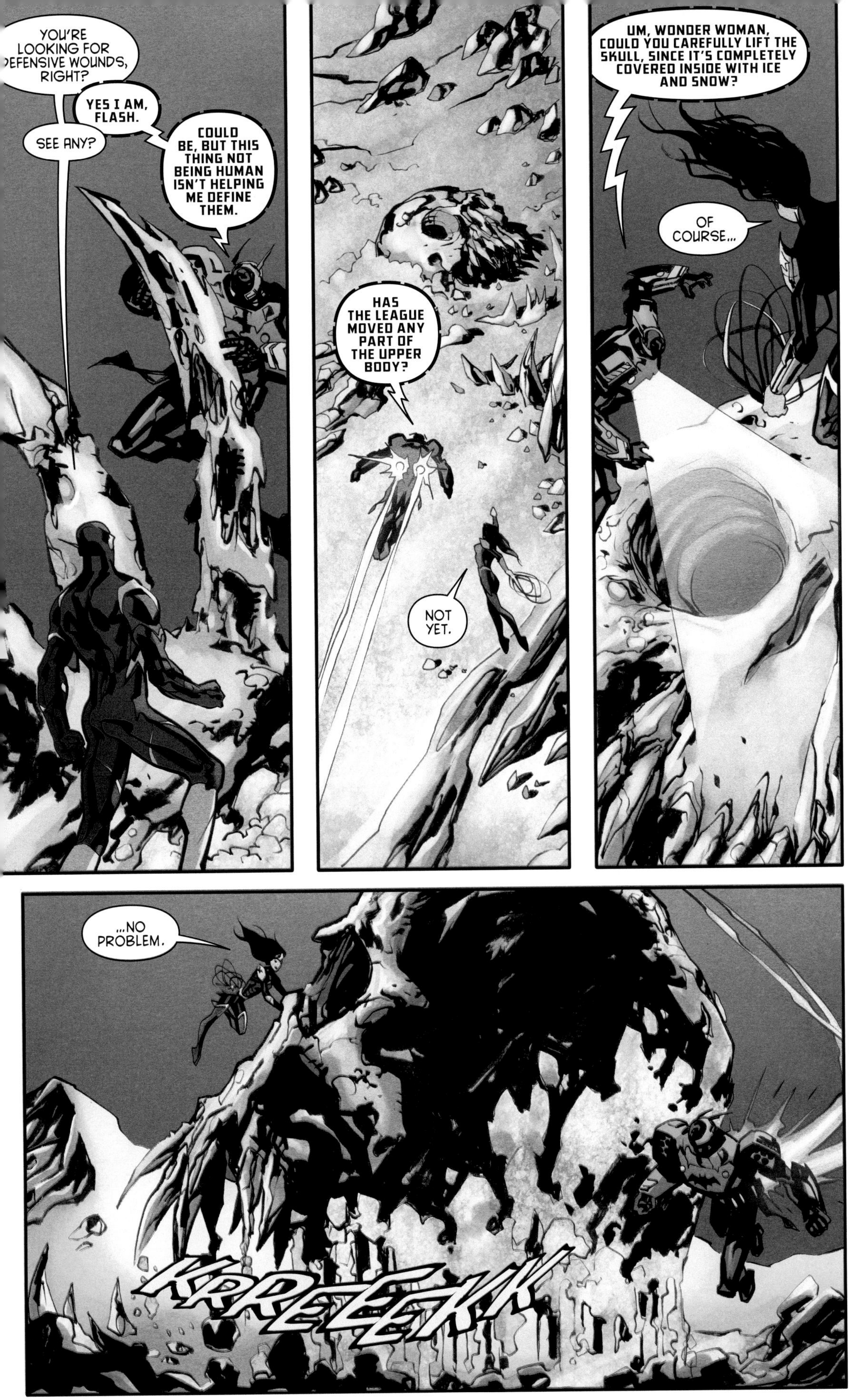

YOU'RE LOOKING FOR DEFENSIVE WOUNDS, RIGHT?
YES I AM, FLASH.
SEE ANY?
COULD BE, BUT THIS THING NOT BEING HUMAN ISN'T HELPING ME DEFINE THEM.
HAS THE LEAGUE MOVED ANY PART OF THE UPPER BODY?
NOT YET.
UM, WONDER WOMAN, COULD YOU CAREFULLY LIFT THE SKULL, SINCE IT'S COMPLETELY COVERED INSIDE WITH ICE AND SNOW?
OF COURSE...
...NO PROBLEM.
KRREEEKK

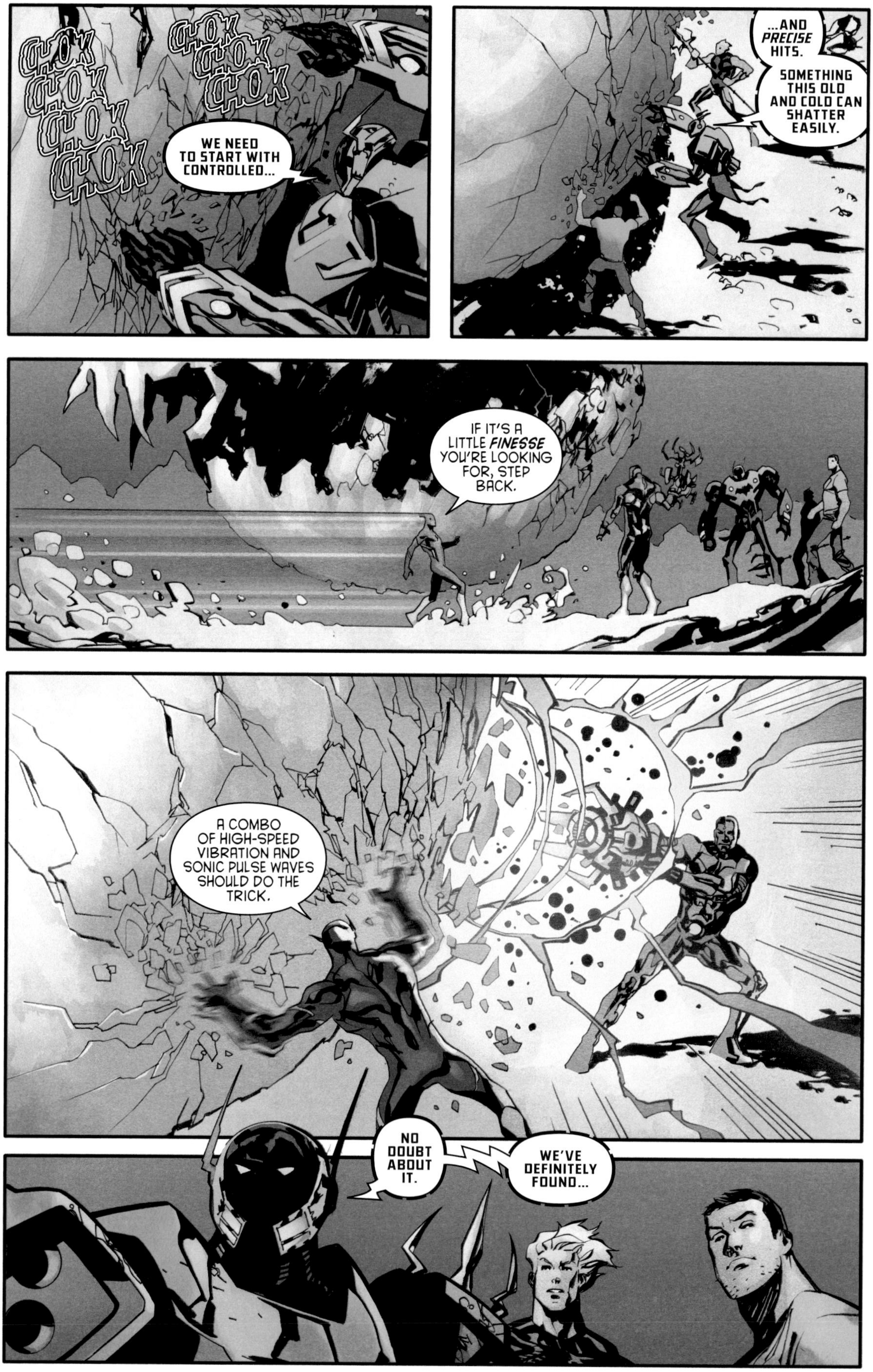
CHOK CHOK CHOK CHOK
CHOK CHOK CHOK
WE NEED TO START WITH CONTROLLED...
...AND PRECISE HITS.
SOMETHING THIS OLD AND COLD CAN SHATTER EASILY.
IF IT'S A LITTLE FINESSE YOU'RE LOOKING FOR, STEP BACK.
A COMBO OF HIGH-SPEED VIBRATION AND SONIC PULSE WAVES SHOULD DO THE TRICK.
NO DOUBT ABOUT IT.
WE'VE DEFINITELY FOUND...

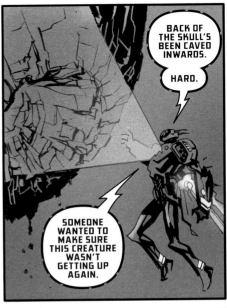

...THE CAUSE OF DEATH.

BACK OF THE SKULL'S BEEN CAVED INWARDS.

HARD.

SOMEONE WANTED TO MAKE SURE THIS CREATURE WASN'T GETTING UP AGAIN.

AND WHOEVER IT WAS HAD TO BE BIG AND STRONG TO CAUSE THIS KIND OF PHYSICAL DAMAGE.

THIS IS A CRIME SCENE.

A *HOMICIDE* TO BE EXACT.

ALL WE NEED TO DO NOW IS FIND...

...THE *MURDER* WEAPON.

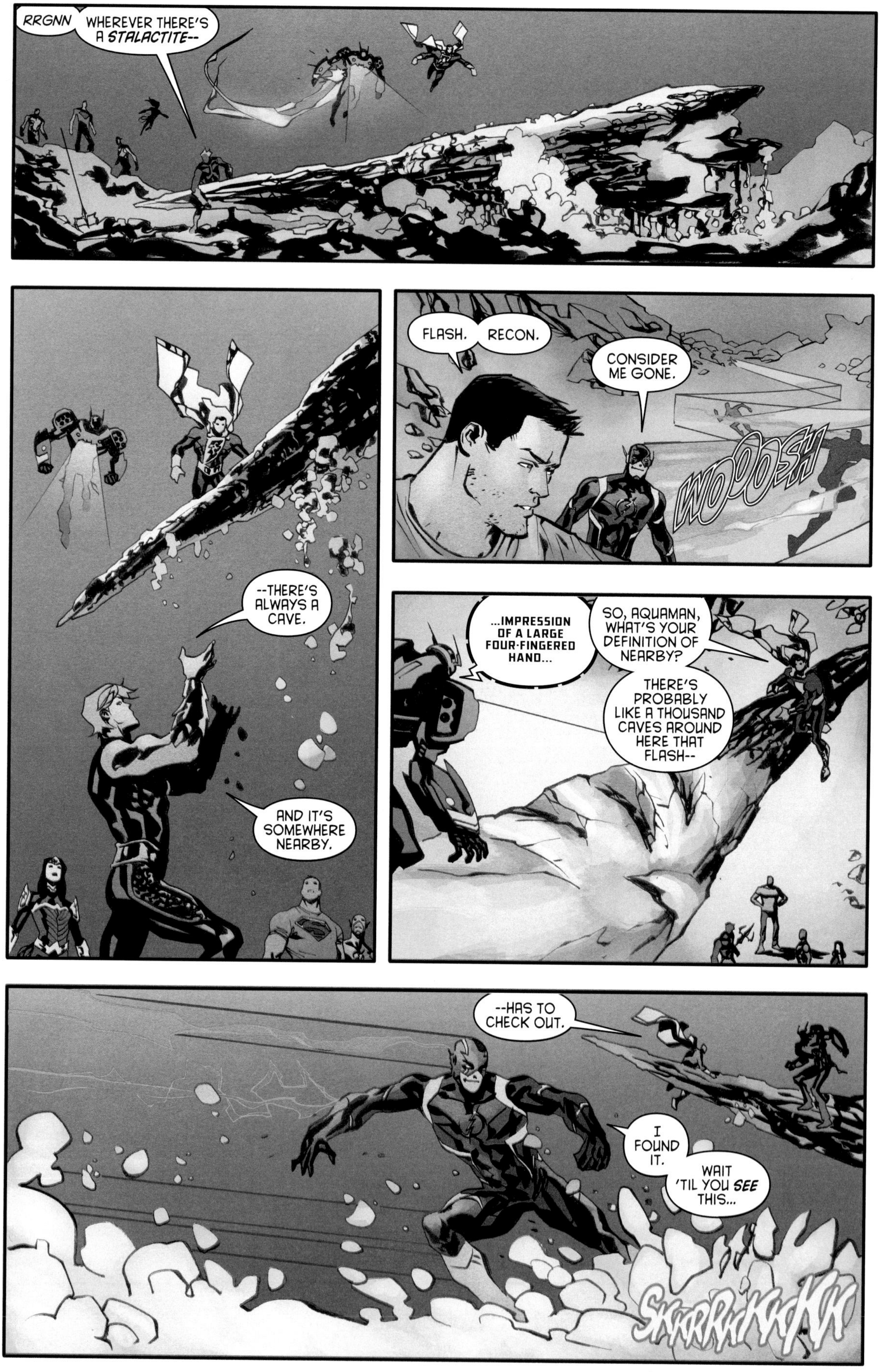
RRGNN
WHEREVER THERE'S A STALACTITE--
--THERE'S ALWAYS A CAVE.
AND IT'S SOMEWHERE NEARBY.
FLASH.
RECON.
CONSIDER ME GONE.
WOOOSH
...IMPRESSION OF A LARGE FOUR-FINGERED HAND...
SO, AQUAMAN, WHAT'S YOUR DEFINITION OF NEARBY?
THERE'S PROBABLY LIKE A THOUSAND CAVES AROUND HERE THAT FLASH--
--HAS TO CHECK OUT.
I FOUND IT.
WAIT 'TIL YOU SEE THIS...
SKRRRKKKK

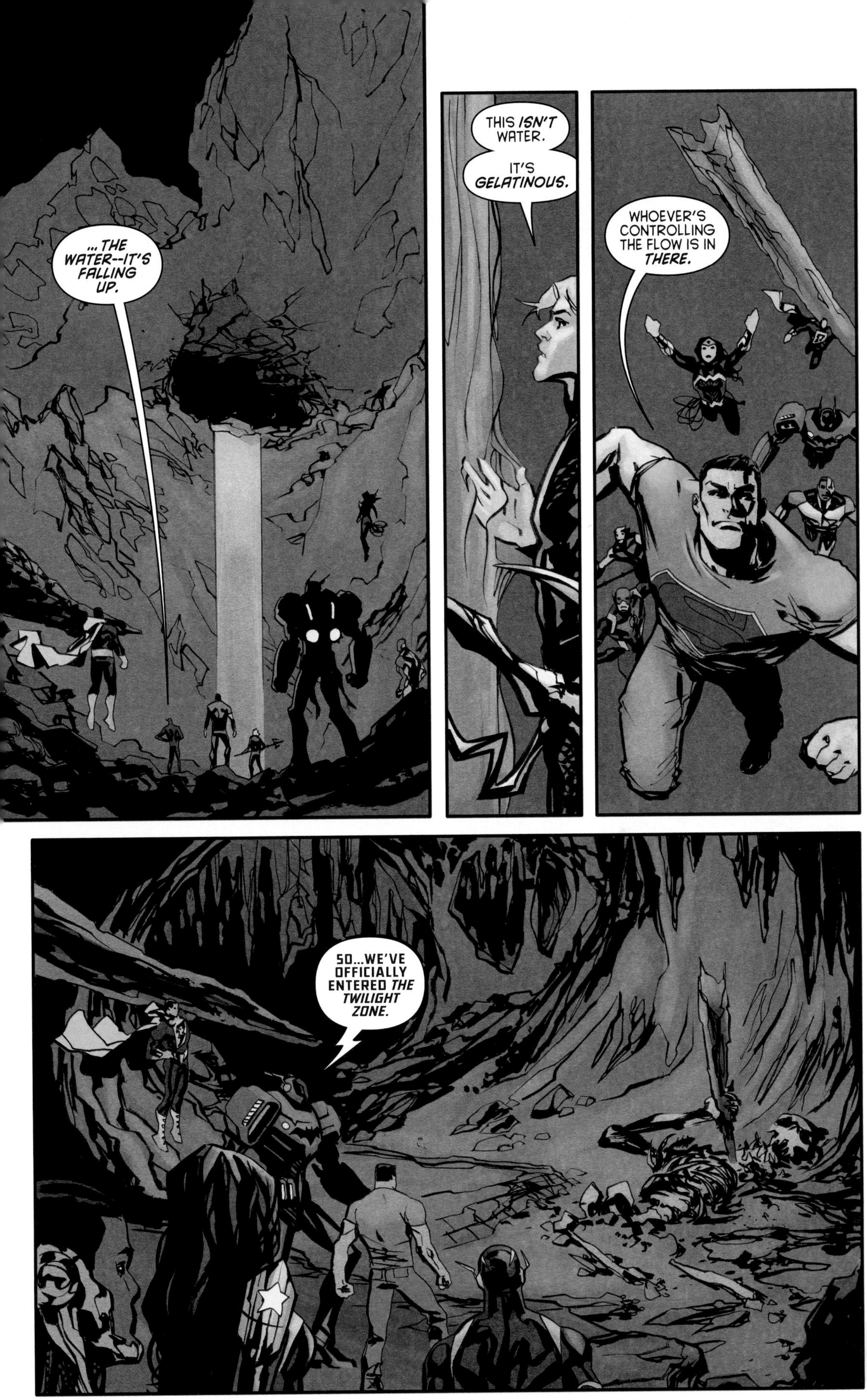
...THE WATER--IT'S FALLING UP.
THIS ISN'T WATER.
IT'S GELATINOUS.
WHOEVER'S CONTROLLING THE FLOW IS IN THERE.
SO...WE'VE OFFICIALLY ENTERED THE TWILIGHT ZONE.

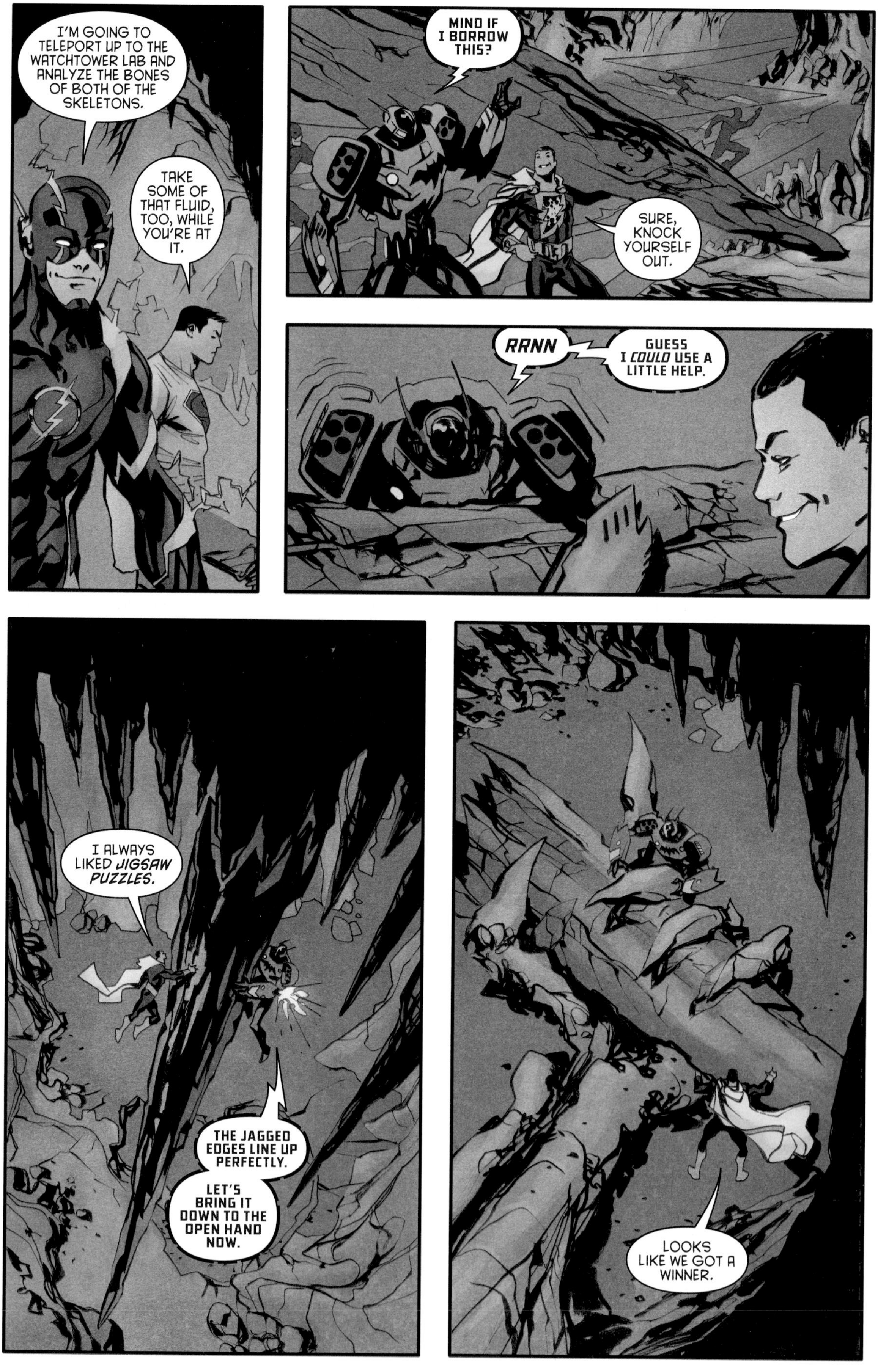
I'M GOING TO TELEPORT UP TO THE WATCHTOWER LAB AND ANALYZE THE BONES OF BOTH OF THE SKELETONS.
TAKE SOME OF THAT FLUID, TOO, WHILE YOU'RE AT IT.
MIND IF I BORROW THIS?
SURE, KNOCK YOURSELF OUT.
RRNN
GUESS I *COULD* USE A LITTLE HELP.
I ALWAYS LIKED *JIGSAW PUZZLES.*
THE JAGGED EDGES LINE UP PERFECTLY.
LET'S BRING IT DOWN TO THE OPEN HAND NOW.
LOOKS LIKE WE GOT A WINNER.

AND IT LOOKS LIKE THIS CREATURE COMMITTED *SUICIDE.*

AND IT LOOKS LIKE THE DISAPPEARANCE OF MOUNTAIN CLIMBERS IN THIS AREA JUST STOPPED BEING A COLD CASE.

OKAY, I'M BACK. THE FIRST SKELETON WE FOUND IS A MALE, AND THIS SKELETON HERE IN THE CAVE IS A FEMALE.

AND THE LIQUID?

AQUEOUS HUMOUR. AND IT'S *HUMAN.*

MMMMMMMMMMM

THAT TIES INTO THE MYSTERIOUS DEATHS AND LOSS OF EYES WE'VE HEARD ABOUT IN THE REGION.

AQUEOUS HUMOUR--THAT LIKE SOME KINDA ICE CREAM FROM A GOOD HUMOR TRUCK?

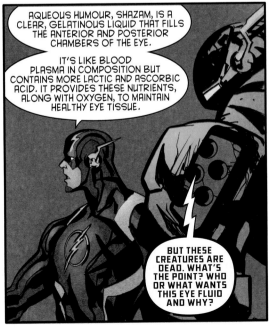

AQUEOUS HUMOUR, SHAZAM, IS A CLEAR, GELATINOUS LIQUID THAT FILLS THE ANTERIOR AND POSTERIOR CHAMBERS OF THE EYE.

IT'S LIKE BLOOD PLASMA IN COMPOSITION BUT CONTAINS MORE LACTIC AND ASCORBIC ACID. IT PROVIDES THESE NUTRIENTS, ALONG WITH OXYGEN, TO MAINTAIN HEALTHY EYE TISSUE.

BUT THESE CREATURES ARE DEAD. WHAT'S THE POINT? WHO OR WHAT WANTS THIS EYE FLUID AND WHY?

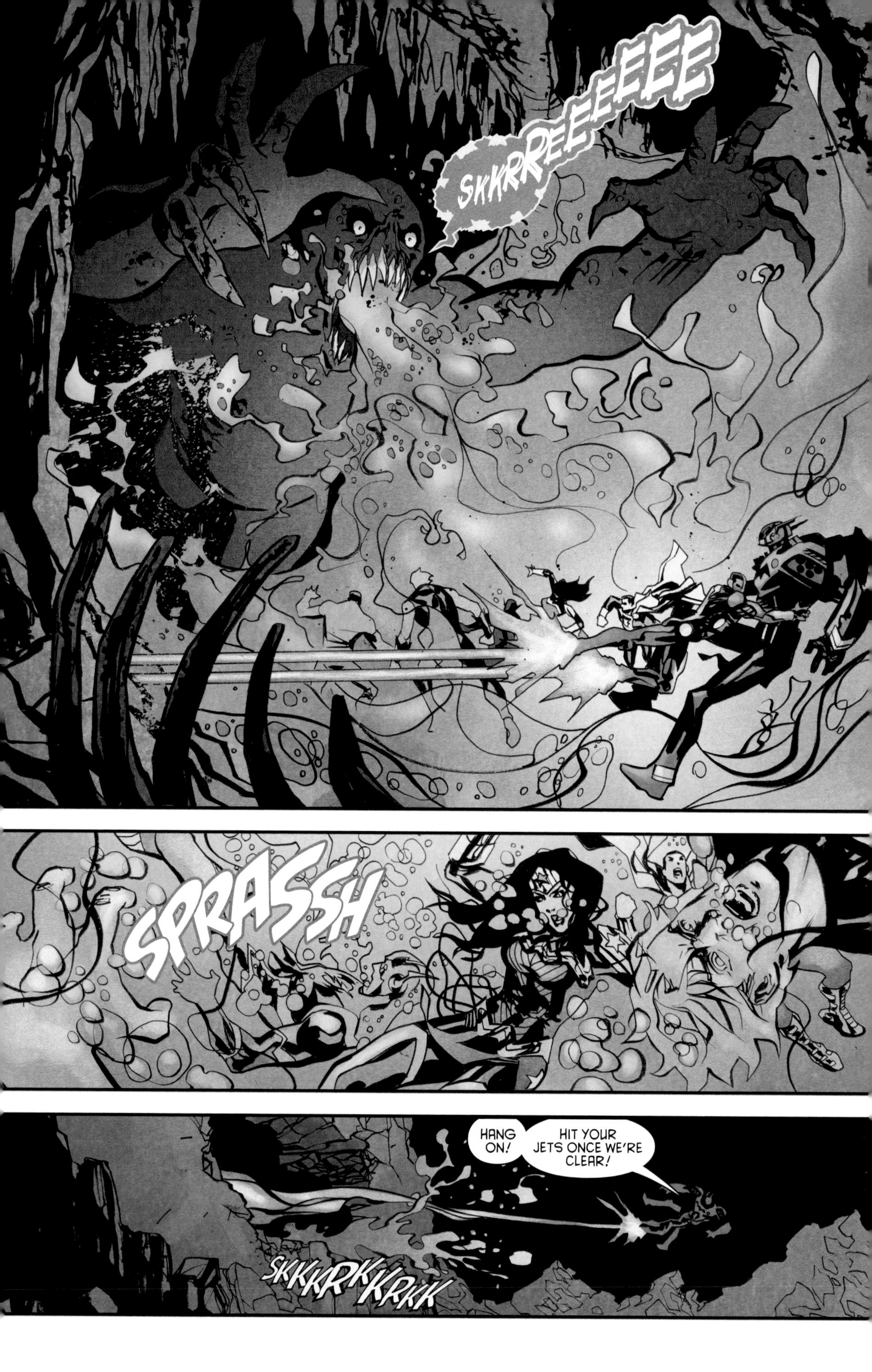
SKKRREEEEEEE
SPRASSH
HANG ON!
HIT YOUR JETS ONCE WE'RE CLEAR!
SKKKRKKRKK

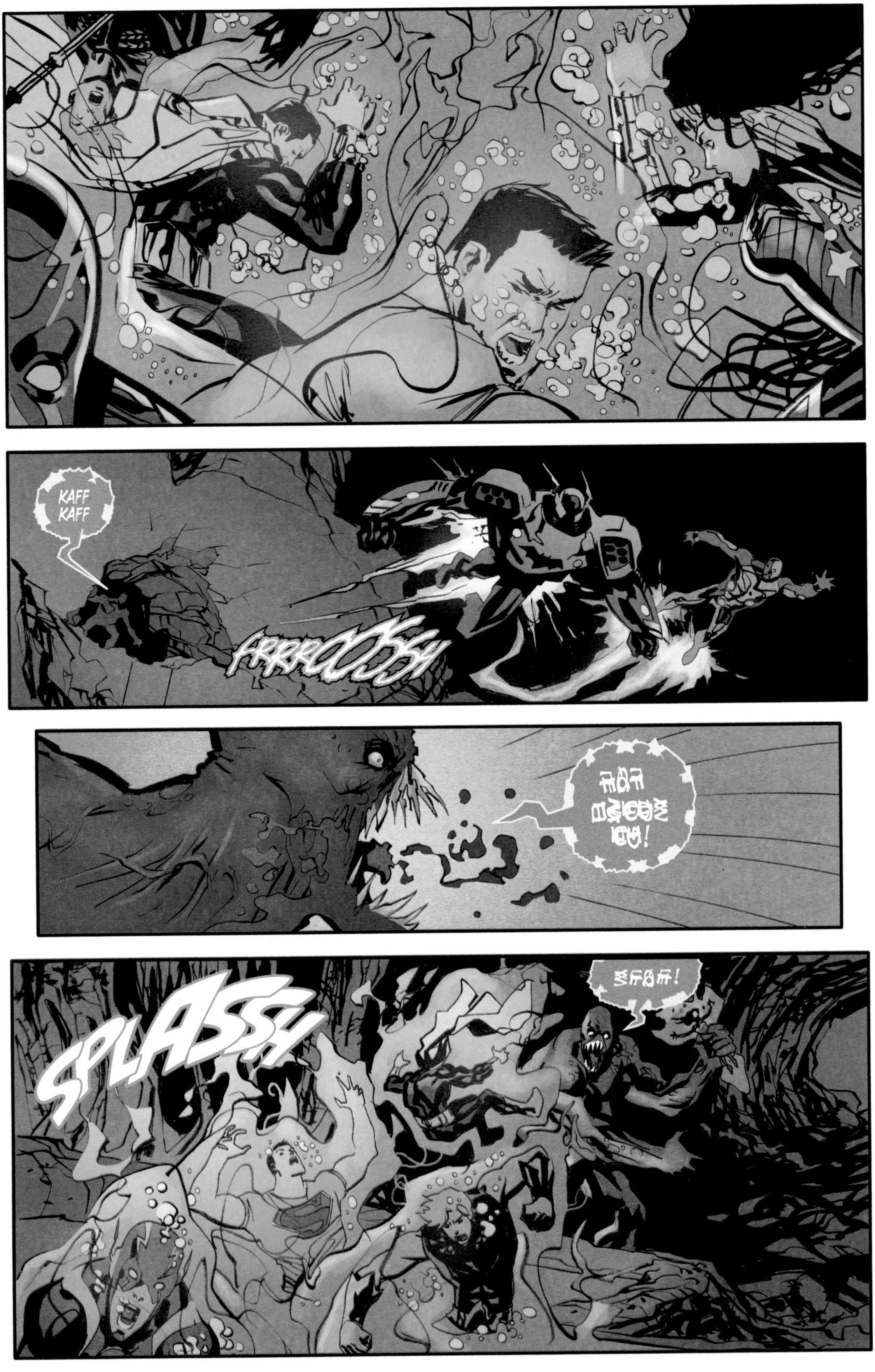
KAFF KAFF
FRRRROOOSSH
SPLASSH

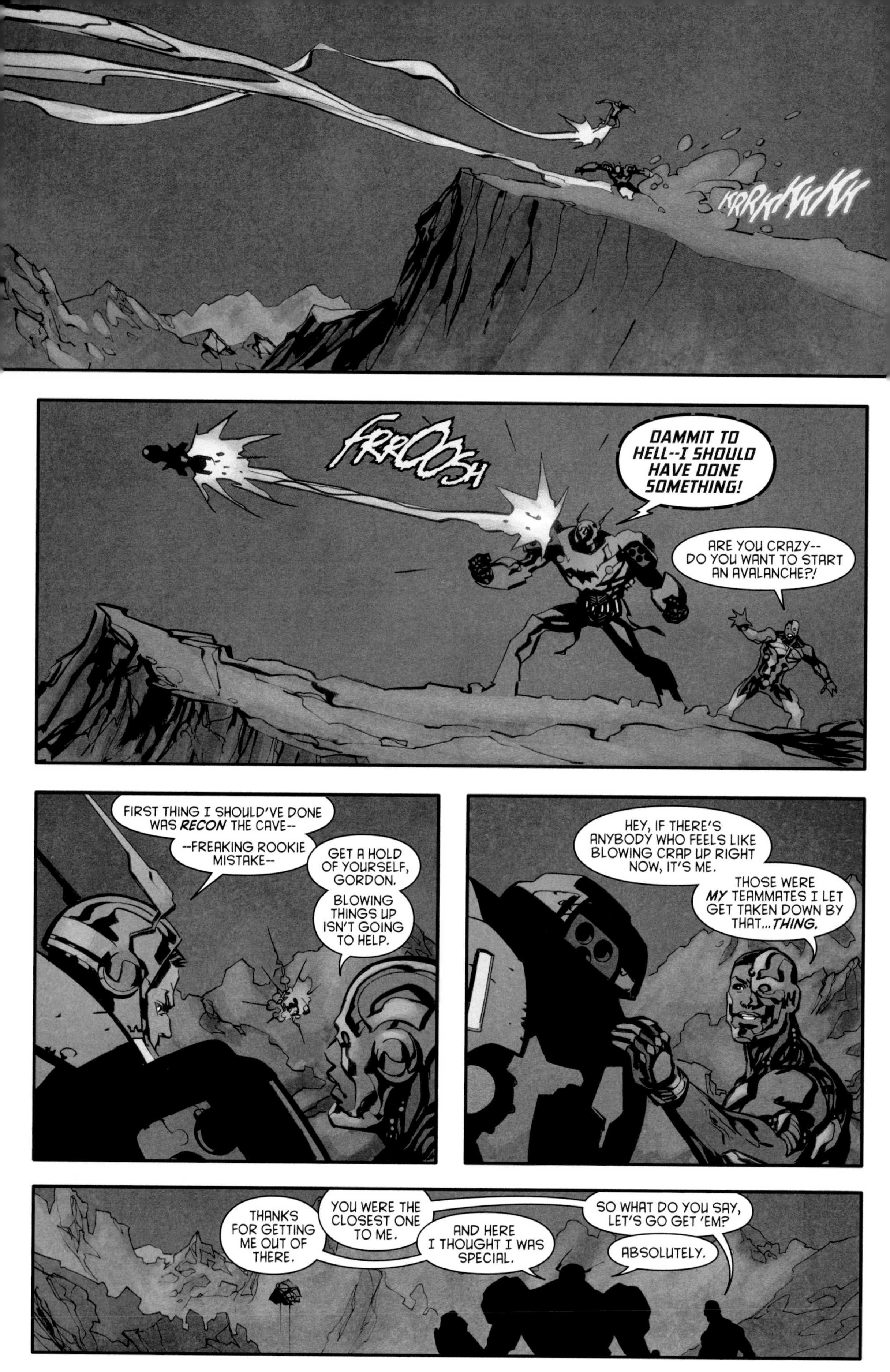

KRRKKKKKKK
FRRCOOSH
DAMMIT TO HELL--I SHOULD HAVE DONE SOMETHING!
ARE YOU CRAZY-- DO YOU WANT TO START AN AVALANCHE?!
FIRST THING I SHOULD'VE DONE WAS RECON THE CAVE--
--FREAKING ROOKIE MISTAKE--
GET A HOLD OF YOURSELF, GORDON.
BLOWING THINGS UP ISN'T GOING TO HELP.
HEY, IF THERE'S ANYBODY WHO FEELS LIKE BLOWING CRAP UP RIGHT NOW, IT'S ME.
THOSE WERE MY TEAMMATES I LET GET TAKEN DOWN BY THAT...THING.
THANKS FOR GETTING ME OUT OF THERE.
YOU WERE THE CLOSEST ONE TO ME.
AND HERE I THOUGHT I WAS SPECIAL.
SO WHAT DO YOU SAY, LET'S GO GET 'EM?
ABSOLUTELY.

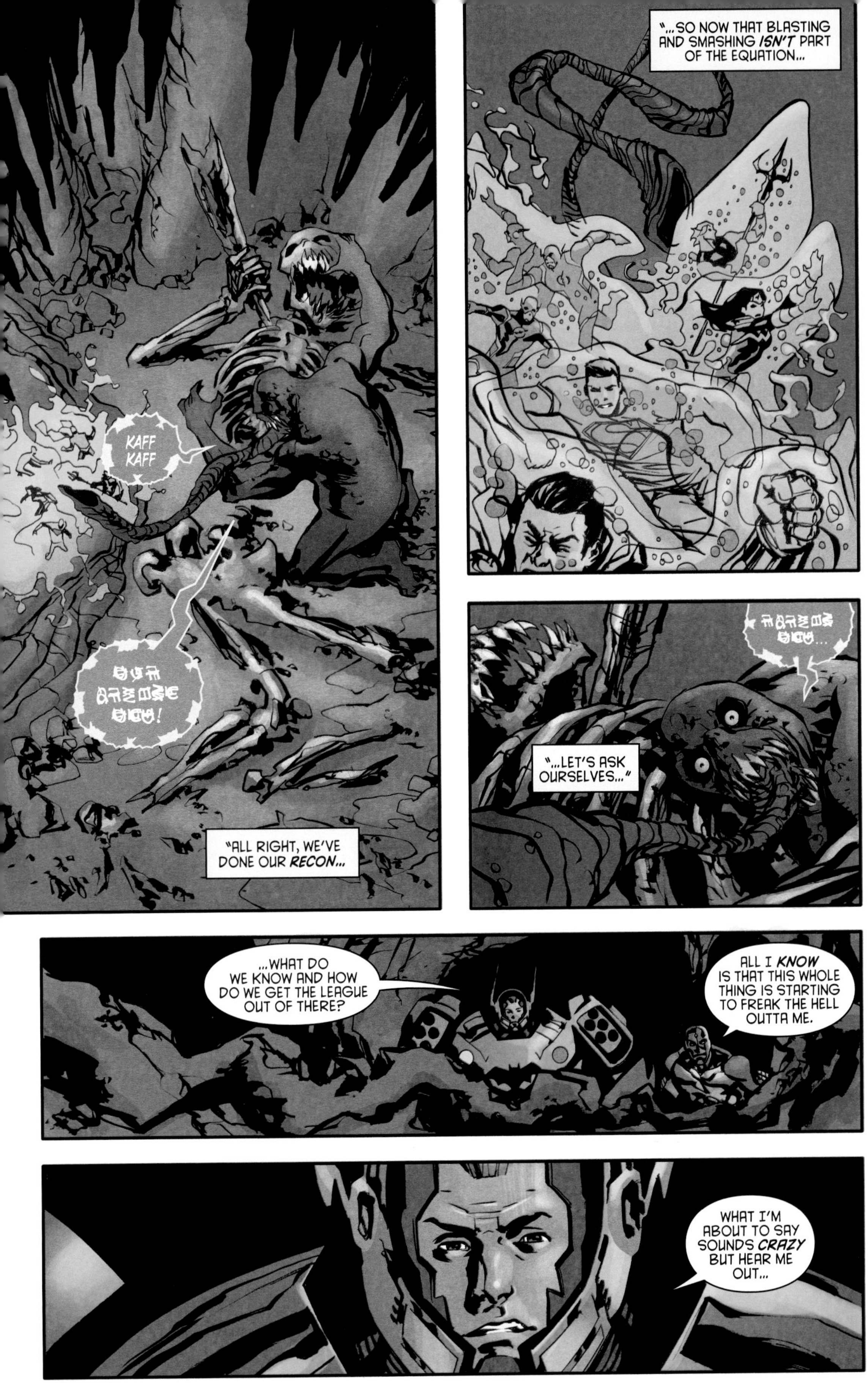
KAFF KAFF
"ALL RIGHT, WE'VE DONE OUR *RECON*...
"...SO NOW THAT BLASTING AND SMASHING *ISN'T* PART OF THE EQUATION...
"...LET'S ASK OURSELVES..."
...WHAT DO WE KNOW AND HOW DO WE GET THE LEAGUE OUT OF THERE?
ALL I *KNOW* IS THAT THIS WHOLE THING IS STARTING TO FREAK THE HELL OUTTA ME.
WHAT I'M ABOUT TO SAY SOUNDS *CRAZY* BUT HEAR ME OUT...

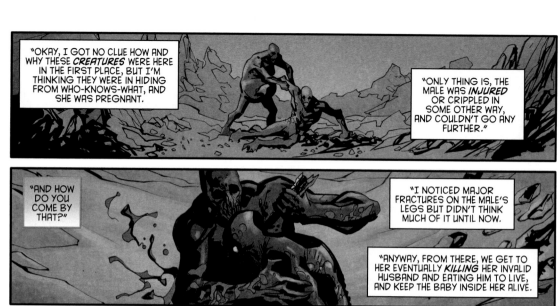

"OKAY, I GOT NO CLUE HOW AND WHY THESE *CREATURES* WERE HERE IN THE FIRST PLACE, BUT I'M THINKING THEY WERE IN HIDING FROM WHO-KNOWS-WHAT, AND SHE WAS PREGNANT.

"ONLY THING IS, THE MALE WAS *INJURED* OR CRIPPLED IN SOME OTHER WAY, AND COULDN'T GO ANY FURTHER."

"AND HOW DO YOU COME BY THAT?"

"I NOTICED MAJOR FRACTURES ON THE MALE'S LEGS BUT DIDN'T THINK MUCH OF IT UNTIL NOW.

"ANYWAY, FROM THERE, WE GET TO HER EVENTUALLY *KILLING* HER INVALID HUSBAND AND EATING HIM TO LIVE, AND KEEP THE BABY INSIDE HER ALIVE.

"SHE HEADS TO THE CAVE AND GIVES BIRTH, FEEDING HER NEWBORN WHAT SHE CAN OF HERSELF...

"...UNTIL FINALLY THERE'S NO MORE FOOD TO KEEP THEM BOTH ALIVE...

"...AND SHE KILLS HERSELF SO THAT THE BABY CAN EAT THE REST OF HER AND *SURVIVE* AS LONG AS IT CAN.

"...ONLY PROBLEM IS, THE BABY WAS ATTACHED TO THE MOTHER, LIKE THE WAY ELEPHANTS ARE IN THE WILD.

"IT WOULDN'T LEAVE HIS MOTHER'S SIDE EVEN AFTER SHE WAS DEAD-- *EXTREME SEPARATION ANXIETY*-- THE ONLY LIFE IT KNEW WAS INSIDE THE WALLS OF THIS CAVE...

"...SO ITS SURVIVAL MECHANISM KICKED INTO OVERDRIVE AND RELEASED SOME KINDA ECTOPLASM--THAT *AQUA* THING FLASH SAID--TO SEEK OUT A SPECIFIC FORM OF NOURISHMENT."

"AQUEOUS HUMOUR."

"RIGHT, WHICH I'M GUESSING IS A KIND OF *BREAST MILK* TO THIS THING, BUT UNFORTUNATELY THE ONLY PLACE TO GET IT IS FROM A HUMAN EYE."

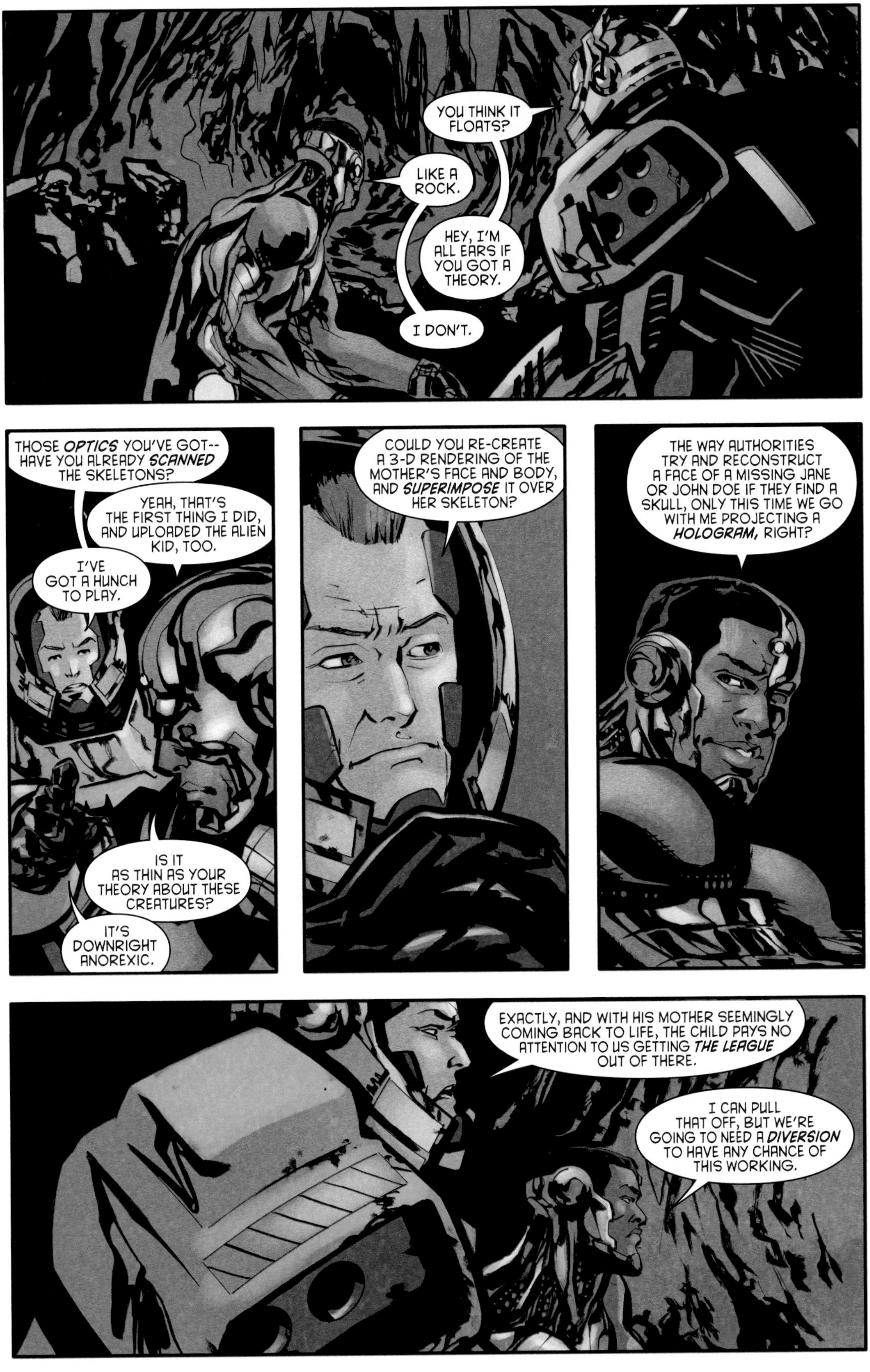
YOU THINK IT FLOATS?
LIKE A ROCK.
HEY, I'M ALL EARS IF YOU GOT A THEORY.
I DON'T.
THOSE OPTICS YOU'VE GOT-- HAVE YOU ALREADY SCANNED THE SKELETONS?
YEAH, THAT'S THE FIRST THING I DID, AND UPLOADED THE ALIEN KID, TOO.
I'VE GOT A HUNCH TO PLAY.
IS IT AS THIN AS YOUR THEORY ABOUT THESE CREATURES?
IT'S DOWNRIGHT ANOREXIC.
COULD YOU RE-CREATE A 3-D RENDERING OF THE MOTHER'S FACE AND BODY, AND SUPERIMPOSE IT OVER HER SKELETON?
THE WAY AUTHORITIES TRY AND RECONSTRUCT A FACE OF A MISSING JANE OR JOHN DOE IF THEY FIND A SKULL, ONLY THIS TIME WE GO WITH ME PROJECTING A HOLOGRAM, RIGHT?
EXACTLY, AND WITH HIS MOTHER SEEMINGLY COMING BACK TO LIFE, THE CHILD PAYS NO ATTENTION TO US GETTING THE LEAGUE OUT OF THERE.
I CAN PULL THAT OFF, BUT WE'RE GOING TO NEED A DIVERSION TO HAVE ANY CHANCE OF THIS WORKING.

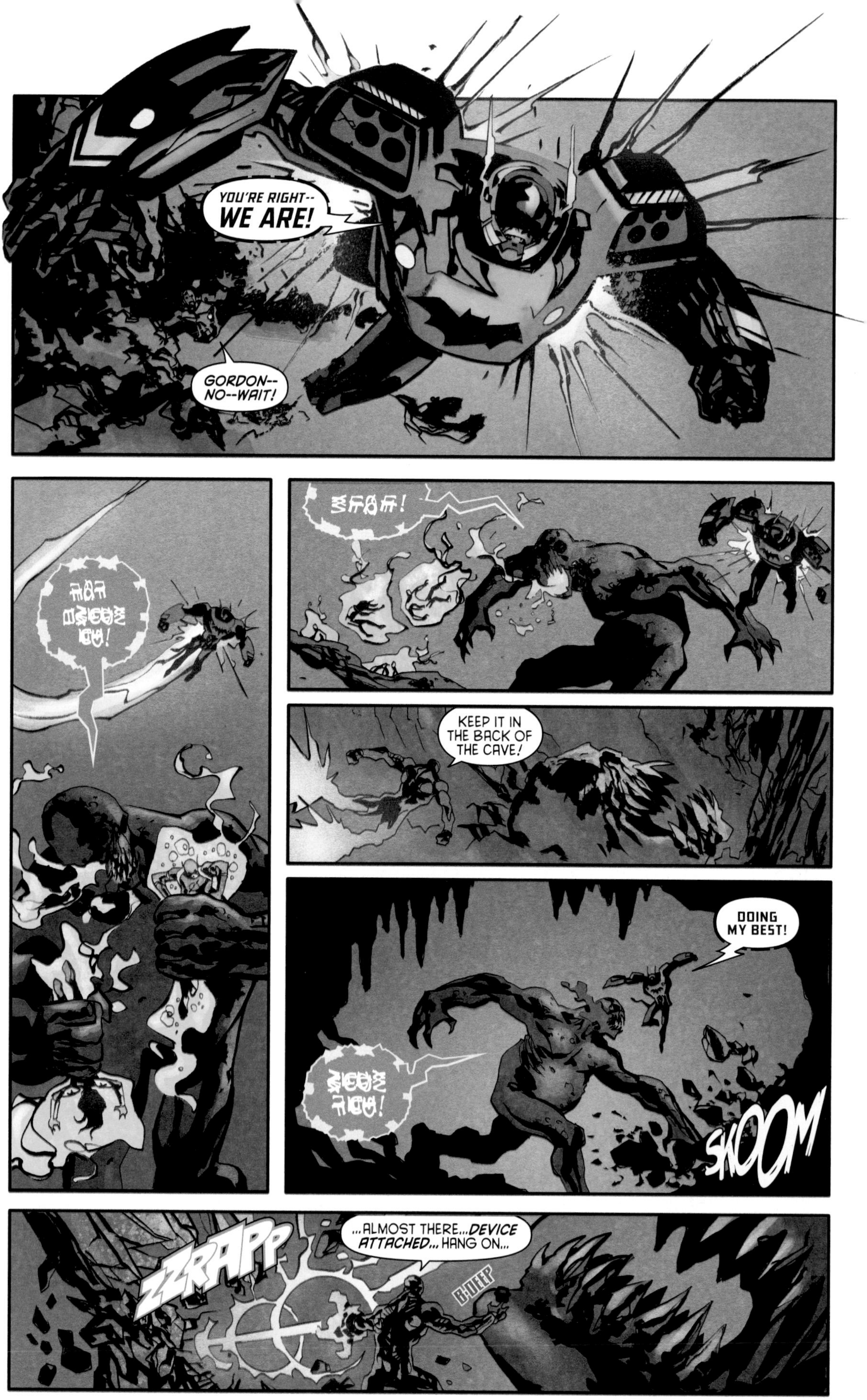
YOU'RE RIGHT-- **WE ARE!**
GORDON-- NO--WAIT!
KEEP IT IN THE BACK OF THE CAVE!
DOING MY BEST!
SKOOM
ZZRAPP
...ALMOST THERE...*DEVICE ATTACHED*... HANG ON...
B-DEEP

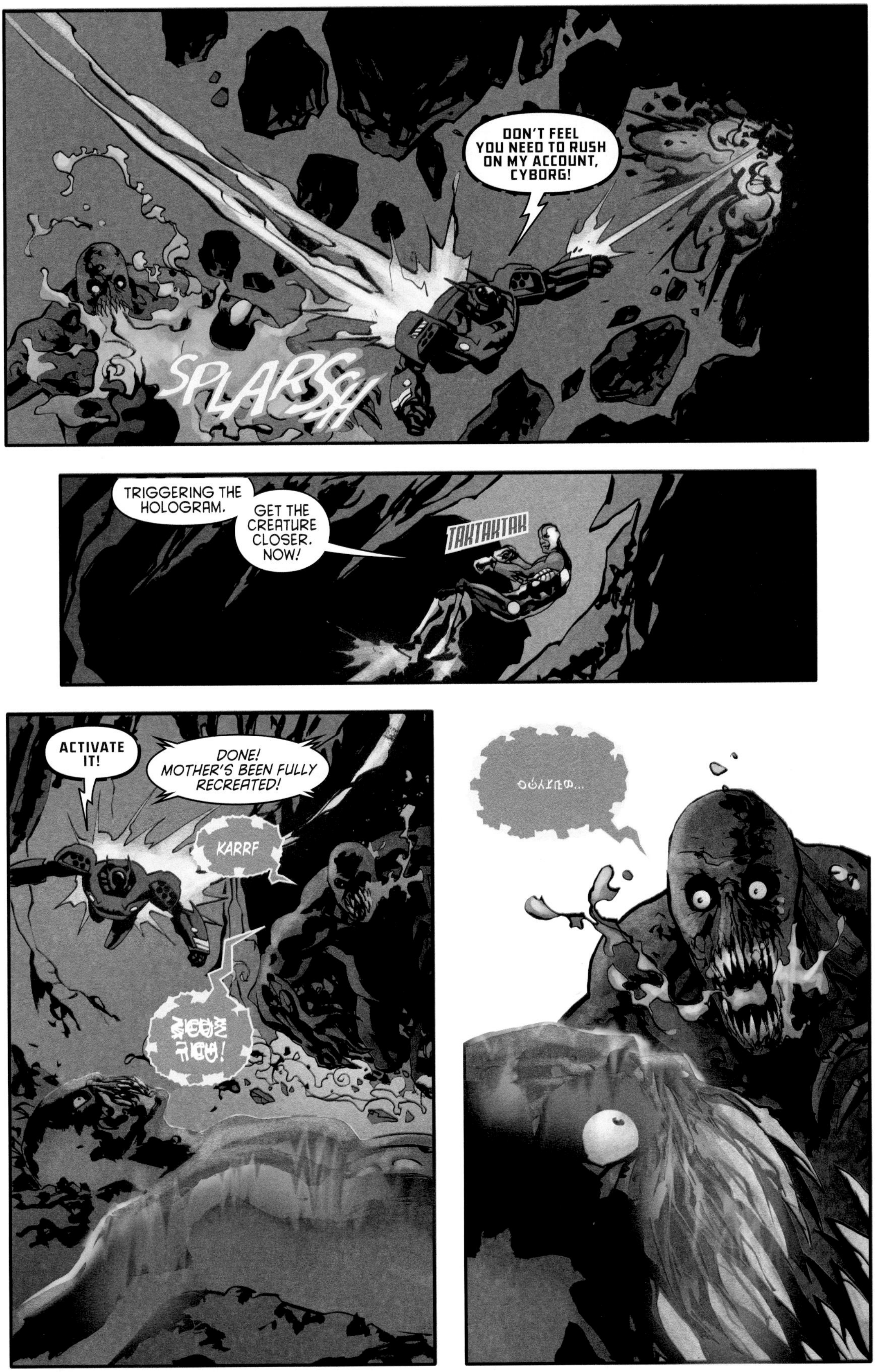
DON'T FEEL YOU NEED TO RUSH ON MY ACCOUNT, CYBORG!
SPLARSSH
TRIGGERING THE HOLOGRAM.
GET THE CREATURE CLOSER. NOW!
TAKTAKTAK
ACTIVATE IT!
DONE! MOTHER'S BEEN FULLY RECREATED!
KARRF

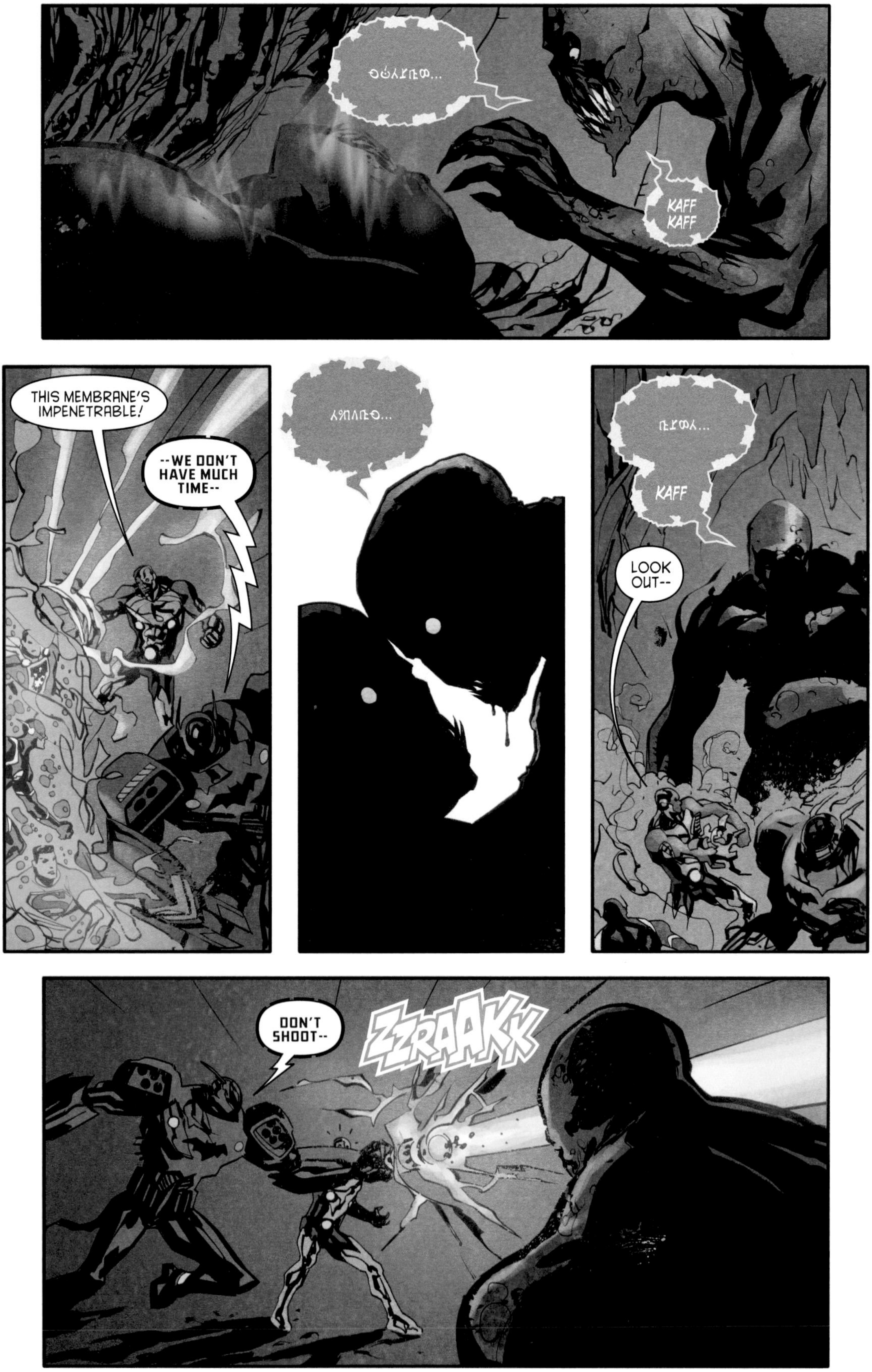
KAFF KAFF
THIS MEMBRANE'S IMPENETRABLE!
--WE DON'T HAVE MUCH TIME--
KAFF
LOOK OUT--
DON'T SHOOT--
ZZRAAKK

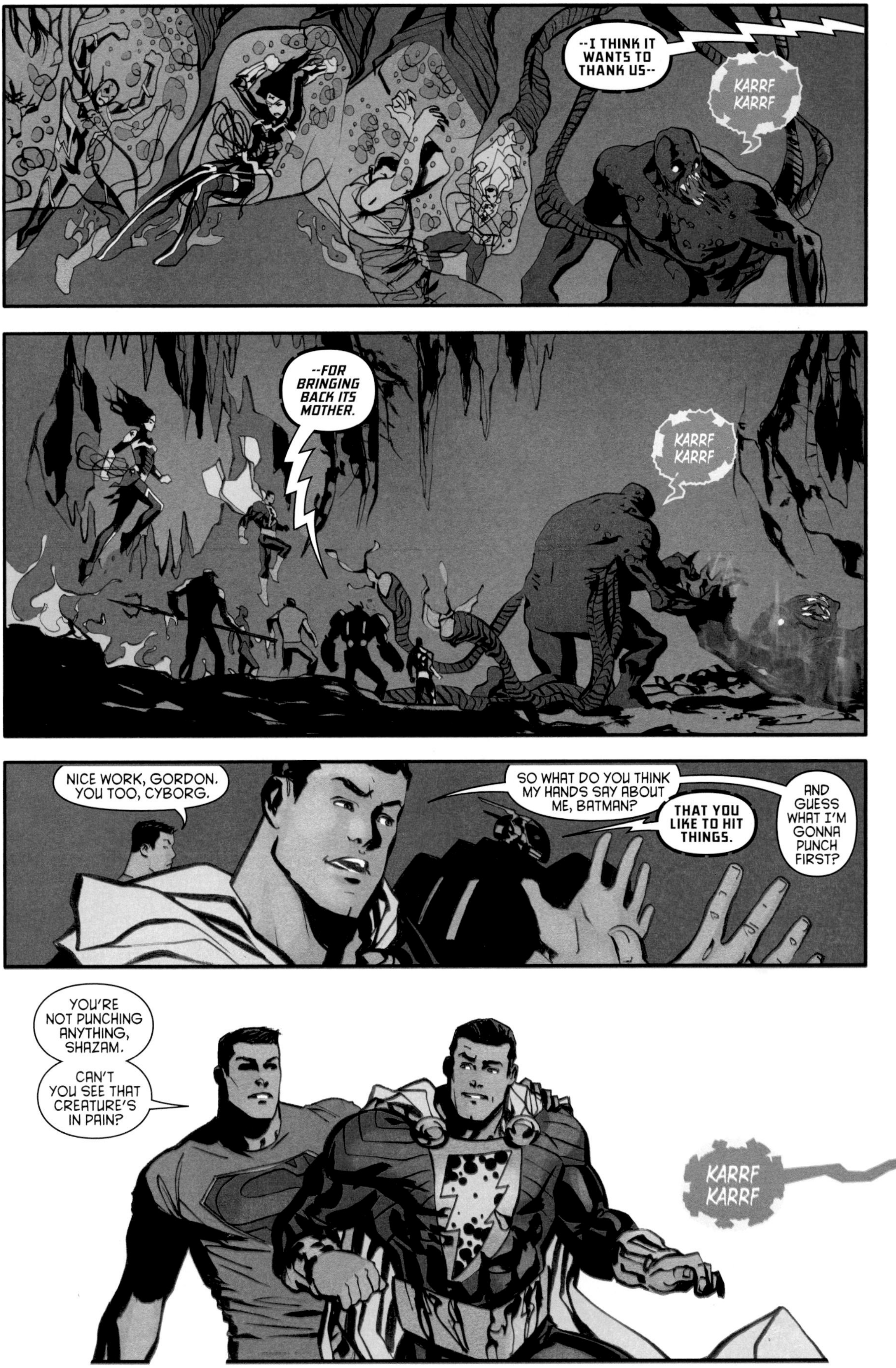
--I THINK IT WANTS TO THANK US--
KARRF KARRF
--FOR BRINGING BACK ITS MOTHER.
KARRF KARRF
NICE WORK, GORDON. YOU TOO, CYBORG.
SO WHAT DO YOU THINK MY HANDS SAY ABOUT ME, BATMAN?
THAT YOU LIKE TO HIT THINGS.
AND GUESS WHAT I'M GONNA PUNCH FIRST?
YOU'RE NOT PUNCHING ANYTHING, SHAZAM.
CAN'T YOU SEE THAT CREATURE'S IN PAIN?
KARRF KARRF

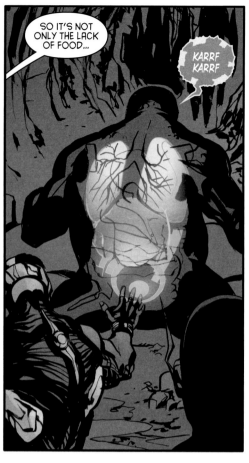

SO IT'S NOT ONLY THE LACK OF FOOD...

KARRF KARRF

...BUT THE EARTH'S OWN *ATMOSPHERE* THAT'S SLOWLY BEEN KILLING IT.

THAT'S WHY THE CREATURE'S STAYED CLOSE TO THE CAVE--IT DIDN'T HAVE THE ENERGY TO TRAVEL AND WANTED TO STAY BY HIS MOTHER'S SIDE.

HEADS UP, PEOPLE-- WE'VE GOT A *CODE BLACK* NEAR EL SALVADOR.

SEVEN POINT FIVE ON THE RICHTER.

AFTER EVERYTHING THAT'S HAPPENED, WE CAN'T JUST LEAVE THIS CREATURE ALONE IN ITS DEATH THROES.

I'LL STAY. YOU DEAL WITH THE EARTHQUAKE.

HOW LONG WILL THE 3-D RENDERING LAST, CYBORG?

'TIL THE END. WHICH, BASED ON THOSE LUNG SCANS, SHOULDN'T BE LONG.

KARRF KARRF

WE'LL CONTACT COLONEL TREVOR OF A.R.G.U.S. HE'LL SEND A SPECIAL SQUAD TO...*ASSIST* WITH THE BONES AND...THE CHILD.

LEAGUE TELEPORTATION ACTIVATED.

THANKS FOR SAVING OUR ASSES, GORDON.

I'D SAY YOU JUST TOOK YOUR FIRST STEP TOWARDS *EPIC.*

VVVMMMMMMMMMMMMMM

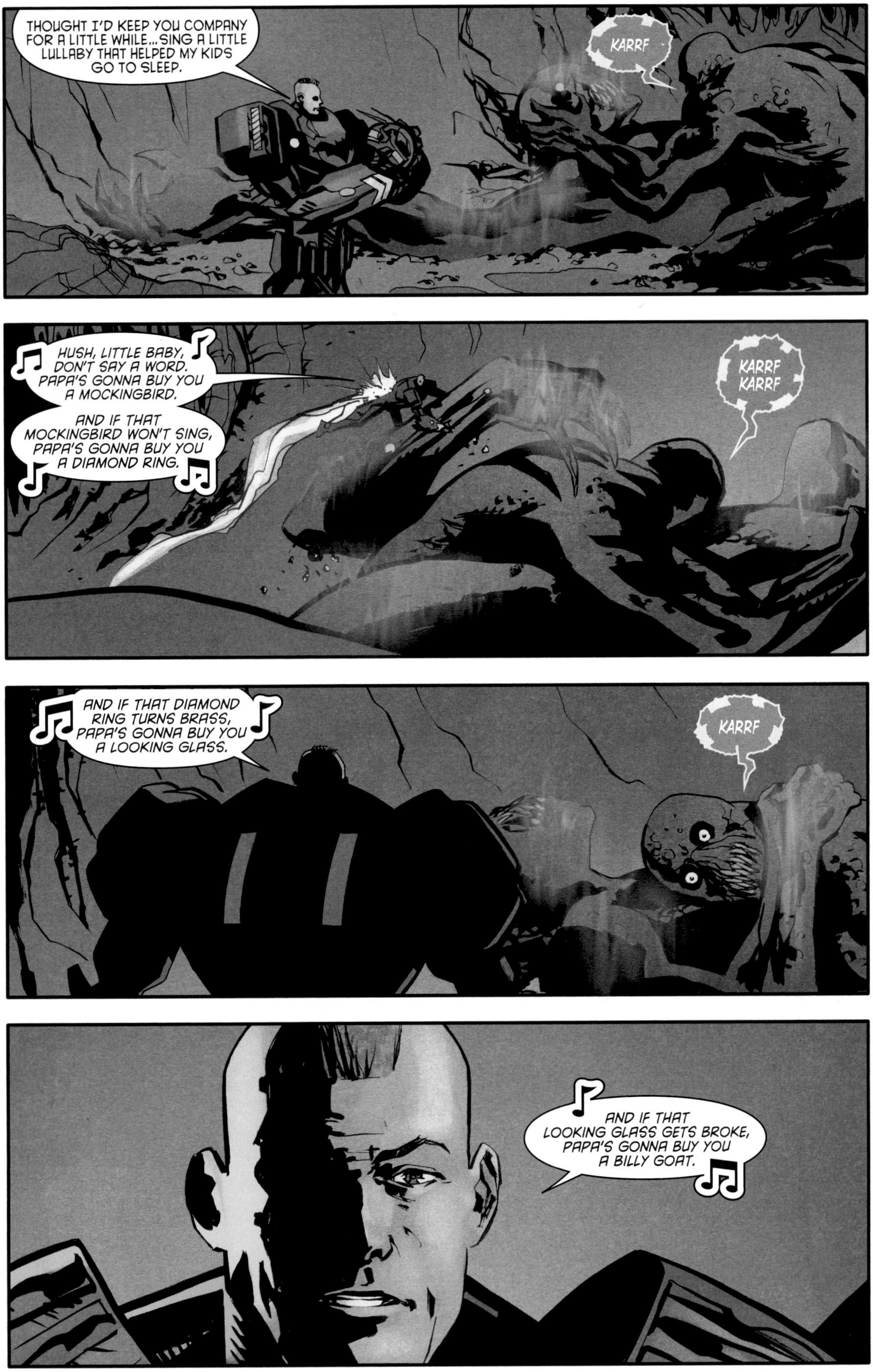
THOUGHT I'D KEEP YOU COMPANY FOR A LITTLE WHILE... SING A LITTLE LULLABY THAT HELPED MY KIDS GO TO SLEEP.
KARRF
HUSH, LITTLE BABY, DON'T SAY A WORD. PAPA'S GONNA BUY YOU A MOCKINGBIRD.
AND IF THAT MOCKINGBIRD WON'T SING, PAPA'S GONNA BUY YOU A DIAMOND RING.
KARRF KARRF
AND IF THAT DIAMOND RING TURNS BRASS, PAPA'S GONNA BUY YOU A LOOKING GLASS.
KARRF
AND IF THAT LOOKING GLASS GETS BROKE, PAPA'S GONNA BUY YOU A BILLY GOAT.

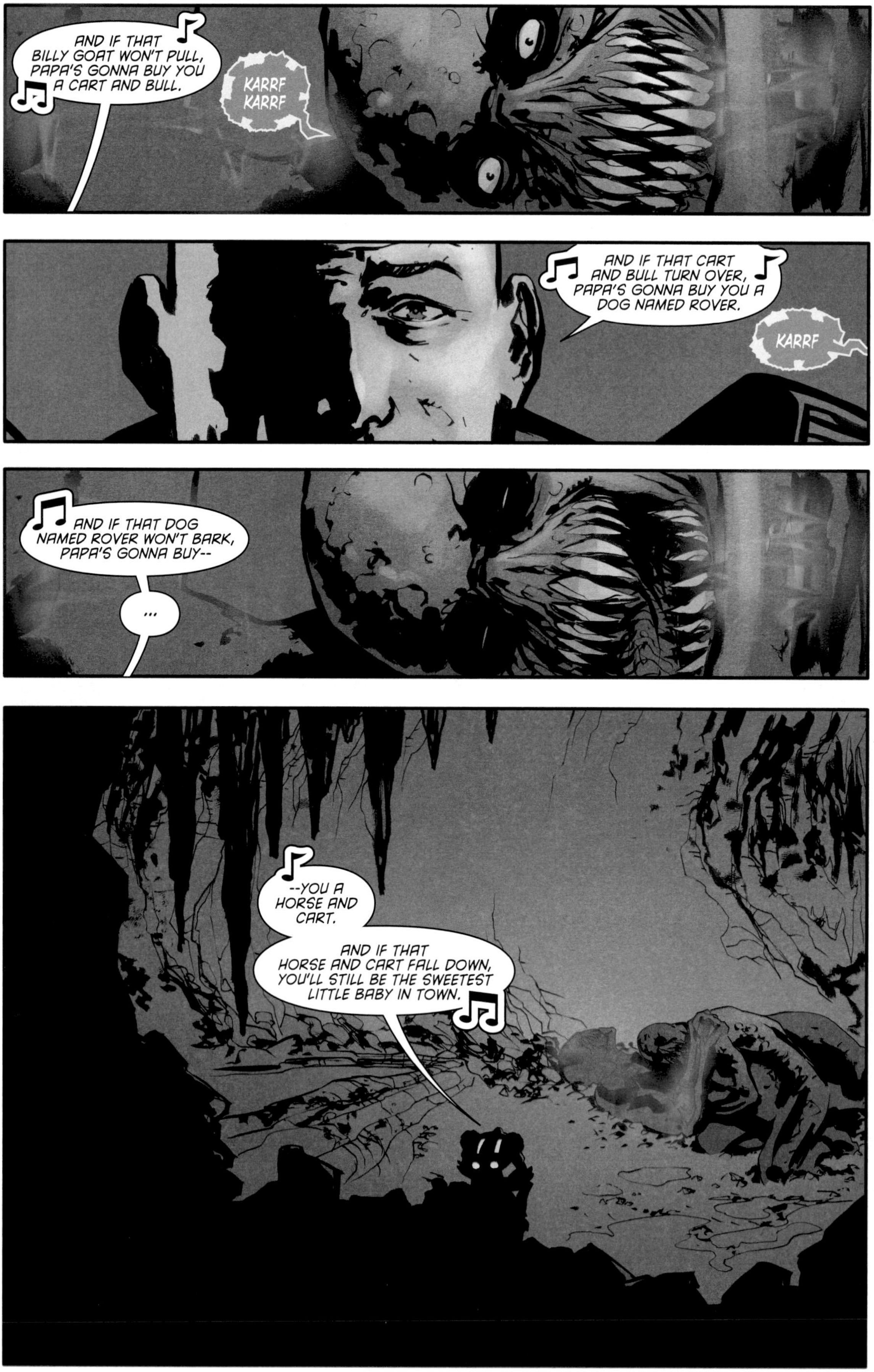
AND IF THAT BILLY GOAT WON'T PULL, PAPA'S GONNA BUY YOU A CART AND BULL.
KARRF KARRF
AND IF THAT CART AND BULL TURN OVER, PAPA'S GONNA BUY YOU A DOG NAMED ROVER.
KARRF
AND IF THAT DOG NAMED ROVER WON'T BARK, PAPA'S GONNA BUY--
...
--YOU A HORSE AND CART.
AND IF THAT HORSE AND CART FALL DOWN, YOU'LL STILL BE THE SWEETEST LITTLE BABY IN TOWN.

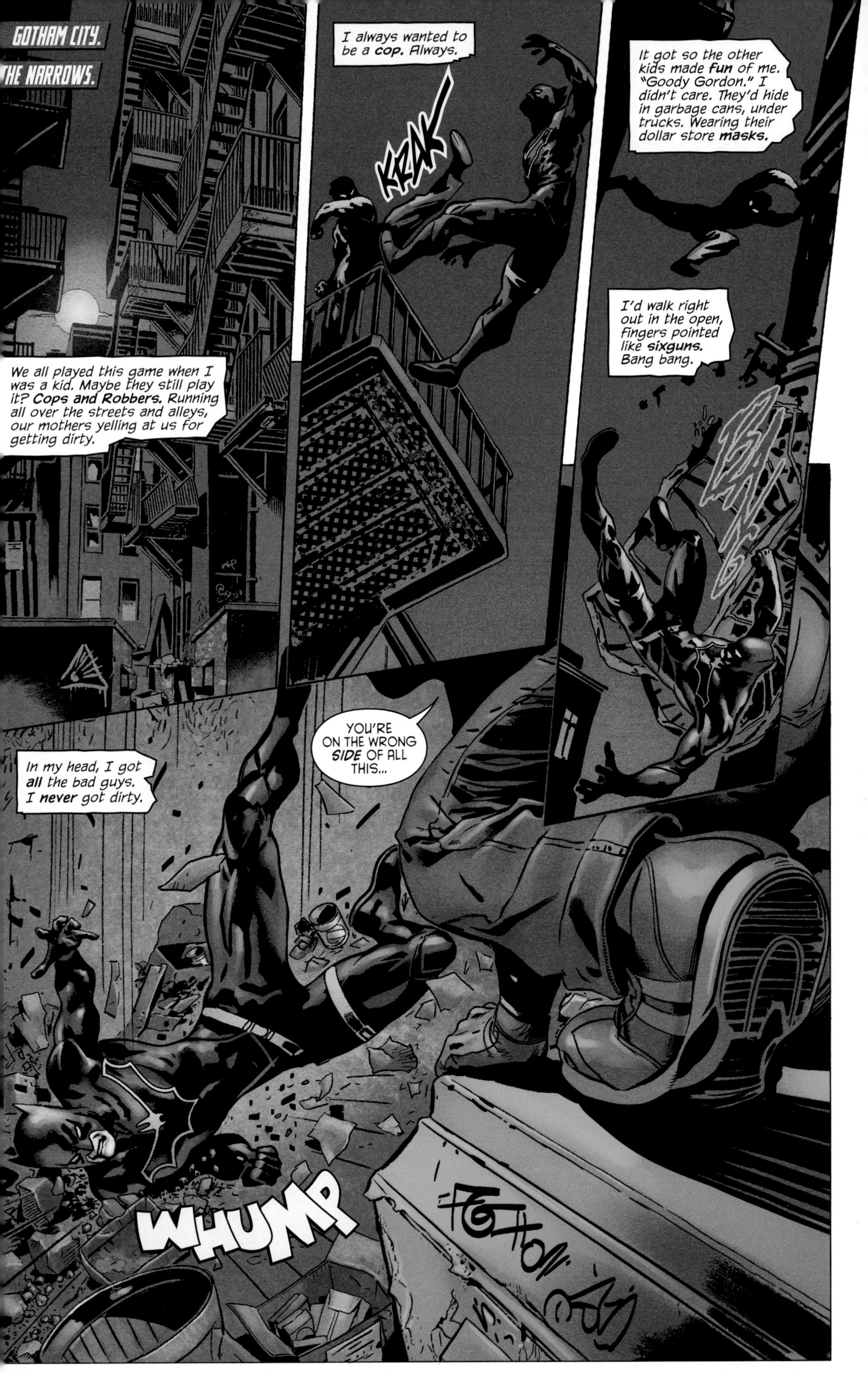
GOTHAM CITY.
THE NARROWS.
We all played this game when I was a kid. Maybe they still play it? Cops and Robbers. Running all over the streets and alleys, our mothers yelling at us for getting dirty.
I always wanted to be a cop. Always.
KRAK
It got so the other kids made fun of me. "Goody Gordon." I didn't care. They'd hide in garbage cans, under trucks. Wearing their dollar store masks.
I'd walk right out in the open, fingers pointed like sixguns. Bang bang.
In my head, I got all the bad guys. I never got dirty.
YOU'RE ON THE WRONG SIDE OF ALL THIS...
WHUMP

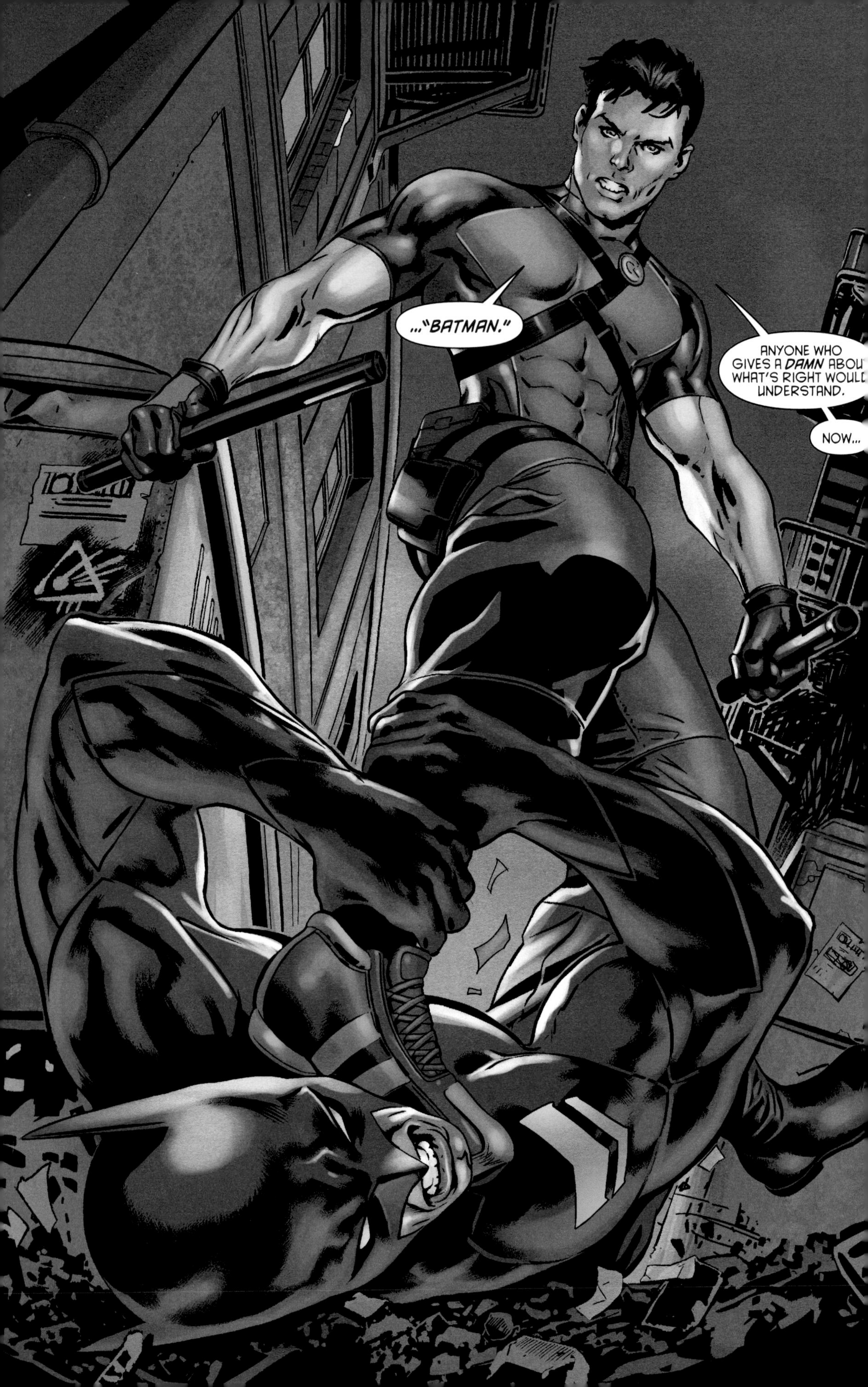
..."BATMAN."
ANYONE WHO GIVES A *DAMN* ABOUT WHAT'S RIGHT WOULD UNDERSTAND.
NOW...

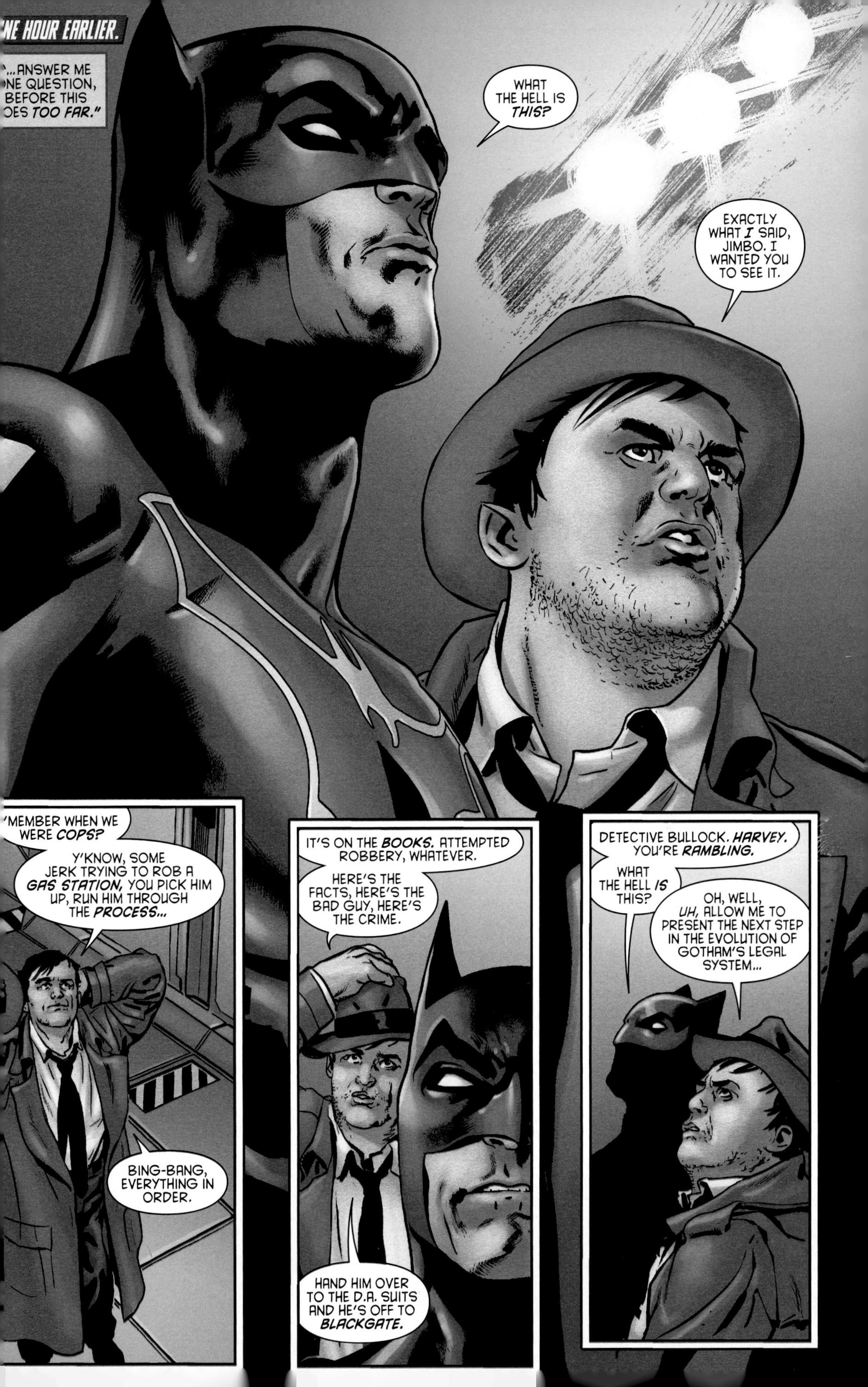
NE HOUR EARLIER.
"...ANSWER ME
NE QUESTION,
BEFORE THIS
OES TOO FAR."
WHAT THE HELL IS THIS?
EXACTLY WHAT I SAID, JIMBO. I WANTED YOU TO SEE IT.
'MEMBER WHEN WE WERE COPS?
Y'KNOW, SOME JERK TRYING TO ROB A GAS STATION, YOU PICK HIM UP, RUN HIM THROUGH THE PROCESS...
BING-BANG, EVERYTHING IN ORDER.
IT'S ON THE BOOKS. ATTEMPTED ROBBERY, WHATEVER.
HERE'S THE FACTS, HERE'S THE BAD GUY, HERE'S THE CRIME.
HAND HIM OVER TO THE D.A. SUITS AND HE'S OFF TO BLACKGATE.
DETECTIVE BULLOCK. HARVEY. YOU'RE RAMBLING.
WHAT THE HELL IS THIS?
OH, WELL, UH, ALLOW ME TO PRESENT THE NEXT STEP IN THE EVOLUTION OF GOTHAM'S LEGAL SYSTEM...

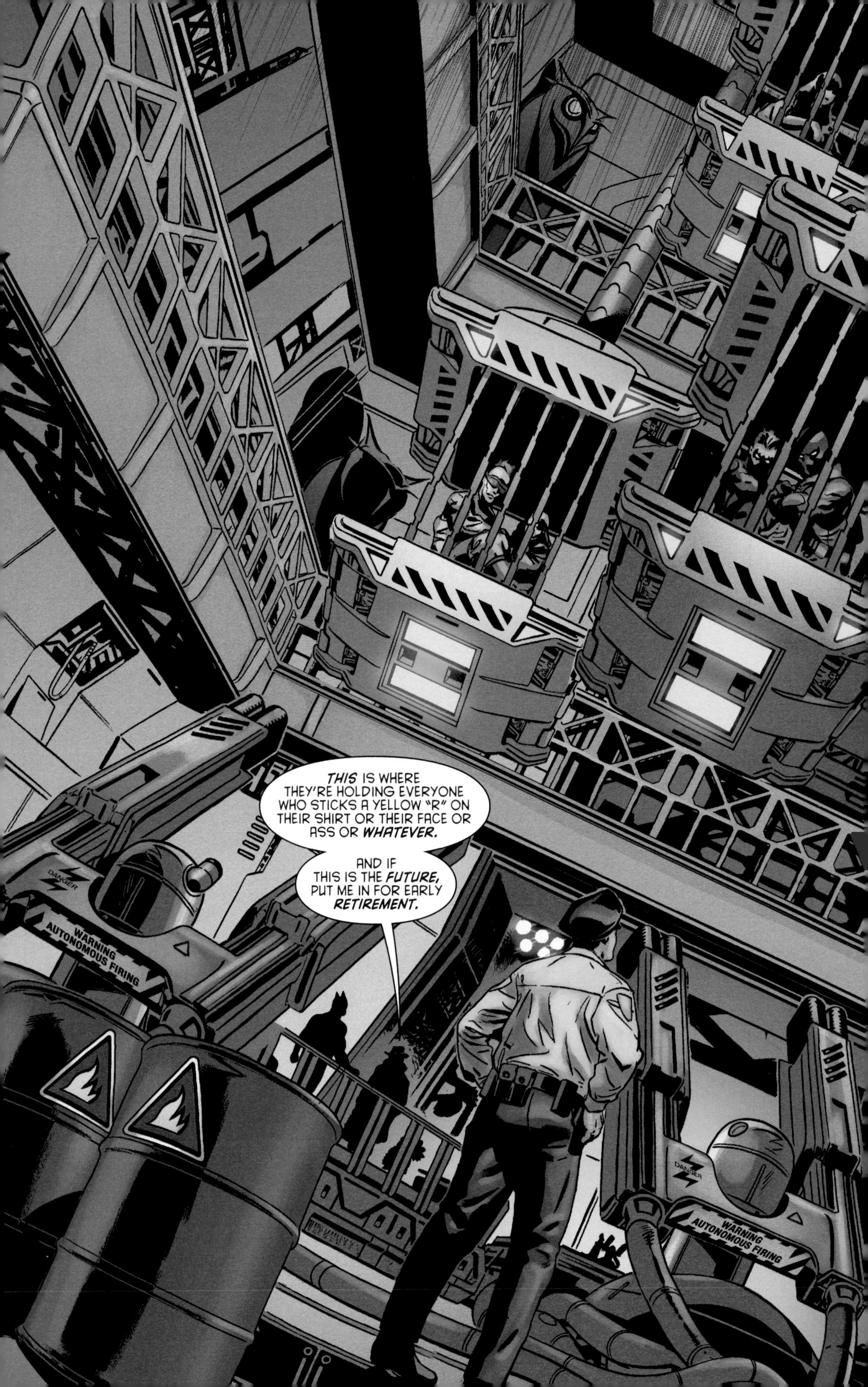
THIS IS WHERE THEY'RE HOLDING EVERYONE WHO STICKS A YELLOW "R" ON THEIR SHIRT OR THEIR FACE OR ASS OR WHATEVER.
AND IF THIS IS THE FUTURE, PUT ME IN FOR EARLY RETIREMENT.
DANGER
WARNING AUTONOMOUS FIRING
DANGER
WARNING AUTONOMOUS FIRING

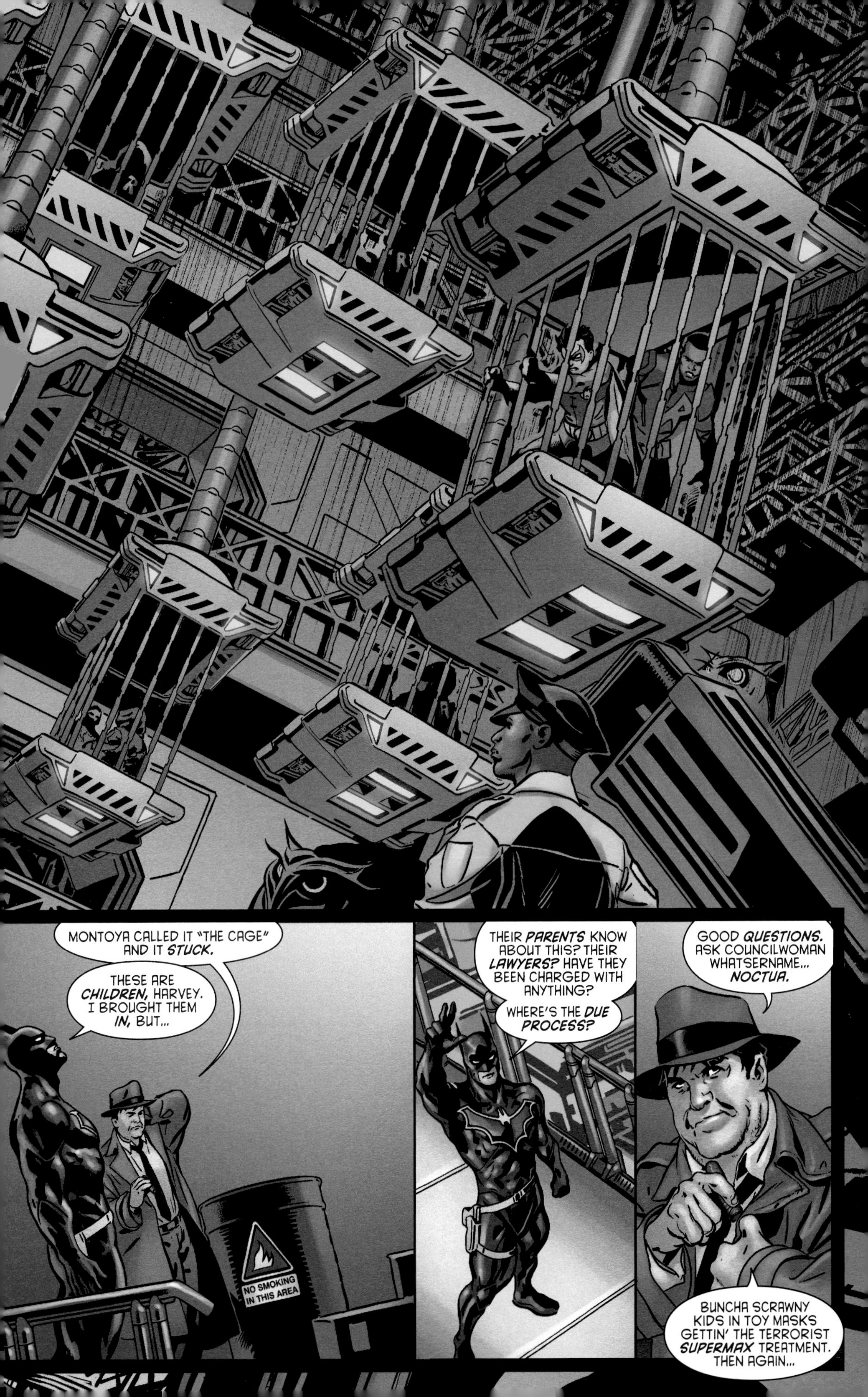
MONTOYA CALLED IT "THE CAGE" AND IT STUCK.
THESE ARE CHILDREN, HARVEY. I BROUGHT THEM IN, BUT...
NO SMOKING IN THIS AREA
THEIR PARENTS KNOW ABOUT THIS? THEIR LAWYERS? HAVE THEY BEEN CHARGED WITH ANYTHING?
WHERE'S THE DUE PROCESS?
GOOD QUESTIONS. ASK COUNCILWOMAN WHATSERNAME... NOCTUA.
BUNCHA SCRAWNY KIDS IN TOY MASKS GETTIN' THE TERRORIST SUPERMAX TREATMENT. THEN AGAIN...

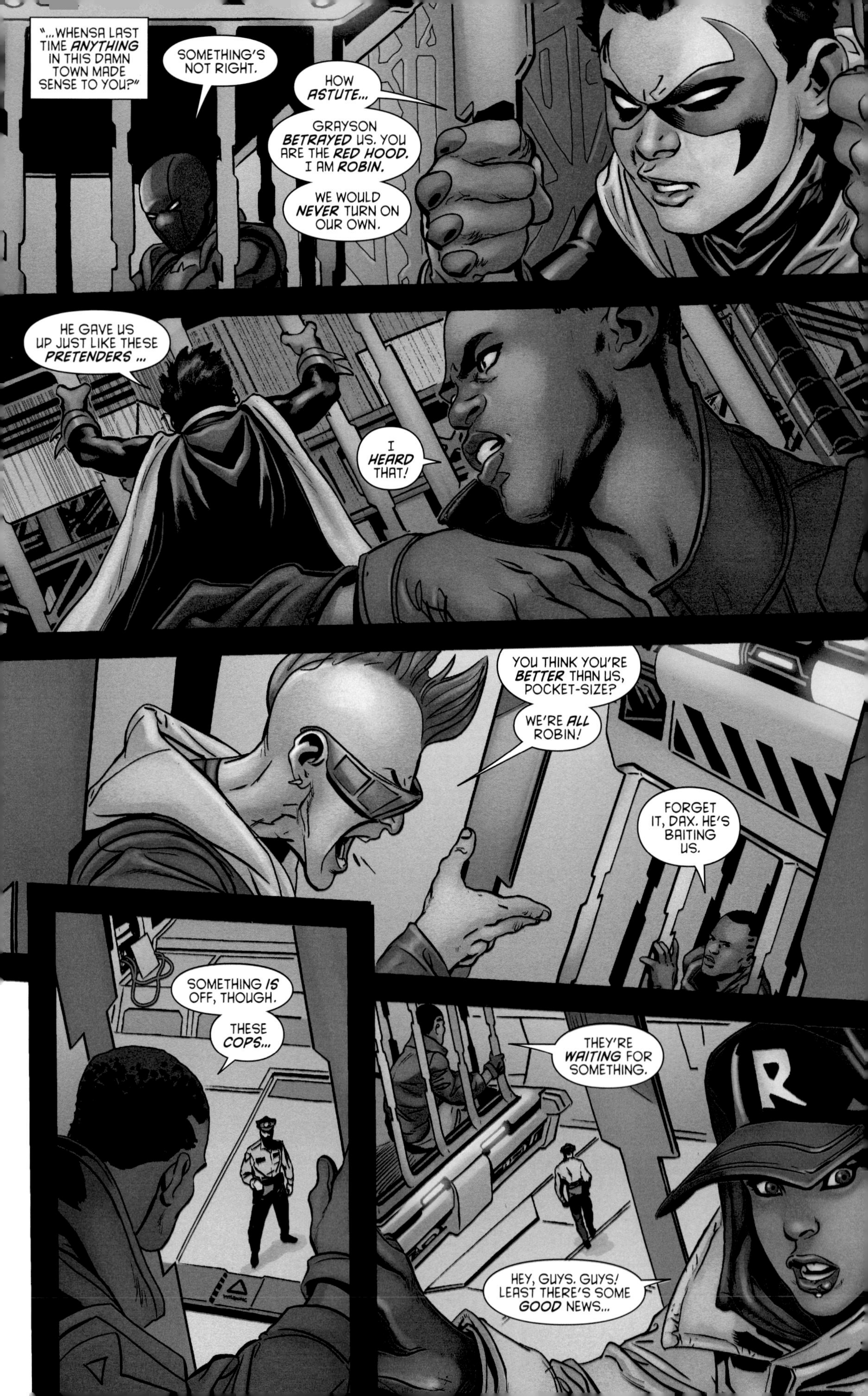
"...WHENSA LAST TIME ANYTHING IN THIS DAMN TOWN MADE SENSE TO YOU?"
SOMETHING'S NOT RIGHT.
HOW ASTUTE...
GRAYSON BETRAYED US. YOU ARE THE RED HOOD. I AM ROBIN.
WE WOULD NEVER TURN ON OUR OWN.
HE GAVE US UP JUST LIKE THESE PRETENDERS ...
I HEARD THAT!
YOU THINK YOU'RE BETTER THAN US, POCKET-SIZE?
WE'RE ALL ROBIN!
FORGET IT, DAX. HE'S BAITING US.
SOMETHING IS OFF, THOUGH.
THESE COPS...
THEY'RE WAITING FOR SOMETHING.
HEY, GUYS. GUYS! LEAST THERE'S SOME GOOD NEWS...

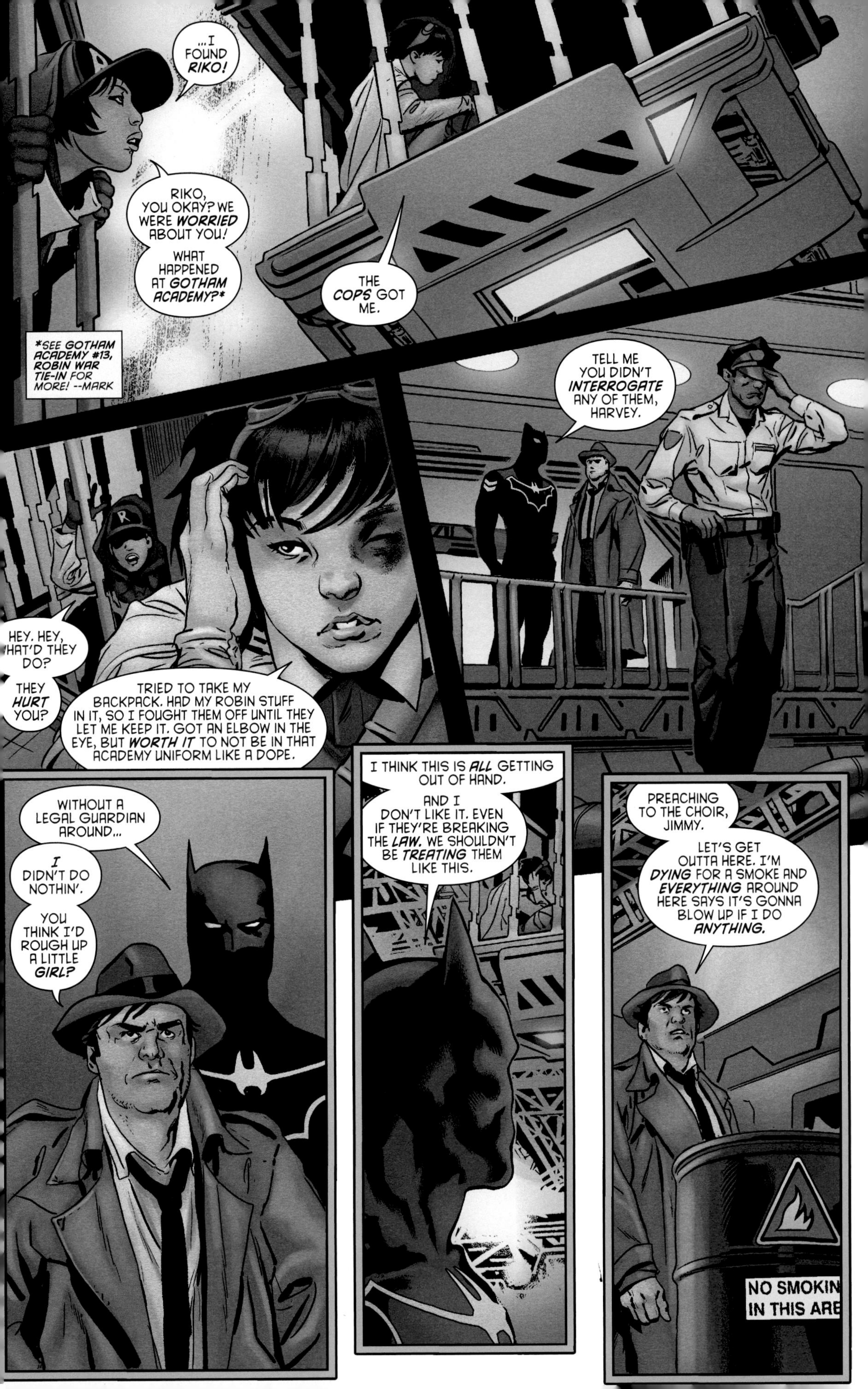

...I FOUND RIKO!
RIKO, YOU OKAY? WE WERE WORRIED ABOUT YOU!
WHAT HAPPENED AT GOTHAM ACADEMY?*
*SEE GOTHAM ACADEMY #13, ROBIN WAR TIE-IN FOR MORE! --MARK
THE COPS GOT ME.
HEY. HEY, WHAT'D THEY DO?
THEY HURT YOU?
TRIED TO TAKE MY BACKPACK. HAD MY ROBIN STUFF IN IT, SO I FOUGHT THEM OFF UNTIL THEY LET ME KEEP IT. GOT AN ELBOW IN THE EYE, BUT WORTH IT TO NOT BE IN THAT ACADEMY UNIFORM LIKE A DOPE.
TELL ME YOU DIDN'T INTERROGATE ANY OF THEM, HARVEY.
WITHOUT A LEGAL GUARDIAN AROUND...
I DIDN'T DO NOTHIN'.
YOU THINK I'D ROUGH UP A LITTLE GIRL?
I THINK THIS IS ALL GETTING OUT OF HAND.
AND I DON'T LIKE IT. EVEN IF THEY'RE BREAKING THE LAW. WE SHOULDN'T BE TREATING THEM LIKE THIS.
PREACHING TO THE CHOIR, JIMMY.
LET'S GET OUTTA HERE. I'M DYING FOR A SMOKE AND EVERYTHING AROUND HERE SAYS IT'S GONNA BLOW UP IF I DO ANYTHING.
NO SMOKIN
IN THIS ARE

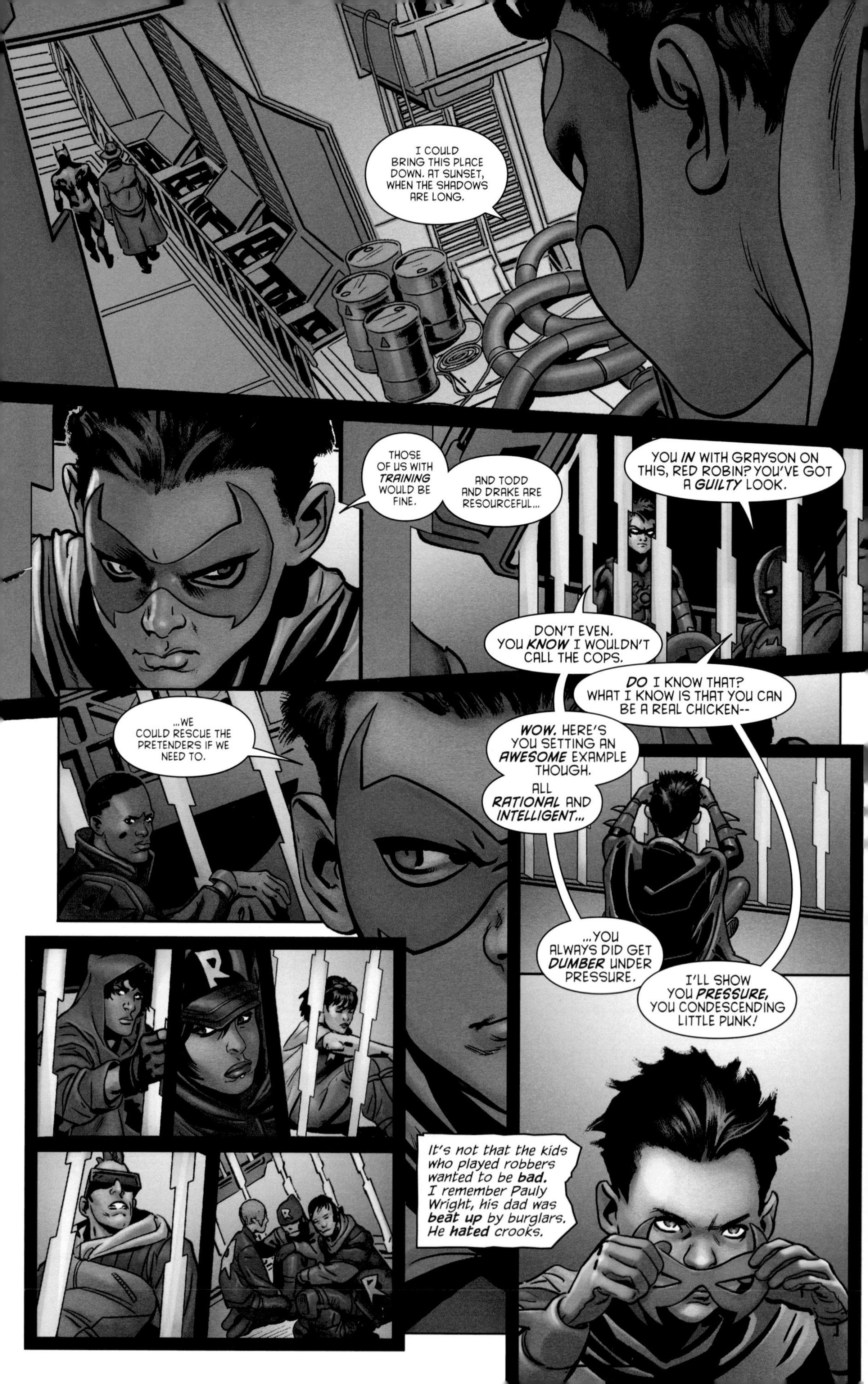
I COULD BRING THIS PLACE DOWN. AT SUNSET, WHEN THE SHADOWS ARE LONG.
THOSE OF US WITH *TRAINING* WOULD BE FINE.
AND TODD AND DRAKE ARE RESOURCEFUL...
YOU *IN* WITH GRAYSON ON THIS, RED ROBIN? YOU'VE GOT A *GUILTY* LOOK.
DON'T EVEN. YOU *KNOW* I WOULDN'T CALL THE COPS.
DO I KNOW THAT? WHAT I KNOW IS THAT YOU CAN BE A REAL CHICKEN--
...WE COULD RESCUE THE PRETENDERS IF WE NEED TO.
WOW. HERE'S YOU SETTING AN *AWESOME* EXAMPLE THOUGH.
ALL *RATIONAL* AND *INTELLIGENT*...
...YOU ALWAYS DID GET *DUMBER* UNDER PRESSURE.
I'LL SHOW YOU *PRESSURE,* YOU CONDESCENDING LITTLE PUNK!
*It's not that the kids who played robbers wanted to be **bad.** I remember Pauly Wright, his dad was **beat up** by burglars. He **hated** crooks.*

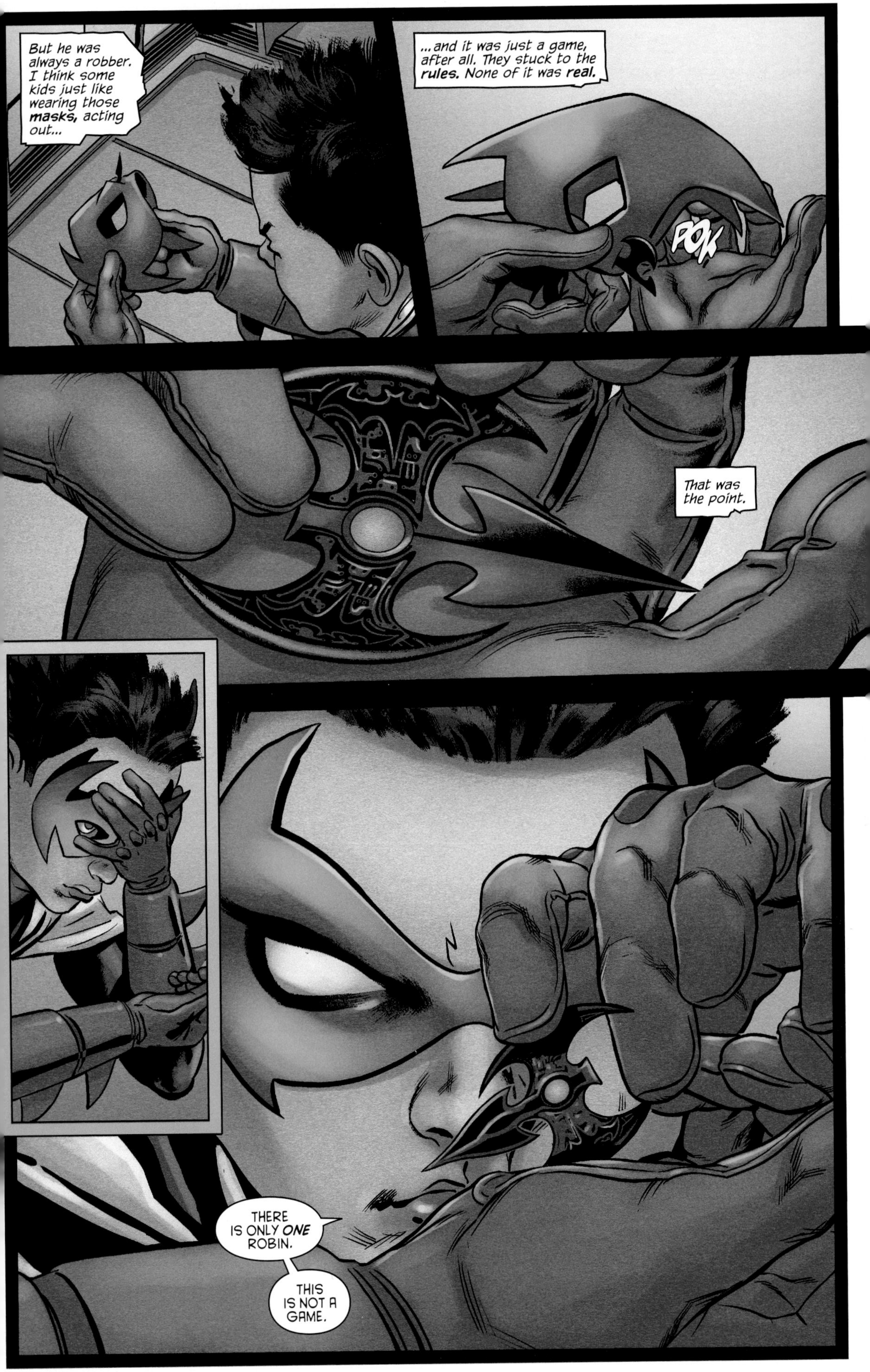
But he was always a robber. I think some kids just like wearing those **masks,** acting out...
...and it was just a game, after all. They stuck to the **rules.** None of it was **real.**
POK
That was the point.
THERE IS ONLY ***ONE*** ROBIN.
THIS IS NOT A GAME.

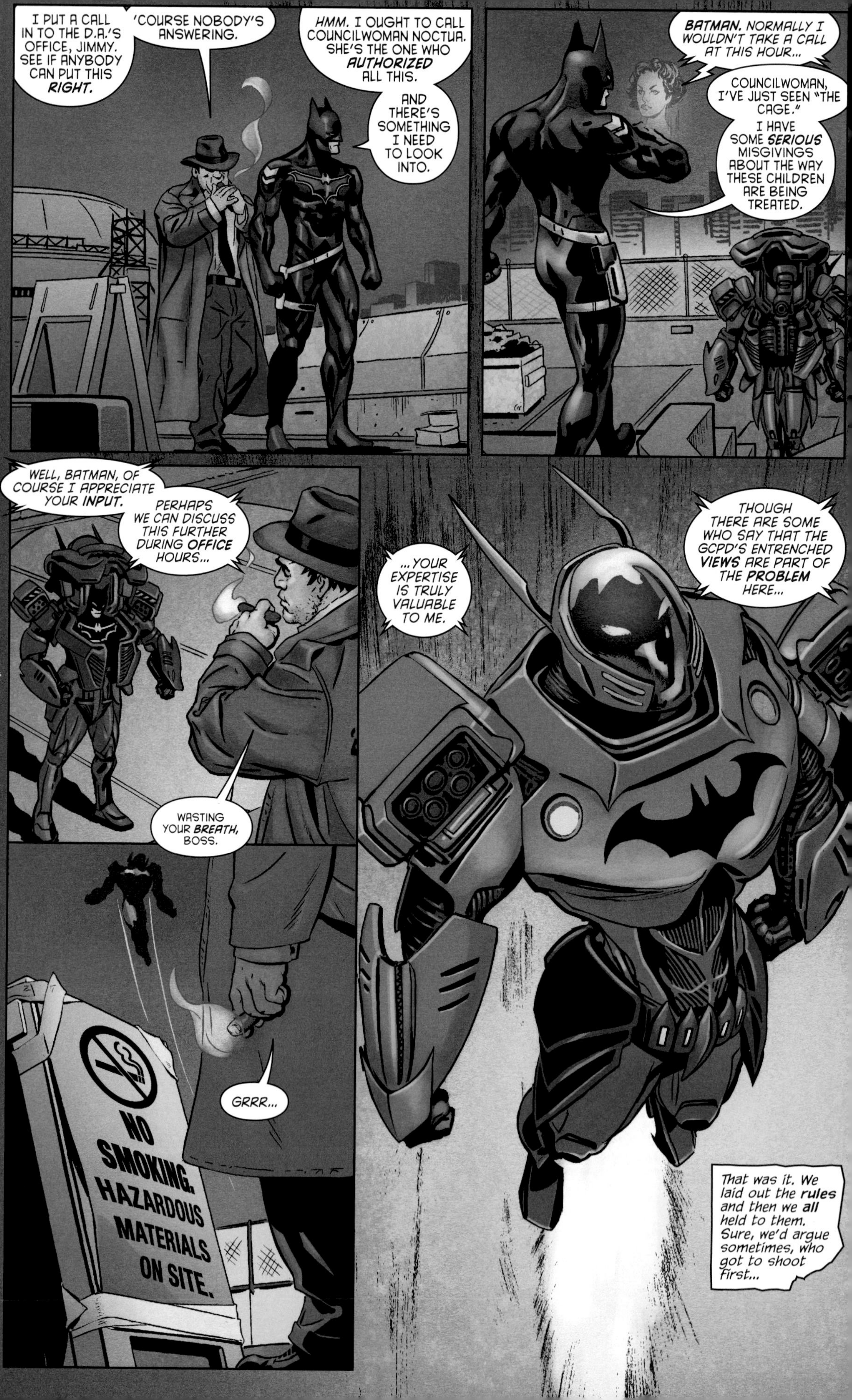
I PUT A CALL IN TO THE D.A.'S OFFICE, JIMMY. SEE IF ANYBODY CAN PUT THIS **RIGHT.**
'COURSE NOBODY'S ANSWERING.
HMM. I OUGHT TO CALL COUNCILWOMAN NOCTUA. SHE'S THE ONE WHO ***AUTHORIZED*** ALL THIS.
AND THERE'S SOMETHING I NEED TO LOOK INTO.
BATMAN. *NORMALLY I WOULDN'T TAKE A CALL AT THIS HOUR...*
COUNCILWOMAN, I'VE JUST SEEN "THE CAGE."
I HAVE SOME ***SERIOUS*** MISGIVINGS ABOUT THE WAY THESE CHILDREN ARE BEING TREATED.
WELL, BATMAN, OF COURSE I APPRECIATE YOUR ***INPUT.***
PERHAPS WE CAN DISCUSS THIS FURTHER DURING ***OFFICE*** *HOURS...*
WASTING YOUR ***BREATH,*** BOSS.
GRRR...
NO SMOKING. HAZARDOUS MATERIALS ON SITE.
...YOUR EXPERTISE IS TRULY VALUABLE TO ME.
THOUGH THERE ARE SOME WHO SAY THAT THE GCPD'S ENTRENCHED ***VIEWS*** *ARE PART OF THE* ***PROBLEM*** *HERE...*
That was it. We laid out the ***rules*** *and then we* ***all*** *held to them. Sure, we'd argue sometimes, who got to shoot first...*

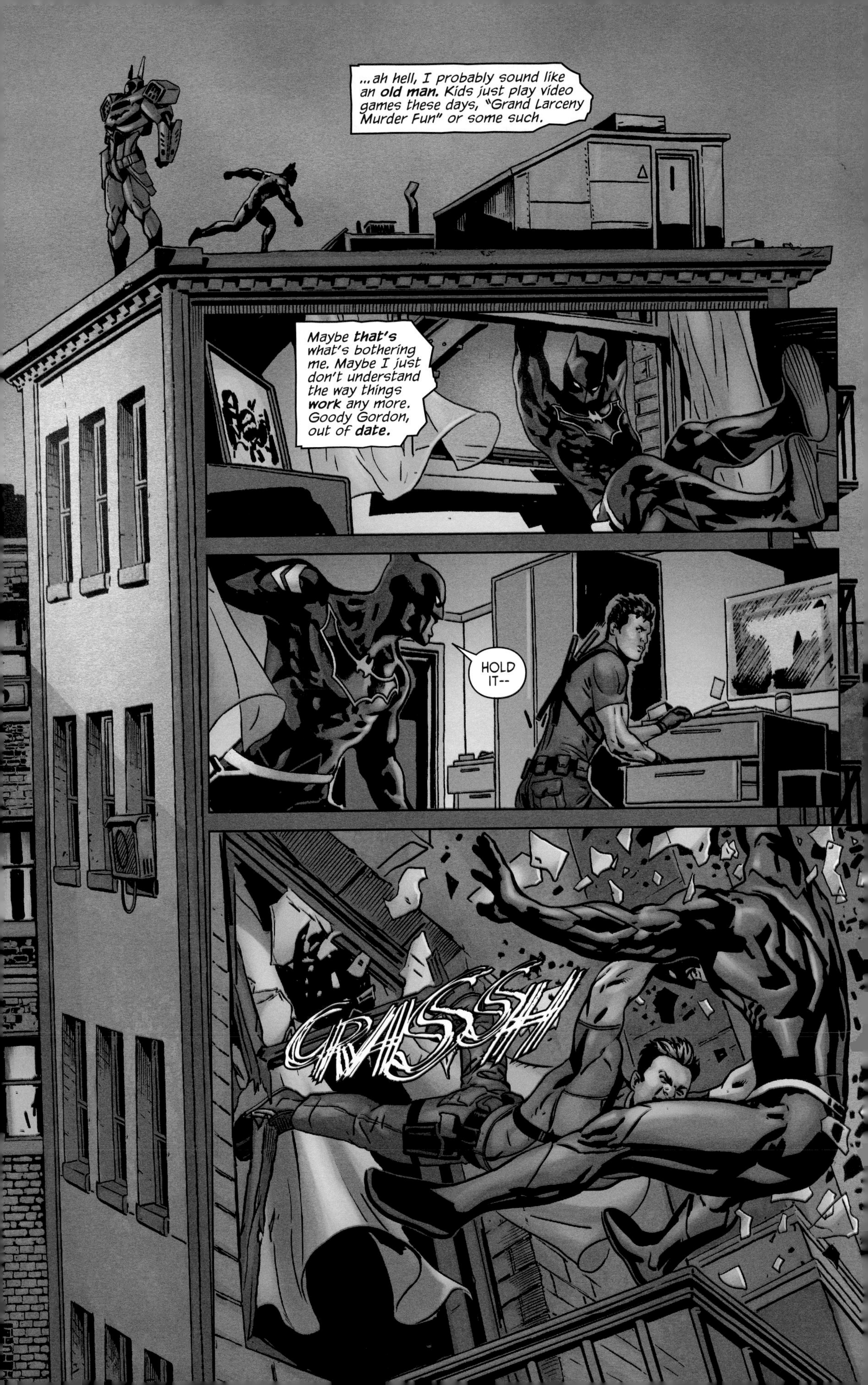
...ah hell, I probably sound like an old man. Kids just play video games these days, "Grand Larceny Murder Fun" or some such.
Maybe that's what's bothering me. Maybe I just don't understand the way things work any more. Goody Gordon, out of date.
HOLD IT--
CRASSSH

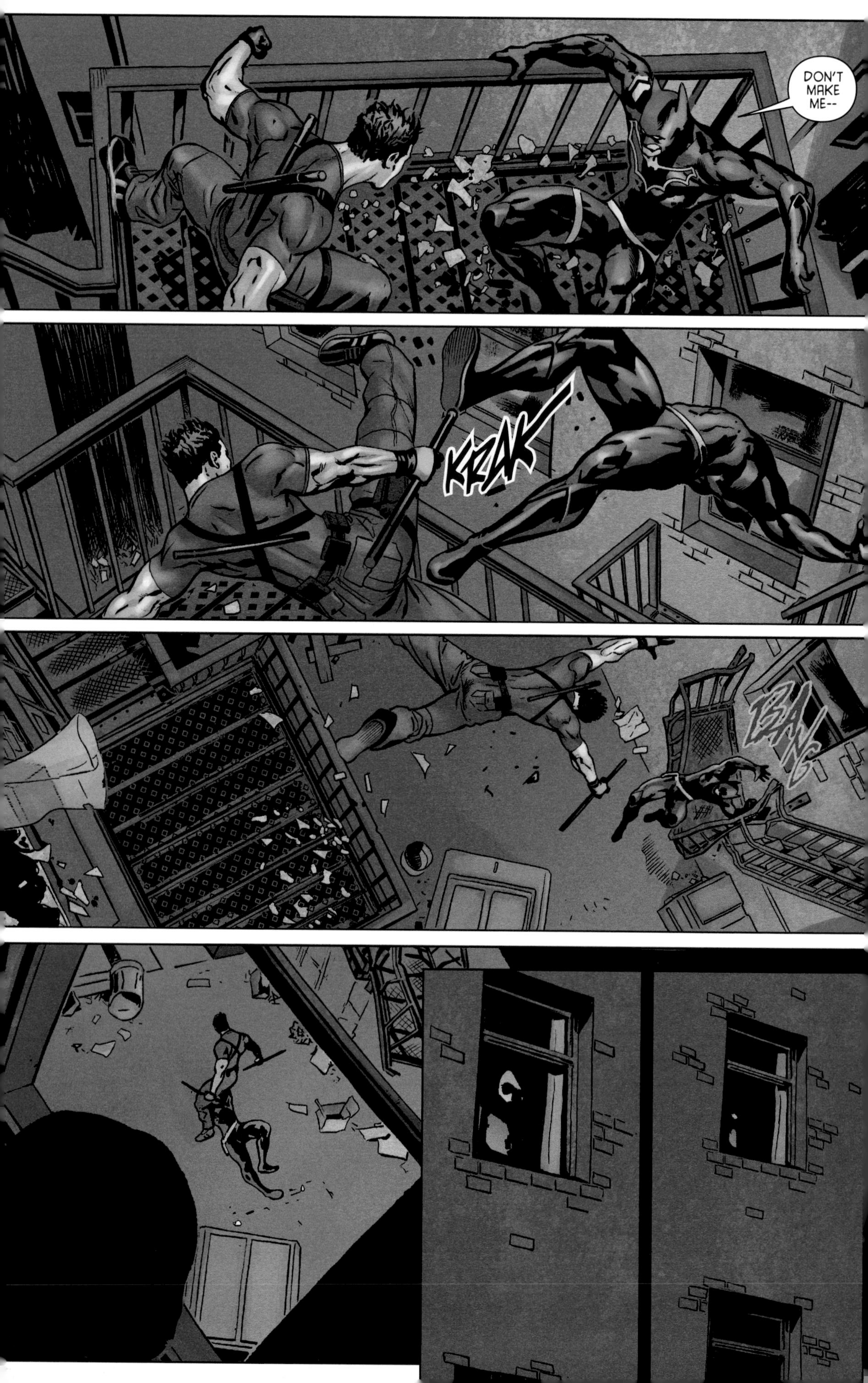
DON'T MAKE ME--
KRZAK
BANG

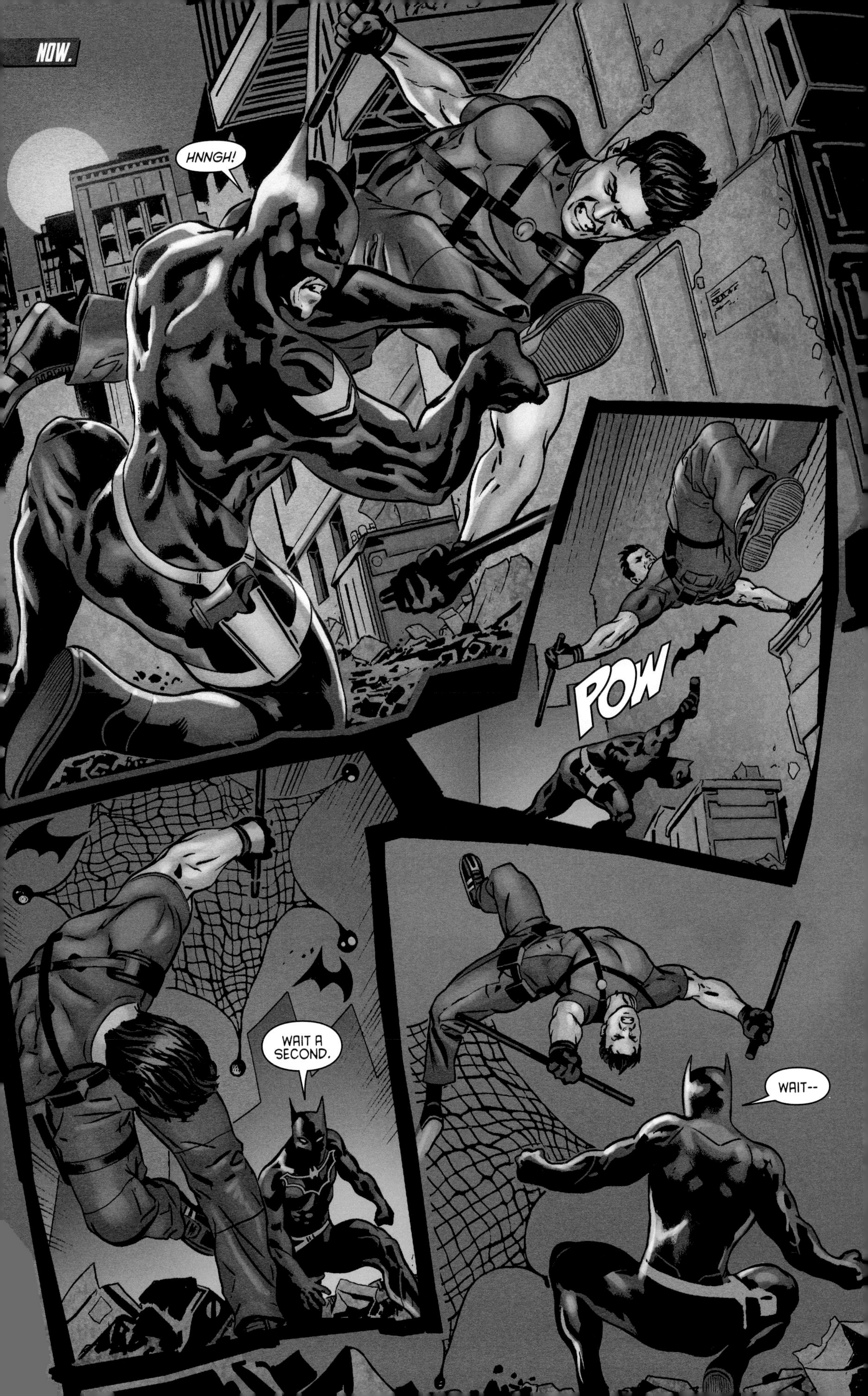
NOW.
HNNGH!
POW
WAIT A SECOND.
WAIT--

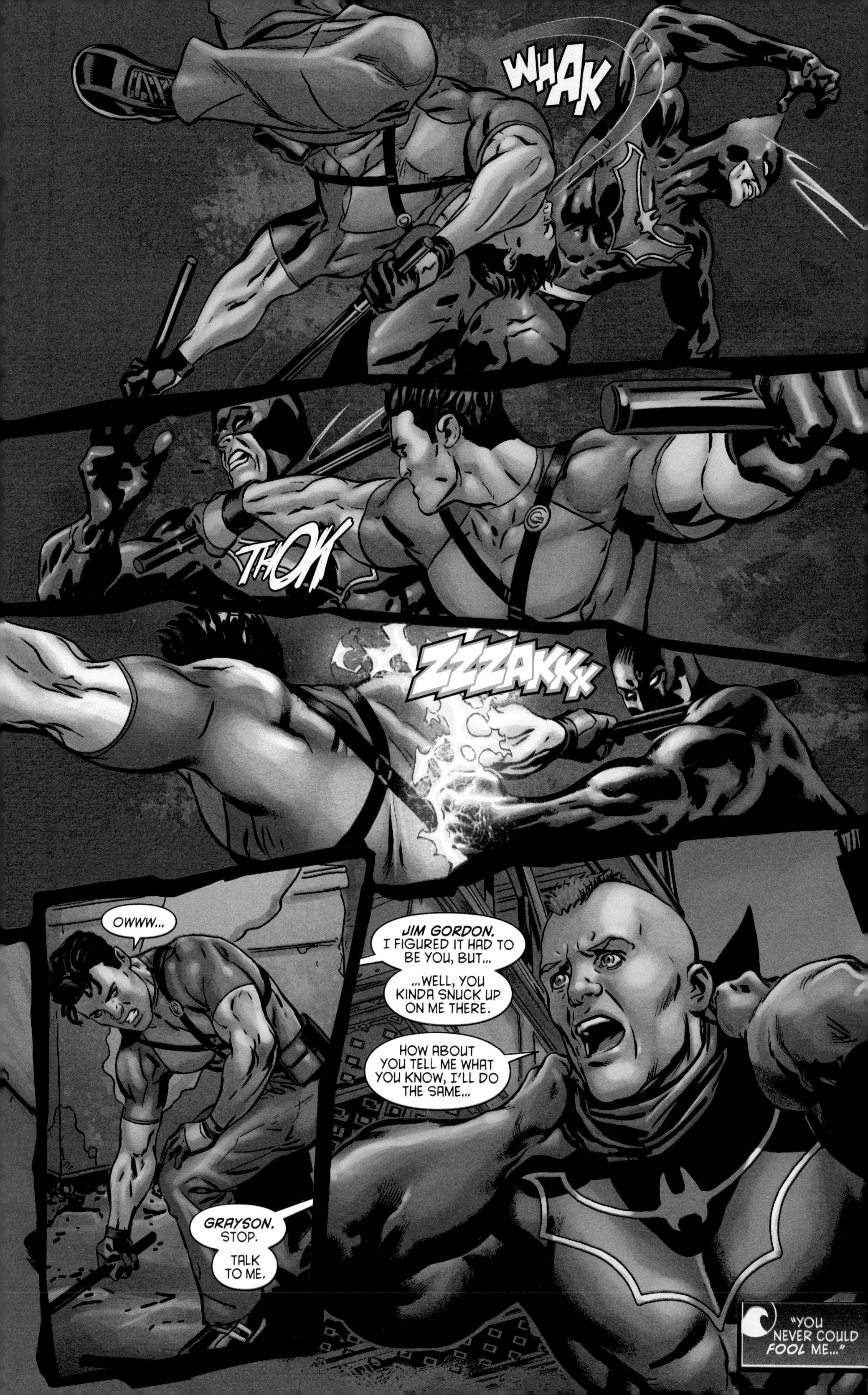

WHAK
THOK
ZZZAKKK
OWWW...
GRAYSON. STOP.
TALK TO ME.
JIM GORDON. I FIGURED IT HAD TO BE YOU, BUT...
...WELL, YOU KINDA SNUCK UP ON ME THERE.
HOW ABOUT YOU TELL ME WHAT YOU KNOW, I'LL DO THE SAME...
"YOU NEVER COULD FOOL ME..."

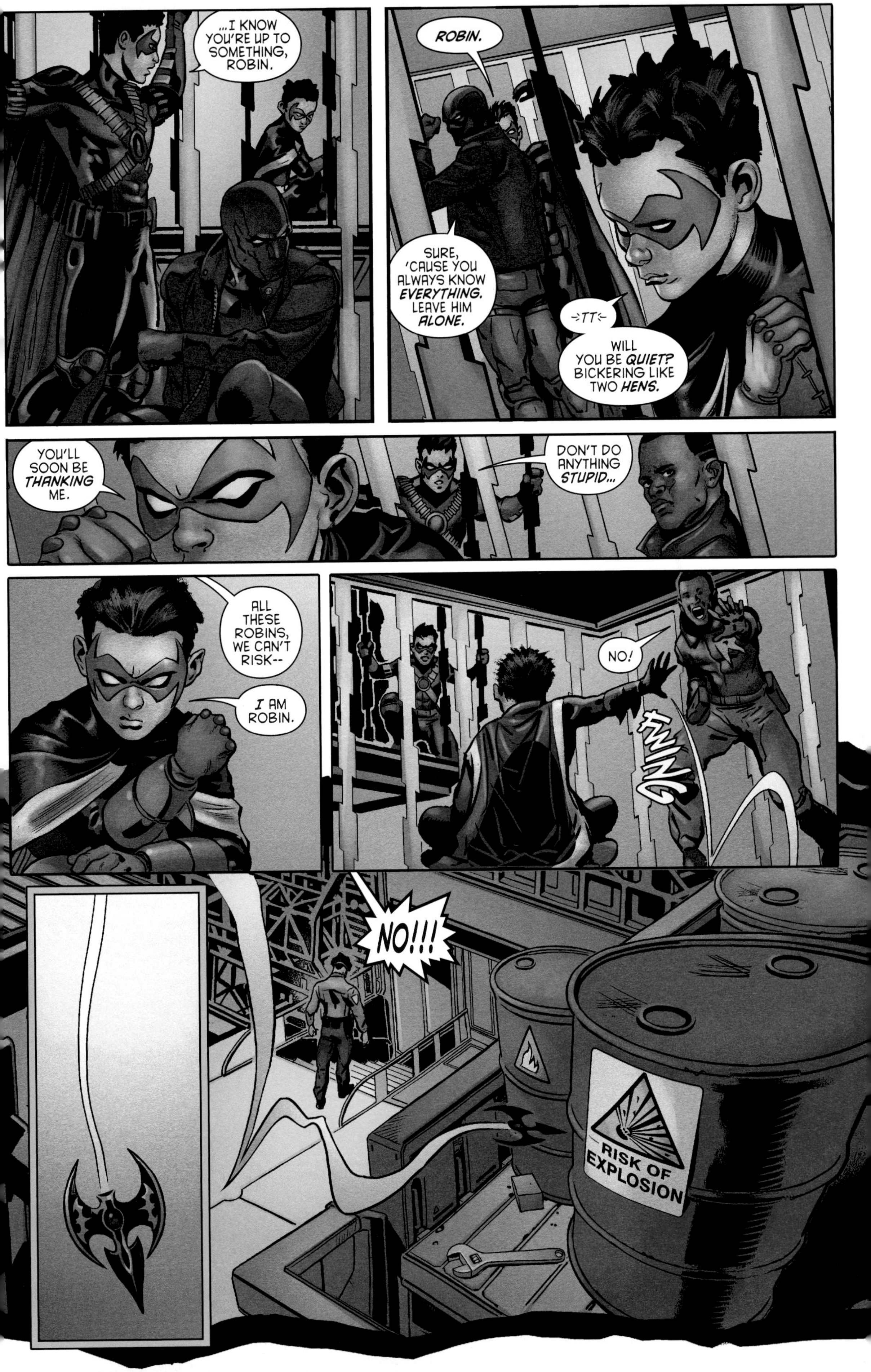
...I KNOW YOU'RE UP TO SOMETHING, ROBIN.
ROBIN.
SURE, 'CAUSE YOU ALWAYS KNOW EVERYTHING. LEAVE HIM ALONE.
TT
WILL YOU BE QUIET? BICKERING LIKE TWO HENS.
YOU'LL SOON BE THANKING ME.
DON'T DO ANYTHING STUPID...
ALL THESE ROBINS, WE CAN'T RISK--
I AM ROBIN.
NO!
FWING
NO!!!
RISK OF EXPLOSION

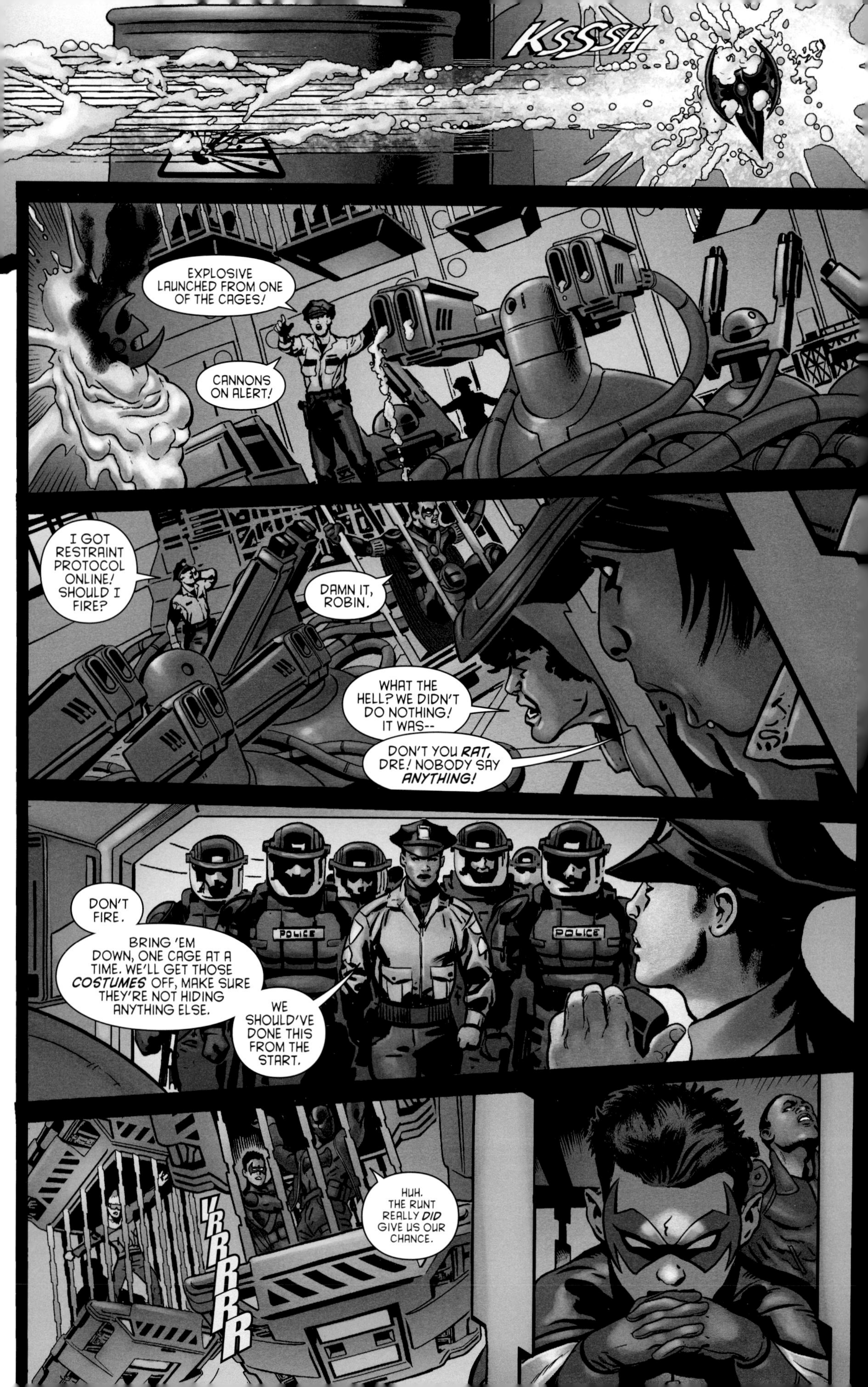
KSSSH
EXPLOSIVE LAUNCHED FROM ONE OF THE CAGES!
CANNONS ON ALERT!
I GOT RESTRAINT PROTOCOL ONLINE! SHOULD I FIRE?
DAMN IT, ROBIN.
WHAT THE HELL? WE DIDN'T DO NOTHING! IT WAS--
DON'T YOU *RAT*, DRE! NOBODY SAY *ANYTHING!*
DON'T FIRE.
BRING 'EM DOWN, ONE CAGE AT A TIME. WE'LL GET THOSE *COSTUMES* OFF, MAKE SURE THEY'RE NOT HIDING ANYTHING ELSE.
WE SHOULD'VE DONE THIS FROM THE START.
VRRRRRR
HUH. THE RUNT REALLY *DID* GIVE US OUR CHANCE.

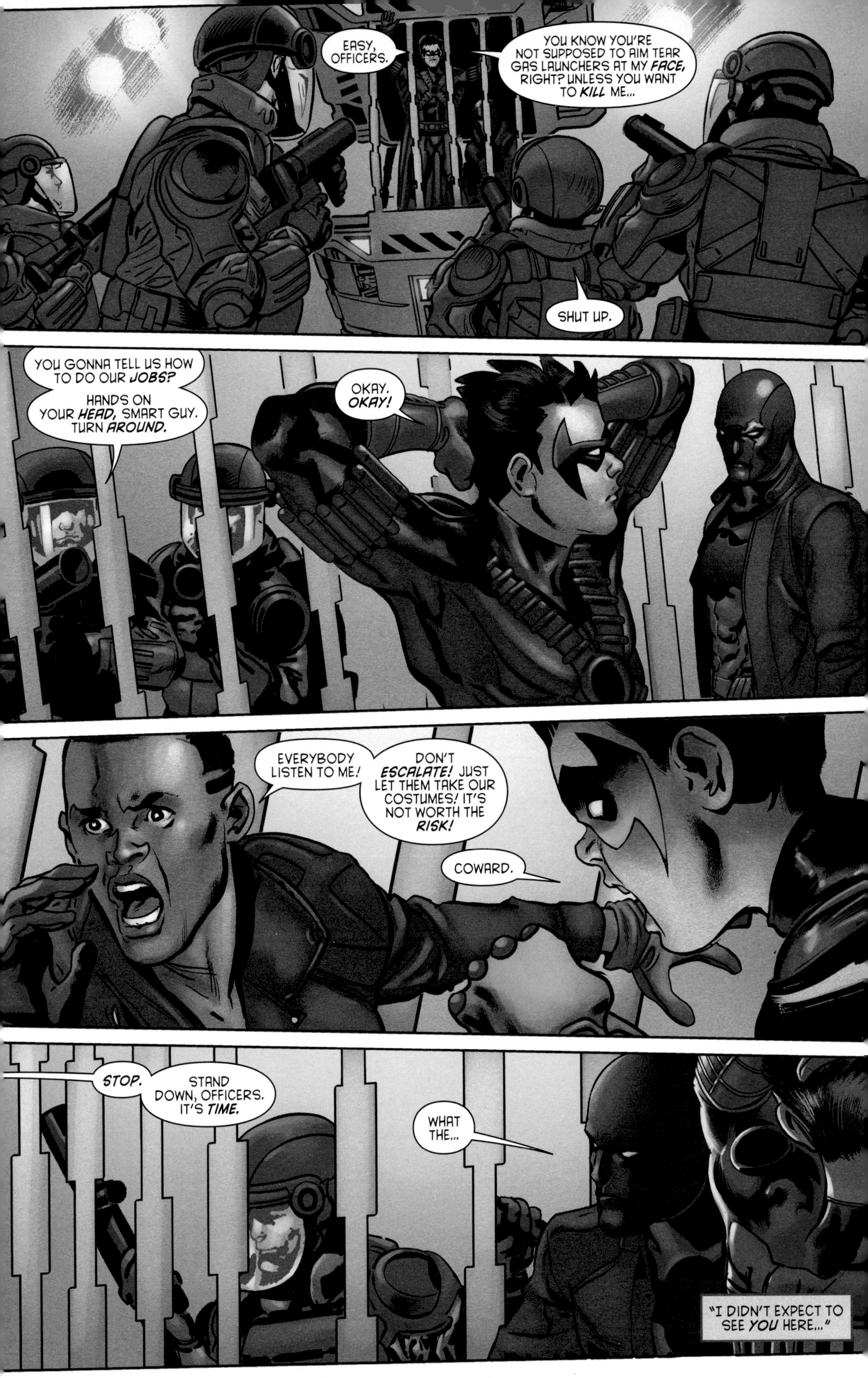
EASY, OFFICERS.
YOU KNOW YOU'RE NOT SUPPOSED TO AIM TEAR GAS LAUNCHERS AT MY FACE, RIGHT? UNLESS YOU WANT TO KILL ME...
SHUT UP.
YOU GONNA TELL US HOW TO DO OUR JOBS?
HANDS ON YOUR HEAD, SMART GUY. TURN AROUND.
OKAY. OKAY!
EVERYBODY LISTEN TO ME!
DON'T ESCALATE! JUST LET THEM TAKE OUR COSTUMES! IT'S NOT WORTH THE RISK!
COWARD.
STOP.
STAND DOWN, OFFICERS. IT'S TIME.
WHAT THE...
"I DIDN'T EXPECT TO SEE YOU HERE..."

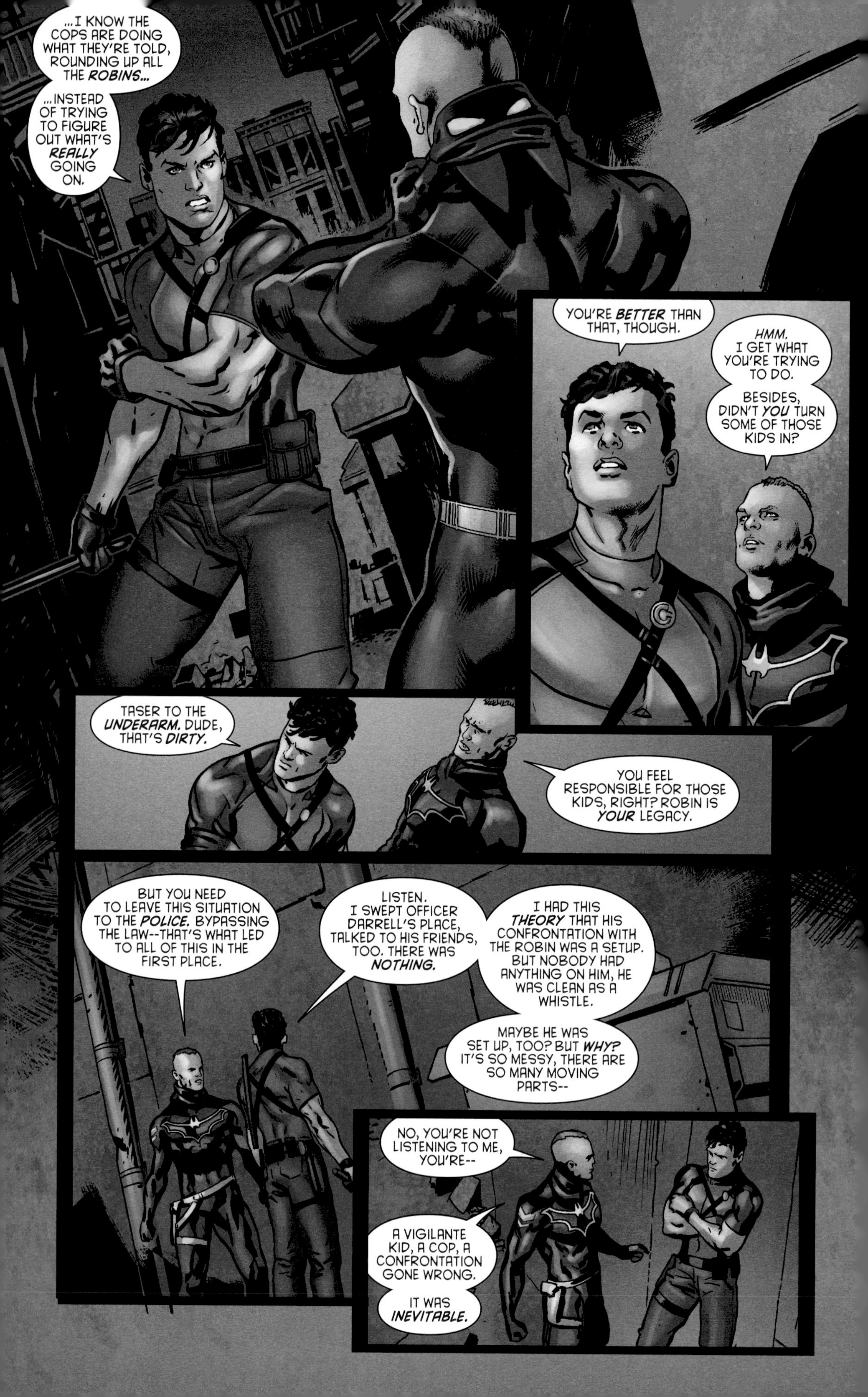
...I KNOW THE COPS ARE DOING WHAT THEY'RE TOLD, ROUNDING UP ALL THE *ROBINS...*
...INSTEAD OF TRYING TO FIGURE OUT WHAT'S *REALLY* GOING ON.
YOU'RE *BETTER* THAN THAT, THOUGH.
HMM. I GET WHAT YOU'RE TRYING TO DO.
BESIDES, DIDN'T *YOU* TURN SOME OF THOSE KIDS IN?
TASER TO THE *UNDERARM.* DUDE, THAT'S *DIRTY.*
YOU FEEL RESPONSIBLE FOR THOSE KIDS, RIGHT? ROBIN IS *YOUR* LEGACY.
BUT YOU NEED TO LEAVE THIS SITUATION TO THE *POLICE.* BYPASSING THE LAW--THAT'S WHAT LED TO ALL OF THIS IN THE FIRST PLACE.
LISTEN. I SWEPT OFFICER DARRELL'S PLACE, TALKED TO HIS FRIENDS, TOO. THERE WAS *NOTHING.*
I HAD THIS *THEORY* THAT HIS CONFRONTATION WITH THE ROBIN WAS A SETUP. BUT NOBODY HAD ANYTHING ON HIM, HE WAS CLEAN AS A WHISTLE.
MAYBE HE WAS SET UP, TOO? BUT *WHY?* IT'S SO MESSY, THERE ARE SO MANY MOVING PARTS--
NO, YOU'RE NOT LISTENING TO ME, YOU'RE--
A VIGILANTE KID, A COP, A CONFRONTATION GONE WRONG.
IT WAS *INEVITABLE.*

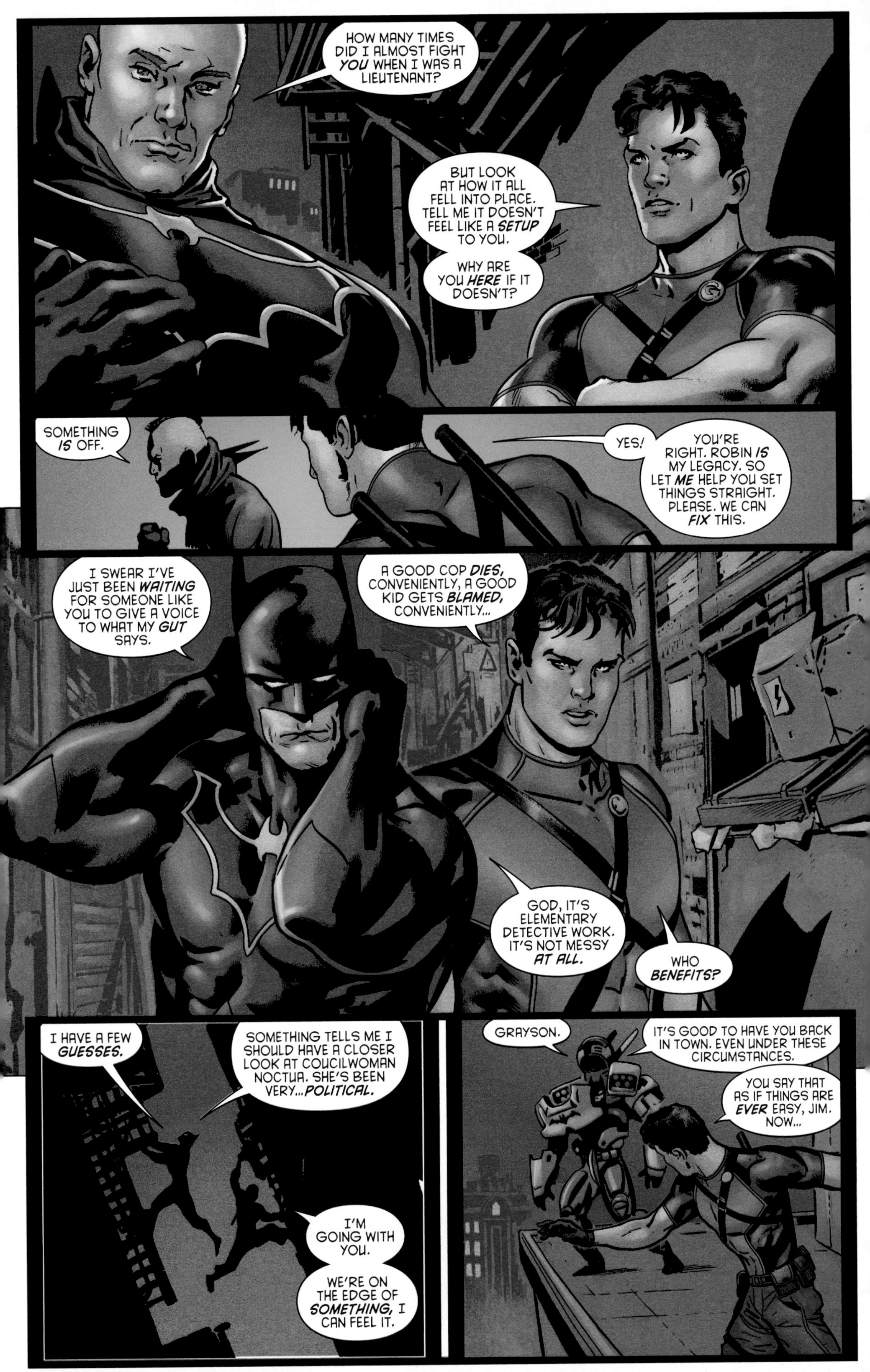
HOW MANY TIMES DID I ALMOST FIGHT YOU WHEN I WAS A LIEUTENANT?
BUT LOOK AT HOW IT ALL FELL INTO PLACE. TELL ME IT DOESN'T FEEL LIKE A SETUP TO YOU.
WHY ARE YOU HERE IF IT DOESN'T?
SOMETHING IS OFF.
YES!
YOU'RE RIGHT. ROBIN IS MY LEGACY. SO LET ME HELP YOU SET THINGS STRAIGHT. PLEASE. WE CAN FIX THIS.
I SWEAR I'VE JUST BEEN WAITING FOR SOMEONE LIKE YOU TO GIVE A VOICE TO WHAT MY GUT SAYS.
A GOOD COP DIES, CONVENIENTLY, A GOOD KID GETS BLAMED, CONVENIENTLY...
GOD, IT'S ELEMENTARY DETECTIVE WORK. IT'S NOT MESSY AT ALL.
WHO BENEFITS?
I HAVE A FEW GUESSES.
SOMETHING TELLS ME I SHOULD HAVE A CLOSER LOOK AT COUCILWOMAN NOCTUA. SHE'S BEEN VERY...POLITICAL.
I'M GOING WITH YOU.
WE'RE ON THE EDGE OF SOMETHING, I CAN FEEL IT.
GRAYSON.
IT'S GOOD TO HAVE YOU BACK IN TOWN. EVEN UNDER THESE CIRCUMSTANCES.
YOU SAY THAT AS IF THINGS ARE EVER EASY, JIM. NOW...

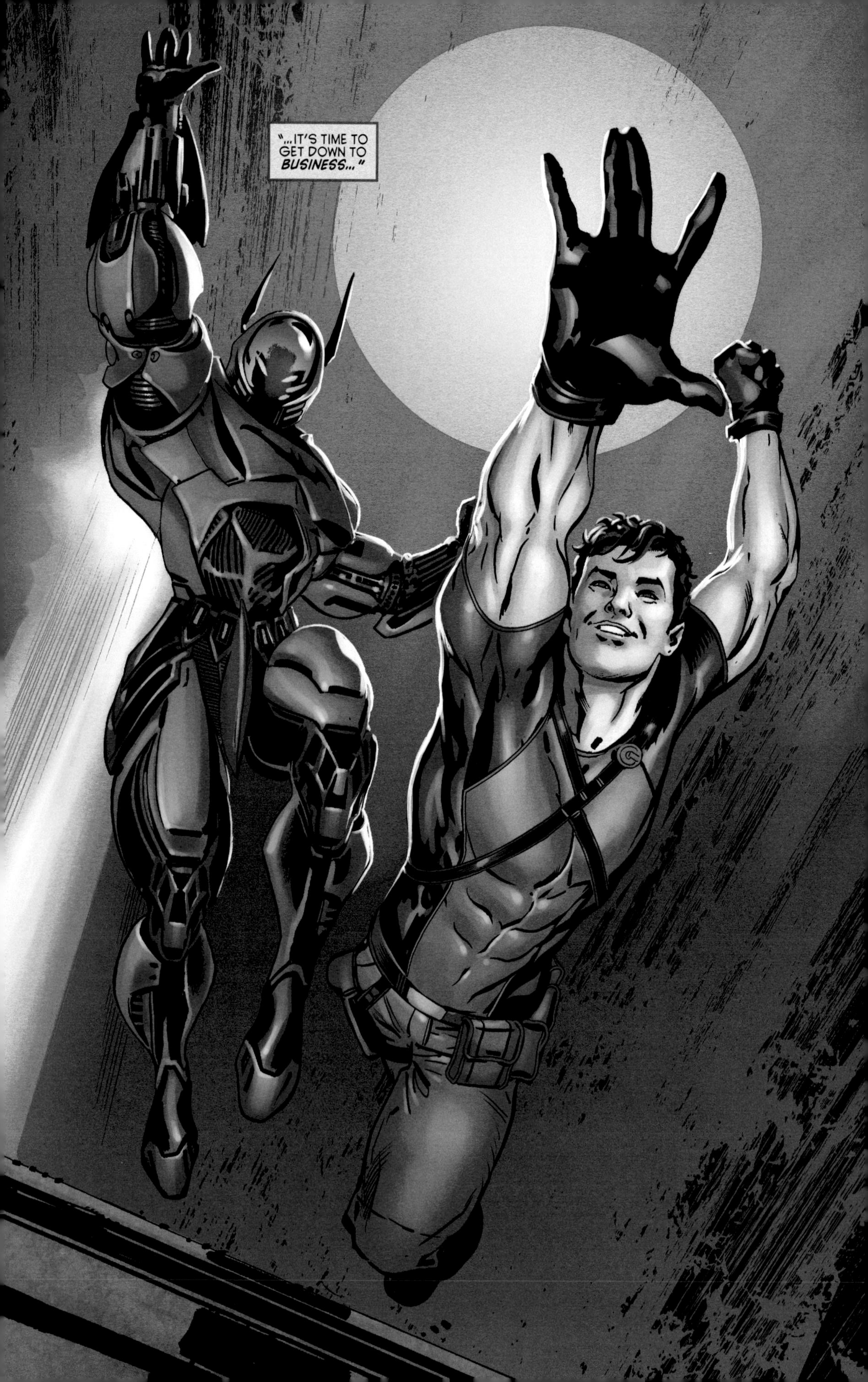
"...IT'S TIME TO GET DOWN TO *BUSINESS*..."

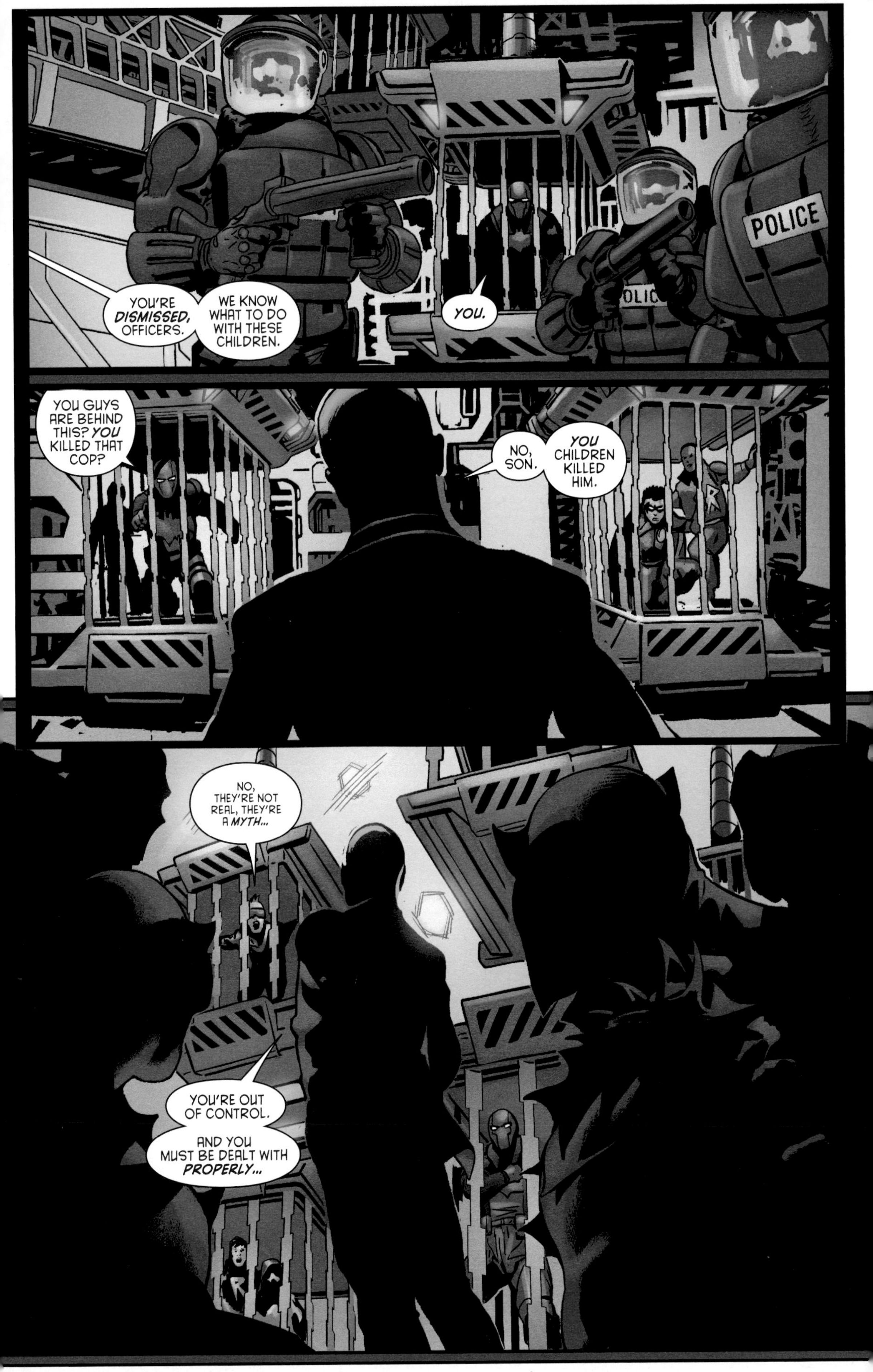
YOU'RE *DISMISSED,* OFFICERS.
WE KNOW WHAT TO DO WITH THESE CHILDREN.
YOU.
POLICE
POLIC
YOU GUYS ARE BEHIND THIS? *YOU* KILLED THAT COP?
NO, SON.
YOU CHILDREN KILLED HIM.
NO, THEY'RE NOT REAL, THEY'RE A *MYTH*...
YOU'RE OUT OF CONTROL.
AND YOU MUST BE DEALT WITH *PROPERLY*...

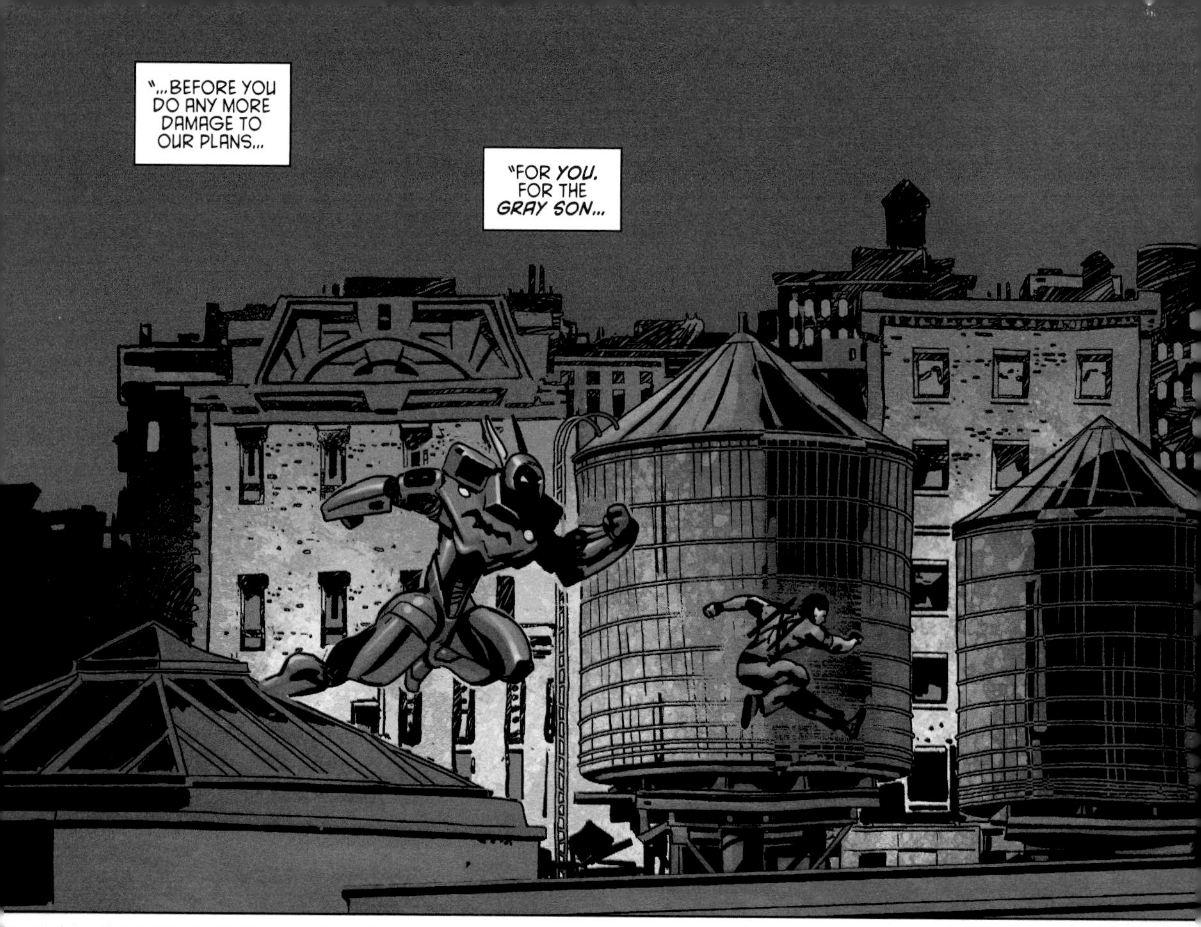
"...BEFORE YOU DO ANY MORE DAMAGE TO OUR PLANS...
"FOR *YOU.* FOR THE *GRAY SON*...

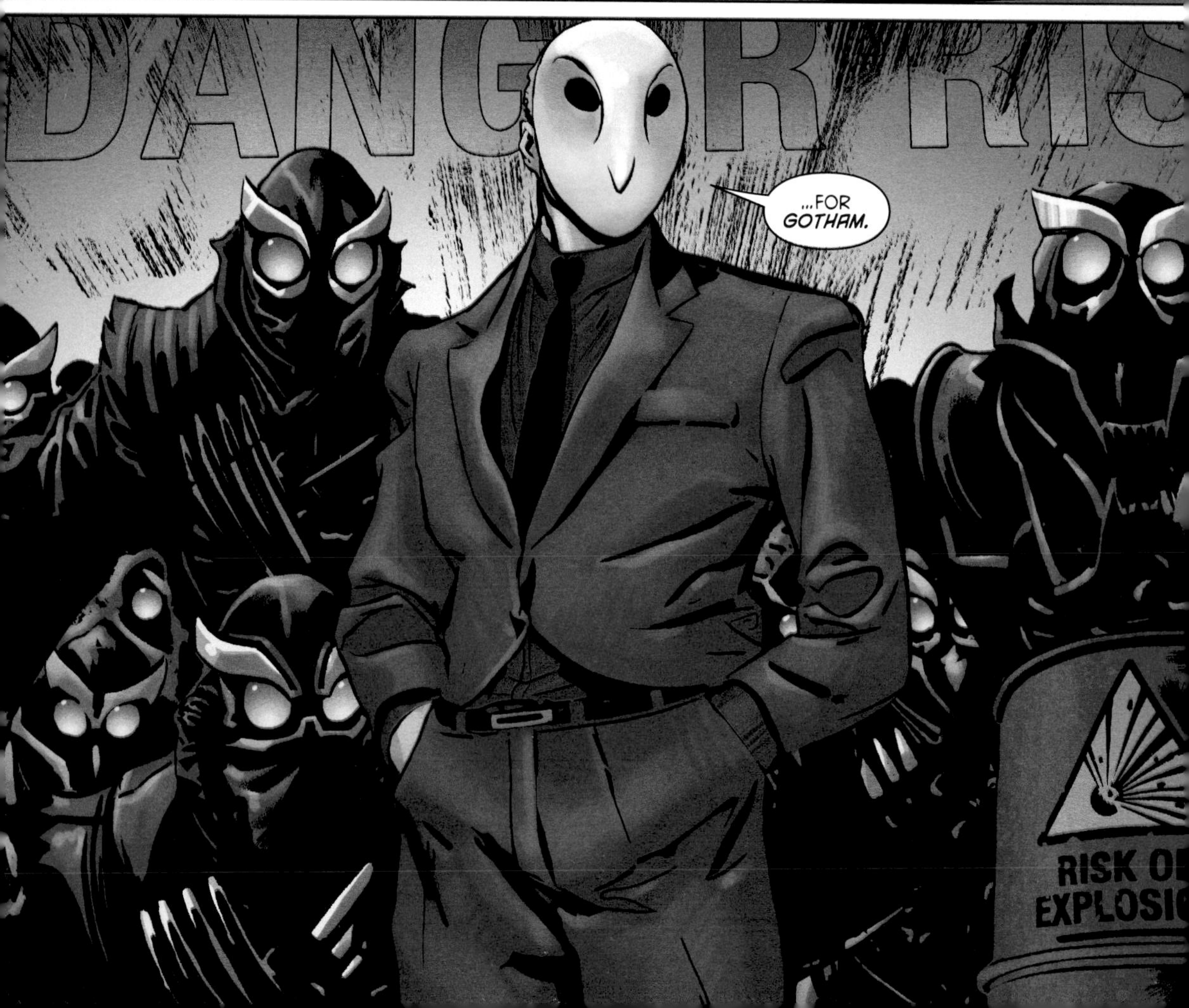
...FOR *GOTHAM.*

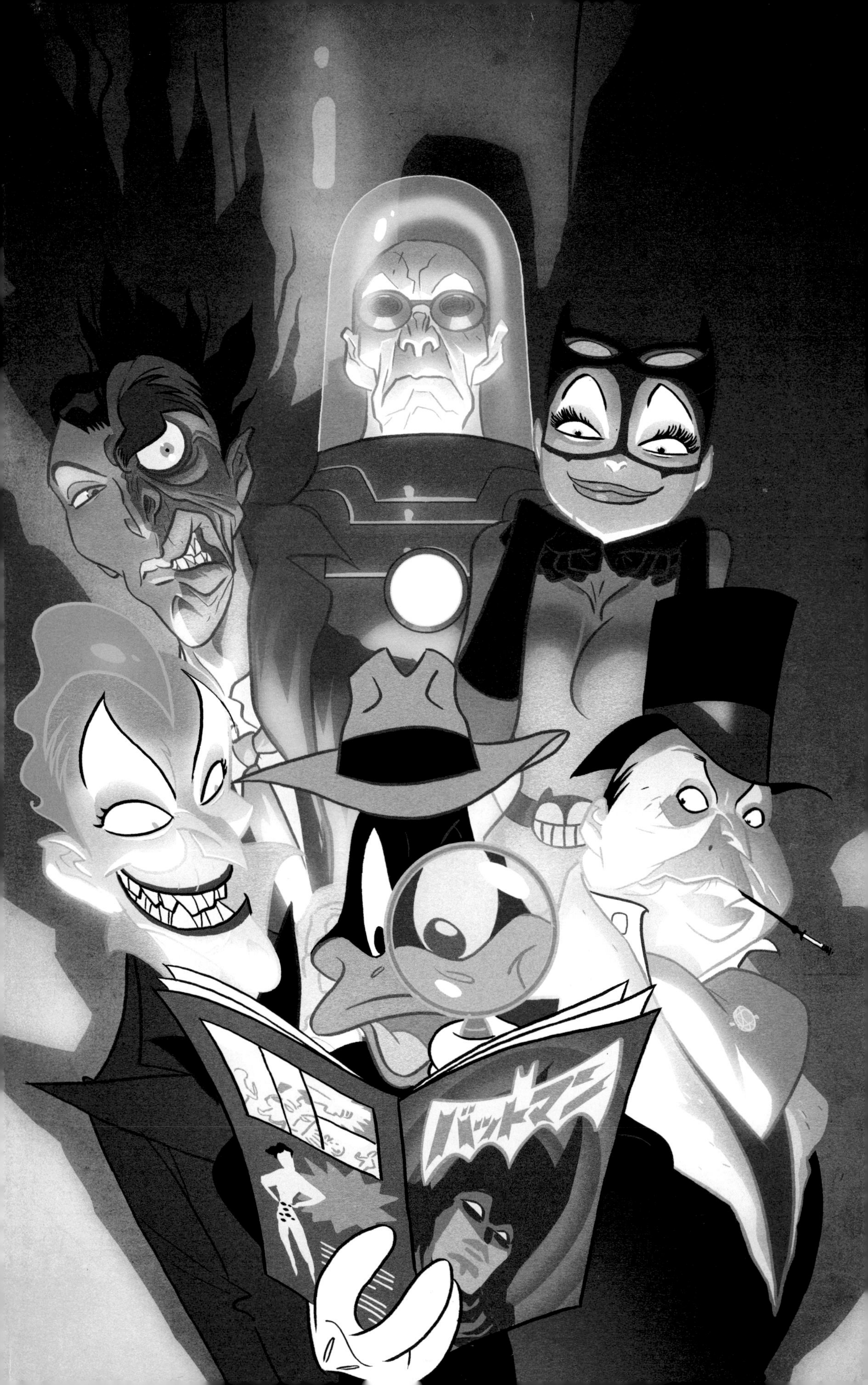
バットマン

"This is your go-to book."—ENTERTAINMENT WEEKLY

"DETECTIVE COMICS is head-spinningly spectacular from top to bottom."—MTV GEEK

START AT THE BEGINNING!

BATMAN: DETECTIVE COMICS
VOLUME 1: FACES OF DEATH

BATMAN: DETECTIVE COMICS VOL. 2: SCARE TACTICS

BATMAN: DETECTIVE COMICS VOL. 3: EMPEROR PENGUIN

THE JOKER: DEATH OF THE FAMILY

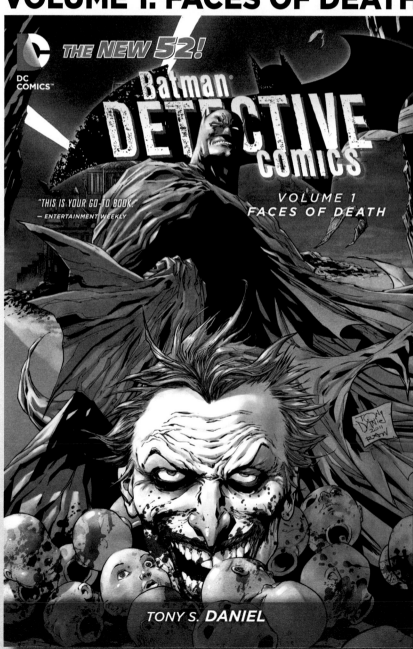